Fundraising Management

IMI

Information Centre & Library

This text [...] guide to [...] *ment,* [...] blending current academic [...] professional practice. [...] than a [...] guide, the text is grounde [...] issues [...] fundraising to provide readers with a comprehensive overview of modern fundraising planning and practice. The text offers key analyses of the critical issues of fundraising as well as acting as a useful tool for the practical side of planning fundraising campaigns.

Topics covered include:

- individual giving;
- Trusts and Foundations;
- corporate fundraising;
- direct marketing;
- community fundraising;
- campaign integration.

The text includes examples and cases from both the UK and the USA, bringing the theory to life. Campaigns discussed include high-profile examples from charities as diverse as RSPCA, Greenpeace, American Humane Society and American Cancer Society. In addition, the text works through the planning stages of fundraising to give readers a rounded understanding of fundraising management.

A truly groundbreaking new text in this area, *Fundraising Management* is essential reading for students of fundraising and non-profit professionals alike.

Adrian Sargeant is Professor of Non-profit Marketing at the University of the West of England and an Adjunct Professor of Philanthropic Studies at the Center on Philanthropy at Indiana University. **Elaine Jay** is a Fundraising Consultant and Director of Sargeant Associates Ltd. She has extensive experience of both the agency and the client side of fundraising in a career that now spans over 15 years.

Fundraising Management

Analysis, planning and practice

Adrian Sargeant and Elaine Jay

Routledge
Taylor & Francis Group

LONDON AND NEW YORK

First published 2004
by Routledge
11 New Fetter Lane, London EC4P 4EE

Simultaneously published in the USA and Canada
by Routledge
29 West 35th Street, New York, NY 10001

Routledge is an imprint of the Taylor & Francis Group

Typeset in Perpetua and Bell Gothic by
Florence Production Ltd, Stoodleigh, Devon

Printed and bound in Great Britain by
TJ International Ltd, Padstow, Cornwall

British Library Cataloguing in Publication Data
A catalogue record for this book is available from the British Library

Library of Congress Cataloging in Publication Data
Sargeant, Adrian.
   Fundraising management/Adrian Sargeant and Elaine Jay.
      p. cm.
   Includes bibliographical references and index.
     1. Fundraising – Management.   I. Jay, Elaine.   II. Title.
   HV41.2.S27 2004
   658.15'224–dc22   2003019260

ISBN 0–415–31701–0 (hbk)
ISBN 0–415–31702–9 (pbk)

Contents

CONTENTS

Plates

Figures

Tables

Exhibits

Chapter 1

The history and development of fundraising practice

'I would leave this work immediately if I thought I were merely raising money. It is raising men that appeals to me.'

Charles Sumner Ward (1905)

LEARNING OBJECTIVES

By the end of this chapter you should be able to:

- Describe how the practice of fundraising evolved in the USA and UK.
- Trace the history of modern fundraising techniques.
- Describe the key changes that took place in fundraising practice in the twentieth century.
- Describe the influence of Charles Sumner Ward on modern fundraising practice.

INTRODUCTION

In this text it is our intention to provide a comprehensive guide to modern fundraising practice, examining commonly used techniques such as the solicitation of major gifts and other less personal forms of communication like direct mail and direct response television. We will also explore the use of emerging new media such as the Internet, digital broadcasting and SMS (short message system) text messaging.

It is our intention to draw on the best of professional experience and academic research on both sides of the Atlantic. The rationale for this is simple. The USA and the UK share a common history and the roots of fundraising are very similar from one country to another – a point that will be developed throughout this first chapter. Importantly, however, the twentieth century has seen a series of contrasting developments in both countries, where the focus has been strongly differentiated and where as a consequence each country can have much to learn from the other. In the USA the practice of major gift fundraising has been greatly refined, and in the latter half of the twentieth century a succession of changes to tax legislation has led to the creation of a number of distinctive products for this market and a creative approach to the stewardship of individual donors as a consequence. In the UK, the approach to fundraising has tended to focus on the solicitation of high numbers of lower value gifts, typically through the use of direct marketing techniques. It thus makes sense to pool this wealth of knowledge and experience and to add it to a rapidly emerging body of academic research focusing on donor behaviour, public perceptions of the voluntary sector and the use and abuse of specific fundraising tools. It is thus not our intention to provide yet another 'how-to' guide based solely on our professional experience. Rather, we blend theory with practice to provide a solid framework against which the organization and fundraising performance of specific non-profits may be assessed.

The result we hope is a text that will for the first time provide fundraisers and students of fundraising alike access to an accumulated body of knowledge about how best to manage and operationalize all the key forms of modern fundraising. It is important to begin, however, by recognizing that the roots of such fundraising lay not in the recent past, but rather through an accumulation of practice over many centuries. Indeed, as will become clear in this chapter, many at first glance modern ideas have actually been around for a very long time.

EARLY PHILANTHROPY AND CHARITY

The word 'philanthropy' comes originally from the Greek and means 'love of mankind'. Robert L. Payton (1984:2) defined it as:

> voluntary giving, voluntary service and voluntary association, primarily for the benefit of others; it is also the 'prudent sister' of charity, since the two have been intertwined throughout most of the past 3500 years of western civilization.

Philanthropy is thus quite dispassionate and impersonal and concentrates on the resolution of the root causes of human issues. It is concerned with improving the quality of life for all members of a society, by 'promoting their welfare, happiness and culture' (Gurin and Van Til 1990:4).

Charity, by contrast, is focused on the poor and is a term drawn from the religious tradition of altruism, compassion and empathy (Ylvisaker 1987). Over the years it has come to be defined somewhat differently from one country to another. In many countries, such as the UK, a charity is a distinctive legal form of organization that has a series of tax advantages enshrined in law. In the USA the term has a wider application, and has come to mean simply serving the poor and needy (Gurin and Van Til 1990).

The concept of charity has been around since the dawn of antiquity, and non-profit organizations of one form or another appear to have been with us since civilization began. References to voluntary giving can be traced back to the beginning of recorded history. The Pharaohs, for example, established some of the earliest charitable trusts, albeit in their case for the somewhat selfish purpose of ensuring the security and perpetuity of their final resting-places. Of course, such early arrangements could hardly be described as philanthropic in nature, since the giving in question served only to ensure the deceased's footprint in history and hopefully a glorious afterlife. It was certainly not the intention of these early trusts to enrich the quality of life for others.

Early references to giving of a rather more 'charitable' nature may be found in the Old Testament. Religious sacrifices were commonly offered and the Old Testament of the Bible notes that the patriarch Jacob promised to give one-tenth of all that God gave him. Indeed, we read that what is now known as the tithe was well established and organized. The Hebrews believed in sharing what they had with the poor who were traditionally, for example, the recipients of the harvest every seventh year.

Other forms of donation from this time include the vast treasures dedicated to the Delphic Oracle (first recorded as early as the fifth century BC) and the earliest recorded school endowments of Plato in Athens and Pliny at Como. Giving in its various forms has thus been around for many centuries.

FUNDRAISING AND THE RELIGIOUS TRADITION

The earliest recorded instances of formal fundraising activity are frequently linked to the activities of religious faiths. Mullin (1995), in particular, charts the significance of organized fundraising activity to early Jewish charity. In this tradition individual volunteers were clearly assigned within each community to take responsibility for specific fundraising tasks. This reflects the positive moral view of the volunteer fundraiser in the Jewish faith; to quote Rabbi Akiba: 'It is a greater virtue to cause another to give than to give yourself.'

In the Christian tradition the now common practice of the weekly church collection dates from the Dark Ages, and in medieval times the Church commonly sent out professional fundraisers (Quaestores) to solicit gifts from the wealthy in order that the Church could both support itself and minister to the poor. Indeed, grand fundraising campaigns were often designed and initiated to support the creation of the great cathedrals across Northern Europe, from the Middle Ages onwards. Frequently, professional fundraisers were employed to ensure success. Detailed analytical planning and market segmentation accompanied much of the fundraising that supported these appeals and, as Mullin (1995) demonstrates, a rich variety of forms of fundraising were undertaken. As an example, Table 1.1 depicts the table of gift allocation associated with the fundraising for Troyes Cathedral; monies that were generated by a volunteer committee supported by professional fundraisers.

Fundraising was not only directed at the rich and powerful in society. Bishop (1898) identifies gifts from fundraising in schools, house-to-house and street collections, community fundraising events and even jumble sales, as significant in the generation of income for Milan's cathedral (See Plate 1.1) in 1386.

Over the centuries the Church developed many effective forms of fundraising practice, including the use of the now infamous 'indulgences'. Until Martin Luther publicly rebelled against the practice in 1517, the Church had for 500 years allowed individuals to pay for their sins by making a worldly donation to the Church. The system was simple. After confessing their sins to a priest, individuals would be set an appropriate penance. Ideally this would be dealt with in life, thereby expunging the sin. However, if the individual died before the penance

Table 1.1 *Troyes Cathedral fundraising (£s)*

	1389–90	1390–91	1412–13	1422–23
Appeals	176 (17 per cent)	186 (13 per cent)	160 (15 per cent)	34 (6 per cent)
Legacies	44 (4 per cent)	5 (4 per cent)	54 (5 per cent)	22 (4 per cent)
Citizens	29 (3 per cent)	386 (28 per cent)	40 (4 per cent)	70 (7 per cent)
Big gifts	440 (43 per cent)	250 (18 per cent)	100 (9 per cent)	100 (17 per cent)
Other	331 (32 per cent)	572 (41 per cent)	695 (66 per cent)	380 (66 per cent)
Total	1,020	1,399	1,049	606

Source: Mullin (1995:6, adapted from Murray 1987)

Plate 1.1
*Milan
Cathedral*

Source: © Mary Ann
Sullivan. Reproduced
with kind permission

had been paid, it would still need to be dealt with before entry to heaven would be permitted. Needless to say, this could delay entry to heaven by a period of some years and was described as a most agonizing and protracted process. The solution to this problem was simple. Having been furnished with an appropriate penance, individuals could buy an 'indulgence' to clear this 'debt'. This would reduce the years of punishment that could otherwise ensue and guarantee a speedy entrance to heaven. Indulgences could be purchased for a variety of good works including churches, hospitals and bridges, and were available from professional fundraisers as well as priests. As Mullin (2002:15) notes, these indulgences 'exploited very private self interest, or harnessed the vulnerabilities of the poor to such self-interest'. The Church has long since abandoned the practice.

THE DEVELOPMENT OF FUNDRAISING IN ENGLAND

Early fundraising in England was conducted against a backdrop of a suspicious state. Social, moral and religious upheavals regularly tore through British society and charities were inevitably bound up therein. One of the oldest surviving charities in England is Week's charity, an organization originally set up in the fifteenth century to provide faggots (bundles of sticks) for burning heretics, an activity supported by the government of the day. The state has therefore long had a vested interest in controlling what should, or should not, be considered charitable in nature. In Tudor times, those seeking to raise funds were well advised to stay within the law or risk fines, flogging, or worse. Even the donors themselves had to be mindful of this legislation, at one stage risking the punishment of having their ears forcibly pierced for giving to the unworthy.

Barbaric though this may sound, Tudor England was much concerned with public order and vagrancy, two concepts which governments of this time saw as inextricably linked. It was thus felt that giving should be strictly controlled to encourage the channelling of alms only to those who were referred to as the impotent poor (i.e. those who, by their age, health or other circumstances, were prevented from earning their own living). The able-bodied poor were to be encouraged to take responsibility for the amelioration of their own condition. In short they should be compelled to find work or starve. Such a preoccupation would, it was felt, preclude the possibility of their finding time to pose a threat to the state. As a consequence all legitimate beggars were licensed and private persons were forbidden to give to anyone not in possession of such a document.

Aside from giving of this very individual and personal nature, there were many great 'general' causes that donors could support at this time. Indeed, many of these are very similar to those we are encouraged to support today. In probably the earliest reference to 'appropriate' charitable causes, William Langland's fourteenth-century work, the 'Vision of Piers Plowman', exalts rich and troubled merchants to gain full remission of their sins and thus a happy death by the fruitful use of their fortunes:

And therewith repair hospitals,
help sick people,
mend bad roads,
build up bridges that had been broken down,
help maidens to marry or to make them nuns,
find food for prisoners and poor people,
put scholars to school or to some other craft,
help religious orders and
ameliorate rents or taxes.

It was not until 1601, however, that English law officially recognized those causes that might be considered as charitable for the first time. The preamble to the Elizabethan Charitable Uses Act of that year appears to have much in common with the fourteenth-century work alluded to above, delineating as it did the legitimate objects of charity:

Some for the Relief of aged, impotent and poore people, some for Maintenance of sicke and maymed Souldiers and Marriners, Schooles of Learninge, Free Schooles and Schollers in Universities, some for Repair or Bridges, Ports, Havens, Causewaies, Churches, Seabanks and Highwaies, some for Educacion and prefermente of Orphans, some for or towards Reliefe Stocke or Maintenance of Howses of Correccion, some for Mariages of poore Maides, some for Supportacion, Ayde and Help of younge tradesmen, Handicraftesmen and persons decayed, and others for releife or redemption of Prisoners or Captives, and for the aide or ease of any poore inhabitants concerninge paymente of Fifteens, setting out of Souldiers and other Taxes.

The Act was significant, not only because it outlined these objects, but also because it acknowledged that trustees and officials of charitable institutions sometimes misused the assets under their care and hence created a means by which they would be made accountable to the public. The law empowered the Lord Chancellor to appoint Charity Commissioners whose responsibility it was to investigate abuses of these charitable uses and to thereby protect the interests of those that had chosen to endow charitable organizations. It perhaps bears testimony to the quality of work undertaken by these early charity legislators that this Elizabethan Act was only repealed in the latter half of the twentieth century. Even today its influence is felt, since the preamble to the Act is still influential in determining those causes that might properly be regarded as being charitable in nature.

Of course, wealth in Elizabethan times was concentrated in the hands of a very small number of individuals, with the vast majority of English society being desperately poor. The wealthy, as now, elected to give by a variety of means. Gifts were made through the Church, directly to other individuals, or perhaps posthumously through the mechanism of a Will. Indeed, the significance of this latter source of charitable donation should not be underestimated. Early records suggest that in the period 1480 to 1660 a variety of causes were supported by this means (See Table 1.2), with the rather low figure donated to religious causes reflecting the

5

Table 1.2 Bequests to charity (1480–1660)

Nature of the cause	Per cent of bequests
Relief of the poor	36
Education (enlarging opportunity)	27
Religious causes	21
Social experiments	10
Fabric of communities	5

Source: Jordan (1964)

increasingly secular nature of the age. Average bequests varied substantially from region to region with the mean bequest to charity from Londoners an almost unbelievably high £255 12s. 2d. In other parts of the country the figure was somewhat lower, in Yorkshire, for example, a mere £28 4s. 6d.

It is interesting to note that this pattern of giving remained relatively static right up until the late nineteenth century which saw a mushrooming in the number of registered charities created. Between 1837 and 1880 there were 9,154 new charities known to the Charity Commissioners and between 1880 and 1900 the number rose sharply to 22,607 (Williams 1989). This proliferation of charities brought with it many problems, notably the increasing number of requests made to the wealthier elements of society for support. It was perhaps, time to broaden the appeal of charities.

THE DEVELOPMENT OF FUNDRAISING IN THE USA

The spirit of private philanthropy in the USA evolved from the attitude of the first settlers who came to America from England and Holland. These individuals continued the pattern of support common in Europe at that time and offered substantial sums of their own monies to build churches, schools and colleges. It is important to note, however, that the spirit and practice of American philanthropy is quite distinctive. While in Europe the state often elected to fund such initiatives through taxation, in the USA public needs often existed before government had been established to cater for them (Boorstin 1963). As a consequence voluntary organizations were formed to provide for basic human needs.

The revolution of 1777 led to the creation of many non-profits as the public was 'swept up in waves of civic enthusiasm and religious fervor' (Hammack 1998:116), with many churches, clinics, schools, orphanages, libraries, colleges and hospitals being built as a consequence. Indeed, the founding fathers had been careful in drafting the constitution to make it difficult for their governments to levy taxes, take vigorous action or grant wealth and power to a privileged few. In the absence of strong taxation religion, education, healthcare and social services had to be funded by alternative means. State legislators responded by making it easier to create non-profit organizations and began shaping them to the needs of society in a variety of ways, notably excluding them from property tax which at the time was the most significant source of government revenue. States also granted non-profits land and began regulating their ability to create endowments.

It is important to note that this tradition of private philanthropy has continued and become what Marts (1966) regards as one of the most durable factors of American life. When Alexis de Tocqueville wrote in 1835 of his travels in America he was impressed by the willingness of the people to give freely of their own funds for social improvements (Probst 1962). He observed that when a community of citizens recognized a need for a church, school or hospital, they came together to form a committee, appoint leaders and donate funds to support it.

Today the Internal Revenue Code permits twenty categories of organization to be exempt from federal income tax and the majority of those that are able to receive tax-deductible contributions also fall into one specific category of the code: Section 501(c)(3). To qualify for this additional benefit organizations must operate to fulfil one of the following broad purposes: charitable, religious, scientific, literary or educational. A number of narrower purposes are also included: testing for public safety and prevention of cruelty to children or animals. The code also requires that no substantial part of an organization's activity should be focused on attempts to influence government, either directly or through participation in political campaigns.

Among the earliest major fundraising campaigns to take place in the USA were those designed to establish the famous Colleges of Harvard in Massachusetts and William and Mary in Virginia. Americans gave generously to create these opportunities for their children, but additional support was often sought from overseas. Since the Colleges of that era existed to educate both laymen and the clergy, ministers were frequently employed to fundraise on behalf of these great endeavours. The first example of this is credited as taking place in the early 1600s when three ministers were despatched from America to England to raise money for Harvard College. One such minister came back with £150 – a pretty good sum at the time. A second stayed in England as a minister, while the third met his death on the gallows, a fact which perhaps illustrates that fundraising has always been a somewhat perilous profession!

Other early fundraisers included Benjamin Franklin who undertook a number of campaigns and was known for the careful manner in which he organized the planning thereof. When asked for his advice he was said to have remarked:

> In the first place, I advise you to apply to all those whom you will know will give something; next, to those whom you are uncertain whether they will give anything or not, and show them the list of those who have given; and lastly, do not neglect those whom you are sure will give nothing, for in some of them you may be mistaken.
>
> (Quoted in Gurin and Van Til 1990:14)

Indeed, much of the fundraising of the day and throughout the nineteenth century was conducted through the medium of personal solicitation, in some cases by paid solicitors. Church collections and the writing of begging letters were also common. It was not until 1829 that the first instance of committed or regular giving is reported. In that year a fundraiser by the name of Matthew Carey sought annual subscriptions of $2 or $3 to support a number of local institutions. Unfortunately only small sums were raised in total and the drive was eventually abandoned.

THE ROOTS OF RAISING MONEY BY MAIL

While direct forms of fundraising from individuals were common in both the UK and the USA prior to and right through the twentieth century, individual solicitations were not the only technique employed by fundraisers. The use of the mail for the purposes of fundraising also has a surprisingly long history. Indeed, there is evidence that professional coaching in the development of fundraising letters has existed since the Middle Ages. A fourteenth-century 'fundraising' handbook developed by monks at a Cistercian monastery in Austria, for example, advocated that an applicant's letter must consist of:

- a honeyed salutation;
- a tactful exordium (an introduction to the purpose of the application);
- a narration (to set the scene with a description of the present situation or problem);
- a petition (the detailed presentation of the application);
- a conclusion (a graceful peroration).

The monks even went so far as to supply twenty-two model letters to illustrate the application of this approach, each of which was framed to offer a different justification for the merit of philanthropy. These included 'generosity to avoid ridicule'; 'the wealthy's obligation to give'; 'do as you would be done by' and 'to be kind is better than being an animal'.

The practice of developing 'model' letters appears to have been consistently adopted throughout the centuries that followed. In 1874 a set of thirty-four directories of such letters were found to be in use in London by a gang of begging letter impostors. The criminal fraternity of the time apparently found it remarkably easy to divest the wealthy of a significant share of their income by using these carefully crafted letters. So widespread was the problem that the London weekly newspaper *Truth* felt compelled to publish a regular gallery so as to issue warnings about such rogues.

THE ROOTS OF MODERN FUNDRAISING AND GIVING

Although individuals have been engaged in fundraising for centuries, fundraising as a serious profession did not really emerge until the mid-eighteenth century. It was common practice at this time to raise funds by assembling a list of suitable wealthy persons and inviting them to a special function or, more usually, dinner. Aside from potential benefactors early fundraising manuals typically suggested that the guests for dinner should include a smattering of 'pretty young ladies' which was seen as essential if high-value gifts were to be solicited. It appears that male donors have always been keen to impress with the size of their charitable wallets.

Fundraising in this form, primarily as a series of dinners and special events, continued throughout the nineteenth century. Given that wealth remained concentrated in the hands of comparatively few individuals there was little motivation for charities to broaden the nature of the charitable appeal.

By the early twentieth century, however, the structure of society and the pattern of wealth distribution was beginning to change. There are many important influences on philanthropy and the fundraising profession that date from the turn of the century.

- The first was the activity of a number of very wealthy philanthropists.
- The second was undoubtedly that of one particularly innovative individual – Charles Sumner Ward.
- The third was the intervention of the Great War.

We will now consider each in turn.

The great philanthropists

The influence of a number of great philanthropists was felt on both sides of the Atlantic around the turn of the century. Multimillionaires such as Andrew Carnegie, and J.D. Rockerfeller in the USA and Joseph Rowntree in the UK in the period from 1885 to 1915, sought innovative ways of disposing of their surplus wealth. This was no easy task, since a way had to be found of diverting resources to those who were most in need and not squandered on those who would not draw benefit from the gift. To quote Carnegie, 'the worst thing a millionaire could do would be to give all his money to the unreclaimably poor'. A mechanism was thus sought to distribute private wealth with 'greater intelligence and vision than the individual donors themselves could have hoped to possess' (Gurin and Van Til 1990:15). It is thus in this period that a number of extraordinarily wealthy charitable trusts or foundations were established for the purpose of distributing the wealth of these great philanthropists. Fundraisers were therefore able to look to this new class of organization for support and the genre of the Trust/Foundation fundraiser was born.

The three charitable trusts set up by Joseph Rowntree in the UK in 1904 were charged with supporting religious, political and social causes. Like their sister organizations endowed by such figures as Carnegie in the USA, these organizations differed from those established in earlier centuries because:

- Their objectives were primarily to achieve some public purpose defined in the deed that established the organization. Such objectives were usually drafted so as to be broad and multiple in nature. The goal of a reorganized Rockerfeller Foundation in 1929, for example, became simply 'the advancement of knowledge throughout the world'.
- They departed from giving to individuals as a means to alleviate suffering, to address the more fundamental and controlling processes (Karl and Katz 1981). Joseph Rowntree wrote into his original trust deeds that much current philanthropic effort was 'directed to remedying the more superficial manifestations of weakness or evil, while little thought is directed to search out their underlying causes' (Rowntree 1904). He criticized the alleviation of Indian famines without examining their causes, and directed that none of this three trusts should support hospitals, almshouses or similar institutions.
- They were legally incorporated bodies whose charitable and public purposes were duly recognized.

Much of the established wealth today has been created over the past 100 to 150 years. Indeed, great wealth has been accumulated by families and individuals over the past few decades alone. In the twentieth century a proliferation of famous philanthropists have emerged such as Clore, Getty, Gates, Hamlyn, Laing, Sainsbury, Weston and Wolfson, all of whom have different interests and motivations for giving.

Some undoubtedly chose to support charity out of their own vanity, perhaps to secure their place in history or to excite a degree of timely public recognition for their works, giving out of a desire for self-aggrandizement, or in the search for some personal advantage or honour. Undoubtedly the majority, however, gave because they felt that it was the moral, religious and socially responsible thing to do with their wealth. As Carnegie famously remarked to Gladstone, 'He who dies rich dies disgraced.'

The rich give by many means. They can of course elect to give cash, but most would typically choose to avail themselves of a tax-efficient form of giving, enjoying the fact that the government must then direct substantial funds to their chosen interest, rather than those of the government of the day. Those with considerable personal wealth may also elect to follow Carnegie and Rowntree's example and establish their own charitable trust for this purpose. Not only does this simplify the administration of tax matters – which need then be dealt with only once a year; it also means that the arduous decision of how much to give to charity need be taken only once a year too. The decision of what to support can then be satisfactorily left to administrators (Hurd and Lattimer 1994).

Other wealthy donors elect to give not only cash, but also the rights to one or more of their services. In the modern era Elton John is particularly well known for his generosity in donating all the proceeds of many of his public performances to charity, and the novelist Catherine Cookson signed away the royalties earned from her novel *Bill Baileys Lot* to charities.

Charles Sumner Ward

Charles Sumner Ward is credited with revolutionizing the practice of fundraising in both the UK and the USA. Indeed, he is regarded by many as the father of modern fundraising. At the turn of the century he was General Secretary of the YMCA in Grand Rapids, Michigan, USA, and spent most of his time raising funds to keep the doors of that organization open. He engaged in the traditional forms of major gift fundraising described above and in an endless round of dinners and public engagements. He was to radically change this approach with the creation of what he later referred to as the first ever 'intensive' campaign in history.

In 1905 he was charged with the task of raising $90,000 for a new YMCA building in Washington DC. Rather than dilute the campaign over a period of many months he reasoned that if plans were made well in advance it should prove possible to limit the fundraising to a single week. In reality Ward met his target well before the week was up and went on to administer many other successful campaigns, notably to help the War effort in 1916.

Ward's 'intensive' or 'whirlwind' campaigns were based on four general principles:

1   *Concentration of time.* Ward believed that businessmen were willing to work for a worthy cause if only they could find the time. By telescoping an appeal for funds into the space of one or two weeks (depending on the size of a city) he was able to secure the active help of those business leaders who were needed to spearhead the drive. Shortening the campaign had the further advantage of keeping it, for its duration, as front-page news in the community. Even when, in later years, Ward directed national campaigns for hundreds of millions and the appeal had to last longer, he always set the shortest feasible time. As he was fond of noting, 'one can raise more money in six days than in six years'.

2   *Organization.* Before the appeal for funds began, the groundwork of a campaign had to be laid with military precision. A large force of the most influential people in a city had to be built up and each individual was carefully informed of exactly what they would be responsible for. Above all, Ward saw the generation of a number of pace-setting gifts as essential. The day the pioneering campaign began, the newspapers carried two front-page pictures, one of J.D. Rockerfeller who contributed $100,000 and one of a local newsboy who had contributed a humble single dollar. The inference was obvious: this was a big-money campaign, but it was also a campaign that concerned the humblest individual in society.

3   *Sacrifice.* In soliciting workers one got nowhere by minimizing the time and effort required. To do that was to cut the ground from under a campaign. Far better to say that the job was a big job and then convince people that the cause was worth it.

4   *Education.* The public must be made to see why it had a stake in the success of the appeal. First of all, the cause must be sound; then it must be brought to the public through all available media of publicity.

In respect of this latter element Ward ensured that in the months before a campaign, news articles slowly built up the need. Civic pride was skilfully manipulated: '*What other cities have done Baltimore can do.*' A notable facet of each campaign was the clock he positioned in conspicuous locations. He would set the hour hand at the Roman numeral XII under which would be written the amount of the goal. As the campaign moved forward the minute hand advanced ever closer to the hour to show how much nearer the goal had become. The clocks generated a substantial amount of public interest and excitement, which Ward complemented with a series of news stories. He was the first to employ publicity directors whose role was to keep all the newspapers supplied with material to keep the campaign on the front page.

Ward was also the first to recognize the significance of arranging a pace-setting gift in advance of a campaign. Such a gift would usually be from one-tenth to one-third of the total and would be conditional on the full amount being raised in the allotted time.

Such was his success that in 1912 Ward was asked to come to England to raise £300,000 for the central YMCA. Needless to say there was some considerable scepticism among conservative London that Ward's methods would curry favour with a British public not used to such brazen 'hard sell' techniques.

The Times editorial, however, was surprisingly supportive:

> It is scarcely necessary to say that this American scheme is no happy-go-lucky attempt, relying for its results on its novelty. Its fame as a new thing, undoubtedly helps it, but the success is really due to a knowledge of human nature and an extremely shrewd application of business principles in securing the advantage at the psychological moment.

Conservative London yielded, and sponsors of the campaign were ultimately to include the Prime Minister, the Lord Mayor and Lord Northcliffe, publisher of *The Times*.

The profession of individual fundraising was changed forever.

The Great War

The advent of the First World War served not only to accelerate the growth in charities registered to address the needs of victims but also to accelerate greater prosperity throughout society, further broadening the potential giving constituency to include all but the poorest elements of society. It was also at this time that 'modern' corporate philanthropy was born and for the first time wealthy corporations began to support need in society.

In the UK charitable appeals linked to the war proliferated, with over 15,000 war charities registered between 1916 and 1918, and significant innovation in fundraising practice occurred as a consequence. Fowler (1999) notes that by the end of the Great War, most of the techniques we are familiar with today had been invented and had reached peaks of varying efficiency:

> During the War itself there were at least three such innovations: flag days, spreading collections to communities overseas, and lotteries. In each case the idea was pioneered by one or more charities, then a host of other bodies copied it.
>
> (Fowler 1999:1)

At the outset of the War contributions to charity poured in from the populace at large. As an example in the UK, the National Relief Fund, established in August 1914, achieved over £2 million within two weeks of its foundation. Seizing an entrepreneurial opportunity, fundraisers quickly developed 'Flower Days' (the then established medium by which cash collections were undertaken) into the more nationalistic Flag Day theme often characterized by the use of ribbons and other symbols of support. It is interesting to note how immediately recognizable this innovation is against the current vogue for charity ribbons and lapel badges. Their success was considerable and the organization behind them not inconsequential.

Donor motivation took on a prescient form. Early appeals for Belgian refugees offered the first real opportunity for ordinary members of the public to contribute to the war effort: 'most people in the movement were motivated at first not by an overwhelming compassion for the refugees – though of course, pity played its part – but by a simple desire to *do*, to be involved in the war effort' (Cahalan 1982:56).

WIDENING THE GIVING CONSTITUENCY

The proliferation of the number of charities around the turn of the century coincided with generally increasing levels of prosperity, a fact which provided the charities of the time with a unique opportunity to begin to expand what had traditionally been very low levels of participation in giving.

Advances in print technology played an important part in promoting the emergence of off-the-page advertising campaigns in newspapers supporting a wide range of appeals from the suffragette movement to the maintenance of private hospitals. Non-profit communications became more generalist in nature and appeal advertisements became commonplace in the popular press. Advertising was generally becoming more sophisticated at this time as the nineteenth-century advertising agencies that had traditionally done little more than sell space on behalf of their patrons reacted to a sharp increase in competition. Agencies found themselves providing an ever wider range of services to their clients in order to secure business and hence their commission from the media owners. Non-profits were initially slow to avail themselves of this service (although Dr Barnardo had already established concerted direct-marketing appeals in the UK before the turn of the nineteenth century), but by the advent of the First World War, with the help of their agencies, non-profits were creating some of the most innovative and exciting advertising of the day. This learning was later developed and integrated with direct marketing by Quaker-inspired commercial philanthropists such as Cecil Jackson-Cole and Harold Sumption (Sumption 1995).

The YMCA ad in Plate 1.2 dates from 1916, yet contains so much of what we would still consider today as 'best practice'. The proposition is a simple one; that everyone can give to help the cause. The ad is written in an informal style and engages the reader with a variety of different typefaces. It also presents bundles of need, illustrating what a donation at each level will achieve, together with a cut-out coupon which the donor can send in noting the amount of their gift. The coupon even carries a 'code' at the bottom so that fundraisers could ultimately assess the efficacy of advertising in many different magazines/newspapers.

The Barnardo's ad in Plate 1.3 was placed in the *Illustrated London News* in the same time period and prompts prospective donors to select the Easter egg they can most afford to send. The range of prompted donations is quite wide, again suggesting that any sum will make a real difference to the children Dr Barnardo's was there to help. In the period 1910 to 1950 advertisements for three categories of charitable cause were particularly commonplace and it seemed as though these were the causes most indelibly printed on the British psyche. As Beveridge noted: 'Britains favour sailors, animals and children – and in that order.'

Advertisements for good causes were also very common in the USA. Indeed, it is interesting to note that the language and style of the early 1900s have many modern parallels. Plate 1.4 depicts a famous ad for the Red Cross which dates from the time of the First World War. The period also saw many other advances in individual fundraising with sales of donated goods, collection boxes and, following a post-regulation slump, charity flag days all proliferating.

In the early 1950s and throughout the 1960s a further revolution in giving behaviour was prompted by concern for famine and poverty abroad made graphically compelling through national newspaper advertisements and the development of structured direct marketing activity. Particularly noteworthy were a series of charity telefons conducted with great success on television channels on both sides of the Atlantic (Seymour 1966, Sumption 1995).

*Plate 1.2
Early YMCA
advertisement*

Common throughout these advances was the importance placed on the identification of need and the donors' effective response to it, stewarded in positive fashion by the professional fundraiser. Yet as direct marketing technology grew cheaper and more accessible to the non-profit sector and as the early fundraising consultant pioneers were joined by others – notably, converts from commercial advertising agency practices (Harold Sumption, Redmond Mullin and George Smith to name but three) – volume of activity increased, and with it public and media scepticism of the methods employed.

It was not until the 1980s, however, that perhaps the greatest changes began to take place in the manner that funds were raised from individuals. Advances in computer technology and the miniaturization thereof now made it possible for non-profits to invest in a database for the very first time. The first to come on to the market were quite simple affairs that did little more than allow the organization to record the names, addresses and gifts made by their donors. More recent developments have allowed non-profits to segment their donor base and target a wide variety of communications at an even wider variety of donor segments.

Fundraisers initially slow to adopt modern marketing concepts and strategies, embraced the methods of the commercial market place whole-heartedly from the early 1970s onwards. Professional institutes were established to promote the distinctive and positive role of the professional fundraiser in both the UK and the USA (Institute of Charity Fundraising Managers

13

Plate 1.3 Early Barnardo's advertisement   **Plate 1.4** Early US advertisement

UK, 1983; National Society of Fundraising Executives USA, 1960). Academic research, textbooks and teaching of non-profit fundraising and marketing were 're-invented' in relation to the new-found skills and disciplines associated with the development of marketing theory (Drucker 1990, Kotler and Andreasen 1991, Clarke and Norton 1992).

In the age of the relational database non-profits can now establish almost one-to-one dialogues with their donors, ensuring that every communication they receive meets the expectations that a donor might have of the organization. For their part professional fundraisers are now 'relationship fundraisers' stewarding and supporting the lifetime value of prospective donors from first gift to – in the case of legacy fundraising – beyond the grave (Burnett 1992, Wilberforce 2001). In essence, contemporary non-profits can develop a *silicon simulacrum* of the relationships that individuals might once have had with their butcher or baker. They can be addressed as individuals at a time that suits them with the products/services and 'asks' which experience tells the non-profit they will find most appropriate.

CONCLUSION

The history of fundraising is much longer than many people believe. While corporate and trust fundraising are comparatively recent phenomena, non-profits and fundraisers have been around since the start of recorded history. For centuries, the task of fundraising from individuals was largely conducted by the Church, the ministers of which employed many of the same methods of solicitation still commonly in use today. Even techniques such as the use of fundraising letters have been known and employed to good effect since the Middle Ages with copies of 'model' requests dating back over 500 years. While there may therefore be little new in individual fundraising, the twentieth century has certainly seen a number of innovations in the way in which these techniques have been deployed. Charles Sumner Ward's carefully integrated 'intensive' campaigns are certainly worthy of note, as are the advances in computer technology that in a way have brought fundraisers full circle. Until Ward's time all fundraising would undoubtedly have consisted of a series of one-to-one requests. The opening up of mass advertising media in the early part of the twentieth century allowed charities to move away from this to a 'one-to-many' approach. While in its simplest form much individual fundraising still falls into this latter category, the evolution of database technology is making it increasingly possible to return to a 'one-to-one' message. Exactly how this might be accomplished and the benefits thereof will form the focus of much of this book.

REFERENCES

Bishop, E. (1898) 'How a Cathedral was Built in the Fourteenth Century – Milan Cathedral', Cited in Bishop Edmund (1918) *Liturgica Historica*, Oxford University Press, Oxford.

Boorstin, D.J. (1963) *The Decline of Radicalism: Reflections on America Today*, Random House, New York.

Burnett, K. (1992) *Relationship Fundraising*, White Lion Press, London.

Cahalan, P. (1982) *Belgium Refugee Relief in England during the Great War*, Macmillan, London.

Clarke, S. and Norton, M. (1992) *The Complete Fundraising Handbook*, DSC, London.

Drucker, P.F. (1990) *Managing the Non-profit Organization*, Butterworth-Heinemann, London.

Fowler, S. (1999) 'Voluntarism and Victory: Charity, the State and the British War Effort, 1914–1918'. Paper presented to the History of Charity Conference, University of Wales, Bangor, September 1999, p. 2.

Gurin, M.G. and Van Til, J. (1990) 'Philanthropy in its Historical Context', in Jon van Til and Associates (eds), *Critical Issues in American Philanthropy*, Jossey Bass, San Francisco, pp. 3–18.

Hammack, D.C. (1998) *Making of The Nonprofit Sector in the United States*, Indiana University Press, Indianapolis.

Hurd, H. and Lattimer, M. (1994) *The Millionaire Givers*, Directory of Social Change, London.

Jordan, W.K. (1964) *Philanthropy in England 1480–1660*, George Allen & Unwin, London.

Karl, B.D. and Katz, S.N. (1981) 'The American Private Philanthropic Foundation and The Public Sphere 1890–1930', *Minerva*, XIX:236–270.

Kotler, P. and Andreasen, A. (1991) *Strategic Marketing for Nonprofit Organizations*, Prentice Hall, Englewood Cliffs, NJ.

Marts, A.C. (1966), *The Generosity of Americans: Its Source, Its Achievements*, Prentice Hall, Englewood Cliffs, NJ.

Mullin, R. (1995) *Foundations for Fundraising*, ICSA, London.

Mullin, R. (2002) 'The Evolution of Charitable Giving', in C. Walker and C. Pharoah (eds), *A Lot of Give*, Hodder & Stoughton, London.

Payton, R.L. (1984) 'Major Challenges To Philanthropy'. Discussion Paper for Independent Sector, August.

Probst, G.E. (1962) 'The Happy Republic: A Reader', in de Tocqueville's *America*, Harper & Brothers, New York.

Rowntree, J. (1904) 'The Founders Memorandum', reprinted in L.E. Waddilove (1983), *Private Philanthropy and Public Welfare: The Joseph Rowntree Memorial Trust 1954–1979*, Allen & Unwin, London.

15

Seymour, H.J. (1966) *Designs for Fundraising*, McGraw-Hill, New York.

Sumption, H. (1995) *Yesterday's Trail-blazing and Pointers for Tomorrow*, Brainstorm Publishing, Hertford.

Wilberforce, S. (ed.) (2001) *Legacy Fundraising*, 2nd edn, DSC, London.

Williams, I. (1989) *The Alms Trade: Charities, Past Present and Future*, Unwin Hyman, London.

Ylvisaker, P.N. (1987) 'Is Philanthropy Losing Its Soul?', *Foundation News*, May/June:3.

The fundraising planning process

Chapter 2

Fundraising planning
The fundraising audit

LEARNING OBJECTIVES

By the end of this chapter you should be able to:
- Outline a process for developing a fundraising plan.
- Explain the purpose of a fundraising audit as the first part of such a process.
- Discuss the key information requirements of a fundraising audit.
- Understand the categories of information gathered in the audit, why this data is important and how it can be used in planning.
- Utilize key tools commonly employed in the audit process such as PEEST, SWOT and portfolio analyses.

INTRODUCTION

In this chapter it is our intention to outline a process that may be employed by non-profits in planning the fundraising activities they will undertake. While the format may differ slightly from one organization to another, at its core a fundraising plan has three common dimensions.

1 **Where are we now?** A complete review of the organization's environment and the past performance of the fundraising function. Only when the fundraising department has a detailed understanding of the organization's current strategic position in each of the donor markets it serves can the organization hope to develop meaningful objectives for the future.

2 **Where do we want to be?** In this section of the plan the organization will map out what the fundraising department is expected to achieve over the duration of the plan. Typically there will be income-generation targets for the department as a whole and a series of 'sub-objectives' for each category of fundraising (e.g. individual, trust/foundation and corporate).

3 **How are we going to get there?** This stage of the plan contains the strategy and tactics the organization will adopt to achieve its targets. The strategy, as we shall see in Chapter 4, specifies in general terms what the broad approach to fundraising will be,

while the tactics supply the minutia of exactly how each form of fundraising will be undertaken.

In this chapter we will provide a generic framework for fundraising planning and concentrate our attention on the first of these three components of a fundraising plan. We will consider the information requirements an organization will have when it commences the planning process, the sources from which this information can be gathered and a range of analytical tools that can be used to help fundraisers interpret this information.

A PLANNING FRAMEWORK

Figure 2.1 contains a generic fundraising planning framework. Many organizations find it helpful to begin the development of the fundraising plan by restating their mission and the objectives that the organization as a whole has set. These objectives will typically be couched in terms of service delivery targets to beneficiaries, changes in societal attitudes towards the cause and so on.

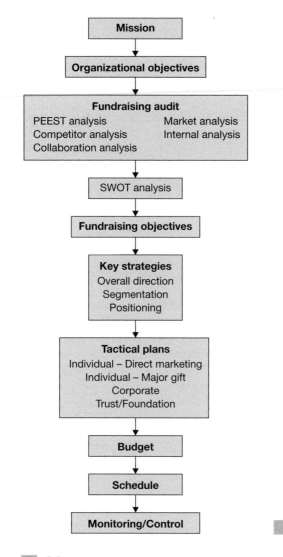

Figure 2.1 Generic planning framework

Restating the mission and organizational objectives serves to focus the minds of fundraisers on what income is likely to be required and why this is necessary. In short it reminds the fundraising team of the reason for their existence and the impact that will be achieved if they are successful in raising the requisite funds. While it may sound a little trite to say this, the nature of the cause is often a strong motivating factor for all members of staff, and fundraisers are no exception. Understanding why funds are needed is thus the fundamental starting point in fundraising planning.

Of course, it is important to recognize that while the Director of Fundraising may have had some input into the mission and organizational objectives, it is unlikely that he or she will have actually written them. They are simply restated here as an overall guide to the fundraising plan that will follow.

A glance through a selection of non-profit publicity material reveals that many non-profits have been intuitively writing mission statements for years, even if they prefer to use alternative terminology such as 'aims', 'purpose' or 'philosophy'. In truth the terminology is unimportant. What matters is that the organization can summarize in a few words its *raison d'être*. Not only does this aid planners in the manner described above, but it can become a remarkably useful reference point for potential donors. Supporters can see at a glance what the organization is trying to achieve and confidently initiate some form of relationship if they feel it will be appropriate.

A selection of 'missions' is given in Exhibit 2.1.

The reader will appreciate that there is a noticeable absence of figures in these examples. Mission statements should address what the organization wishes to achieve, but in such a way that the mission can be adopted consistently for a reasonable period of time. It should not be necessary to readdress the mission on an annual basis, since it should serve only to provide the most general of signposts.

EXHIBIT 2.1 MISSIONS

The European Blues Association is a non-profit organization and educational institute. Our aim is to be 'the resource' for our members and the general public who are interested in the historical past and the modern progression of the blues. We are dedicated to the appreciation and understanding of all aspects of the music and the African American culture from which it evolved.

Environmental Defense is dedicated to protecting the environmental rights of all people, including future generations. Among these rights are clean air and water, healthy and nourishing food, and a flourishing ecosystem.

The mission of Planned Parenthood is:

- to provide comprehensive reproductive and complementary health care services in settings which preserve and protect the essential privacy and rights of each individual;
- to advocate public policies which guarantee these rights and ensure access to such services;
- to provide educational programs which enhance understanding of individual and societal implications of human sexuality;
- to promote research and the advancement of technology in reproductive health care and encourage understanding of their inherent bioethical, behavioral, and social implications.

Indeed, the specific detail of what an organization seeks to accomplish within each planning period would normally form part of the content of the organizational objectives. Drucker (1955) isolated what he believed to be eight aspects of operations where organizational objectives could be developed and maintained. These have been modified slightly below to relate them more specifically to the context of non-profit organizations:

1   Market standing
2   Innovation
3   Productivity
4   Financial and physical resources
5   Manager performance and development
6   Employee/volunteer performance and attitude
7   Societal needs to be served
8   Public/social responsibility

Clearly each of these areas has some relevance for fundraisers, even if many do not relate specifically to the fundraising function. It is important to realize that these objectives are stated for the organization as a whole to work towards. Their achievement will require a co-ordination of effort across all divisions/departments within the organization. Managers with responsibility for finance, human resources, service delivery and so on, will all have their part to play in ensuring that the organization delivers what it says it is going to deliver. It is for this reason that it is usual to restate the organizational objectives at the beginning of the fundraising plan. Fundraisers should then be able to isolate what they as individuals need to be able to achieve over the planning period to facilitate the achievement of these wider objectives. There would be little point, for example, in the fundraising department concentrating on raising funds for aspects of the organization's work that are not perceived as congruent with the organization's current goals and failing to raise money for those that are.

THE FUNDRAISING AUDIT

As noted above, the fundraising planning process can be conceptualized as having three key components:

1   Where are we now?
2   Where do we want to be?
3   How will we get there?

The fundraising audit specifically addresses the first of these elements. As such it is arguably the most crucial stage of the whole planning process since without a thorough understanding of the organization's current position it will be impossible for planners to develop any kind of vision of what they can expect to accomplish in the future. The fundraising audit is essentially a detailed review of any factors that are likely to impinge on the organization, taking into account both those generated internally and those emanating from the external environment. The fundraising audit is thus a systematic attempt to gather as much information as possible about the organization and its environment and, importantly, how these might both be expected to change and develop in the medium and longer term futures. A typical framework for a fundraising audit is provided in Figure 2.1. While the list of information requirements may appear regimented and prescriptive, it is essential to impose some structure to ensure that valuable data are not overlooked.

Macro factors

It is usual to begin the process by examining the wider or 'macro' environmental influences that might impact on the organization. Often these may be factors over which the organization itself has little control, but which will nevertheless affect the organization at some stage during the period of the plan. The framework utilized for this analysis is typically referred to as a PEEST analysis and comprises the following elements:

- **Political factors**: Political factors impacting on fundraising might include government attitudes to the non-profit sector and recent or forthcoming legislative or regulatory changes that might affect the fundraising environment or fundraising performance (e.g. privacy legislation, the repeal of the estate tax or additional fiscal incentives to increase giving). Likely changes to government structures such as the devolving of power to local bodies would also be considered under this heading. Trends in the international political environment would also be considered here in terms of likely impact on the economy and/or changes in social attitudes.
- **Economic factors**: Economic trends are relevant primarily as predictors of future donor behaviour. Trends in wealth, employment, tax, consumption and disposable income impact on all categories of funders from corporate givers and foundations through to individuals.
- **Environmental factors**: Environmental factors will be of particular interest to non-profits working in related fields, but are also relevant as indicators of personal beliefs and behaviours. Environmental trends might include the prevalence of recycling, interest in sustainability issues and growth in the market for organic products and renewable energy sources.
- **Socio/cultural factors**: Key data here will include data on demographics and social attitudes, plus evidence of likely behavioural changes or significant shifts in societal values that might occur over the duration of the plan. For example, trends in levels of civic participation, changes in the formation of families, in levels of trust and confidence in the non-profit sector and in patterns of working would be considered here.
- **Technological factors**: Crucial here will be factors such as the likely impact of developments in technology on the non-profit sector and on fundraising techniques. Developments in web communications, mobile phone technology, automated bank payments and interactive TV would all, for example, fall into this category.

In each case the aim is to accumulate a list of all the pertinent factors and how these are expected to change over the planning period. At this point in the process it is best not to spend too much time deliberating over the impact that these factors may have on the organization, but rather to note them, detail how they might change and move on. The danger of precipitating a discussion at this stage is that other clues as to the impact these PEEST factors may have will tend to emerge as the audit process progresses. It is therefore better to consider potential impacts *en masse* when the audit itself is complete. A sample PEEST analysis for an environmental charity is provided in Exhibit 2.2.

In researching these 'macro' trends the main challenge lies in the selection of accurate and pertinent information, and in the production of summaries setting out the main points for the reader succinctly. Data for PEEST analyses are gathered through secondary sources via desk research, i.e. information is found through existing publications rather than being sourced through the commissioning of new (or primary) research. In gathering information for a PEEST analysis one would look at practitioner and academic journals, books and reports, often via

EXHIBIT 2.2 PEEST ANALYSIS FOR A UK ENVIRONMENTAL CHARITY

Political

- Government implementation of the charity sector review.
- Implications of the Data Protection Act.
- Recent changes to tax-efficient giving legislation.
- Centralizing of landfill and aggregate tax funding bodies.
- Imposition of recycling targets nationally and locally.
- Forthcoming European legislation on recycling.
- Changes to European social funding.

Economic

- Gloomy economic forecasts.
- Potential rise in interest rates.
- Falling levels of disposable income.
- Rising unemployment.

Environmental

- Increased levels of recycling.
- Continuing interest in sustainability and bio-diversity issues.
- Purchase of organic products up 30 per cent in past five years.

Socio-cultural

- Changing patterns of work/increase in home working.
- Ageing population.
- Changing family patterns.
- Falling levels of civic participation.
- Increased migration to rural areas.

Technological

- Digital TV now widely available.
- Growth in automated online banking.
- Availability of new Internet channels.
- Growth in use of e-mail and SMS messaging.

online information databases such as ProQuest available through libraries and academic institutions or by searching the web more generally. Reports and publications published by trade bodies such as the Association of Fundraising Professionals in the USA and the Charities Aid Foundation in the UK would also be utilized. Many non-profits find that much of the necessary information for the production of PEEST analyses is already held internally in the form of publications and reports, or that staff have knowledge of where such information may be sourced internally or externally. The role of the 'auditor' is often therefore to interview staff, find out what information they have on file or can help with, and manage the gathering of those data. In this scenario the auditor would then seek to update the data where appropriate, and fill in any gaps through further research.

It is important to note however, that simply identifying the key factors, is not enough, and that it is vital that as much data as possible are gathered against each factor to ensure that decision-makers are fully informed. For example, most non-profits would identify 'increasing use of the Internet' as a key technological trend. Having identified this, the auditor would need to relate this factor to the context of the specific organization. They might hence collate information on the likely growth in users over the duration of the plan, new features and developments, and on the current use of the Internet in fundraising. Likewise, predicted falls in disposable income levels among members of the public might be identified as an important economic factor, but this would mean little if data on the recorded impact of a fall in disposable income on fundraising and non-profit performance were not included in the PEEST.

Analysis of competitors

Accurate and full information on the activities, size and market position of competitor organizations is of vital importance to any non-profit putting together a fundraising plan. The non-profit marketplace is complex and crowded, with many organizations competing for a limited pool of support. In seeking to successfully raise funds it is therefore essential that an organization conducts a detailed analysis of the activities of key competitors and uses this information to inform its own subsequent fundraising strategy.

Of course the starting point in conducting an analysis of the competition is to decide which competitors the organization should profile. There are a number of options:

- *Industry leaders*: The fundraising team will undoubtedly be aware of those competitor organizations that they regard as particularly outstanding in their fundraising activity. It may be possible to learn a great deal from these industry leaders about successful fundraising practice and to borrow exciting new and innovative ideas in respect of the best ways to solicit funds. These non-profits may be working in the same field, but could equally be working elsewhere in the sector serving entirely different needs. They are thus selected purely on the basis of the quality/originality of the fundraising they undertake.
- *Other non-profits serving the same cause*: Some non-profits will assess the strategy and performance of those charities they perceive to be in direct competition with themselves since they serve the same broad category of cause (e.g. children, animal welfare, environmental defence). The goal here is to gather sufficient data to benchmark the activities of the focal non-profit against those of its key competitors. The nature of the activities undertaken, the quality of the promotional materials produced and the estimated or actual cost-effectiveness of the fundraising undertaken will all be of interest.
- *Non-profits of a similar size*: A further strategy employed by some non-profits is to look at organizations of a similar size to themselves irrespective of the category of cause served. This is a strategy particularly favoured by larger non-profits who want to ensure that their performance is comparable with organizations of similar size and stature. Once again, organizations will look at the forms of fundraising undertaken, the promotional materials produced and the performance achieved. This information may be used to assist in benchmarking the performance of the focal organization and in highlighting areas of weakness.

Irrespective of the approach adopted there are a number of common categories of information that are typically gathered:

- *Financial performance*: It will generally be instructive to look at how key competitors are performing. This might include the levels of various categories of income they are able to generate and the investment they have made to secure this. This will give the auditor a sense of the returns that might be expected from various forms of fundraising and how the performance of the focal non-profit might compare with this. It will also be useful to scrutinize those organizations that seem to be achieving significant growth, or doing particularly well at certain forms of fundraising. The reasons for this performance may be ascertained and the data used to inform an organization's own fundraising strategy. If only a few competitors are to be scrutinized it may be possible to obtain copies of their annual reports and to use these as the starting point. If larger numbers of organizations are involved in the USA it is possible to obtain the 990 returns that non-profits seeking tax exemptions must file. The 990 provides very broad-brush data in respect of the performance of US non-profits and may be viewed online (alongside other useful information) at the non-profit website www.guidestar.org. In the UK, data may be obtained from the Charities Aid Foundation or from the Charity Commission. Indeed, at the time of writing a UK version of the Guidestar website is also planned. More detailed benchmarking data are available in the UK from the Institute of Fundraising and the Centre for Inter-Firm Comparisons (which produces a study entitled Fundratios). In the USA the most comprehensive benchmarking study of fundraising performance has been conducted by Patrick Rooney and others at the Indiana Center on Philanthropy. Benchmarking is a subject we return to in detail in Chapter 15.

- *Competitor objectives and ambitions*: Unfortunately, while published accounts provide a reasonably reliable picture of the past performance of non-profit competitors, what is typically of greater interest is how these competitors might behave in the future. It is thus of immense value to research what the objectives and ambitions of those key competitors might be. Clearly if a non-profit involved in related work has plans for greatly expanding its work, it could prove to be a particularly aggressive competitor for funds in the months and years ahead. It is essential to be aware of changes such as these and to prepare a strategic response.

- *Past, present and future strategies*: Finally, it will also be useful to obtain data about the fundraising strategies/tactics of key competitors. The fundraiser will want to ask questions such as: What kinds of fundraising have they been engaged with in the past? How successful were these? Why was this performance achieved? Which audiences were addressed? What fundraising is being conducted now? How might this change in the future? What is unusual or distinctive about this fundraising? How does it differ from our own? The answers to all these questions have the capacity to inform how an organization can defend itself against competition and improve the quality of its own fundraising activity. Of course, tracking down this kind of information is not easy, but the sector press or local/national media can often contain a lot of information about aspects of fundraising strategy.

One of the most useful ways to gather information on the fundraising activity of competitor organizations is through 'mystery shopping' (i.e. sending in a donation to the organization, and then monitoring the subsequent communications received). Many non-profits run an ongoing programme of 'mystery shopping' across a range of competitors to track strategies, tactics and creative approaches.

When information has been gathered the auditor will need to present and summarize it in a suitable format. This may involve a comparative study, or an exercise plotting the position of competitors against various axes. One useful tool is to run an analysis of the apparent strengths and weaknesses of each competitor, and an assessment of how their activities might impact on the focal organization in the future.

Potential collaborators

Of course there may be many instances where instead of viewing other non-profits as competitors, it makes more sense to partner with them to the advantage of all concerned. Such partnerships may open up access to new sources of funds, new markets or simply allow the partner organizations to take advantage of economies of scale and thus lower their costs of fundraising. In the USA, for example, it may not be economic for smaller non-profits to undertake corporate fundraising working on their own. Forging an alliance with other 'complementary' or related non-profits can create a pool of shared resources that would facilitate fundraising from this potential new audience.

Many forms of community fundraising are also conducted collaboratively, where smaller non-profits get together to run a joint campaign for the benefit of a local community and share the costs associated with promoting the campaign and associated events. Non-profits can also collaborate by sharing lists of donors. This is a practice common in the UK, although it tends to be limited to lower value supporters. Non-profits tend not to share the details of their highest value givers!

Thus in conducting a fundraising audit it will be instructive to consider examples of where organizations have collaborated successfully in the past and the factors that led to that success. The non-profit should look to see what it could learn from these collaborations and whether there might be any way in which it could work in partnership with others. If this is felt to be desirable it will be instructive to conduct background research into potential partners and to explore how such relationships might develop. An approach to one or more partners could then be included in the fundraising strategy/tactics.

Market factors

The next stage of the audit concerns the gathering of data in respect of the various donor markets the organization is addressing. It may therefore be sensible to structure this section by considering each donor market (e.g. Individuals, Corporates, Trusts, Foundations, Community) in turn. Each of these sections should then be further subdivided into identifiable segments or groups of donors, with current performance and likely future developments considered for each group.

Typically a non-profit needs to understand:

- *Who donates to their organization*: Are there certain types of people, corporates or foundations that have elected to offer their support? In the case of individuals, do these individuals have distinctive demographic or lifestyle characteristics that help the organization to understand more about the nature of their target audience?
- *Donor motivations*: Why do each group of donors elect to support the organization? What, if anything, do they expect to gain in return for their gift? How can the organization best reflect these motives in their fundraising communications?
- *Donor needs/preferences*: What kinds of communications do donors find appropriate? How do they view the communications they currently receive? Could these be improved in some way?
- *Donor behaviour*: Organizations need to understand how donors behave when they give to the organization. How much do each group or segment of donors give? Do higher value donors have any distinctive characteristics or needs? Are certain types of donor more likely to terminate their support than others? What are the primary reasons why donors terminate their support? Is there anything that may be done to address this?

In gathering this information it would again be wise to start with the material that is already available within the organization. Many non-profits (especially those that use cold list mailings in donor recruitment) commission lifestyle profiling on their donor base and on segments of that base, and generate reports from the donor database which detail the demographics and giving history of supporters. Likewise, fundraisers dealing with major givers, corporates, trusts and foundations and community groups are likely to have reports on file which provide considerable insight into the nature and distinguishing characteristics of the people or organizations they receive income from.

These data should then be supplemented through desk research, looking at the most recent published sources on the key segments and seeking to provide data on the size, growth and trends within each identified customer group. Using internal documents, database analysis and key secondary sources on lifestyle, demographic and charity-giving trends, current audiences can be compared against identified market potential to elicit information on each segment. This process will identify opportunities to gather further support from some audiences, attract new groups of donors, or may in some cases identify audiences which are saturated or shrinking, and where the non-profit might therefore need to consider whether further investment is wise.

Key sources of fundraising data are described in Chapter 3. In some cases it may also be necessary to conduct additional new or 'primary' research. This will also be developed in detail in Chapter 3.

The internal environment

Having summarized the key external influences on the organization it is possible to move on to consider an audit of the organization's own fundraising activity. The aim here is to scrutinize past fundraising performance and to carefully appraise what has worked well in the past and what has not. Current fundraising activities, trends in performance and the current structure and support systems that underpin fundraising activity will all be considered.

It is impossible to be prescriptive about the exact information requirements but it is likely that the auditor will wish to research:

- The past performance of each form of fundraising undertaken, trends in this performance and whether this might vary by the region in which the fundraising is undertaken. The auditor will wish to examine the revenues that are accumulated, the costs incurred and the returns generated.
- These data should also be examined by the group or segment of donors addressed. What success has the organization had in addressing discrete donor segments? Have some segments proved more responsive than others? If so, why has this been the case? All these data can be valuable in selecting future donors for contact and suggest the optimal ways in which funds could be solicited.
- Organizational processes: A review of the processes that support fundraising is also warranted. In particular the auditor will want to examine whether these processes are optimal and whether any problems have arisen in caring for donors over the period of the last plan. These processes will include donation processing and handling, mechanisms for dealing with donor communications and queries, internal co-ordination of strategy with departments such as press/public relations/campaigning, mechanisms for dealing with data protection/privacy issues (see Chapter 16).
- Organizational structure: The auditor will also want to look at the manner in which the fundraising function is organized and to explore whether this is optimal. In particular the split between the use of paid staff and volunteers will warrant investigation, as will the management reporting structures for each fundraising function. Does it make sense to organize the fundraising department in this particular way, or would it be valuable to explore making changes to these reporting structures? If the organization is involved in

regional fundraising and managing a network of fundraisers working from home it may also wish to explore whether the definition of these regions is optimal and whether the number of managers is appropriate given the number and spread of employees/volunteers in the regions.

Data for the internal audit are usually gathered through a mixture of desk research and meetings and interviews with staff. Directors and senior staff will be able to provide information on past strategy, tactics and performance, and will also provide the necessary data on financial performance, human resource strategy, and issues concerning governance and the general direction of the organization. It is often necessary to interview non-fundraising senior staff at this stage, such as the Finance Director and the CEO, to paint the full background picture of the non-profit and to establish the positioning and importance of fundraising within the organization.

It is then necessary to talk to individual fundraising staff to establish an understanding of the current fundraising work undertaken, to understand what has happened in the past and how the organization has come to have a particular fundraising mix, and to gather information on perceived opportunities and barriers. The auditor undertaking such interviews should also prompt for records and data at these interviews to illustrate, add to and verify the information provided by the interviewee. It is good practice to record the interviews, write them up, and then to check the written versions with the interviewees for accuracy and to ensure that they have not been misunderstood or their views misrepresented. Again, it often proves necessary to interview non-fundraising staff where areas of work overlap, or where other work areas may impact on fundraising (e.g. within the communications or trading functions and in IT resourcing). If external agencies are retained, especially where those agencies give strategic or planning support, it will also be necessary to interview their staff to get a full picture of the fundraising effort.

As with the external audit, the internal data gathering should be an iterative process, with checks being performed throughout to ensure that full and accurate information is being gathered and expressed. The financial, structural and performance information gathered may be used to provide benchmarking data for comparison against other organizations.

ANALYTICAL TOOLS

The audit of internal factors allows the auditor to capture a wealth of data on the performance of existing fundraising products or services. In essence each form of fundraising that the organization undertakes can be scrutinized to see whether it is worth continuing, what future performance might look like and how it compares with other similar forms of fundraising undertaken by other organizations. While it may be perfectly plausible to draw out a series of such conclusions from raw audit data, it may be preferable to use one of a number of analytical models which can assist the auditor in interpreting the mass of data accumulated.

Product/service lifecycle

One of the most fundamental concepts in marketing is the idea that a product or service will pass through several distinctive stages from the moment it is first introduced until it is ultimately withdrawn from the market. An understanding of these stages can greatly aid a fundraiser, since the appropriate tactics for the successful management of the product/service will often vary greatly between each stage of its lifecycle. Wilson *et al.* (1994:274) summarize the implications of the lifecycle concept as follows:

1   products/services have a finite life;
2   during this life they pass through a series of different stages, each of which poses different challenges to the organization;
3   virtually all elements of an organization's strategy/tactics need to change as the product/service moves from one stage to another;
4   the profit potential of products/services varies considerably from one stage to another;
5   the demands upon management and the appropriateness of managerial styles will also vary from stage to stage.

This idea is illustrated in Figure 2.2. During the introductory stage of the lifecycle the product/service will take time to gain acceptability in the market and take-up will hence be relatively low. At this stage the organization will be unlikely to have recouped its initial set-up and development costs and profitability remains negative. Over time, as the product begins to gain acceptability in the market, take-up will experience a period of sustained growth and provision of the product should at this stage become profitable. With the passage of time the volume/value of donations will eventually begin to level off as the market becomes saturated, until ultimately the product/service becomes obsolete and take-up begins to decline. At this stage the organization may wish to consider discontinuing the service, as with the lower volume of transactions the costs of provision may prove prohibitive. In employing the model the organization can monitor either the volume of fundraising transactions generated, or the value of such transactions. Either approach is acceptable.

Of course, to use this model the fundraiser has to define what he or she means by a product/service. This is trickier than would be the case in for-profit organizations where products/services are typically well defined. In fundraising it may make sense to examine forms of fundraising (i.e. individual, corporate, Trust/Foundation) or it may make sense to examine specific offers, which may be either bundles of need, or ways in which each category of donor might give (e.g. adopt a dog, charity of the year, challenge events, payroll giving, badger conservation). There is no one right way to use the lifecycle model; it simply depends on which is the best way of looking at the fundraising activities the organization undertakes.

The lifecycle concept has been much criticized over the years, but it still offers fundraisers considerable utility in that it can help shape the fundraising mix that may be adopted at each

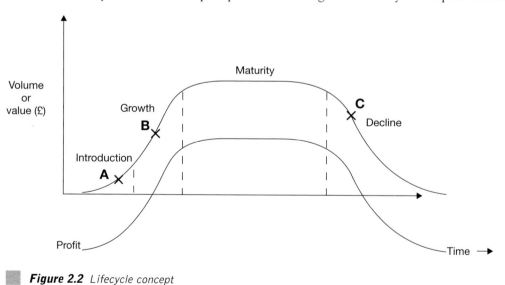

Figure 2.2 *Lifecycle concept*

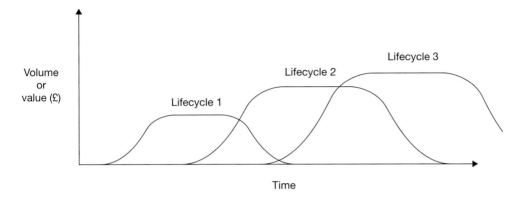

Figure 2.3 *Using the lifecycle for planning*

stage. As an illustration of this point, consider the role of promotion in supporting a fund-raising product. At point (A) in Figure 2.2 the role of promotional support would almost certainly be to inform the potential market that the product exists and the potential benefits it might offer. Raising awareness would be a key task at this stage. As the product moves to point (B) in the lifecycle, however, the nature of the market has changed. If the product was new and innovative, other non-profits will have started to copy the idea and the focus of promotion will need to change. A continual emphasis on awareness would be inappropriate since it would only serve to increase the overall level of demand in the market and thus benefit all competitor non-profits too. Instead a more useful strategy would be to differentiate the product from that provided by the competition. The emphasis would change to providing a clear positioning in the minds of target consumers/donors. By the time the product moves to point (C) in its lifecycle, promotional support may be withdrawn altogether to reduce costs, or additional monies may be spent in an attempt to 'prop-up' ailing demand in the market.

The lifecycle model may also be used to plan the introduction of new fundraising products. As an organization realizes that one product is soon to decline it can plan the introduction of new products. This idea is illustrated in Figure 2.3. In this case the organization is attempting to time new product introductions to ensure that the volume/value of donations from this particular source remains relatively constant, or ideally increasing, over time.

It should be noted, however, that non-profits normally have more than one fundraising product available at any one time and the lifecycle concept has the significant drawback that it tends to focus management attention on each product individually without viewing the organization's portfolio as a coherent whole. Indeed, a fundraising department may be viewed as a set of activities or projects to which new ones are intermittently added and from which older ones may be withdrawn. These activities and projects will make differential demands on, and contributions to, the organization as a whole. Hence some form of 'portfolio' analysis may prove a useful tool in deciding how the product mix might be improved, given the resource constraints that are valid at any one time.

Portfolio analysis

While there are a variety of portfolio models that have been employed over the years, these have been developed largely in the business context and are thus difficult to apply to the context of fundraising. In particular fundraisers should studiously avoid any portfolio model that has as its base the concept of market share, since this concept cannot be meaningfully applied to the realm of fundraising. This is the case for two reasons:

1   The sheer scale of the non-profit sector and the fact that fundraising performance is reported in aggregate terms only means that it would be impossible to properly quantify market share for particular products/services.
2   Portfolio models employing market share assume that the performance of a product is related to market share (i.e. that there are economies of scale). This is simply not the case with many forms of fundraising.

However, the model depicted in Figure 2.4 can offer considerable help to fundraisers in appraising the current health of their portfolio of products/services. To utilize the model it is necessary to begin by examining in detail the components of the two axes, namely external attractiveness and internal appropriateness. If we consider first the question of external attractiveness, not all of an organization's fundraising products will be equally attractive to potential funders. Some fundraising products will be more appealing than others and thus more worthy of investment. While the specific factors that drive how attractive a product might be to funders will vary from one organization to another, external attractiveness may typically depend on:

■   the level of general public concern about the 'content' of the product;
■   the number of potential donors (i.e. the potential/actual size of the market);
■   the perceived impact on the beneficiary group;
■   the uniqueness or novelty offered by the product;
■   ease of participation in the product.

It is important to recognize that this list is not exhaustive, and the beauty of this model is that organizations can employ whatever factors they perceive as being relevant to their own environment and circumstances.

Turning now to the question of internal appropriateness, this relates to the extent to which the product fits the profile of the organization providing it. In other words, is it appropriate to provide this product given the skills, expertise, organizational structure and resources available? Relevant factors here might include the following:

1   the extent to which the organization has relevant staff expertise;
2   the extent to which the organization has past experience of this product;

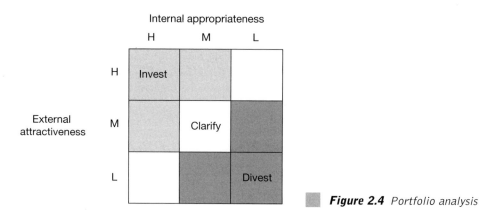

Figure 2.4 *Portfolio analysis*

3 the fundraising returns generated by the product;
4 the availability of volunteers.

Once again this list can be expected to vary from context to context and an organization should look to identify those factors which are most pertinent to its particular circumstances.

Having now defined the components of both internal appropriateness and external attractiveness the reader will appreciate that not all the factors identified may be seen as having equal importance to a given organization. For this reason it is important to weight the factors according to their relative importance. Beginning first with external attractiveness this is illustrated in Table 2.1. The reader will note that the weights for the components of each axis should all add up to 1. In the example given, the key factor driving external attractiveness is the perceived impact on the beneficiary group. This therefore receives a relatively high weighting. The issues of novelty and ease of participation are less important and therefore warrant only a low weighting.

The next step is to take each activity in which the organization is engaged and give it a score from 1 (very poor) to 10 (excellent) in terms of how it measures up against each of the components listed. To make this process clear a fictional example (let us call it Activity A – for the sake of argument a child sponsorship product) has been worked through in Tables 2.1 and 2.2. Considering first the issue of external attractiveness, Table 2.1 makes it clear that this product offers a very clear benefit to the beneficiary group and we thus rate this a 10 out of 10. The product also scores highly against the level of public concern. Unfortunately the product is also

Table 2.1 *External attractiveness*

Factor	Weight	Rating	Value
The level of general public concern about the 'content' of the product	0.2	8	1.6
The number of potential donors	0.2	5	1.0
The perceived impact on the beneficiary group	0.4	10	4.0
The uniqueness or novelty offered by the product	0.1	2	0.2
Ease of participation in the product	0.1	5	0.5
Total	1.0		7.3

Table 2.2 *Internal appropriateness*

Factor	Weight	Rating	Value
The extent to which the organization has relevant staff/volunteer expertise	0.4	8	3.2
The extent to which the organization has past experience of this product	0.1	5	0.5
The fundraising returns generated by the product	0.4	10	4.0
The availability of volunteers	0.1	7	0.7
Total	1.0		8.4

available from many other non-profits and cannot be considered unique. The rating against this dimension is thus only 2 out of 10. The product also offers only average performance in terms of the size of the market and ease of participation in the product. The product thus rates only 5 out of 10 against these dimensions.

Multiplying the weights by the ratings assigned produces a value for each factor. Summing these values gives an overall score for (in this case) the external attractiveness axis of product A of 7.3.

The process is identical for internal appropriateness. Each pertinent factor is assigned a weight, and each activity in which the organization engages is given a rating according to its performance in respect of each factor. Once again 1 = very poor, 10 = excellent. Returning to our analysis of Activity A we see that internal appropriateness for this organization is largely driven by staff/volunteer expertise and the returns generated by the product. These factors have relatively high weightings. The returns from our child sponsorship product (Activity A) are obviously excellent and the level of staff/volunteer expertise is also good. Multiplying the weights by the ratings gives us a value for each item and summing these generates an overall score for Activity A of 8.4 on the internal appropriateness axis.

These figures may then be plotted on the matrix in Figure 2.5 where the position of Activity A has been clearly indicated. If it is conceptually useful some organizations choose to take the analysis one stage further and draw a circle around the plotted position, the diameter of which is directly proportional to the percentage of fundraising income it generates. In this way managers can see at a glance the relative significance and position of each of the products in their portfolio. Of course for this to happen, all the products that a particular organization provides would have to plotted in this way, just as in Figure 2.5. Only then could an analysis be undertaken of the health and balance of the portfolio as a whole. Depending on the location of each activity within the matrix, the organization can then either look to invest further in its development, divest the activity and use the resources elsewhere, or subject the activity to further evaluation if the position still remains unclear.

Activities in the top left-hand corner of the matrix are clearly those that are highly attractive to their respective market and which the organization is well placed to deliver. These are clear candidates for continuing development.

Activities in the bottom right-hand corner, however, are clearly those that could be causing an unnecessary drain on resources. They are not seen as attractive by the target funders and the organization has no particular skill in delivering the products. Activities in this area of the matrix should be scrutinized with a view to termination or divestment. After all, if these products are not attractive and the organization is not good at providing them, what could be the

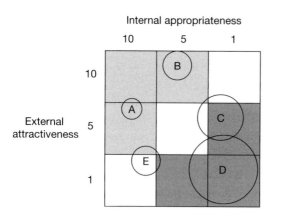

Figure 2.5 *Example portfolio analysis*

possible rationale for continuing? Of course this is only a model and the activity would have to be scrutinized very carefully before a divestment decision was taken, but the analysis has at least yielded considerable insight into the potential for valuable resources to be conserved and perhaps put to other, more appropriate, uses.

This leaves the question of activities falling within the central diagonal. These should be carefully evaluated as they are only moderately appropriate for the organization to provide and they have only limited external attractiveness.

The lifecycle matrix

In examining the health of a portfolio it is also possible to employ an adapted version of a matrix originally developed by consultants at Arthur D. Little Inc (See Hofer and Schendel 1978). The matrix is illustrated in Figure 2.6. In this matrix the user plots competitive position against lifecycle stages. The diameters of the circles around each activity are once again proportional to the fundraising revenue that they generate. The goal of using this matrix, as with that detailed above, is to guide investment decisions in fundraising products. In Figure 2.5 Activity A could be labelled a developing winner, Activity B a potential loser, Activity C an established winner and Activity D a loser. The power of this particular matrix is that it illustrates graphically how the products are positioned in respect of various stages of evolution. This may well be important in deciding when to create new products and to divest those at the end of their lifecycle which lack a clear rationale for their continuing existence.

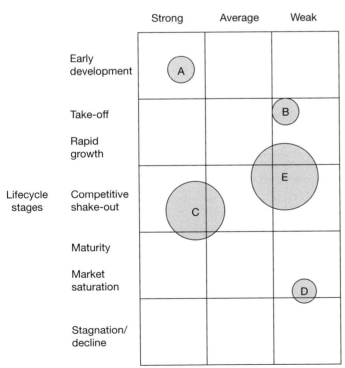

Figure 2.6 *Lifecycle matrix*
Source: Hofer and Schendel (1978)

The decision over where to place an activity on the competitive position axis depends on how that activity rates against a variety of factors. These typically include:

- how well the organization's strengths match the success factors in the particular fundraising market;
- the profitability associated with an activity;
- the extent to which the organization has the requisite fundraising skills;
- the extent to which the organization has developed a reputation in delivering that activity;
- the perceived costs/benefits to the donor of engaging with the activity.

A combination of these factors will determine how strongly positioned a particular fundraising product might be in its market. In employing the matrix, non-profits can either take an entirely subjective view of the 'score' or they may construct a weighted axis as with the previous matrix to impose a little more rigor on the analytical process.

In interpreting this matrix, it is possible to draw a number of conclusions in respect of how the performance of particular products might change over the duration of the plan. Similarly, the matrix may be used to guide investment decisions and in particular to highlight those products that should simply be divested. Those products towards the end of their lifecycle where the organization does not have a strong competitive position are clear candidates for this.

Drawbacks of portfolio models

In electing to employ a portfolio model it is essential that the user be aware of some of the disadvantages of such models.

- *Definition of market*: It is not always clear how the market should be defined when drawing conclusions about the position of a product on a given axis. When examining corporate fundraising products, for example, is the market: the whole corporate marketplace, only those corporations that give presently to non-profits, only those companies in particular sectors, or only those companies of a particular size? In using a portfolio model it is essential that the market is clearly defined and that the implications of this definition are fully understood.
- *Innovation*: The difficulty with some models is that they can understate the significance of an innovative new product. When such products first appear on a matrix they are characterized by low profitability/revenues and a weak market position as they fight to become established. Thus a cursory glance at a portfolio model might suggest that such products are struggling and that divestment is warranted. This is clearly not the case and care is required in interpretation.
- *Divesting unwanted products*: It should be recognized that while a number of fundraising products may be highlighted as candidates for divestment, this may frequently not be desirable. While it makes little financial sense to continue with a particular product, there may be a number of good human reasons why it should be continued. Perhaps volunteers have a long and proud tradition of managing the product and there are strong emotional attachments to its continuation. It may also be the case that some products gain the organization very welcome publicity that assists in the fulfilment of the mission, even though the performance of the activity itself is poor. Non-profits thus need to subject the recommendations to emerge from a portfolio analysis to greater scrutiny before divestment decisions are actually taken.

- *The desirability of growth*: Finally, most portfolio models assume that an organization is looking to achieve growth in fundraising income, and the prescriptions offered by such models may therefore not be appropriate to the circumstances facing every organization.

THE SWOT ANALYSIS

Clearly at this stage the output from the fundraising audit may be regarded as little more than a collection of data, and in this format it is as yet of limited value for planning purposes. What is required is a form of analysis, which allows the fundraiser to examine the opportunities and threats presented by the environment in a relatively structured way. Indeed, it should at this point be recognized that opportunities and threats are seldom absolute. An opportunity may only be regarded as an opportunity, for example, if the organization has the necessary strengths to support its development. For this reason it is usual to conduct a SWOT analysis (Strengths, Weaknesses, Opportunities and Threats) on the data gathered during the fundraising audit. This is simply a matter of selecting key information from the audit, analysing its implications and presenting it under one of the four headings. The important word here is 'key'. It is important that some filtering of the data gathered at this stage is undertaken so that the analysis is ultimately limited to the factors of most relevance for the subsequent development of strategy. The SWOT addresses the following issues:

- What are the strengths of the organization? What is the organization good at? Is it at the forefront of particular fundraising developments? Does it have access to a donor segment that is not reached by competitors? Does it have a strong database system/great support agencies/high local awareness?
- What are its weaknesses? In what ways do competitors typically outperform the organization? Are there weaknesses in terms of internal support or structures? Are there barriers to future development in some areas?
- What are the main opportunities facing the organization over the duration of the plan? Are there new fundraising techniques to test, new audiences to attract? Are new developments within the organization likely to present extra opportunities for fundraising?
- What are the major threats facing the organization? Is a major competitor likely to launch a new capital appeal? Will economic changes impact on certain core funders and leave them with less to give? Are planned changes to legislation likely to curtail fundraising activity?

Good SWOT analyses share a number of distinctive characteristics:

- They are relatively concise summaries of the audit data and are typically no more than four to five pages of commentary focusing on key factors only.
- They recognize that strengths and weaknesses are differential in nature. This means that a strength is only a strength if the organization is better at this particular activity or dimension than its competitors. Similarly, weaknesses should be examined from the perspective of where the organization lags behind the competition.
- They are clear and easy to read. Quality suffers if items are over-abbreviated and the writer concentrates on micro rather than macro issues. As MacDonald (1995:406) notes: 'If a SWOT analysis is well done, someone else should be able to draft the objectives which logically flow from it. The SWOT should contain clear indicators as to the key determinants of success in the department.'

- A separate SWOT should be completed for each segment of donor crucial to the organization's future. What may be perceived as a strength in relation to individual donors may well be a weakness when approaching corporate donors. Thus, the global SWOT analyses that are conducted so frequently by fundraising departments can often tend towards the meaningless. For all but the smallest and simplest organizations a series of highly focused SWOTs will be warranted.

CHAPTER SUMMARY

In this chapter we have introduced the fundraising audit as the first key component of the fundraising plan. We established that it provided an organization with the 'Where are we now?' component of a plan. We have also outlined the information requirements that a non-profit will have at the commencement of the planning process and suggested why this information is important. In Chapter 3 we shall explore in further detail where a non-profit can source much of this material and, in cases where existing sources prove unhelpful, the tools and techniques of marketing research that may be used to plug the gaps.

We have also examined a range of product and portfolio models that may be used to assist in the manipulation and interpretation of audit data. The use of such models can greatly enhance the quality of insight gained through the audit process, although it is important for the auditor to understand the underlying assumptions made by these models and the implications for the derivation of subsequent fundraising strategy.

Finally, we have introduced the SWOT analysis as a tool to summarize audit data. This is also essential since it draws out the key factors driving, or likely to drive, fundraising performance in the future. A good SWOT analysis should not only summarize the audit data, but also suggest to planners what might be realistic objectives to achieve over the planning period. The SWOT analysis will also suggest the strategy/tactics that may best be employed to achieve these objectives. These are subjects that we return to in Chapter 4 when we examine the final two components of the fundraising plan, namely 'Where do we want to be?' and 'How are we going to get there?'

DISCUSSION QUESTIONS

1   Fundraising audits can be undertaken by external suppliers (agency staff or consultants), or the task can be allocated to internal staff. What do you think would be the advantages and drawbacks associated with each of these routes?

2   List five political, economic, environmental, economic and technological factors likely to impact over the next three years on a US-based animal welfare non-profit.

3   Explain the strengths and weaknesses of portfolio modelling for non-profits.

4   You are the fundraising director of a medium-sized UK non-profit where no formal fundraising planning has been undertaken over the past five years. Prepare a set of notes to be used in a presentation to your trustees on the advisability of investment on a fundraising planning process.

REFERENCES

Drucker, P.F. (1955) *The Practice of Management*, Heinemann, London.

Hofer, C.W. and Schendel, D. (1978) *Strategy Formulation: Analytical Concepts*, West Publishing, St Paul, Minn.

MacDonald, M. (1995) *Marketing Plans: How to Prepare Them, How to Use Them*, Butterworth Heinemann, Oxford.

Wilson, R.M.S., Gilligan, C. and Pearson, D.J. (1994) *Strategic Marketing Management*, Butterworth Heinemann, Oxford.

Chapter 3

Marketing research for fundraising

LEARNING OBJECTIVES

By the end of this chapter you should be able to:

- Explain the relevance of market research to fundraising planning.
- Distinguish between primary and secondary research.
- Distinguish between qualitative and quantitative data.
- Utilize a wide range of secondary sources of data.
- Identify and employ relevant primary research methods.
- Present marketing research data.
- Brief and monitor the work undertaken by external research agencies.

INTRODUCTION

In the previous chapter we explored a range of information needs typically encountered by a non-profit in writing a strategic marketing or fundraising plan. While this list seems extensive it must be remembered that good information can be used to great effect in guiding the decisions and policies an organization might adopt and is therefore invaluable.

The sheer number of non-profit organizations presents donors and other supporters with a vast array of choice. Donors often have multiple opportunities to support very similar (if not identical) causes and programmes. Given this, to compete successfully for funds organizations need to understand their position in the market, the activities of key competitors and also the behaviour of the donors themselves. In respect of this latter category, issues such as why people give, the value they place on the exchange, how they select between competing demands on their resources and so on are all of relevance. If these were all rational 'objective' decisions on the part of the donor there would be little need for marketing research. Fundraisers could take an educated guess about how individuals might think and behave and be right some 90 per cent of the time. Sadly, human beings frequently do not behave rationally and base their decisions on a range of subjective and emotional factors. These are not immediately obvious even to those with considerable experience of a sector, and thus research is necessary to identify donor perceptions of each of these dimensions. It is important to stress from the outset that conducting such research need not be an expensive exercise. As we shall shortly see, much can be learned for comparatively little time, effort and expenditure.

Of course market research should not be seen as a substitute for good managerial decision-making. The role of market research is not to usurp executive experience or judgement. Rather market research provides the basic data that managers can use to help *inform* the decision-making process. It thus reinforces good decision-making rather than replacing it.

It is also important to note that there is an element of risk associated with every management decision and that decision-making in the absence of research data simply exposes an organization to unnecessary additional risk. In the non-profit sector this risk is all the more acute because of the agency role that non-profits play in stewarding the resources supplied by donors. If, for example, a fundraising campaign goes badly wrong and loses the organization money, it will effectively be wasting the resources donated to the organization by previous donors and will put the organization in breach of their trust. Non-profit managers are thus under a considerable obligation to ensure that the risk inherent in decision-making is held to a minimum.

There are thus a number of advantages to an organization in conducting thorough research in relation to each of the issues highlighted in Chapter 2. Given the plethora of information needs and the equal plethora or potential information sources, there is no shortage of data to be had about the fundraising function or the environment in which it operates. Sadly this is frequently irrelevant, incompatible with the specific information need or excessive in terms of volume. Problems can also arise when managers fail to understand the nature of the information presented and then, even in the presence of high-quality data, the wrong decisions can be taken.

In this chapter we will navigate some of the pitfalls associated with conducting marketing research, outline a process that may be used to manage the activity, explain the research tools and techniques available, and finally explore how to brief and manage external agencies that might be employed to assist an organization in capturing data.

DEFINITION

Before beginning with this process it is important to begin by clarifying exactly what we mean by marketing research. Over the years there has been considerable confusion between the terms 'marketing' and 'market research'. Although market research has tended to be used as a synonym for marketing research there was originally a distinction drawn between these two terms by virtue of their scope. Market research was regarded as research into markets (e.g. in the case of fundraising, individual donors, corporate supporters and foundations) whereas marketing research applies more broadly to every aspect of marketing. This would thus include researching the activities of competitors, trends in the external environment, the performance of an organization's own fundraising activity and so on.

The American Marketing Association (1961) defined marketing research as 'the systematic gathering, recording and analyzing of data about problems relating to the marketing of goods and services'.

More recently Kotler (1967) prefers to emphasize the goals of marketing research and defines it as: 'systematic problem analysis, model building and fact finding for the purposes of improved decision making and control in the marketing of goods and services.' Thus marketing research is concerned with the disciplined collection and evaluation of data in order to aid managers in understanding the needs of their target audiences more fully. It may be used to reduce risk in decision-making and to control (to some extent) the risk surrounding each aspect of fundraising.

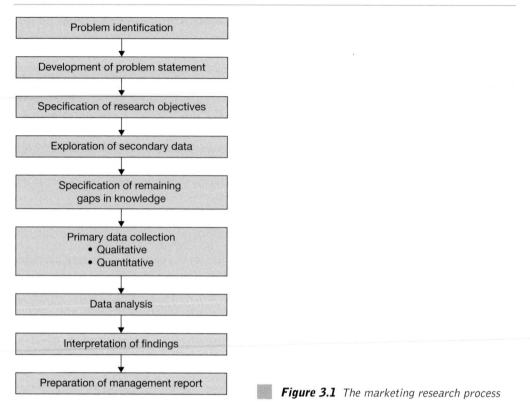

Figure 3.1 *The marketing research process*

While perspectives on the research process frequently differ from one organization to another, the approach adopted will always share a number of common features as outlined in Figure 3.1.

The marketing research process is typically initiated by an organization realizing that it has a problem or issue to resolve. To operationalize this for the purposes of research it must first be expressed as a series of specific research objectives. These objectives are then addressed through initial desk research of existing data. In some cases this may yield all the answers an organization needs, in which case an appropriate analysis of this material may result in the preparation of the requisite report for management. It is frequently the case, however, that not all of the information needs can be met in this way and that new or *primary* data may have to be collected and analysed for this purpose.

In the sections below we will discuss each element of this process beginning with the specification of the research problem.

STATING THE RESEARCH PROBLEM AND RESEARCH OBJECTIVES

The first stage of the research process involves a clear specification of the fundraising problem on which the research is expected to focus. This is essential if the organization is to achieve a satisfactory outcome from the research process, particularly if external agencies are to be employed for the purposes of data collection.

Where it is intended that the organization will work with an agency it is important that both management and the research team work closely together in this crucial task of developing a problem statement. Unless the agency thoroughly understands the issues facing the client it is quite possible that the research objectives designed to provide information to resolve these problems will be irrelevant or possibly even counter-productive.

Having defined the problem it is then possible to design the research objectives. This requires the organization and/or agency to turn the problem into a series of information needs. Thus, for example, if the problem facing the organization is a fall in bequest income, the research objectives could be written to explore why this might be the case and offer insight into what might be done about it.

In this example the research objectives might appear as follows:

- to quantify and establish trends in the decline in bequest giving;
- to explore the extent to which this decline is unique to the organization in question or shared by the sector as a whole;
- to assess the motives of bequest givers for offering a bequest;
- to assess donor perceptions of the bequest solicitation process;
- to explore the utility (and donor perceptions) of the various communication channels that may be used to solicit bequests;
- to explore the role of intermediaries in facilitating bequests;
- to identify the barriers to bequest giving.

This list is by no means exhaustive and, depending on the circumstances facing a particular organization, the actual content of this list will vary considerably. The point is that the problem must be broken down into a series of research objectives that will address each of the likely causes for the decline, providing enough information for managers to take remedial action. Again, if an agency is to be employed for the purposes of data collection it must also be involved in selecting research objectives, since they may well have insight into the issues which could help shape these objectives, and also because they need to understand the rationale underlying each information need and how it pertains to the problem as a whole.

SECONDARY VERSUS PRIMARY DATA

The next stage in the research process is typically to conduct a desk research of existing information sources. Typically, many of the organization's information needs can be met adequately and cheaply by simply reading through the trade press, research reports or specialist journals. Collectively, this is known as secondary data.

Secondary data are data that have already been collected for some purpose in the past. The data have thus *not* been collected specifically to address the issues at hand. Such data may typically be found within the non-profit organization in management/consultancy reports or in an analysis of database records, but more frequently they will be found outside the organization in government publications, syndicated research, trade/professional reports, electronic databases, professional/academic journals and so on. A summary of key secondary sources of data is supplied in Exhibit 3.1.

Secondary data are always the starting point in seeking to satisfy research objectives since they have the advantage of being cheap to collect and will typically be a fraction of the cost of the collection of new fundraising research (e.g. surveys, focus groups). There are however, a number of distinct disadvantages in that:

- Data may have been collected for another purpose that may not meet the exact information needs of the organization.

EXHIBIT 3.1 KEY SOURCES OF SECONDARY DATA

United Kingdom

The Institute of Fundraising (www.institute-of-fundraising.org.uk)

The Institute is the professional body that represents the interests of UK fundraisers to the media, government and other interested parties. It provides a range of training courses, information about fundraising and sponsors research into the field.

The Giving Campaign (www.givingcampaign.co.uk)

Provides research data on a range of fundraising topics such as corporate giving, tax-efficient giving (Giftaid) and share giving.

National Council of Voluntary Organizations (www.ncvo-vol.org.uk)

Provides an excellent range of publications covering many aspects of non-profit management. Research department also provides statistics on giving, the use of fundraising techniques and so on.

Charities Aid Foundation (www.cafonline.org)

Provides a range of research reports covering topics such as fundraising costs, donor life-time value and the behaviour of grant-making trusts. Also provides annual statistics in respect of the performance of the Top 500 charities.

Directory of Social Change (www.dsc.org.uk)

Provides a wide range of publications covering every aspect of non-profit management. Particularly good at providing information for the smaller non-profit. Also has an interest in the cost of fundraising and has published in this field.

Charity Commission (www.charity-commission.gov.uk)

The body responsible for regulating registered charities in the UK. Provides a range of publications offering guidance to charities and also has a database of charity accounts, which must be lodged with the commission each year.

Guidestar

At the time of writing, this web-based service has yet to be established, but is likely to open up access to Charity Commission data and hence to the annual accounts of all registered charities in the UK. It is also likely that some degree of analysis and commentary will be provided on these data.

Fundraising UK (www.fundraising.co.uk)

This excellent site hosted by Howard Lake provides news and information about all aspects of fundraising. Also offers a range of links to other pertinent sites.

Caritas Data (www.caritasdata.co.uk)

Caritas has for many years provided financial data and analysis in respect of the performance of UK charities. Its new service 'charitiesdirect.com' allows donors to access information about their chosen charity and presents key analytical ratios.

HM Government

Key government departments such as the Treasury or the Home Office have an active interest in the voluntary sector, and their website often features pertinent reports, policy papers and so on.

Academic institutions

Many universities have established research centres that provide fundraising information. These include the Centre for Voluntary Sector Management at Henley Management College, the Centre for Charity and Trust Research at South Bank and the VOLPROF Centre hosted in City University's Business School.

Professional journals

There are also an array of professional journals that serve the sector such as *Third Sector*, *Professional Fundraising* and the *Charity Times*.

USA

Association of Fundraising Professionals (www.afpnet.org)

The professional body that represents the fundraising profession in the USA and other countries worldwide. It provides training, a major annual conference, fundraising publications and sponsors research.

Council for Advancement and Support of Education (www.case.org)

CASE, as the name suggests, is the professional body for fundraisers working in the field of education. While we list it here as a US organization it actually serves the needs of fundraisers all over the world with local chapters established in many countries. It provides training, conferences, news/information and a range of publications.

National Committee on Planned Giving (www.ncpg.org)

The professional association for people whose work includes developing, marketing and administering charitable planned gifts. Those people include fundraisers for non-profit institutions and consultants, and donor advisers working in a variety of for-profit settings. It provides a wide range of services and publications.

Charity America (www.charityamerica.com)

This site is effectively an online village designed to unite donors, volunteers, businesses and charity professionals. It contains a wealth of information for all these various stakeholder groups.

American Association of Fundraising Counsel Trust for Philanthropy
(www.aafrc/trust/index.html)

The Trust provides many excellent research publications scooping the non-profit sector and its activities. Giving USA is produced by the AAFRC, as is the Annual Yearbook of American Philanthropy.

Guidestar (www.guidestar.org)

This site allows users to access financial information in respect of US non-profits. Those users wishing to access a more detailed financial analysis of non-profits may also obtain this service from Guidestar.

Indiana Center on Philanthropy (http://philanthropy.indiana.edu/)

The IU Center conducts, co-ordinates and supports research, building a broad base of knowledge about the causes and consequences of philanthropic behaviour involving individuals, communities and institutions. It offers a range of research data and publications, together with an annual conference allowing practitioners to access latest research.

Social Welfare Research Institute at Boston College (www.bc.edu/research/swri)

The Institute publishes a range of research papers and reports of interest to the fundraising profession. It has tended to focus (although not exclusively) on wealth transfers and major gift fundraising. Many resources may be downloaded free of charge.

Trade Press

There are numerous trade publications in the USA including the *Nonprofit Times*, *Chronicle of Philanthropy*, *Fund Raising Management* and the *CASE journal*.

- Data are often out of date, having been collected a year or more prior to the current investigation.
- Data may be of dubious quality, and thus a careful consideration of the source and the methodology adopted will be warranted to ensure that the data offer appropriate validity and reliability.

Having exhausted the sources of secondary data the organization may then return to the research objectives and determine those that have not been fully addressed with this extant data. Where information gaps remain, it will be necessary to commission primary research to supply the missing information. Primary research involves collecting new data specifically for the purpose of answering the questions posed by the current research objectives. This is typically an expensive exercise and will not be undertaken lightly by the commissioning organization. Primary research may be either qualitative or quantitative.

QUALITATIVE RESEARCH

Fundraisers are frequently concerned with issues such as how donors view the organization, what motivates them to support it, what they like and do not like about the communications they receive and so on. If the organization lacks an understanding of the factors likely to be at work in each case, it would be advised to begin by conducting what is known as *qualitative* research. This form of research is designed to provide such an insight and is a good way of gathering data about people's attitudes, feelings and motives. It is impressionistic in style rather than conclusive and it probes for data rather than counting responses. The most common qualitative research methods include focus groups (group discussions), detailed 'depth' interviews and projective techniques.

Depth interviews

The use of this technique involves the researcher in a free-flowing discussion with members of the group whose opinions are being sought. Discussions are conducted on a one-to-one basis, so that there is no need for the interviewee to feel under any pressure to respond in a socially acceptable way, or to worry about what other participants in the research process might think of their views. It is thus a very open and non-threatening research setting and interviewers are trained to put their subjects at ease. Such interviews can be either unstructured or semi-structured, depending on the level of knowledge the researcher has about the factors likely to be of interest. Where a detailed knowledge is lacking the interviewer will find an unstructured approach of most value and facilitate a general discussion of the research question, and allow the conversation to focus on whatever factors emerge.

Focus groups/group discussions

This technique requires the researcher to assemble a group of six to ten respondents who agree to take part in (typically) a one- to two-hour discussion that addresses the research objective(s). This discussion may be held at the organization's premises or at a centrally located venue that is easy for the respondents to access. The researcher carefully facilitates a discussion of the topic and ensures that the views of each member of the group are elicited. He or she may also have to deal with 'difficult' personalities who attempt to either dominate the discussion or fail to express a point of view. It is important that the views of every participant are considered equally, and the process of facilitation is thus a highly skilled task. Focus group proceedings are typically either audio- or video-taped, so that they can subsequently be analysed by the research team.

The biggest drawback of this technique is the expense, with a typical focus group costing between US$1,000 and $1,200 and a range of six to eight groups typically being necessary to address a given research task. Basing decisions on a smaller number of groups can be risky, since focus group participants may prove to be highly unrepresentative of the donor (or other) population and thus the results misleading. The insights gained from focus groups can be of considerable value, but this is frequently gained at substantial cost.

Projective techniques

The use of projective techniques has moved in and out of fashion over the past fifty years. They are said to generate considerable insight into feelings, beliefs and attitudes that individuals find it difficult to articulate by other means. A number of techniques are in existence, where research subjects can express their views by 'projecting' those views on to objects, pictures or third parties.

An organization interested in the perception of its brand might thus provide a group of eight to ten individuals with a set of cards and crayons and ask them to create an image that for them embodies the brand. This may also be achieved through the use of clay, where subjects create a physical representation of the brand. The shapes and pictures created can then be subject to expert analysis to identify the common themes to emerge.

A further common technique would involve asking subjects to create a personality for an organization or brand. Thus 'if this organization were a well-known celebrity – who would it be?' The description and subsequent rationale can then form the basis for discussion.

Projective techniques have also been used in the context of cartoons, where research subjects are presented with a cartoon illustration of a social situation embodying the research objective(s). Blank dialogue boxes (or speech bubbles) will be provided and the subject asked to supply appropriate speech. An example is provided in Figure 3.2. The technique works because

Figure 3.2 *Projective techniques*

subjects may find it easier to address some topics by projecting their own values and beliefs on to these cartoon characters, thereby expressing views they would feel uncomfortable voicing in a traditional interview. Again, this speech can be subject to a content analysis at the end of the research process and common themes elicited.

A caveat

It should be noted that qualitative techniques themselves do not constitute valid market research. The samples are inadequate, the method of questioning inconsistent and the means of interpretation subjective. Two or three people (or agencies) doing the same piece of qualitative research can often come up with very different results. This is simply because the use of eight to ten individuals in a focus group is rarely representative of the 'population' as a whole and the results will therefore always have a high degree of bias. To take a fundraising example, one might commission a series of focus groups to determine the reasons why donors support the organization. Such a group would likely generate an excellent list of reasons, but it could never tell you what proportion of the donor base might be motivated by each rationale for support. It is thus only half a story. The real strength of the technique lies in its ability to generate *hypotheses* about how the donor population as a whole *might* feel or *might* behave. To be used to inform fundraising strategy an organization might typically test these hypotheses with quantitative techniques and a larger, more representative sample of the population.

QUANTITATIVE RESEARCH TECHNIQUES

Quantitative research typically involves the gathering of numerical information about the market or particular audience with which the researcher is concerned. Unlike qualitative research the goal is to quantify the number of members of a particular group that hold certain views, donate in particular ways, are motivated by particular factors and so on.

Quantitative research techniques include:

- *Personal interviews*: These may be conducted by a trained researcher in the home, office or a central location/street. Both qualitative and quantitative data could be gathered, although cost and time restraints frequently confine data collection to quantitative data. The interviewer follows a set script and simply poses a range of questions, noting down the replies he or she receives for subsequent analysis.
- *Telephone interviews*: Increasingly marketing research is being conducted by phone. Researchers from the organization or agency ring a sample of individuals and again follow a set script, posing each question in turn. Modern technology now facilitates a process known as CATI (Computer Assisted Telephone Interviewing) where the questions appear on a screen in front of the interviewer and, when each response is given, it is typed into the database (or the appropriate box clicked through). Depending on the nature of the response the interviewer is then prompted by the system to ask the next appropriate question.
- *Postal questionnaires*: Here the contact with the research sample is impersonal. A series of questions are developed, printed on to a questionnaire and dispatched to members of the target audience whose opinion is sought. Often the response is incentivized in some way and facilitated through the inclusion of a reply paid or freepost envelope.
- *E-mail questionnaires*: The recent rise in computer ownership and access to the Internet has now made the acquisition of market research data much more affordable. Sudman and

Blair (1999) argue that electronic surveys will replace telephone surveys over the next quarter century as more and more individuals become comfortable with the medium. Surveys can easily be e-mailed to donors or other categories of supporter. Alternatively if the questionnaire is lengthy, it is possible to post the questionnaire on an organization's website and then to e-mail respondents asking them to visit the site and complete it. Sudman and Blair (1999) recommend locating the questionnaire in a password-protected part of the site, so that responses from members of the sample do not become confused with those of other site users who decide to complete the questionnaire during their visit.

- *Fax questionnaires*: In the USA the fax is a medium now commonly employed for advertising and other forms of marketing solicitation. Its use is more common in the context of business-to-business marketing, although home faxes are growing in number and significance. In some instances, if involved in research with corporate organizations, it may thus be appropriate to consider employing a fax survey, which respondents may complete and fax back to the non-profit. Such forms of research are unlikely to work in the UK at present where the fax is regarded as highly intrusive.

TAKING A SAMPLE

In undertaking quantitative research it may be possible to solicit the opinions of everyone in the whole group or **population** of interest. Under these circumstances the researcher is effectively conducting a **census** since everyone of interest can be contacted and asked for their views.

More frequently, however, it is not practical to pose questions of everyone in a target population, by virtue of the sheer number of contacts involved, the costs of soliciting their views, or the difficulty of contacting them, perhaps because of their geographic spread. In such circumstances researchers take a sample of the members of the population and calculate statistics about that sample, which allow them to make statements and estimates about the population as a whole without the need to contact everyone.

There are four main methods for sampling of relevance to fundraisers, namely random sampling, systematic random sampling, stratified random sampling and quota sampling. Random sampling is referred to as **probability sampling**, while quota sampling is referred to as **non-probability sampling**. This difference matters because it impacts on the way we may interpret the results of the research undertaken.

Under random sampling each member of a population has an equal chance of being selected in the sample. Because of this it is possible to calculate a **level of confidence** and limit of accuracy from the results of such a sample. A level of confidence is a statement about how confident we can be about the results from the sample holding good across the population as a whole. At the 95 per cent level of confidence, for example, there is only a 5 per cent (or 1 in 20) chance that the sample results do not hold good for the whole population. Confidence levels may be set higher than this to offer greater accuracy, but this would add substantially to the cost since it would require the extraction of a larger sample.

It is important to note that we are not saying that probability samples are necessarily more representative than non-probability samples. Indeed, the converse may often be true. The point is that probability samples allow for the calculation of **sample error** or the extent to which errors in the results occurs because a sample was used rather than asking the whole population for their views. You cannot do this with non-probability samples since no objective method is used in the first place to gather the sample.

We now consider each form of sampling in turn.

Random sampling

To generate a random sample, as noted above, every member of the population must have an equal chance of selection. To take a random sample it is thus necessary to begin by defining or assembling a *sampling frame*. This is simply a complete list of all the individuals in the target population. This may, for example, be a list of names on a database, a directory of organizations or a list of contacts. Each name on this list would then be assigned a number and all the numbers entered into a hat. If a 10 per cent sample of individuals is required, 10 per cent of those numbers and associated names would then be drawn at random out of the hat.

Of course, modern technology now makes this process much less cumbersome, and many modern software programs generate numbers at random which may be used to generate a random sample for the researcher. Indeed, in many cases the researcher will be oblivious to the process since it is necessary only to request this kind of sample from the database software.

Systematic sampling

There are occasions, however, when a truly random sample is not practical, perhaps because the sampling frame is supplied in a list format and where the number of contacts on that list is large. Assigning numbers and then selecting numbers at random from the list would then be time-consuming and potentially costly. Under these circumstances it may be more practical to take a *systematic random sample*. Suppose we wish to take a 10 per cent sample from a list of 1,000 names. We could then proceed by selecting a random start point and thus selecting at random a number between 1 and 10. Suppose we select the number 4. We would then work down through our list taking the 4th name, the 14th name, the 24th name, the 34th name and so on until we had completed the list and extracted the 10 per cent of contacts required. This is a random sample.

Stratified random sample

To illustrate the need for this form of sampling let us consider the example of a non-profit wishing to explore the reasons why its donors stop giving, or lapse in their support of the organization. To investigate this issue it has been proposed that a 10 per cent sample of the lapsed portion of the database be sent a questionnaire to ascertain their views. Intuitively the fundraising team feel that these reasons might vary by the age of the individual. Now suppose that the age profile of lapsed donors is as depicted in Table 3.1.

Table 3.1 *Age profile of donors*

Age category	Percentage of lapsed file
Under 20	10
21–40	20
41–60	30
61–80	20
80+	10

By taking a purely random sample of 10 per cent of these individuals it is possible, however unlikely, that a sample could be generated where all the individuals contacted are over age 80. This could greatly bias the results. Instead researchers would better proceed by deciding in advance that of their sample 10 per cent will be under age 20, 20 per cent will be aged 21 to 40, 20 per cent will be aged 41 to 60, 20 per cent will be aged 61 to 80 and 10 per cent will be aged 80+. In other words the composition of the sample mirrors that of the population to ensure that each category or *strata* is properly represented.

Non-probability sampling

With non-probability sampling the chances of selection are not known; therefore the ability to generalize about a population based on the results of a sample are much reduced. Indeed, Kumar *et al.* (1999) argue that the results of non-probability sampling may contain biases and uncertainties that make them worse than no information at all. Not all writers are as pessimistic however, and the decision of whether or not to use probability-based sampling will be a function of the degree of accuracy required, the likely costs of error, the population variability and the type of information needed (Tull and Hawkins 1996).

Non-probability sampling does not require the use of a sampling frame and thus the project's costs might be reduced. The sample is chosen at the convenience of the researcher to fit the needs of the particular project. Samples can be created by convenience sampling (simply selecting individuals convenient to the research project), purposive sampling (where individuals are selected who are felt appropriate to the project objectives) or quota sampling.

In quota sampling researchers make a clear effort to ensure that the sample they construct mirrors the characteristics of the sample as a whole. Thus if a non-profit were looking to assess the awareness of their organization/brand among members of the local population, the researchers could proceed by identifying the demographic profile of that population. They might do this by age and gender, for example. They would then create a quota such as that depicted in Table 3.2 to ensure that the balance of people whose opinions they solicit reflects that of the population as a whole.

It is important not to confuse quota sampling with stratified sampling. The major difference is that in the former the interviewer/researcher selects the individual respondent; in the latter the selection process is carried out by random selection.

Table 3.2 Derivation of quota sample

	Percentage of population	Quota sample (50 individuals)
Male (aged 20–40)	10	5
Male (aged 41–60)	16	8
Male (aged 60+)	26	13
Female (aged 20–40)	14	7
Female (aged 41–60)	10	5
Female (aged 60+)	24	12
Total	100	50

Sample size

The question of how big a sample to use for research is not an easy one to answer as it depends on a number of factors. Much depends on the type of sample, the statistics that will be calculated, the homogeneity of the population and the resources (time, people and money) that are available. It is impossible in this chapter to cover all the pertinent factors, but it is worth noting that there are now a number of tables, calculator functions and software programs that will prompt the user with the relevant questions and generate an appropriate sample size. There are also many websites hosted by research agencies that have sponsored online tools to help the inexperienced researcher.

An often surprising point to consider when calculating the sample size is that it has nothing to do with the size of population. The reason for this is quite straightforward. Rather than the size of the population being the key, it is the extent to which all the members of the population have the same value or response. If you had 20,000 people in a population who all responded in exactly the same way to a direct marketing solicitation, then obviously you would need a sample of only one of them to ascertain the behaviour of the others. Not a very likely scenario. Typically not everyone mailed will give and individuals will give different amounts. Thus what affects the sample size that will be necessary is the variability of the population. Obviously the greater the variability, the larger the sample required to estimate aggregate behaviour with any precision.

QUESTIONNAIRE DESIGN

General advice

In designing a research questionnaire there are a number of points to bear in mind.

Overall length

People quickly get bored with completing surveys, particularly in face-to-face or telephone situations. In these circumstances the length of the questionnaire should be held to an absolute minimum with the questions posed tightly integrated with the overall research problem. Postal questionnaires can be somewhat longer since respondents may complete them at their leisure, but researchers employing questionnaires of over four pages will note a sharp drop-off rate in the achieved response rate.

Questions should be clear and unambiguous

Questions should be written in the language of the target audience. It should be remembered that while a fundraiser may be highly conversant with the language employed by the cause, members of the public may not understand much of the specialist terminology and even fewer of the mnemonics. These must be studiously avoided or explained.

Each question should also be written and checked for clarity. The question should also avoid ambiguity and the notorious 'and' word. Consider the example at the top of page 53.

If this question seems appropriate at first glance, consider how a donor might answer if donating to the organization gives them a sense of pride, but they hate the communications they receive. Each question in a questionnaire should address one dimension only.

Please indicate the extent to which you agree with the following statement employing the following scale:

1 = Strongly disagree
2 = Disagree
3 = No opinion
4 = Agree
5 = Strongly agree

Donating money to this charity gives me a sense of real pride and I enjoy receiving the communications they send me.

1	2	3	4	5

Use closed questions wherever possible

It is important when designing a questionnaire to consider how the data will be analysed. Closed questions are much easier to analyse since they only allow respondents a range of options in respect of their response. The example below is thus a closed question.

Please indicate your age category:

☐   Under 20
☐   21–40
☐   41–60
☐   61–80
☐   81+

Open questions by contrast invite the respondent to offer an answer which then has to be coded into categories (or interpreted) *post hoc* by the researcher (e.g. Please tell us what you think of our donor communications). It is this latter dimension that makes the inclusion of open questions undesirable since they can substantially slow down the speed of the analysis undertaken and greatly increase the costs of analysis as a consequence. It should be noted however that the use of closed questions requires researchers to have a firm grasp of the subject area in advance, since they must ensure that the options available to respondents are comprehensive. Where doubt remains, some researchers add a final category – namely 'Other – please specify'.

Classifications should be carefully designed

Where closed questions are employed, researchers should take great care to design the categories appropriately. Each option should be discrete, unlike the example given on page 54 where it is possible to tick two boxes if one is aged, 20, 40, 60 or 80.

Similarly, confusions may arise as to the meaning of some categories. In the author's experience asking for occupation can be a particular problem since in one instance an individual chose to describe his occupation as 'bank director' when in reality his role involved greeting customers at the door and directing them to the correct counter!

Please indicate your age category:

- ☐ Under 20
- ☐ 20–40
- ☐ 40–60
- ☐ 60–80
- ☐ 80+

Avoid leading questions

Leading questions are those that direct the respondent to give a specific answer; thus 'Did the recent financial scandal affect your giving?' is doomed to failure from the outset. Less obviously asking a donor whether they have read a particular magazine or communication may simply prompt them to say 'Yes'. If a researcher is interested in recall of specific communications or the media exposure of a particular individual he or she will be advised to generate a list of communications and to ask the respondent which of them he or she can recall or has read, respectively. Respondents are then less likely to answer in an 'ego-defensive' manner.

Order questions in a logical sequence

In designing a questionnaire it is also important to group together questions that pertain to a particular issue so as not to confuse the respondent as to what specifically is being asked. Similarly, it is appropriate to seek to 'funnel' responses from general questions about the issue as a whole down to the specifics of exactly what data are being sought. In other words, questionnaires should be constructed in a logical order that guides the respondent in an orderly manner through the topic.

Keep personal questions until the end

If it is necessary to ask any sensitive questions of respondents (e.g. their ethnic background, income level, religion, or attitudes to tough social issues), it is better to ask these at the end of the questionnaire rather than at the beginning. Asking these questions up front is likely to put off the respondent from completing the questionnaire as he or she is likely to assume that the whole questionnaire will probe for such personal data. Asking for this at the end of a questionnaire, when a respondent has already invested considerable time in the process, and when some form of relationship has been established, is far less likely to result in non-completion.

Pilot test

It is absolutely essential that any questionnaire be piloted before rolling it out to a particular audience. While all the questions posed might seem entirely logical and appropriate to the researcher, there are inevitably a few that create confusion, fail to be understood, or attract answers that the research team were not expecting. A pilot test may be undertaken at low cost with a small percentage of the sample and any necessary changes made before the time and expense of the full survey roll-out are incurred.

Scaling techniques for surveys

There are two important scaling techniques that are typically used by researchers in surveys: Likert scales and Semantic differential scales. There are others, but these are the most commonly employed.

LIKERT SCALES

A Likert scale is a list of statements with five (or sometimes seven) possible choices such as 'Strongly agree, Agree, Neutral (or no opinion), Disagree and Strongly disagree'. The scale is used against a battery of questions that are given to respondents. The researcher is then able to measure the attitudes of respondents. Typically the items included in the battery will have been generated from prior qualitative research or secondary sources. An example battery of questions is provided below.

Thinking back to the first time you supported Arthritis Care, how important were the following factors in influencing your decision to start giving? Please circle the appropriate point on the scale.

FACTORS	Very unimportant			Very important	
I believed Arthritis Care's management to be professional	1	2	3	4	5
I felt it was expected of me	1	2	3	4	5
I felt pressured into giving	1	2	3	4	5
I felt that someone I know might benefit from my support	1	2	3	4	5
I felt that Arthritis Care had a good reputation	1	2	3	4	5
I found Arthritis Care's original approach to me professional .	1	2	3	4	5
I thought my family/friends would expect me to give	1	2	3	4	5
I wanted to give in memory of a loved one	1	2	3	4	5
My family had a strong link to this charity	1	2	3	4	5

In presenting the results from questions designed in this format it is now common practice to present the mean and/or median scores calculated from all the respondents who answered each question. Thus the higher the average score, the greater the degree of agreement with each of the statements listed.

SEMANTIC DIFFERENTIAL SCALES

These scales are designed to measure differences between words. As previously, qualitative work may have identified a series of constructs or ways in which people think about the organization and its services. An attitude battery consisting of bipolar constructs may then be developed. A 5- or 7-point rating scale is frequently used. As an example the name of a particular organization could appear at the top of a page on a questionnaire. Respondents could then be asked to rate this organization using each of the scales in the battery. Computed results could then allow the researcher to compile an attitude profile, perhaps comparing perceptions of their own organization with those of a key competitor.

In this example the bipolar constructs could include:

Amateur	Professional
Traditional	Modern
Caring	Uncaring
Listens	Ignores
Well known	Unknown
High quality	Low quality

The profile of two organizations could then be compared as indicated in Figure 3.3.

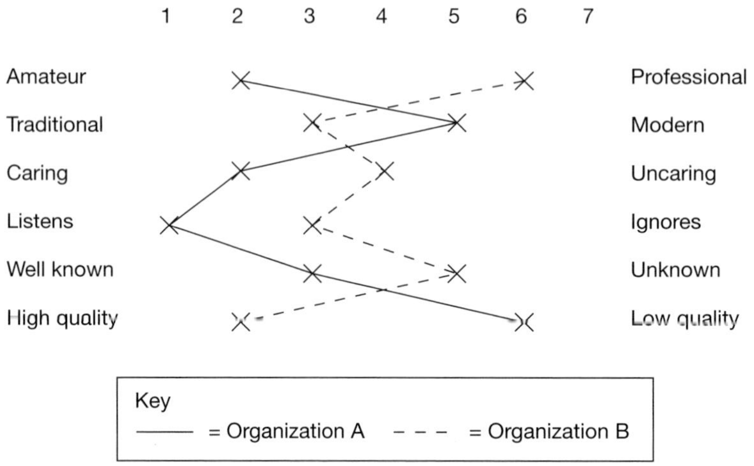

Figure 3.3 *Brand profile of two non-profits*

DATA ANALYSIS

Qualitative data

The process of data analysis differs greatly between qualitative and quantitative data. Qualitative data from interviews and focus groups are typically transcribed from recordings of the original research. The resultant text is then input into a software package such as NUD*IST or NVIVO which allows the researcher to examine and code each aspect of the content.

The majority of qualitative software packages operate in a similar way and allow a researcher to highlight a line or lines of text that contain a particular idea. This idea is then assigned a code. Subsequent text containing similar ideas will also be assigned this particular code. In a typical analysis of focus group data there may be a hundred codes or more that reflect different facets of the discussion and the response thereto. Text can also be coded according to who is speaking, and reflect gender, income, age and so on.

In writing up the results researchers can then request that the software groups the text of the discussions by code – and thus the themes to emerge from each facet of the discussion can easily be written up and peppered with direct quotations from respondents to illustrate why a particular conclusion has been drawn. One may also explore, again using the codes, whether the views of participants varied by categories such as age, gender, income and so on.

An example of this form of analysis and how it is written up is provided in Exhibit 3.2 (see page 58). In this example the researchers were interested to explore the impact of a merger between two or more non-profits on their subsequent fundraising activity. A series of depth interviews were conducted with senior fundraisers who had experienced the merger process and its outcomes. In the brief abstract reproduced below the researchers report their findings in respect of the crucial success factors that drive success in post-merger fundraising. Notice how each idea raised in the interviews is expressed in turn, described, and illustrated where appropriate with a direct quotation. This is typical of the format of many qualitative research reports.

Quantitative data

Software packages are also available to analyse quantitative data and these vary in terms of sophistication and cost. Among the most commonly employed are SNAP (which also aids in questionnaire design) and SPSS (Statistical Package for the Social Sciences). There are then a range of statistics that may be calculated to assist the researcher in summarizing and interpreting the results they have achieved. Such analysis is beyond the scope of this text, but interested readers may wish to consult Hair *et al.* (1995).

The most common forms of summary that are used to represent this form of data include tables, bar charts, histograms and simple numerical summaries such as the mean, median and standard deviation.

Charts

Bar charts or frequency diagrams are probably the most common forms of graphical representation of statistical data. They consist of a series of bars, the height of which is either proportional to the frequency with which a particular outcome occurs, or to the probability that this outcome will occur.

A simple bar chart is presented in Figure 3.4. In this example the total donations to a range of fundraising products are presented for the period shown. While the same information could be presented in tabular form the reader will appreciate the greater degree of impact that can be achieved with a graphic presentation. It is immediately obvious to the eye which of the fundraising products has performed the best.

A second type of chart commonly employed for the presentation of data is the histogram (see Figure 3.5). In this case it is not only the height of the bars that is significant but also the dimensions of the base. In this example the Dolphin Sanctuary has plotted the response rates that it has historically received to one of its most popular recruitment mailings. It seems clear that a common outcome for this particular mailing would be to achieve a response rate of *circa* 1 to 1.5 per cent.

Descriptive statistics

MEAN

One of the most commonly encountered descriptive statistics is the mean – denoted by $\bar{x}$. It is also one of the simplest to calculate. You simply add up the results of a given set of measurements and then divide by the number of measurements. This is shown in the following mathematical notation (page 60):

EXHIBIT 3.2 RESULTS OF ANALYSIS

Critical success factors

The interviews began by exploring the facets of the merger process that respondents believed could contribute to successful post-merger fundraising activity. All respondents agreed that a primary factor here was the quality of communication that had been undertaken with donors and other stakeholder groups:

> It is absolutely essential that the reasons for merger are clear and laudable and those reasons are communicated effectively to all stakeholders in such a way that they feel a part of the process.

The notion of involvement was addressed by several respondents who clearly felt that all potential funders should be kept appraised of developments and, where appropriate, consulted over the action that should be taken. While this is clearly easier in the case of non-profits who have a few, perhaps institutional funders, it was still felt to be practical even with direct mail donors.

> We felt it was important to involve all our donor groups in the decision-making, but since we have a database of over 500,000 individuals it was clearly not going to be practicable to consult everyone. We settled on a survey which actually gave us a very useful insight into the issues and concerns that these individuals had.

Aside from the desire that had been expressed to be as inclusive as possible in the decision-making processes, there were often more pragmatic reasons for keeping organizational funders 'in the loop'. In the case of one particularly large merger, for example, the resultant organization would have had 'embarrassingly' high levels of reserves. Indeed, some informants were also of the view that the accounting SORP (Statement of Recommended Practice) had highlighted reserves as a particular issue, drawing the attention of potential donors specifically towards this facet of the organization.

> We spent a lot of time thinking about what a merged organization might look like. We thought about each aspect of the organization, its services, structures and financial profile. We recognized that in the case of the latter, the nature of the case we make for support might require change and also that issues such as fundraising ratios and reserves could potentially trip us up in the future.

Other key financial matters of relevance and concern to fundraising management were restricted income funds and endowments, where income/capital may be spent only on specific objects due to limitations applied by previous donors to the charity.

> It is important to look carefully at the nature of the restrictions in order to ensure that the funds can be transferred into the new organization, and/or that the restrictions can be preserved. With funds that are not technically restricted, they can be earmarked or designated in order to respect the wishes of donors if this is thought advisable.

It was noted that consent is required from funders to transfer a restricted fund, and this can be a complex procedure. It therefore proves important to educate funders so that they are aware of the distinction between restricted and unrestricted funds and do not pull out under the impression that the charity has access to more funds than it does in practice.

A further key issue was felt to be the treatment of volunteers. Without exception all respondents felt that volunteers should be treated in the same way as paid fundraising staff during the merger and should thus be consulted and kept fully informed throughout. A number of informants had established within their organization a merger committee whose role was to work with key stakeholders such as volunteers, but also service users, charity workers, subscribers, members, patrons and funders to ensure that these key stakeholders are carried along with the merger plans and do not block change. Three respondents had even decided on a joint retreat for key staff from the parties to a merger, the purpose of which was to address questions or concerns and to increase productivity and morale during the merger period. It was deemed essential, however, that merger negotiations were not protracted and that agreement be reached as soon as was practicable.

Consequences of merger

Over two-thirds of informants had recorded a decline in fundraising income at the time of the merger and immediately thereafter. There were felt to be a number of key reasons for this phenomenon. First, the level of reserves of the newly merged body (as noted above) was deemed to deter many institutional funders. Second, in the case of some of the mergers investigated it was the case that a significant percentage of the database of individual and corporate supporters was shared between the two parties to the merger. Following merger these individuals/organizations tended to offer only one gift where previously there had been two.

> Despite a big push, promoting the efficiencies the new organization had to offer and the enhancements to service provision it could supply, we were disappointed that individuals who appeared on both of the original databases were now largely giving just one gift to the new charity at the same level they would have supported both previously.

Informants also felt that despite the publicity accruing to the merger, many of the individual donors were confused about the identity of the organization and did not recognize the campaign materials from the new organization as being of relevance to them.

> Many of our donors are elderly and we found that many did not recognize the materials we had sent were from us. With hindsight we should probably have made better use of the facets of our brand such individuals would have recognized. The new corporate livery was very different and that was a mistake.

Indeed, the informants agreed the consequences of merger activity would vary by category of funder, and that a strategy which recognized the needs of each group before, during and after the merger was therefore essential.

$$\bar{x} = \left(\sum_{i=1} x_i\right)/n$$

In this case the formula simply indicates that to calculate the mean one has to calculate the sum of the values of x from the first observation to the last and then divide by the number of observations (denoted by n).

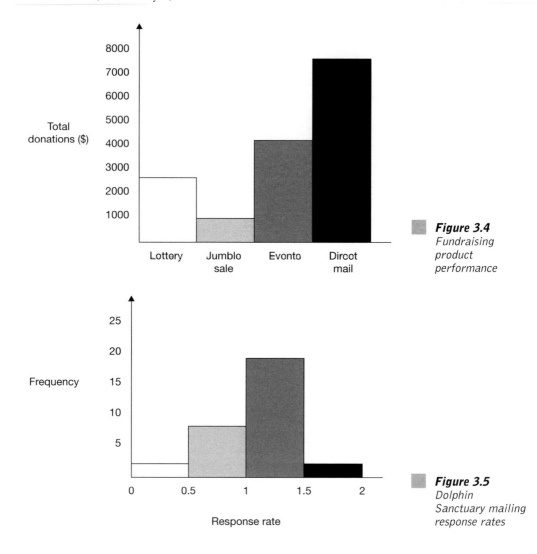

Figure 3.4
Fundraising product performance

Figure 3.5
Dolphin Sanctuary mailing response rates

MEDIAN

A second commonly used descriptor is the median. This is simply the measurement that falls in the middle of a given set of observations or 'distribution'. There are many occasions when it is preferable to quote the median rather than the mean. Specifically the median is preferable where there are a number of outliers in the distribution that would bias the mean and thus give a misleading picture of the nature of the distribution. Suppose, for example, we were interested in reporting the 'average' salaries earned by donors. We take a small sample of the salaries earned for five individuals and obtain $20K, $22K, $23K, $24K and $70K. In this case the median value would be $23K while the mean distorted by the outlier would be $31.8K. The median would thus be a more reasonable representation of this distribution than the mean.

STANDARD DEVIATION

Both the mean and the median give the researcher some idea of where the centre of a distribution is located. While this is clearly useful information researchers are usually also interested to know how spread around this distribution might be. One possible way that this measure might be derived would be to take the difference between each measurement and the mean and then to calculate the average of this deviation. The problem with this approach however is that the deviations will be both positive and negative. Consider a distribution containing the measurements 1, 2 and 3. In this case the mean would be 2 and the deviation −1, 0 and +1. The mean deviation in this case would be zero and we would therefore be no further forward in attempting to find a measure of spread. The way around this difficulty is to calculate the deviations from the mean as previously and then to square these numbers (which removes any negative signs), add these squared numbers together, divide by the number of measurements and then take the square root of the answer. In our previous example the square deviations would be 1, 0 and 1 and their sum would be 2. If we then divide this by three to get the mean of the squared deviations and take the square root of the answer we obtain a result of *circa* 0.8. This somewhat wordy description is represented in mathematical notation as follows:

$$s = \sqrt{\left[\left(\sum_{i=1} (x - \bar{x})^2\right)/n\right]}$$

The more spread out a given distribution might be, the greater will be its standard deviation.

RANGE

In cases where the median has been used to describe the 'average' point on a distribution a good measure of spread to accompany this value is the range. The range is simply the highest value observed minus the lowest value. While this is a useful figure it is helpful to recognize that this too can be strongly influenced by outliers. For this reason some researchers prefer to quote the inter-quartile range. This is simply the difference between two points. The lower of these corresponds to a point below which one quarter of the observations lie (the lower quartile) and the second to the point above which a quarter of the points lie (the upper quartile).

   In the example provided in Exhibit 3.3 we reproduce an extract from a quantitative research report. Here the researchers have chosen to present the data in tabular form and to cite many of the statistics listed above. The objective of this research was to compare the demographic profile and attitudes of individuals who have pledged a bequest to a non-profit with members of the standard (i.e. non-pledger) supporter base. In this extract the researchers provide the details of their demographic comparison. It is interesting to note that alongside their comparison they have also performed a number of statistical tests to determine whether differences they note between pledgers and supporters are 'significant' differences, represented in the population as a whole, or not significant since they might well be due to sampling errors and the operation of random chance. Comparisons of this type are common in market research and the exact statistical tests that may be employed are a function of the categories of data being examined. This is beyond the scope of this text, but the illustration shows how useful this additional form of analysis can be.

61

EXHIBIT 3.3 PROFILE OF RESPONDENTS

Tables 3.3 to 3.8 present the details of the demographic profile of respondents. The results are presented for both legacy pledgers and supporters. The results in Table 3.3 illustrate the slight female bias present on many charity databases. There is no significant difference however in the balance of gender between the supporter and pledger groups.

The occupation of each group is depicted in Table 3.4. It may be noted that both the supporter and pledger groups have a high concentration of office/clerical and professional individuals, reflecting the bias towards socio-economic groups B and C1 in giving. The high concentration of teachers/lecturers is also noteworthy and again typical of the profile of many charitable databases. No significant differences between pledgers and supporters could be identified.

The income profile of respondents is reported in Table 3.5. In this case it may be seen that pledgers report a significantly lower annual income than supporters (X^2 = 46.98, Significance level 0.000).

Significant differences between the two groups were also reported when examining the marital status of respondents. Pledgers are significantly more likely to be living alone, either because they are single or because they have been widowed (Goodman and Kuskal Tau value 0.061, Significance level 0.000). This difference is also supported in Table 3.7 where it will be seen that pledgers are significantly less likely to have children (X^2 = 107.55, Significance level 0.000).

Table 3.3 *Gender of respondents*

Gender	Supporter (%)	Pledger (%)
Male	40.2	35.1
Female	59.8	64.9

Table 3.4 *Past/present occupation of respondents*

Occupation	Supporter (%)	Pledger (%)
Director	5.4	4.2
Housewife/husband	8.5	6.4
Manager	6.9	7.8
Manual/factory	0.9	1.4
Office/clerical	12.6	16.9
Professional	27.0	23.7
Self-employed	6.6	8.0
Shop assistant	0.9	0.8
Skilled tradesman	2.1	2.0
Supervisor	0.7	1.6
Teacher/lecturer	17.0	18.1
Other	11.4	9.0

Table 3.5 *Current income profile of respondents*

Category	Supporter (%)	Pledger (%)
Up to £4,999	3.6	4.6
£5,000–£9,999	8.4	17.5
£10,000–£14,999	13.8	17.3
£15,000–£19,999	11.1	14.2
£20,000–£24,999	12.1	14.4
£25,000–£29,999	8.4	7.0
£30,000–£39,999	13.6	10.1
£40,000 +	29.0	14.9

Table 3.8 presents the remaining demographic data captured in the survey and in addition presents the total amount donated by each group to the charity sector in the past year. As the results indicate the mean age at which both pledgers and supporters completed their full-time education is very similar, suggesting that many individuals were educated to degree level. No significant difference between the two groups was reported. It may be seen however that pledgers are significantly older than supporters, having a mean age of 68.4 years.

No differences could be discerned between the two groups in relation to the total amount given to charity each year with supporters offering £601 per annum and pledgers £701. It should be noted that the distributions in each case were highly skewed and that as a consequence a better measure of the typical amount given per annum is the median. The median amount donated per annum by both supporters and pledgers was found to be £300.

Table 3.6 Marital status

Status	Supporter (%)	Pledger (%)
Single	18.7	34.9
Married	55.1	33.3
Separated	0.3	1.8
Divorced	5.4	5.7
Living with partner	6.2	5.0
Widowed	14.3	19.4

Table 3.7 Presence of children

Children	Supporter (%)	Pledger (%)
No	31.1	61.3
Yes	68.9	38.7

Table 3.8 Demographic and behavioural characteristics

Variable	Supporter mean	Pledger mean	F	Sig
Age at which full-time education completed	20.9	19.0	1.27	0.26
Age	59.2	68.4	53.06	0.00
Amount given to charity each year	£600.64	£701.26	2.41	0.12

USING EXTERNAL RESEARCH AGENCIES

At the beginning of the chapter we stressed the need, where external agencies are to be employed in the capturing of data, for senior agency personnel to be involved in defining both the research problem and the research objectives. When an agency is involved in this way it will be necessary to construct a research brief which would include the agreed problem definition and research objectives. If a relationship already exists with a particular agency this can simply be handed over to the respective organization to progress. More usually, however, the brief is used as the basis for competitive tendering, so that the non-profit can ensure that it is getting the best value for money possible from its agency.

In the case of this latter scenario, the agencies invited to pitch should be asked to respond to the brief with a research proposal document that interprets the research objectives, specifies the data requirements and indicates what methods will be employed to gather the requisite data. This document will also provide details of the proposed costs, and in the case of quantitative research, some sense of the level of accuracy of the findings that will be delivered.

The non-profit is then in a position to select between the competing bids. This will be based partly on the quality, originality and cost of the proposal. It will also be based on past experience with the organization concerned, its track record with the specific techniques being proposed and the extent to which it has worked with competing organizations – which could be either an advantage or disadvantage depending on the task in hand. Most organizations will want to employ an agency experienced in dealing with the sector, but may not want to work with an agency also assisting a competitor, as there could be conflicts of interest and concerns over the confidentiality afforded the project.

In assessing research proposals the following points are relevant.

Methodology

Do the proposed research methods look appropriate given the objectives of the organization? Remember that qualitative and quantitative techniques have their own sets of strengths and weaknesses and are better suited to certain kinds of objectives. The non-profit must therefore ensure that the agency appears to have selected an appropriate methodology.

The nature of the sample

In the case of quantitative research, is the sample proposed representative of the population? It would be usual for researchers to identify the key variables of interest from the outset (perhaps age and gender), and to ensure that the sample comprises an appropriate mix of both. The balance in the sample should reflect the balance in the population.

The size of the sample

Again, in the case of quantitative research the size of the sample may be an issue. As was noted above, bigger isn't always better! An appropriate sample size is a function of the variability of the population, the number of variables of interest, the analytical techniques it is intended to use and the desired degree of accuracy that is required. Non-profits should tend to be suspicious of samples, however, where the population is known to be large, variable, and the agency is proposing a sample size of fewer than a couple of hundred individuals. It is surprising how many studies based on very small and potentially very unrepresentative samples are commissioned.

Response rate/non-response bias

Many management reports talk about a survey of X individuals. Let us say for the sake of argument that a researcher claims to have surveyed 2,000 individuals. Often this is the only fact reported. It is only later that one realizes that the response rate obtained was only, say, 10 per cent. Their results would thus be based on the views of only 200 individuals. We would have concerns about this since it would put the survey towards the lower end of achievable response rates, but it would not necessarily invalidate the results. The real test is whether the individuals that responded are still representative of the population. There are various ways of testing this. One could look at the characteristics of these individuals, perhaps by age, gender, income, and compare the profile of the respondents with the profile of the population as a whole. If they are broadly similar we might place more faith in the results. We could also take the further step of comparing the responses of the individuals who responded first with those who responded last and again test for differences. The argument goes that, for example, in the case of postal surveys, those individuals who respond last are likely to resemble most the non-responders who by definition never got around to responding at all. Thus if there are differences between these groups we may conclude that there is a strong risk of the views/characteristics of non-responders being quite different from those who responded, thus invalidating the results of the survey. Of course there are many ways of dealing with non-response and from a managerial perspective it is just worth posing the question to an agency of how they intend to deal with this dimension.

The degree of accuracy

Reputable agencies and researchers should be able to provide an estimate of the likely accuracy of their research. There is always a likelihood, no matter how small, that the findings of a study may have occurred purely by chance. Before basing a strategy on the findings of a given piece of work it is useful to clarify how confident one might be in the findings.

Variables versus constructs

Simple variables such as age, gender, income, height and weight may be measured by a single question. It is necessary to be wary of surveys that claim to be able to measure complex social phenomena such as, for example, trust and confidence, by also asking a single question of

To what extent would you trust voluntary organizations to undertake each of the activities listed?

	Low degree of trust				High degree of trust		
To always act in the best interest of the cause	1	2	3	4	5	6	7
To conduct their operations ethically	1	2	3	4	5	6	7
To use donated funds appropriately	1	2	3	4	5	6	7
Not to exploit their donors	1	2	3	4	5	6	7
To use fundraising techniques that are appropriate and sensitive	1	2	3	4	5	6	7

respondents. Such things are best regarded as 'constructs' and should be measured in a variety of different ways to ensure that the researcher is actually measuring the real phenomena of interest. Thus, rather than asking individuals whether or not they trust charities, which could mean almost anything, it is better to ask them the extent to which they trust charities to use donated funds appropriately, not to exploit their donors and so on (as shown in the example on page 65). A single and much more robust measure of trust may then be constructed from the responses to this battery of questions. It is thus worth asking an agency how it would propose to measure key constructs of interest to the organization.

Having selected a particular agency on the basis of the brief it will then be necessary to monitor progress as the agency begins to develop the project. Most agencies will allocate a client director who will keep the non-profit appraised of progress. If the organization has commissioned a two-stage project, perhaps beginning with qualitative research, it would be worthwhile asking the agency to report at the end of the first stage before it begins work on a second perhaps quantitative phase. This allows the organization to appraise the quality of the work undertaken and to conduct a 'reality' check of the preliminary research findings. There would be little point in progressing with an expensive quantitative study if it were based on an obviously flawed understanding of the particular research issue.

CHAPTER SUMMARY

There will always be a role for high-quality research to aid decision-making in our sector. In this chapter we have proposed a process that organizations can adopt to assist them in managing the research process. We have stressed the need for a clear statement of the research problem and the derivation of specific research objectives. Typically the process then proceeds with an examination of secondary data sources to see whether the requisite information already exists and may be acquired cost-effectively. In cases where this is not possible it will be necessary to conduct primary research that may be either qualitative or quantitative depending on the nature of the research objectives. We have also outlined in this chapter how both categories of data can be analysed and written up for the purposes of informing managerial decision-making. In the next chapter we move on to consider how this research may be used to inform the development of fundraising strategy.

DISCUSSION QUESTIONS

1   Distinguish, with examples, between qualitative and quantitative marketing research.

2   As the fundraising manager of a small children's charity looking to explore the motives for legacy giving, explain and justify a programme of marketing research you would propose to adopt to explore this issue.

3   In your role as the fundraising director of a medium-sized arts charity you have been asked by your chief executive to commission a piece of donor research. Explain to her the criteria you would use to select between the agencies likely to compete for this business.

4   Prepare a marketing research plan to explore why donors stop giving to an organization of your choice (i.e. why they lapse in their support).

REFERENCES

American Marketing Association (AMA) (1961) *Report of the Definitions Committee*, American Marketing Association, Chicago.

Hair J.F., Anderson R.E., Tatham, T. and Black, W.C. (1995) *Multivariate Data Analysis With Readings*, Prentice Hall, Englewood Cliffs, NJ.

Kotler, P. (1967) *Marketing Management: Analysis, Planning and Control*, Prentice Hall, Englewood Cliffs, NJ.

Kumar, V., Aaker, D.A. and Day, C.S. (1999) *Essentials of Marketing Research*, John Wiley & Sons, New York.

Sudman, S. and Blair, E. (1999) *Sampling in the Twenty First Century*, Academy of Marketing Sciences, Greenvale.

Tull, D.S. and Hawkins, D.I. (1996) *Marketing Research: Measurement and Method*, 6th edn, Macmillan, New York.

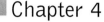

Chapter 4

Strategic planning
The fundraising plan

LEARNING OBJECTIVES

By the end of this chapter you should be able to:
- Develop SMART fundraising objectives.
- Develop appropriate strategic direction.
- Segment a range of individual and organizational markets.
- Develop a positioning strategy.
- Develop a case for support.
- Integrate plans for specific forms of fundraising into the aggregate fundraising plan for the organization.

INTRODUCTION

The generic format for a fundraising plan identified in Chapter 2 is reproduced in Figure 4.1. In Chapter 2 we dealt with the early stages of the plan, highlighting the significance of the fundraising audit and suggesting categories of data that the fundraising department should look to assemble before writing the operational sections of the plan. The significance of this material lay in developing a detailed picture of where the organization stood currently in relation to its donor markets, competitors and so on. We also reviewed the role and contribution of the SWOT analysis in summarizing this data and suggested that in most cases it would be appropriate to conduct a SWOT analysis on the organization from the perspective of each major category of donors. These, we argued, would provide a good working summary of 'where the organization is now'.

In this chapter we will move on to consider the remaining two components of the plan, namely 'Where do we want to be?' and 'How will we get there?' We will consider the role and derivation of fundraising objectives, the characteristics of good objectives and the role they play in control. We will also consider aspects of fundraising strategy, including overall direction, segmentation and positioning.

As you read this chapter it is important to bear in mind that non-profits vary widely in terms of size, available resources and structure. There is therefore no 'one correct' structure for a

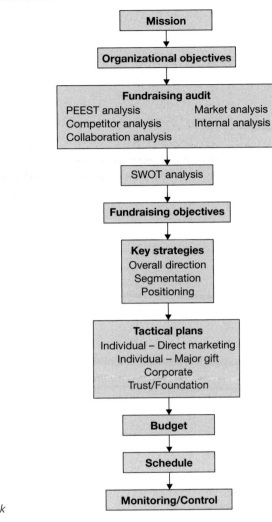

Figure 4.1 *Generic planning framework*

fundraising plan and no one 'right way' of organizing fundraising activity. The outline we present in Figure 4.1 is an aggregate fundraising plan, which contains the detail of all the fundraising that the organization will conduct over the planning period (e.g. one year, three years, five years). It contains objectives, generic fundraising strategy and an overview of the tactics the organization will adopt in relation to each form of fundraising undertaken. While this is a common format, some organizations prefer to generate separate documents for each specific form of fundraising, and a plan will thus be generated for corporate fundraising, trust/foundation fundraising and individual fundraising. Other organizations prefer a hybrid, where an aggregate fundraising plan exists, typically for use by senior management and the Board of Trustees, with more detailed sub-plans being created at the departmental level for each form of fundraising.

Thus in seeking to provide an overview of fundraising planning we have chosen to structure our debate around one of these alternatives and to focus on a holistic fundraising plan. The detail of planning for distinct forms of fundraising such as corporate, Trust/Foundation, individual, major gift will be dealt with in subsequent chapters.

SETTING FUNDRAISING OBJECTIVES

Once the organization has identified its current position in the donor market and reviewed what has been accomplished to date it is in a position to decide what might realistically be achieved in the future. As Drucker (1990: 107) notes, objectives have a particular significance for non-profit organizations:

> In a non-profit organization there is no such [thing as a] bottom line. But there is also a temptation to downplay results. There is the temptation to say: We are serving a good cause. We are doing the Lord's work. Or we are doing something to make life a little better for people and that's a result in itself. That is not enough. If a business wastes its resources on non-results, by and large it loses its own money. In a nonprofit institution though, it's somebody else's money – the donor's money. Service organizations are accountable to donors, accountable for putting the money where the results are and for performance. So, this is an area that needs special emphasis for non-profit executives. Good intentions only pave the way to hell!

In Drucker's view non-profits should thus be accountable for how they choose to spend their income and that includes what they spend on fundraising. Fundraising objectives ensure that the organization gives adequate consideration to exactly what will be achieved and at exactly what cost.

Objectives are also an important part of the plan as they are the only mechanism by which its success can be measured. If a plan achieves its stated objectives we might reasonably conclude that it has been a success. Without them, one can only speculate as to the planner's original intent and the effectiveness of the activities undertaken. Valuable resources (donated by donors!) could be being wasted, but the organization would have no mechanism for identifying that this was in fact the case.

As a minimum therefore, fundraising objectives should address the following three issues:

1   the amount of funds that will be raised;
2   the categories of donors that will supply these funds (i.e. individual, corporate, foundation/trust);
3   the acceptable costs of raising these funds.

They can also address more specific issues such as the donor attrition rate (i.e. the percentage of donors lost each year), changes in the lifetime value of donors (see Chapter 6), donor perceptions of service quality, and metrics such as average gift, response rate (to postal appeals), return on investment and so on.

For many organizations it may be appropriate to split these objectives out and to consider writing separate objectives for restricted and unrestricted funds, for committed/uncommitted givers and/or for capital campaigns as against the annual fund. This is frequently appropriate since these forms of fundraising differ greatly. The terms are explained below:

■   *Restricted/unrestricted funds*: This terminology simply reflects the fact that donors can offer two distinct types of funds to an organization. Restricted funds are funds donated for a specific scheme and may not be used for general purposes. Thus if a donor donates US$1 million to support the extension of a school library, the organization may not use these restricted funds to support teaching costs or management overheads. Unrestricted funds, by contrast, are funds that are donated to support the work of the charity and are not designated to be spent on a particular project or programme. Since many non-profits desire the maximum possible flexibility the emphasis within fundraising appeals is frequently on unrestricted funds. As the reader will appreciate it makes sense to write objectives for both categories of funds, since the degree of flexibility associated with each category is very different.

■ *Capital campaigns/annual fund*: These terms are more frequently encountered in the USA and refer to two classic forms of fundraising that may be undertaken. As the title suggests, the capital campaign is designed to raise 'capital' for a specific and often major project. Thus if a non-profit needs a new building to house its operations, create a resource centre for adults with disabilities or build a sensory garden for visually impaired children, it will run a capital campaign to raise the requisite funds. The annual fund, by contrast, is the term given to fundraising designed to fund the ongoing running costs of the organization. Non-profits would typically write a separate plan for each form of fundraising – but in some cases the plan is merged to ensure the maximum possible synergy from the two appeals, in which case it is standard practice to specify specific objectives for each set of activities.

■ *Uncommitted/committed givers*: This terminology is widely employed in the UK to distinguish between donors who have signed up to a regular payment to a charity deducted monthly, quarterly or annually direct from their bank account or credit card. These donors are frequently distinguished separately in fundraising objectives since separate appeals would typically be conducted to recruit committed givers, and they tend to receive a tailored programme of communication once they have been recruited which reflects their enhanced value to the organization. The term 'uncommitted donors' is often used to denote donors who prefer to send a series of occasional donations, perhaps writing a cheque in response to ongoing appeals. Since the term can sound derisory of donors who are often very loyal and generous to the organization, some non-profits prefer to use the terms 'cash' or 'one-off' donors instead.

It is important to realize that the style in which the objectives are written is also a significant issue. Objectives are of value only if it is possible to use them as an aid to managing the organization's resources, and hence vague terms and needless ambiguity should be studiously avoided.

> Vague objectives, however emotionally appealing are counter-productive to sensible planning and are usually the result of the human propensity for wishful thinking which often smacks more of cheerleading than serious marketing leadership. What this means is that while it is arguable whether directional terms such as decrease, optimize, minimize, should be used as objectives, it seems logical that unless there is some measure, or yardstick, against which to measure a sense of locomotion towards achieving them, they do not serve any useful purpose.
>
> (MacDonald 1984: 88)

Hence to be managerially useful, good objectives should exhibit the following characteristics. They should be:

1 *Specific*: Related to one particular aspect of fundraising activity and/or one particular category of donor. Objectives that relate simultaneously to diverse aspects of fundraising are difficult to assess since they may require the organization to use different techniques of measurement and to look across different planning horizons. Attempting to combine activities may therefore lead to confusion, or at best a lack of focus.

2   *Measurable*: Words such as 'maximize' or 'increase' are not particularly helpful when it later becomes necessary to assess the effectiveness of fundraising activity. To be useful, objectives should avoid these terms and be capable of measurement. They should therefore specify quantifiable values whenever possible (e.g. to achieve a 10 per cent increase in legacy/bequest income).

3   *Achievable*: Fundraising objectives should be derived from a thorough analysis of the content of the fundraising audit, not from creative thinking on the part of managers. Objectives which have no possibility of accomplishment will serve only to demoralize those responsible for their achievement and to deplete resources that could have had a greater potential impact elsewhere.

4   *Relevant*: Fundraising objectives should be consistent with the objectives of the organization as a whole. They should merely supply a greater level of detail, identifying specifically what the fundraising function will have to achieve to provide the non-profit organization with the resources it needs to continue to offer the desired level of service provision.

5   *Time-scaled*: Good objectives should clearly specify the duration over which they are to be achieved. Not only does this help to plan the strategies and tactics by which they will be accomplished but it also assists in permitting the organization to set in place control procedures to ensure that the stated targets will indeed be met. Thus monthly 'sub-targets' for each form of fundraising could be set and corrective action initiated early in the duration of a plan as soon as a variance is detected.

Thus good fundraising objectives should be SMART! (Specific, Measurable, Achievable, Relevant, Time-scaled).

Having now outlined the rules, it might be helpful to actually demonstrate what typical fundraising objectives might be:

- to attract $250,000 in voluntary income from individual donors by the end of the financial year;
- to attract $150,000 of (cash) corporate support by the end of November 2004;
- to attract 100,000 new committed givers by the end of December 2005;
- to lower the annual attrition rate of individual cash givers to 15 per cent per annum by the end of December 2006.

KEY STRATEGIES

Having specified the objectives it is intended that the plan will achieve, it is now possible to address the means by which these objectives will be accomplished. The broad approach to be adopted is termed 'fundraising strategy' and it is useful to consider this in relation to the following three categories:

1   overall direction
2   segmentation strategy
3   positioning strategy.

Each will be considered in turn below.

OVERALL DIRECTION

Overall direction pertains to the selection of fundraising methods that will be used to raise funds. Where the organization requires additional funds to those raised in the previous year there are four key strategic directions it can follow if growth is required (Ansoff 1968). These are illustrated in Figure 4.2. All the options involve making decisions about the range of fund-raising activities that will be conducted and the markets into which they will be delivered. Each strategic option is outlined below.

- *Market penetration*: The first strategic option that may be adopted to achieve growth is market penetration. As the figure indicates this involves the fundraiser in attempting to raise more funds from existing donor markets. Existing fundraising activities are continued, but the organization seeks to solicit greater levels of participation from the target donor group. Thus if an organization is employing direct marketing to attract new donors it may elect to follow a strategy of market penetration and solicit funds from an ever greater number of these individuals. Similarly, if a non-profit is soliciting funds from major donors in a particular city, it could follow a strategy of market penetration and attempt to find other individuals living in this area who are sufficiently wealthy and who have sufficient interest in the cause to offer a major gift.

  It is important to recognize that this strategy involves the least risk of any of the four options. This is simply because the organization employs only those fundraising activities with which it is already familiar and contacts only those categories of donor with which it has direct experience of dealing. By definition it will therefore have a firm grasp of what to expect, and the likelihood of the strategy failing due to serious errors on the organization's part is greatly diminished.

- *Activity development*: This option engenders a higher degree of risk, because here the organization achieves growth by developing new forms of fundraising which it will attempt to utilize to solicit funds from existing donor groups. Charities employing direct mail to raise funds might create new products such as 'Adopt a Child' or 'Sponsor A Dog' that may be used to generate greater commitment and loyalty from the donor base. Equally, those charities working in the realm of community or local group fundraising could introduce raffles, competitions, jumble sales and so on to bolster the range of products they can offer to solicit funds.

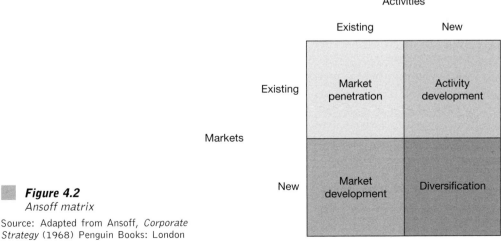

Figure 4.2
Ansoff matrix

Source: Adapted from Ansoff, *Corporate Strategy* (1968) Penguin Books: London

- *Market development*: Market development involves the organization in seeking new markets for its existing fundraising products or activities. Thus it will look to target new groups of donors who previously have not been addressed by the organization. Non-profits could seek to enter new counties, cities or geographical regions of the country. They could also decide to target different types of people or organizations than have previously been approached. This strategy also contains a degree of risk, since while the organization is familiar with the techniques that will be used, it has no prior experience in dealing with these donors and therefore no direct knowledge of how they may react.
- *Diversification*: This constitutes the highest risk strategy of all. It involves targeting new donors with new products and thus the organization has no experience on which it can rely. Non-profits, for example, may take a decision to enter the retail or mail order market for the first time and to raise funds by selling products. Others may choose to establish a website to target younger categories of donors. Similarly, in the USA, a non-profit might decide to explore 'planned giving' for the first time (see Chapter 9). These are all examples of diversification.

All attempts to raise additional funds may be classified under one of these four headings and while in itself this may not appear a useful exercise, the real utility of the model lies in providing a structured way for organizations to actively consider *all* of the alternatives available to them, before they decide on those they will actually pursue. In using the model non-profits should be prepared to brainstorm every possible strategic alternative and then to begin a process of deciding which of the available alternatives is the most appealing and which balances the degree

Table 4.1 *Fundraising activities/products undertaken in the USA and UK*

Individual fundraising	Corporate fundraising
Personal solicitation	Personal solicitation
Direct mail	Charity of the Year
Press advertising	Payroll giving
Press/magazine inserts	Staff fundraising events
Direct response television ads	Sponsored events (e.g. walks)
Radio advertising	Special events/dinners/galas
Face-to-face (on-the-street recruitment)	Cause-related marketing
Door-to-door (soliciting gifts on the doorstep)	Challenge events
Street collections	
Telephone fundraising	
Trading (charity shops/mail order catalogues)	
Flag days	
Sales of raffle/lottery tickets	
Jumble sales	
Special events/dinners/galas	
Sponsored events (e.g. walks)	
SMS text messaging	
Internet fundraising	
Challenge events	

of risk to which the organization is exposed. In practice non-profits will therefore tend to opt for a mix of a number of the four available options.

Table 4.1 contains a summary of the key fundraising activities that are currently conducted in both the UK and the USA. In employing the Ansoff model fundraisers can decide which of these could potentially be employed and site them appropriately in the matrix. A more detailed analysis of how appropriate each might be can then be undertaken and decisions made about the activities that will be advanced. Organizations often do this by looking at what activities will be adopted in the short, medium and long term, since commencing a completely new form of fundraising is likely to take time to accomplish.

Of course there may be a number of circumstances when the non-profit does not wish to raise additional funds, or to continue with a particular form of fundraising. Thus two additional strategies warrant consideration.

- *Consolidation*: There may be circumstances when the non-profit has had a particularly good year, or where it has rapidly grown a new fundraising activity to the point where existing volunteer and staff resources are stretched. In either of these two scenarios the non-profit could look to consolidate its position and, rather than grow voluntary income from these sources, it could merely look to sustain it.
- *Withdrawal*: This strategy may be appropriate where the levels of voluntary income generated by an activity have fallen significantly, or where the cost of conducting a particular activity can no longer be justified. In these circumstances it may be appropriate to follow a strategy of withdrawal and to terminate the activity altogether.

MARKET SEGMENTATION: SEGMENTING INDIVIDUAL DONOR MARKETS

This process of identifying suitable groups of donors to target is known as 'market segmentation'. Kotler (1991:66) defines it as 'the task of breaking down the total market (which is typically too large to serve) into segments that share common properties'. In a similar vein Wilson *et al.* (1992:91) define it as 'the process of dividing a varied and differing group of (donors) or potential (donors) into smaller groups within which broadly similar patterns of needs exist'.

Segmentation thus allows the fundraiser to develop a specific offer likely to appeal to the needs/interests of certain groups of donors. Segmentation is worthwhile only where different groups of donors have different needs, or must be approached in a different way from others. The rationale for segmentation is simply that by focusing on a distinctive set of needs or interests, the non-profit can develop a fundraising programme which uniquely addresses these issues. The fact that this adaptation has taken place makes it more attractive for these donors to give to the organization, and enhanced response rates and donations are likely to result.

There are a variety of criteria that may be used to segment both individual and organizational markets. These are outlined below.

Demographic segmentation

It may be possible to segment a market on the basis of variables such as age, gender, socioeconomic group, family size, family lifecycle, income, religion, race, occupation or education. Collectively, these are referred to as demographic variables. In most cases a combination of some or all of these demographic variables will be used in building a profile of existing and prospective donors. Demographic data have been collected over many years and a great deal is known about the behaviour of each grouping in terms of the likely needs, wants, sympathies and preferences of each.

Age, gender, family lifecycle stage, income/occupation and race/ethnicity are possibly the most frequently cited demographic variables used in non-profit profiling and prospect segmentation.

- *Age*: A huge proportion of giving to non-profits stems from the older sections of the population. Recent analysis of the Family Expenditure Survey in the UK indicated that for every increase of ten years in the age of the head of the household there is an increased likelihood of giving of 3 per cent, and an increase in the value of donations of 30 per cent (Banks and Tanner 1997). Age tends to be a reliable indicator of the sources of information an individual is likely to use, and the social influences they are likely to be susceptible to (Philips and Sternthal 1977).
- *Gender*: Many studies of giving have demonstrated that women and men give differently. It appears that women tend to spread their giving among a greater number of charities, and so tend to give smaller amounts to each (Sargeant 1999). Most non-profit donor databases are weighted markedly towards females. Studies in for-profit marketing have shown that the manner in which women respond to information is radically different from men, and that the sexes respond very differently, for example, to direct marketing

Table 4.2 *Family lifecycle*

	Stages in the family lifecycle	Buying patterns
1	Bachelor stage: Young single people living at home	Few financial commitments – recreation and fashion orientated
2	Newly married couples: Young no children	High purchase rate of consumer durables – buy white goods, cars, furniture
3	Full nest 1: Youngest child under 6	House buying is at a peak. Liquid assets are low – buy medicines, toys, baby food, white goods
4	Full nest 2: Youngest child 6 or over	Financial position is improving – buy a wider variety of foods, bicycles and pianos
5	Full nest 3: Older married couples with dependent children	Financial position is improving still further. Some children now have jobs and wives are working. Increasing purchase of desirables – buy furniture and luxury goods
6	Empty nest 1: Older married couples, no children, head of household still in workforce	Home ownership is at peak – savings have increased and financial position improved. Interested in travel, recreation and self-education. Not interested in new products – buy luxuries and home improvements
7	Empty nest 2: Older married, no children living at home, head of household retired	Substantial reduction in income. Buy medical products and appliances that aid health, sleep and digestion
8	Solitary survivor in the workforce	Income still high, but may sell home
9	Solitary survivor retired	Same medical and product needs as group 7. Substantial cut in income. Need for attention and security

Source: Wilson *et al.* (1994). Reproduced with kind permission of Elsevier Ltd

Table 4.3 Socio-economic groups

UK		USA	
Category	Description	Category	Description
A	Senior professional/ managerial	Upper-uppers	Social elite living on inherited income
B	Middle professional/ managerial	Lower-uppers	Individuals often from the middle class who have earned very high levels of income from success in business or the professions
C1	Junior management, clerical or supervisory	Upper-middles	Professionals or managers with unexceptional wealth
C2	Skilled manual labour (e.g. electrician)	Middle class	White and blue collar workers on 'average' levels of pay who live on the 'right' side of town
D	Unskilled manual labour (e.g. labourer)	Working class	Blue collar workers on 'average' income leading working class lifestyle
E	Unemployed, students, etc.	Upper-lowers	Employed in the workforce but earning income frequently just above poverty levels
		Lower-lowers	Living on welfare, public aid or charity

Note: US categories adapted from work of Richard P. Coleman (1983)

communications. As a consequence some non-profits develop 'male' or 'female' copy in their recruitment appeals depending on the target audience.

■ *Family lifecycle*: The concept of a family lifecycle was first put forward by Rowntree over a century ago. The version now used was that developed by Wells and Gubar in 1966, which is illustrated in Table 4.2. As a composite model made up of age, number of years married, ages of children and working status, the concept of the family lifecycle has proved more useful in many cases than simple segmentation based on age alone. However, it is based on the traditional concept of the nuclear family, and is obviously no longer completely valid as such when one views the current and changing patterns of family life and women's employment. Despite these criticisms, the model remains widely used, and is a helpful indicator of propensity to donate.

■ *Income/occupation*: Income has also been proved to be a useful base for segmentation and, despite difficulties in identifying a true picture of income for any particular group, has been shown to be a powerful indicator of propensity to give, and of likely donation levels. Some segmentation systems combine information on income levels and occupation into a single model. In both the USA and the UK this has led to the development of socio-economic groups. Table 4.3 illustrates the categories of occupation that are included in each group. It is interesting to note that the higher and lower socio-economic groups tend to give a higher proportion of their income to good causes than do those on 'middle' incomes.

■ *Race/ethnicity*: Race and ethnicity are used in demographic segmentation by US non-profits. Different issues impact upon different racial and ethnic groups, and these groups differ in their media habits and organizational ties, with all the major minority groups having a plethora of specific newspapers, magazines, radio and television programming, which permit very precise targeting of messages. Creative images and messages may also be tailored to appeal to the various racial and ethnic groups and segments.

Geographic segmentation

In terms of historic development, segmentation on the grounds of where people lived was the first system developed. Non-profits would tend to look for support from individuals living close to the headquarters of the organization. However, segmentation and profiling on the basis of location alone is now very rare and it tends to be used in concert with one or more of the other bases for segmentation that are available. Geodemographics is an attempt to improve significantly on some of the limitations of the simple geographic model.

Geodemographics

In geodemographics information on geographical location is combined with lifestyle information to provide descriptions of neighbourhoods. In the USA this approach is typified by the PRIZM system, which is based on the core notion that people who live near each other are likely to have similar interests and behaviours. PRIZM was developed by the Claritas Corporation. Claritas collects a vast amount of information on the 42,000 Zip code areas of the USA, including standard demographic data, product and service purchases and media use. Clustering procedures are used to group Zip code areas into sixty-two categories and fifteen social groups, which are given names such as 'Shotguns and Pickups', 'Money and Brains' and 'Second City Elite'. Fundraisers can use the PRIZM system to help define markets and target areas which appear to match those of existing donors. Other systems such as ACORN, ClusterPlus and MicroVision are also available to US non-profits.

UK geodemographic studies arose from work carried out by Webber in 1973. He was interested in studying urban deprivation and classified neighbourhoods using cluster analysis techniques to produce a system comprising twenty-five neighbourhood types, each of which exhibited different mixes of problems and required a different type of social policy. Using census data he was later able to extend this analysis to derive thirty-eight neighbourhood types with which to classify the whole of the UK.

Webber's work was developed further by the British Market Research Bureau which overlaid purchasing patterns on to the neighbourhood types. There are now a number of commercially available geodemographic systems in the UK such as MOSAIC, ACORN and PINPOINT. All the systems use census data that are updated every ten years when every household in the country receives a questionnaire gathering data on some 300 variables. Census information is published only at the level of the 'enumeration district', which typically contains around ten postcodes. The geodemographic systems match the census data to the relevant postcodes and then reduce the high number of census variables to a manageable number that are capable of explaining key differences in consumer behaviour. To develop market segments a technique such as cluster analysis is then used to group together postcodes with similar behaviours.

All the major suppliers of geodemographic data employ slightly different sets of census data and different statistical techniques to derive the final segments that will comprise their system. Typically, this includes information on: age, marital status, household composition, household size, employment type, travel to work, unemployment, car ownership, housing tenure, amenities, housing type, socio-economic group. Some of the suppliers conduct additional market research among representative samples of each of their segments to provide additional data on purchasing behaviour by group.

Systems such as ACORN and MOSAIC may be purchased as additions to non-profit data-bases so that geodemographic data are appended automatically to every donor record, or data from the existing base can be exported and classified by the data providers as a 'one off' or occasional profiling exercise to see which of the set categories predominate. This information may then be used in list selection or the purchase of other media. Geodemographic systems are sometimes criticized as being too homogeneous, with the groupings used described as subjective and potentially misleading.

Behavioural segmentation

In the commercial arena individuals are segmented according to their 'knowledge, attitude, use, or response to a product' (Kotler 1991:272). This form of segmentation does not trans-late readily into non-profit donor recruitment, since by definition the organization has had no contact with these individuals before, and as a consequence holds no data on their behaviour. It is widely used, however, in donor development communications where the organization looks to establish a relationship with the donor over time. The Royal Society for the Protection of Birds, for example, segments donors according to the level of interest and knowledge that they have on the subject. They send different forms of communication to committed bird-watchers than they do to individuals who merely like to attract birds to their domestic garden and in reality understand very little about them. Organizations also target donors with specific campaigns based on their value (i.e. how much they have given in the past) and have a separate strategy for dealing with major givers (i.e. personal contact) than they do the remainder of the fundraising database.

Psychographic and lifestyle segmentation

There are also a number of bases for segmentation that may be considered as psychological or psychographic variables. Some researchers have argued that personality can be used as a suitable basis for segmentation and several studies have demonstrated links between personality variables and consumer buying behaviour.

In the non-profit sector, segmentation by attitudes, values and value systems is more common, especially where organizations are actively attempting to change societal attitudes and behaviours. Data on the values and attitudes of existing donors can be gathered through survey instruments and used to add to the picture of the ideal prospect.

Lifestyle has been defined as 'a person's pattern of living in the world as expressed in the person's activities, interests and opinions. Lifestyle (as a consequence) portrays the whole indi-vidual interacting with his/her environment' (Kotler 1991:171). It can therefore be considered to be different to personality. Personality variables describe the pattern of psychological charac-teristics an individual might possess but say nothing of that individual's hobbies, interests or activities. Lifestyle data supply these missing variables. When the term 'lifestyle' was first intro-duced into marketing research it was viewed as consisting of three basic components: activities (work, hobbies, social life, entertainment, shopping, sports), interests (family, home, job, community, recreation, media, achievements), and opinions (of oneself, social issues, politics, business, education, products and culture).

The basis of lifestyle profiling and segmentation is that very substantial numbers of people can be persuaded to provide comprehensive information about themselves, their households, their possessions, behaviour and interests. A huge amount of lifestyle information on millions of individuals is available commercially. Lifestyle data providers collect information at the level of the individual. Huge databanks are compiled from product registration cards and large consumer surveys that are often over 200 questions long (with some questions 'sponsored' by individual companies), and are incentivized to encourage completion.

Lifestyle data houses will take existing donor lists (or lists of 'best' donors) and match the names and addresses against their file. If a match rate of 10 per cent or more is attained a 'reliable' profile of the donors can be provided, illustrating characteristic lifestyle variables and indicating the extent to which the donors differ from the 'norm' in the display of these characteristics. The key weakness of lifestyle data is that they contain a self-selected, and therefore unrepresentative, sample. It is therefore not possible to extrapolate from a lifestyle study to make a universal statement. Where non-profits use direct mail in recruitment and development communication, lifestyle bases remain valuable and are made up of mail-responsive people. Where different, non-direct mail-responsive donors are recruited lifestyle data may be inappropriate.

SEGMENTING BUSINESS MARKETS

In preparing a strategy for corporate fundraising, it is equally essential to decide exactly which segments of the market should be targeted. It is unlikely that the non-profit will have global appeal, but it may have resonance with a number of very specific commercial organizations.

In the commercial context segmentation operates at two levels. The non-profit has, first, to consider which organizations it will target and, second, who within these organizations should be contacted. This is not so straightforward as it may at first appear, as the decision to support a non-profit may be taken not by one individual, but by a number of people within the organization. Marketers refer to this group as the decision-making unit or DMU. It typically comprises the following:

- *Initiators*: Those within the organization who raise awareness of the nature of the cause, or trigger the initial consideration of whether or not to offer a gift. They may have personal links to the cause, or have raised the issue with management in response to a communication from the charity. Either way they are important since they initiate the decision-making process.
- *Deciders*: Those individuals who will effectively take the decision over whether support will be offered. They may be managers, or more senior staff such as a Director or the Chair if higher value forms of support are being suggested. They may have no direct contact with the non-profit and simply take the decision on the basis of evidence presented to them by other members of their team.
- *Participants*: Members of this group are nominated by the corporate to take responsibility for the decision. They may serve on a committee or meet on an *ad hoc* basis to consider the merits of a particular approach from a non-profit. In some cases, where the decision is to be taken by a committee, their views will carry equal weight. In other cases, their views are sought to inform the decision that will be taken by the responsible manager (i.e. the decider).
- *Influencers*: These may be influential people within the organization or they may be external contacts or consultants. These members of the DMU are important since their views are highly regarded by other members of the group. Again, they may have no direct contact with the non-profit and may have no direct interest in the support that will be offered. They are merely opinion leaders.

- *Gatekeepers*: These individuals 'guard' the senior staff in a corporate and thus make it difficult for the non-profit to get its message across. Frequently, a secretary or personal assistant will filter calls to senior members of staff and will intercept mail, binning anything perceived as not being of relevance. They are thus an important category to consider since they control access to other members of the DMU.

Indeed, all these categories are important, since the non-profit needs to ensure that it develops a separate strategy for getting its message across to as many of these groups as is practical. Each will likely have very different information needs and aspirations, and this should be reflected in a segmented approach to fundraising practice.

Wind and Cordozo (1974) suggest that business segmentation should be undertaken in two stages. The first stage involves defining the segments in terms of size, profitability, industrial sector, and Standard Industrial Classification (SIC) code (a two- to four-digit code which defines the company's industry and the nature of its work). The second stage they advocate is to define the segments in terms of the behavioural characteristics of their DMUs. The result is a hybrid segmentation system which reflects not only the type of business, but also the manner in which it operates. To help illustrate the variety of criteria that are available it is worth briefly reviewing the work of Bonoma and Shapiro (1983) who developed one of the most comprehensive reviews of industrial segmentation currently available. The criteria the authors identify are given in Exhibit 4.1. The authors originally suggested that these criteria are arranged in descending levels of importance. In the context of fundraising, however, many of the criteria towards the bottom of the list can actually offer considerably more utility than those towards the top. As an example, companies whose customer profile would be likely to match the profile of a non-profit's typical donors would clearly warrant consideration with an appropriately tailored approach.

Similarly, the purchasing approaches adopted will have considerable relevance. Those organizations who would be likely to make a genuinely philanthropic gift would require rather different treatment from those who would look to measure the 'success' of their donation by its impact on the bottom line.

Since criteria such as company size and location will clearly determine the likelihood and amounts of funding to be supplied it would seem that charities should give the greatest consideration to a mix of demographic, purchasing approach and personal characteristic variables when considering how best to segment the corporate donor market.

EVALUATING THE SUITABILITY OF SEGMENTS

By now the reader will appreciate the diversity of variables that could potentially be used as the basis for market segmentation. While there are many potential segments that an organization could look to pursue, it is almost certain that only a few will actually be worth exploiting. The difficulty facing fundraisers is exactly how to evaluate the possibilities.

In practice there are seven criteria that may be used to evaluate the potential offered by each segment proposed. Only if the analysis is favourable in each case should the segment be pursued. The segment must be:

1   *Measurable*: The segment should be easily measurable and information about the segment and its characteristics should therefore exist or be obtainable cost-effectively.
2   *Accessible*: It should be possible to design a fundraising approach to target the segment cost-effectively. One would therefore need to look, for example, at appropriate media opportunities that could be used with the minimum of wastage.

EXHIBIT 4.1 CRITERIA FOR SEGMENTING OF INDUSTRIAL MARKETS

Demographic

- Industry type – Which industries should be targeted?
- Company size – What size of company should be targeted?
- Location – In what geographical regions should firms be targeted?

Operating variables

- Technology – What kinds of technology do potential customers employ?
- User status – Would they be heavy, medium or light users of the service?
- Customer capabilities – Should customers having many or few needs be concentrated on?

Purchasing approaches

- Buying criteria – What would customers be looking for? Cost, convenience, service?
- Buying policies – Are decisions made locally or centrally, and what duration of relationship would be desirable?
- Current relationships – Should the organization focus on only those customers who have a track record of support?

Situational factors

- Urgency – Should customers with immediate needs be targeted?
- Size of order – Should customers requiring high- or low-value relationships be targeted?
- Applications – Should customers looking to use the association in different ways be targeted?

Personal characteristics

- Loyalty – Should only companies exhibiting high degrees of loyalty to their suppliers be targeted?
- Attitudes to risk – Should risk-taking or risk-avoiding customers be targeted?
- Buyer–seller familiarity – Should companies with similar characteristics to the seller be targeted?

Source: Adapted from Bonoma and Shapiro (1983)

3 *Substantial*: It should be cost-effective to fundraise from the segment. Clearly the segment should be large enough in terms of volume of donations (or small with sufficiently high margins) to warrant exploitation.

4 *Stable*: The segment's behaviour should be relatively stable over time to ensure that its future development may be predicted with a degree of accuracy for planning purposes.

5 *Appropriate*: It should be appropriate to approach a certain segment given the organization's mission, resources, objectives and so on. A children's charity, for example, may wish to avoid seeking donations from corporations that have links to companies in the Third World which exploit child labour.

6   *Unique*: The segment should be unique in terms of its response (to fundraising activity) so that it may be distinguished from other segments.

7   *Sustainable*: Sustainability is an issue that is rapidly growing in importance. It refers to the extent to which particular categories of donor can be sustained by the organization. The National Trust, for example, would only hope to attract members/donors who will treat their properties with appropriate respect, stick to signposted paths, take home their litter and so on. Not every segment of society will thus be sustainable and fundraising activity, particularly where membership is offered as a product, will need to take this into account.

Criterion 6 warrants elaboration. A segment may meet all the other criteria but may behave identically to other segments in terms of its response to different types and timing of strategy. If this is the case, Kotler and Andreasen (1991:170) identify that 'although it may be conceptually useful to develop separate segments in this way, it is not managerially useful'. As an example, many charities now have two distinctive demographic groups in their direct marketing database. Older individuals (i.e. aged 60+) and younger donors (aged 25 to 40) are recruited through one or more of the new media channels (see Chapter 6). The fundraiser responsible for donor development could look at the demographic differences and decide on the basis of this that he/she is looking at two distinct segments and develop a separate communications programme for both. However, this makes sense only if these individuals differ in their response to different forms of communication. If they react in an identical way to receiving direct mail, find the same topics/issues of relevance and are stimulated to give by the same motives, it does not make sense to treat these two groups differently. Segmentation is not necessary.

As a further example Figure 4.3 shows the allocation of a fundraising budget between two geographically separate markets, North and South. It may be seen from the slope of the two graphs that the North is more fundraising elastic (i.e. more sensitive to fundraising expenditure) than the South. The points FS1 and FN1 represent equal fundraising expenditures in the two markets. This allocation strategy yields total response results of (RS1 and RN1). However, if the expenditure is shifted around between the two regions and $2,000 is moved from the South to the North, then the total amount raised will rise (RS2 + RN2), even though total expenditures remain unchanged. Clearly fundraisers should continue shifting their fundraising

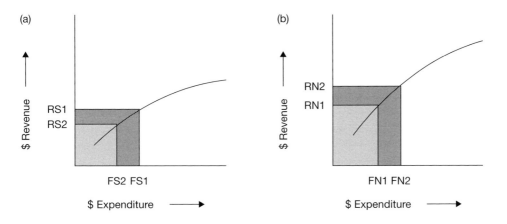

Figure 4.3 *Hypothetical responses of two markets to fundraising activities*
Source: Kotler and Andreasen (1991). © 2003 adapted by permission of Prentice Hall Inc, Upper Saddle River, NJ

budget to the North until such time as the incremental gain in one market equals the incremental loss in the other. One would normally take advantage of any differential responsiveness until there is no variation in total responsiveness given any small changes that might be instigated. It should be remembered that in this simple example the only variable under consideration was fundraising expenditure. In reality segments may exhibit differential responsiveness to a wide range of differing criteria and these data can be used to great effect in fundraising planning. Clearly, if no differential responsiveness is exhibited, one might question the value of segmenting the market on that basis since no managerial advantages accrue.

POSITIONING STRATEGY

Once the organization has decided on appropriate segments for the fundraising plan to address, it will be necessary to develop a strategy that will shape the message which the non-profit wishes to project in the minds of these targets. This is in essence what marketers refer to as 'positioning', and it may be defined as:

> The act of defining in the minds of the target audience what a particular organization stands for and can offer in relation to other non-profits.

In simple terms positioning defines what is unique about an organization and thus what distinguishes it from other non-profits seeking to raise funds from similar sources. Positioning is key since it indicates to donors the distinctive nature of the work that is being undertaken and/or the distinctive nature of the benefits that might accrue as a result of being a member or donor. It is important that donors are clear from the outset about the nature of the work the organization undertakes and why this is different from that undertaken by other non-profits they could look to support. Positioning is thus a general statement about perceptions of the organization as a whole and will later drive the specific 'case for support' that is created for each segment of donors, or, in the case of major donors, each individual donor. It should be reflected in all the communications the organization sends out and be linked closely to the issue of branding (see Chapter 13).

As an example, the UK has a number of large national children's charities. Figure 4.4 gives an example of how these different organizations might be positioned in terms of key organizational facets.

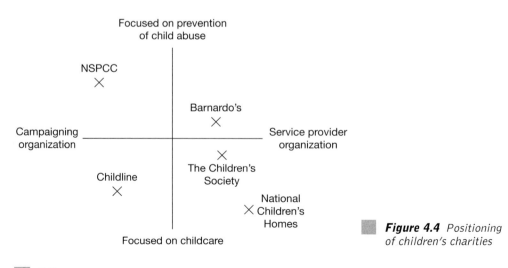

Figure 4.4 Positioning of children's charities

STRATEGIC WEAR-OUT

Thus far in our discussion of strategy we have been considering the overall direction an organization will take towards the fulfilment of its fundraising objectives, the segments of donors who will form the basis of the target audience for each form of fundraising undertaken and how the organization wishes to be perceived by the individuals or organizations that comprise this audience. These three dimensions comprise the overall fundraising strategy of the organization.

It is important to recognize that this organizational strategy can easily become obsolete and inappropriate, particularly if the organization fails to undertake a regular fundraising planning exercise. This is known as 'strategic wear-out'. Its causes include:

- *Changes in the macro-environment*: For example, changes in legislation can limit the range of fundraising techniques available or make them uneconomic.
- *Competitor activity*: The strategy adopted by other non-profits could impact negatively on an organization's ability to raise funds if it does not take account of their activities.
- *Lack of investment*: Some non-profits fail to achieve targets, or set over-ambitious targets that cannot realistically be met given the level of investment. A direct mail strategy, for example, can easily become stale and inappropriate if the organization does not keep up adequate investment in database technology.
- *Management complacency*: The single biggest cause of strategic wear-out is management complacency where fundraisers believe that they have adopted the optimum strategy and there is no reason to consider change, or even to monitor it. Such individuals and/or fundraising departments are frequently overtaken by changes in the environment and recognize this only when it is too late to respond.

In seeking to prevent strategic wear-out fundraisers need to conduct regular and systematic planning exercises where all pertinent factors and changes are considered. The process of debating audit data and competitor activity should be open and constructive, and all members of the fundraising team should be permitted and encouraged to challenge current ways of thinking and operating. The internal culture of the non-profit should be stimulated to regard change as positive and an essential part of being responsive to donor needs and expectations. Finally, regular and ongoing communication within the fundraising team and with other departments or functions within the organization is essential. Often other teams working in service provision, IT or other areas may be aware of changes that could impact on the organization's future fundraising practice. Clearly the earlier this is shared and discussed with the fundraising team, the stronger the likelihood that the organization can develop a cogent response.

TACTICAL PLANS

Aggregate or activity sub-plans

Having defined the strategy, or overall approach that will be adopted, the next section of the plan contains the fine detail of the fundraising that will be undertaken. Thus separate plans will be provided here for direct marketing, major gift fundraising/planned giving, corporate fundraising, Trust/Foundation fundraising and community/local group fundraising. In smaller non-profits, or those conducting only a limited range of fundraising activities, this may consist only of a list of actions to be taken (i.e. an action plan). In larger organizations, or those involved in a range of fundraising techniques, a separate sub-plan will be created for each form of fundraising and only the key points will be reported in the aggregate fundraising plan. If 'sub-plans' are used they will typically be structured in a very similar way to the aggregate plan and will have their own objectives, action plans, budget, schedule and series of controls.

Rather than elaborate further here, later chapters will consider each form of fundraising in detail.

Case for support

In writing the plans for each form of fundraising, the organization will need to consider the development of an appropriate case for support for each target audience. In the case of corporate, Trust/Foundation and major individual donors, this case for support may be individually tailored, but it will still retain a number of common ingredients.

The case for support is the expression of the cause and why it warrants support. It must be well articulated and be capable of being thoroughly understood by all the charity's donors. When creating and managing the case for support the non-profit must consider three key elements.

1   *Compiling case resources*: The Fund Raising School at Indiana University (1999) suggests that non-profits should collate a pool of resources which can be used to write the case for support and update this material on an ongoing basis. These resources may be existing documents, or they may have to be created for the first time as part of this process. They include:

- The mission statement and ultimate goals of the organization.
- The specific objectives that the organization is now seeking to achieve.
- An outline of the programmes and services that the non-profit provides. Here the organization should clearly express how it implements its objectives and the impact it has on the cause or the people it aims to assist. This must be much more than a bland statement of operational strategy, and should stress the real impact the non-profit is having on people's lives.
- A description of the governance structure, namely the composition of the Board, how it is elected or appointed and its relevance to the beneficiary group. This is particularly important for social welfare organizations since potential funders will often look to ensure that the Board is representative of those it exists to serve.
- Staffing plans. The non-profit should express how both paid staff and volunteers will be used in the appropriate and effective delivery of programmes.
- Statement of non-financial resources. This consists of a description of the facilities the non-profit can offer and a list of the resources that can be brought to bear on service or programme provision.
- Financial statements. A detailed set of the organization's accounts should be included in the pack of case resources, including both the published accounts and the more detailed management accounts. Fundraisers may also solicit the help of the finance or programmes departments to secure any meaningful graphics, which help illustrate how resources are expended, or current levels of financial need.
- Planning documents. It would be helpful to include both a statement of the nature of the planning process itself and copies of any organizational or strategic plans the non-profit may have produced.
- History. A brief summary of when and why the organization was created and a list of its past achievements

(Adapted from The Fund Raising School 1999)

2   *Understanding donor needs*: The organization should distil information gathered from the fundraising audit in respect of the current and likely future needs of donors. While much of giving remains genuinely philanthropic, it is important to recognize that some segments of donors may have very specific needs or expectations of the organization. Such needs must be genuinely understood if the case for support, however worthy it might be, is to be made relevant and attractive to donors.

3   *Writing case expressions*: In writing a case expression the fundraiser seeks to use all of the above-mentioned resources to explain clearly and straightforwardly the benefits the organization provides and why it would warrant support. It needs to engender a sense of immediacy, excitement and importance. It should also draw on the positioning strategy and make it clear why the particular organization is distinctive. It will typically be helpful to write a case expression for each segment of donors approached and, in the case of major funders such as corporates and major donors, to tailor it to the likely interests of the individual. The same process will also be necessary in the case of Trusts/Foundations, but the form that the case expression must take will often be defined by the foundation in its application literature.

BUDGET

Having detailed the steps that it will be necessary to take to achieve the fundraising objectives, the writer of the plan should then be in a position to cost the various proposals and to derive an overall fundraising budget for the planning period. This is the optimal approach. Of course, in reality life is often not that neat. Cost will undoubtedly have been in the minds of fundraising planners even before they commenced the audit. At the very least the development of a suitable budget is likely in practice to have been an iterative process, with proposals being re-evaluated in the light of budgetary constraints.

There are a variety of ways of determining the fundraising budget. The ideal would clearly be to specify the strategy and tactics that are felt necessary to achieve the fundraising objectives and then to cost these to arrive at an overall budget. This is often referred to as the 'task' method of setting a fundraising budget. Of course, in practice this method is seldom employed since financial pressures from senior management, the budget/accounting practices of the organization and uncertainty will all hamper the derivation of an appropriate budget. In practice, therefore, budgets tend to be set by the following methods:

- *Percentage of previous year's donations*: Perhaps 10 to 20 per cent of income may be set aside to fund the following year's fundraising activities. While easy to calculate, this approach suffers from two key drawbacks. First, the budget may bear no resemblance to the cost of raising the requisite funding for the coming year's operations and, second, setting the budget in this way can have the effect of lowering the fundraising spend when income levels fall. It could be argued that this is the exact opposite of what should happen in these circumstances where many organizations would look to invest in new forms of income generation to secure the non-profit's long-term future.
- *Percentage of budgeted donations*: This approach eliminates the weaknesses alluded to above, but requires great care in calculating an appropriate percentage. Different fundraising techniques vary widely in the returns they are capable of generating and an aggregate percentage allocation can therefore be very simplistic.
- *Competitor matching*: Some non-profits choose to monitor the expenditure undertaken by those they regard as their key competitors. While a careful choice of competitor against which to benchmark can often be insightful in suggesting the ballpark figures an

organization might look to invest, this approach again fails to take account of the non-profit's own objectives and need for funds, which could be quite different from those of a competitor.

■   *What can be afforded*: This is perhaps the least rational of all the methods of budget calculation and involves members of the senior management of the organization deciding what they believe they can afford to allocate to the fundraising function in a particular year. Once again, little or no reference is made to the fundraising objectives.

Irrespective of the method actually employed, in practice it would be usual to specify how the eventual budget has been allocated and to include such a specification in the fundraising plan itself. It would also be normal for an allowance to be made for contingencies in the event that monitoring by the organization suggests that the objectives will not be met. Sufficient resources should then exist for some form of corrective action to be taken.

SCHEDULING

The reader will appreciate that a large number of tactics will have been specified in the main body of the plan. To ensure that these tactics are executed in a co-ordinated fashion over the duration of the plan it is usual to present a schedule that clearly specifies when each activity will take place. This would often take the form of a Gantt chart (an example is provided in Figure 4.5). If the responsibilities for various fundraising activities are split between different groups of staff the schedule will act as an important co-ordination mechanism. Indeed, if responsibilities are split in this way it would be usual to add an additional section to the plan specifying the individual post-holder who will have responsibility for the implementation of each component of the plan.

	Jan	Feb	Mar	Apr	May	June	July	Aug	Sept	Oct	Nov	Dec
Direct mail	X			X				X				X
Press ads	X										X	X
Display ads	X						X					
Telemarketing		X			X				X			X

Figure 4.5 *Gantt chart*

MONITORING AND CONTROL

As soon as the plan has been implemented, fundraising management will take responsibility for monitoring the progress of the organization towards the goals specified. Managers will also need to concern themselves with the costs that have been incurred at each stage of implementation and monitor these against the budget. Thus control mechanisms need to be put in place to monitor:

1   the actual donations achieved against the budget;
2   the actual costs incurred against those budgeted;

88

3   the performance of specific forms of fundraising;
4   the appropriateness of the strategy/tactics adopted.

In the case of financial objectives, such as (1) and (2) above, it would be usual to crack out the aggregate target for a given year into monthly targets, perhaps for each form of fundraising undertaken, each donor segment and so on. It should also stipulate how much variation it is prepared to tolerate from these monthly 'sub-targets' before the alarm is raised. The organization can then monitor actual performance against its targets each month and, where performance falls outside the band of permissible performance, the matter is brought to the attention of fundraising managers who then have the opportunity to instigate some form of corrective action.

CHAPTER SUMMARY

In this chapter we have reviewed the final components of an aggregate fundraising plan. We have stressed the need for SMART objectives to guide the direction of the plan and to act as an effective form of control to ensure that scarce resources are applied appropriately across the range of fundraising techniques adopted. We have also examined the key elements of fundraising strategy, namely determining the overall direction that will be adopted, the donor groups that will be addressed with the plan, and in general terms how the organization is distinctive in relation to its competitors (i.e. positioning). We have also explored how tactical plans for each category of fundraising undertaken can be integrated into an aggregate fundraising plan, and in subsequent chapters we will explain how each form of fundraising can be planned, implemented and controlled. Finally, we outline the need to consider the fundraising budget, schedule and controls.

DISCUSSION QUESTIONS

1   What role do objectives play in the fundraising plan? What factors should be born in mind when setting fundraising objectives?

2   Distinguish between positioning strategy and the fundraising 'case for support'.

3   What is meant by the term 'segmentation'? How might a large national charity concerned with child welfare segment the market for corporate donations?

4   You are the fundraising director of a medium-sized non-profit concerned with wildlife conservation. Your organization currently serves four counties and is considering using direct mail to solicit donations for the first time. Prepare a report for your Board indicating how the individual donor market might be segmented and highlighting the research you would propose to implement to explore this potential.

REFERENCES

Ansoff, I. (1968) *Corporate Strategy*, Penguin Books, London.

Banks, J. and Tanner, S. (1997) *The State of Donation*, London, IFS.

Bonoma, T.V. and Shapiro, B.P. (1983) *Segmenting the Industrial Market*, Lexington Books, Lexington, MA.

Coleman, R.P. (1983) 'The Continuing Significance of Social Class To Marketing', *Journal of Consumer Research*, December: 265–280.

Drucker, P.F. (1990) *Managing The Non-Profit Organization*, Butterworth-Heinemann, Oxford.

Kotler, P. (1991) *Marketing Management: Analysis, Planning, Implementation and Control*, 8th edn, Prentice Hall, Englewood Cliffs, NJ.

Kotler, P. and Andreasen, A. (1991) *Strategic Marketing For Nonprofit Organisations* (5th edn), Prentice Hall, Englewood Cliffs, NJ.

MacDonald, M.H.B. (1984) *Marketing Plans: How To Prepare Them, How To Use Them*, Heinemann, London.

Mullin, R. (1997) *Fundraising Strategy*, ICSA Publishing, London.

Philips, L.W. and Sternthal, B. (1977) 'Age Differences in Information Processing: A Perspective on the Aged Consumer', *Journal of Marketing Research*, 14(4): 444–457.

Sargeant, A. (1999) *Marketing Management for Nonprofit Organizations*, Oxford University Press, London.

The Fund Raising School (1999) *Principles and Techniques of Fund Raising*, Indiana University Center on Philanthropy.

Wells, W.D. and Gubar, G. (1966) 'Lifecycle Concept in Marketing Research', *Journal of Marketing Research*, 12(2): 301–335.

Wilson, R.M.S., Gilligan, C. and Pearson, D.J. (1992) *Strategic Marketing Management*, Butterworth-Heinemann, Oxford.

Wind, Y. and Cordozo, R. (1974) 'Industrial Market Segmentation', *Industrial Marketing Management*, 3(1): 153–165.

Part II

Fundraising from individuals

Chapter 5

Understanding giving

LEARNING OBJECTIVES

By the end of this chapter you should be able to:

■ Describe economic theories of giving and understand the implications for fundraising.
■ Compare and contrast a number of composite models of giving behaviour.
■ Understand who gives to charity and the motives for their support.
■ Understand the criteria that donors use to select between charities.
■ Understand why donors stop giving to specific organizations.

INTRODUCTION

In the USA total giving to the charitable sector in 2001 stood at $212 billion, representing a 0.5 per cent increase over the previous year (AAFRC Trust 2002). Just under 90 per cent of Americans offer donations to non-profits with people giving on average around 2 per cent of their income and contributing nearly 85 per cent of the total accruing to the sector (the balance coming from corporates and foundations). In the UK the picture is less impressive, although individuals still contributed £6.1 billion in 2001 and a further £1.5 billion in the form of bequests/legacies (Pharoah 2002). Individuals give an average of 1.3 per cent of weekly household income, but participation rates are noticeably lower than in the USA with only 68 per cent of the total population supporting non-profits (Passey *et al.* 2000).

The issue of why individuals elect to offer their support in this way has puzzled philosophers and economists since the dawn of antiquity (Wispe 1978). In recent times researchers from a variety of fields have studied the topic. Notable here is the contribution of the economics literature which has always had something of a problem in explaining charitable support. Neoclassical economic theory prefers to regard man as an entirely rational creature who takes decisions on the basis of the utility that will be afforded to the individual (so-called *homo-economicus*). Under this scenario 'charitable' support can only be explained when some tangible economic benefit accrues to the individual as a consequence of his or her gift. While this may explain some aspects of giving, where perhaps gifts are made to support an art-form enjoyed by the donor, the vast majority of gifts do not appear to match this profile.

More recent economic theory has tended to regard giving as a 'softer' exchange where the utility may take a variety of different forms. Andreoni (2001) notes three distinct perspectives:

1   *Public good theory* – which postulates that people will support non-profits because they recognize that society as a whole will benefit from the donation. They are thus rational since as a member of that society they too will derive benefit from the donation.
2   *Exchange theory* – which posits that donors will give because of the tangible rewards they receive for their donation. This may take the form of membership benefits that may accrue as part of their subscription, or it may take the form of acknowledgement devices such as plaques or citations on a roll of honour.
3   *Warm glow effect* – some economists believe that the utility offered by a gift can be psychological in nature and thus completely intangible. People give because they feel better about themselves for having made the donation.

In general, however, economic theories of giving have generally lacked empirical support and have been shown to offer only partial explanations for why individuals decide to give.

In this chapter it is therefore our intention to provide a detailed review of why people give, drawing on a broad theoretical and practical base. We will examine the characteristics of donors, their motives for support, the criteria they use to select between non-profits, and finally, the reasons why they terminate their support.

What is striking about the evidence presented is the degree of similarity in donor behaviour between the USA and the UK. It is therefore our intention to highlight the generally applicable research indicating where necessary any differences that might exist between the two countries.

WHO GIVES?

As was noted earlier, a large proportion of the population in the UK and USA donate funds to non-profits. In the UK the Family Expenditure Survey tracks the involvement of the public in purchasing a variety of goods and services. It also includes details of any charitable giving that might be undertaken and as a consequence can overlay the profile of the 'typical' giving household on these data. We therefore understand a great deal about the charitable behaviour of certain categories of individual (see Table 5.1). The table makes reference to a range of demographic variables that can impact on giving (e.g. income, age, education), and over the years considerable research has been conducted into how giving behaviour might vary by each of these categories. We will discuss each of the major variables in turn.

Age

According to Royer (1989), 60 per cent of charitable gifts in the USA come from people aged between 60 and 76. A similarly skewed profile of charitable support has been reported in the UK (Banks and Tanner 1997). While the young have always been less inclined to give to charity a trend has emerged in recent years and, in general, the younger generations in our society appear to be less motivated to give to charity than would have previously been the case. As Simpson (1986:33) puts it:

> (in the UK) this generation seems less inclined to believe in philanthropy. They are much more consumption driven, they buy things for themselves. Young people today like to spend money on eating out, on clothes and other things – more than people did 20 years ago.

Table 5.1 _Key characteristics of donor households_

Key characteristic	Probability of giving	Effect on levels of giving
Income	For each 10 per cent increase in household income, there is a 1.2 per cent increase in participation in giving	For every 1 per cent increase in expenditure, there is a 1.1 per cent increase in size of donations
Age	For every increase of 10 years in the age of the head of the household, there is an increased likelihood of giving of 3 per cent	For every increase of 10 years in the age of the head of the household, there is a 30 per cent increase in the value of donations
Children	Households with children are 3 per cent more likely to give than those without	(no information)
Wealth	Home owners are 6 per cent more likely to give than non-home owners and the effect of each additional room is to raise the likelihood of giving by 1 per cent	Home ownership increases size of donations by 14 per cent
Education	Households where the head has A levels are 5 per cent more likely to give and, where college-educated, 11 per cent more likely to give	The effect of having A levels is to increase the size of donations by 38 per cent and the effect of college education is an 80 per cent raise
Employment status	Households where the head is self-employed are 11 per cent less likely to give; where unemployed they are 7 per cent less likely to give	Those not in work are likely to give 20 per cent less than where the head is self-employed or employed

Source: Walker and Pharoah (2002), adapted from Banks and Tanner (1997). Reproduced by kind permission of Hodder Arnold

Even in the USA there has been an apparent resurgence of materialistic values among younger US consumers and fewer young people are electing to give to good causes as a consequence (Yankelovich 1981).

Despite the apparently contracting pool of donors, however, not all authors are pessimistic about likely patterns of future giving. Some writers account for the skewed age distribution of givers by explaining that older people experience less social interaction than do their younger counterparts. This results from a physiological decline (impacting on mobility), age-related losses (including retirement and the death of a spouse – Atchley 1987) and a less positive self-image due to a lack of control and self-determination (Ward 1977). Elderly members of society may thus be able to experience _pseudo-social interaction_ through the relationships they build up with charities and in essence exchange one form of social interaction with another (Caplow 1984). Given that the elderly of today are much more likely to be wealthy than their predecessors, this represents a considerable future opportunity for charities to address and not necessarily a threat (Moschis 1992).

It is also worth noting that our preference for categories of cause seems to change as we get older. Health issues become more important with the passage of time and 18- to 24-year-olds have a marked preference for children's charities, homelessness, famine relief and environ-mental causes (Reed 1998). Some writers prefer to regard these differences as a function of 'lifestage' rather than age *per se*. The motivation for giving to a number of charities, notably those connected in some way with medical research, may be related to a great extent to the level of involvement an individual may have with the problem addressed by a charity. Those individuals who either suffer from a particular complaint or who are perhaps related to a sufferer will be somewhat more disposed to giving than those who have no such association.

Gender

A number of gender differences have been reported in relation to giving. In the USA the Council of Economic Advisors used data from the 1998 Survey of Consumer Finances to examine the giving behaviour of donors who had given $500 or more in 1998. They determined that women tended to give more frequently than men, although they donate very similar amounts in aggre-gate. What this means in practice is that individual non-profits looking at the behaviour of their database will notice that while they have more women on their database they appear to be less generous than men. This is simply because they are spreading their giving across a wider range of organizations. It is interesting to note that this pattern is mirrored in most other Western countries.

There are further attitudinal and behavioural differences. Braus (1994), for example, identi-fied that women tend to want more information about how the money is actually going to be used, prefer one-off donations as opposed to regular (or committed) giving and to give more 'from the heart than the head' (p.48). This again reflects practitioner experience, and a number of organizations have had success through direct mail by using gender-specific copy.

Differences in preferences have also been reported, with Marx (2000) identifying that women are more likely to support human service organizations. Stirling (2000), in a study of capital campaigns conducted between 1988 and 1998 in formerly all-female or all-male liberal arts colleges, analysed planned giving by former students. She found that women tended to prefer outright bequests (legacies) rather than other planned giving vehicles such as pooled income funds and charitable gift annuities (for a discussion of these forms of giving see Chapter 9).

Social class or socio-economic group

Fundraisers often segment their approach to donors on the basis of socio-economic group or social class. In the USA social scientists have used an amalgam of variables such as income, occupation and education to create six distinct social classes: (1) upper uppers, (2) lower uppers, (3) upper middles, (4) lower middles, (5) upper lowers, and (6) lower lowers. In the UK the related concept of socio-economic group is widely used.

In the case of both models, the notion is that the level of disposable income will rise as one moves up the social scale. Of course it is important to recognize that these systems are very simplistic and were developed at a time when society was much more static than is the case today. Movement between the categories is now not unusual, and the link between group and disposable income is far more tenuous than would have been the case thirty or forty years ago.

Nevertheless, these categories are of interest since variable income is an important deter-minant of charitable behaviour. In general, and very much as one would expect, the wealthier individuals in society tend to give larger sums than do those on lower incomes. It is interesting to note that in the USA, the poor and extremely wealthy give a much higher proportion of their income than the middle class (Silver 1980). In the UK this does not hold true with the poorest 10 per cent of households giving 3 per cent of their weekly household expenditure to good causes while the wealthiest 20 per cent give only 0.7 per cent of their expenditure. This highlights an interesting cultural difference between the two countries!

It is also important to note that lower income earners differ in their rationale for support of non-profits. Radley and Kennedy (1992) identified that the lower socio-economic groups tend to see the needy as a group to be pitied because of their treatment at the hand of fate. Promotional messages stressing the ability of even a small gift to alleviate pain and suffering are therefore likely to be most effective. The higher socio-economic groups by contrast, particularly those from the professions, give not only for the amelioration of suffering but also for the longer term change in their situation. Support is thus prompted by a need to make a change in a social structure, and promotional messages could perhaps reflect this motivation.

Higher value givers are also distinctive in the sense that they tend to favour certain categories of cause. They tend to avoid causes involving the overtly poor such as homelessness and are much more likely to patronize organizations that they, or members of their social class, can draw benefit from. As Ostrower (1997:133) notes, they 'carve out a separate and exclusive arena for themselves quite distinct from the "philanthropic arena" of the economically disadvantaged, supporting causes such as the arts, education and healthcare'.

Education

The level of education an individual has achieved has also received attention in the literature. The level of education attained by the head of the household impacts both on the likelihood that donations will be offered and also on the level of the gift that will be made. Those individuals who have achieved a college/university degree are the most likely both to participate in giving and to give the highest sums (Sargeant 1999).

Religion

The many countries and cultures of the world have developed long and distinctive histories of individual giving. It is impossible here to fully address the impact of the world's great faiths and their traditions of giving, but it is probably fair to say that all have promoted voluntarism and the need to support the welfare of others. As Pharoah (2002: 38–39) notes:

> In Islam the concepts of zakat and sadaqa enshrine the giving of money or gifts in kind. In Hinduism the central concept of daanam (the act of giving) takes many forms. Sikhism has the concept of kar seva (service to each other). Confucian teachings highlight 'humaneness,' and there is a long history of private benevolence for public good in China. Jewish concepts of charity have both long religious and secular traditions.

Given this history it is perhaps not surprising that an individual professing a religious faith has been found to be more likely to engage in giving funds to non-profits. Studies have also indicated that the strength of that faith can be an issue, with individuals professing a stronger sense of faith being more likely both to give and to give at higher levels.

Ethnicity

Comparatively little research has been conducted into the impact of ethnicity on giving. This is due in part to the complexity surrounding the difference between race and ethnicity (hampering categorization) and also to the sensitivity surrounding the issue, making it difficult for researchers to handle the matter in an appropriate way. Nevertheless there is now a body of evidence to suggest that individuals from particular ethnic backgrounds tend to support causes which benefit others matching that profile. This seems to be true even for second or third generation immigrants to a particular country, where the giving patterns of parents and grand-parents seem to be reflected in the priorities of the current generation. In many communities of colour, for example, there is a strong sense of tradition and desire to express a unique identity. Such philanthropy is often characterized by small groups of people getting together to help others only marginally less privileged than themselves and is thus highly distinctive. It has played an important role historically and continues to play a vital role in supporting individuals who might otherwise not reach their full potential.

In a study of various ethnic communities in the USA, Millett and Orosz (2001) conclude that the following motives predominate:

- *African Americans*: Give because of a determination to meet the needs of other African Americans, their primary interests being religion, education, health and human services. Fifty-nine per cent of their donations are made to religious causes.
- *Latinos*: Motives are as diverse as the various Latino cultures themselves. They give to religious organizations, family/extended family and Latino non-profits. They send a significant proportion of their money outside the USA, and give to 'give back' to their Latino community and accelerate opportunities for other members of their ethnic group.
- *Asian Americans*: Again, a diverse pattern of motives was found to exist. Giving was found to be closely tied to family and social circles. Giving was seen as a duty or obligation and billions of dollars are sent abroad to support the extended family overseas in the country of origin. First donations to 'mainstream' non-profits tend to be those to the United Way or their Alma Mater.
- *Native Americans*: Giving is considered a form of power or prestige and may be seen as a way of honouring future generations and clan members. It differs from giving in other communities in that gifts are often made to equals rather than the rich giving to the poor. In Native cultures, human beings are seen as stewards of the natural world and not consumers. As a consequence their gifts are based on a consideration of what is necessary (i.e. need-based) and anonymous.

Personality

The personality of a given individual does not in general appear to be a good indicator of charity support (Penrod 1983). Of the evidence that is available a number of studies have highlighted that the 'self-confident' are more likely to donate to non-profits than other categories of individual. There is also evidence that intrinsically motivated people do more for charity than self-centred, external reward seekers (Reykowski 1982). Of course, while this may be interesting it is difficult to use this knowledge for the purposes of fundraising since these characteristics are very difficult to identify a priori. As a consequence interest has tended to focus on lifestyle rather than on personality *per se*.

Lifestyle

Kotler (1991: 171) defines lifestyle as a 'person's pattern of living in the world as expressed in the person's activities, interests and opinions'. Lifestyle as a consequence portrays the whole individual interacting with his or her environment. It may therefore be viewed as distinct from personality. Personality variables describe the pattern of psychological characteristics an individual might possess, but say nothing of that individual's hobbies, interest, opinions or activities. Lifestyle data, however, can supply some of these missing variables.

Lazer (1963), who first introduced the term 'lifestyle', viewed it as consisting of three basic components: activities (work, hobbies, social events, entertainment, shopping, sports), interests (family, home, job, community, recreation, media, achievements), and opinions (of oneself, social issues, politics, business, education, products, culture).

Lifestyle does offer considerable utility for fundraisers, since individuals are far more willing to support causes that relate to their hobbies/interests or to facets of life about which they hold strong opinions. Donors with pets are thus more likely to support the Humane Society or the Royal Society for the Prevention of Cruelty To Animals. Similarly, donors who enjoy walking in the countryside are more likely to offer their support to conservation organizations.

WHY DO PEOPLE GIVE?

Having examined who gives to charity, it will be instructive to return to the issue of why they give. A variety of potential motives for giving have been identified including self-interest, altruism, sympathy, empathy, fear, guilt, pity, social justice and the existence of social norms. In this section we address the most widely cited of these variables.

Self-interest versus altruism

We have already alluded in the introduction to classic economic theory and the notion of self-interest. This may manifest itself in a variety of different ways including:

- *Self-esteem*: Donors can be motivated to give because it offers them the opportunity to feel better about themselves for having made the gift (Piliavin *et al.* 1975).
- *Atonement for sins*: Some donations may be motivated by the desire to atone for past sins – again with the ultimate goal of allowing the donor to feel better as a consequence of having made the gift (Schwartz 1967).
- *Recognition*: Donors may also be motivated by the recognition they will receive from the organization, their family, peers or the local society in which they live (Dowd 1975).
- *Access to services*: Donors may give to a non-profit because they believe that they may benefit from the work it undertakes at some point in the future. Donations to cancer research, for example, may be driven by a donor's fear of developing the disease themselves.
- *Reciprocation*: Equally donors may give in reciprocation for assistance or services that have been provided in the past. Donors whose lives have already been touched in some way may feel obligated to give to 'reciprocate' for the services offered. It is interesting to note that the notion of reciprocation also has a wider application, since we know from the psychology literature that sending tangible 'gifts' to donors can also generate the need for reciprocation. Plate 5.1 depicts a direct mail solicitation based on this principle, where the donor is sent 2p by the Children's Food Fund in the hope that it will be returned with a donation.
- *In memorium*: Donors frequently give in memory of a friend or a loved one. In such cases the gift acts as a celebration of the individual's life and/or allows donors to express their feelings of loss and perhaps solidarity with those left behind. Such gifts are often intensely personal and may offer the donor considerable utility in bringing meaning to the loss of a loved one.

99

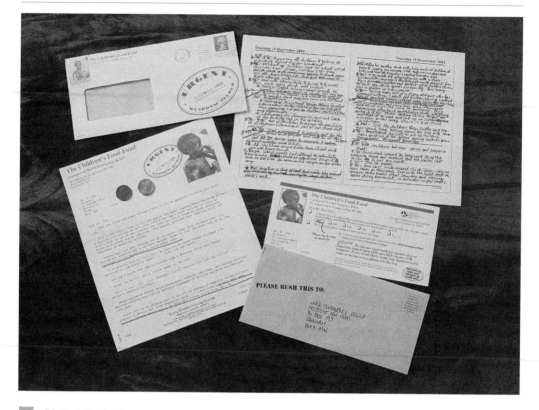

Plate 5.1 *Children's Food Fund Appeal*
Source: © Children's Food Fund Appeal. Reproduced with kind permission

- *Tax*: There is considerable empirical evidence from the USA that the smaller the cost to donors of making a gift, the more likely they are to contribute. A number of studies have examined the relationship between income tax rates and charitable support, and although there has been considerable variation in their findings the responsiveness of individual giving to changes in taxation appears relatively great. A change in the price of donating of a given percentage results in a 24 per cent greater percentage change in donations. Thus a shift in the marginal tax rate from 40 per cent to 30 per cent results in a 15 per cent increase in the cost of giving and would therefore reduce giving by some 18.6 per cent (i.e. 15% × 1.24) (Weisbrod 1988).

The notion of tax relief on giving is considered an important motivator of charitable giving in the USA, and as Odendahl (1987:21) notes:

> the saving of taxes is not ever far from a person's motivation . . . it is in mine, and it is in almost everybody's I know. I think if it were not for the savings in taxes – the notion that the government really is participating in a gift – I think there would be an awful lot less giving.

Nevertheless, it is important not to overstate the influence of taxation. Whatever way one looks at giving and whatever the marginal rate of taxation, donors will always be better off not making a donation and keeping their money to themselves. Indeed, this is reflected in studies that have sought to rank motives for giving, where the impact of favourable tax breaks is typically a long way down the list.

There have also been arguments raised in favour of so-called altruistic giving, whereby donors recognize a need and decide to offer a gift even in circumstances where they themselves will be likely to derive none of the benefits alluded to above. Becker (1976) argues against the existence of altruistic motives for support, claiming instead that what at first glance may appear a selfless act can ultimately be traced back to some form of self-interest motive. Simmons (1991: 16) takes the middle ground and argues that the underlying motive should not really be of interest. Helping acts remain admirable even when inspired by subtle self-rewards:

> such as the desire for one's life to matter, to improve one's self picture, to feel happier about life and self, to relieve the distress of empathy with the victim, or to obey religious or societal norms.

This is a view echoed by De Tocqueville as long ago as 1835 who noted that Americans:

> enjoy explaining almost every act of their lives on the principle of self interest properly understood. It gives them great pleasure to point out how an enlightened self love continually leads them to help one another and disposes them freely to give part of their time and wealth for the good of the state.
>
> (De Tocqueville [1835], 1966: 526)

It seems sensible to conclude that whether or not one believes in the existence of truly altruistic motives for giving is a function of how broad and 'impersonal' one is prepared to make the definition of 'self-benefit'. If one assumes that any benefit to society is likely to result in a degree of self-benefit, it will be possible to post-rationalize almost any donation as being made for selfish purposes, even when the donor may have had no such intention at the time.

Empathy

The arousal of empathy in a donor has consistently been shown to precipitate donations. Empathy may be defined as an individual's emotional arousal elicited by the expression of emotion in another (cf. Shelton and Rogers 1981). Thus donors are motivated to give because they are themselves distressed by the suffering endured by another. Numerous studies have found that the higher the level of empathy the greater the likelihood of a donation being made – up to a point. To be truly effective the arousal of empathy must be powerful enough to overcome indifference and stimulate giving, but not so powerful that it becomes personally distressing to the donor. In such circumstances the message will be ignored (Fultz *et al.* 1986). Images in fundraising communications thus have to strike an appropriate balance.

Sympathy

The motive 'sympathy' has also received attention from researchers. Sympathy is a *value-expressive function* that allows the donor to conform to personally held norms (Clary and Snyder 1991, Schwartz 1977). In other words when confronted with a request to give donors will feel sympathetic if they believe it is inappropriate for the beneficiaries to be suffering in the manner depicted in the fundraising communication. Again, there would appear to be a relationship between the degree of sympathy engendered and both the propensity to donate and the chosen level of support (Batson 1990, Fultz *et al.* 1986). Greater sympathy leads to a higher level of gift.

101

Social justice

Miller (1977) argued from social justice motivation theory that if people witness undue suffering their belief in a just world will be threatened – consequently they will be motivated to respond to restore their faith in that just world. Donors with this motivation have a strong sense of equity and believe that people 'get what they deserve'. They will thus be more motivated to respond to a campaign raising funds for breast cancer victims than for lung cancer victims, whom, rightly or wrongly, they may regard as partially responsible for their own condition.

Miller also identified that helping behaviour would be increased when the need is not widespread and the duration of the need (persistence) is short. It is interesting to note that most charity communications appear based on the exact opposite of this position. Appeals tend to stress the ongoing nature of the need for support and make much of the number of individuals currently being impacted with the affliction/cause for concern.

Norms

Giving may be motivated by a desire on the part of the donor to conform to social norms. Donors will give if they believe that other, similar individuals have also given to support the non-profit. Indeed, there is now considerable evidence to support the proposition that people pay considerable attention to what others contribute. In a detailed experiment Reingen (1978) illustrated that showing prospective donors a fictitious list of others who had contributed to the cause tended to generate higher numbers of gifts and higher levels of gift. He identified that the length of the list was also an issue, with longer lists outperforming shorter ones. Judgements in respect of giving are therefore made in terms of beliefs about what is normative for the group (Clark and Word 1972, Bryan and Test 1967).

The concept of group is of particular significance, since individuals perceive themselves as members of some groups but not others (Hogg and Abrams 1988). Research has consistently shown that individuals tend to support other individuals perceived as similar to themselves, and thus the perception of group membership is key for fundraisers to understand and exploit in their solicitation activity.

THE IMPACT OF CHARITY APPEALS

Thus far in our discussion we have concentrated specifically on the characteristics and motives of donors. At this point it is our intention to move on to consider the 'inputs' to the donor's decision-making process and to consider the impact that factors such as branding, the mode of ask and the content of fundraising communications may have in stimulating giving.

Branding

Non-profits currently engage in a variety of different fundraising techniques employing media such as direct mail, telemarketing, face-to-face canvassing, door-to-door distribution, press advertising and increasingly, radio advertising and DRTV (Direct Response Television). The use of each of these media is potentially capable of generating a response from the prospects targeted. In the case of a number of the larger charities it has been argued that this process has been greatly facilitated by the presence of a well-known and 'trusted' brand.

Roberts Wray (1994) was one of the first to explicitly debate the relevance of branding to the charity sector, with more recent work by Saxton (1995) suggesting that in the voluntary sector context a strong brand should both draw on, and project the beliefs and values of, its various stakeholders. While these are perhaps rather less tangible than the facts about why an organization exists and the nature of the beneficiary group, this latter class of variables can greatly aid a donor's understanding of the charity concerned and suggest very potent reasons why it might be worthy of support (Dixon 1997). It is only comparatively recently, however, that there has been much formal interest in branding within the sector, but while, as Tapp (1996:335) notes, 'charities do not describe much of what they do as "branding", organizations have long been concerned with maintaining a consistent style and tone of voice and conducting periodic reviews of both policies and actions to ensure that a consistent personality is projected'. In the author's view, the clarity with which this 'personality' is projected will have a direct impact on an organization's ability to fundraise. In effect donors will assess whether the personality of the organization is such that it can be trusted to act appropriately in the use of funds. Charities with an established brand therefore have a distinct advantage since donors already feel that they understand something of what the organization does, its values and the methods it uses to achieve its goals. Brands thus act to reduce risk for the donor in making a donation – a theme we shall return to again in Chapter 13.

Mode of ask

The variable 'mode of ask' is also important, because charities can clearly elect to approach donors in a variety of different ways. Reference has already been made to the variety of media that may be used for the purposes of solicitation and we know from professional experience that the profile of the donors recruited by each of these means will vary in terms of their demographic, lifestyle and behavioural characteristics (see e.g. Sargeant and McKenzie 1998). In short, certain types of people will respond to certain types of ask. It is impossible to generalize about these characteristics since they will vary by the nature of the cause and the number and nature of the modes by which the donor can reply and make a donation (e.g. sending through a cheque, making a regular gift, promising a bequest). An example of face-to-face donors (i.e. individuals who are recruited to a regular gift by agency fundraisers approaching them on the street) is provided in Figure 5.1.

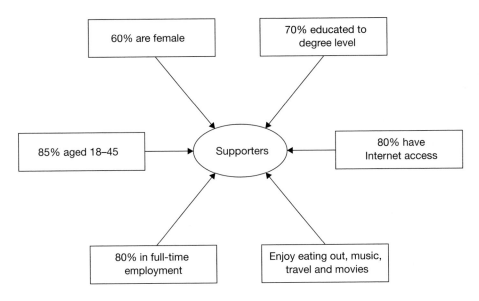

Figure 5.1 Profile of face-to-face supporters

Non-profits need to recognize that the profile of their support will vary depending on the nature of the techniques employed, and they may wish to take steps to ensure that an appropriate breadth of support is maintained. Over-reliance, for example, on direct mail may lead to an increasingly elderly profile of donor and make it difficult for the organization to sustain income in the medium to long term.

Role models

In seeking to solicit funds a number of non-profits make use of celebrities or community leaders who demonstrate their support of the organization and act as a 'role model' for others. The provision of role models can influence giving behaviour by leading to the creation of social norms, thereby legitimizing and encouraging the giving behaviour (Krebs 1970). Role models can be provided at events, by the presence of well-known high-profile donors and also in indirect forms of communication such as direct mail. While role models can be provided in a variety of contexts they work particularly well in circumstances where it is necessary to encourage behaviours that are relatively rare. In the charity context this may be when an organization is looking to solicit funds from a new audience for the first time, or when making a request for donors to give in a way that may previously have not been considered. In such examples donors exhibit a degree of 'social ambiguity' (Festinger 1954) and are unsure of how to behave. It may therefore be helpful to use a role model to indicate the appropriate behaviour and hence an appropriate response. Plate 5.2 contains an example of a communication designed to solicit a legacy/bequest. Here the charity has invited a celebrity who is well known to the target audience to endorse the organization's work and to encourage others to offer a legacy gift. For many this will undoubtedly be a form of giving they may not have considered before.

Plate 5.2 *Use of role models in legacy/bequest solicitation*

Portrayal of beneficiaries

The manner in which recipients of the charitable 'product' are portrayed can have a considerable impact on attitudes towards support and actual giving behaviour. Donors will tend to support those charities that represent the needy in an acceptable way (Eayrs and Ellis 1990). Pictures (for example, of an overtly handicapped child) have been shown to actually decrease the response to fundraising solicitations. Donors can find such images distressing and ignore the communication concerned. Reactance theory (Brehm 1966) also suggests that individuals have what they like to regard as a number of behavioural and attitudinal freedoms. A hard-hitting campaign can thus fail because it may threaten donors' ability to choose to spend their monies elsewhere. It is thus somewhat ironic that a picture of an aided beneficiary can be much more effective, because donors then feel they have the freedom not to give and are statistically much more likely to give as a consequence (Bendapudi and Singh 1996).

Similarly, appeals for charities concerned with disability often emphasize how dependent on the organization's work individuals with the disability are. There is now considerable evidence that such appeals are very successful in engendering feelings of sympathy (Brolley and Anderson 1986, Feldman and Feldman 1985) and feelings of guilt and pity (Feldman and Feldman 1985, Krebs and Whitten 1972, Pieper 1975). A key issue for fundraisers, however, is the extent to which dependency should be exhibited. While one might assume that depicting a greater degree of dependency is desirable and that it would be best to maximize it, this need not necessarily be the case. It depends on whether the dependency on the organization is perceived as temporary or permanent. Wagner and Wheeler (1969) identified that when the need is perceived as permanent, the level of dependency has no effect on the amount likely to be given. However, if the need is only temporary, increasing the level of dependency depicted in fundraising communications will increase the number of donors who both give and give at higher levels.

Interestingly Adler et al. (1991) identified that portraying recipients as succumbing to their condition (in contrast to coping) has no impact on the pattern of donations. They do however identify a strong impact on the subsequent attitudes of the donor towards the recipient group. This latter point is of particular interest since many authors argue that portraying people with disabilities as dependent may well harm the long-term interests of the beneficiary group by reinforcing negative stereotypes and attitudes (Elliot and Byrd 1982, Harris and Harris 1977). Positive portrayals on the other hand seem to engender positive attitudes (Harris 1975, Shurka et al. 1982), and fundraisers thus need to ensure that they take adequate steps to preserve the best interests of the community they serve, consulting as widely as possible before running a potentially contentious campaign. Those messages likely to raise the most funds can on occasion be entirely inappropriate given the nature of the cause and the wider needs of the beneficiary group.

Finally, other work on the portrayal of beneficiaries has suggested that attractive people are perceived as more worthy of support than unattractive people (Latane and Nida 1981) and that female subjects are considered more worthy of support than male subjects (Feinman 1978, Gruder and Cook 1971). The portrayal of the responsibility of recipients for their own condition can also impact on a willingness to support. Piliavin et al. (1975) identified that the extent to which an individual could be blamed for his or her needy condition would impact directly on both the number of donations and the levels of support proffered.

Fit with self-image

Coliazzi et al. (1984) noted that individuals are more likely to help those who are perceived as being similar to themselves. They will thus tend to filter those messages from charities existing to support disparate segments of society. Of course, charities exist to support work, not only with other members of human society but also wider environmental or ecological concerns from which every segment of society can ultimately stand to benefit. Dichter (1972) offers some explanation for support of this category of cause, suggesting that giving can greatly aid one's self-image or self-worth. Indeed, generous giving to all manner of different causes has long been a source of prestige for individuals in the USA. Donors may thus prefer to concentrate on those categories of cause which are either perceived as most relevant to their segment of society, or which are perceived more widely as supporting how they wish to see themselves, or have others see them. As Schwartz (1967) notes, donating can confer an identity on both the recipient and the donor. Work by Yavas *et al.* (1980) suggests that possessing a generous, loving self-image is more important for donors than for non-donors. Donors should therefore be portrayed in communications as generous and loving to help them project the self-image that they would wish others to accept (Douglas *et al.* 1967).

Strength of the stimulus

A variety of authors have chosen to focus on the strength of the stimulus generated by a particular non-profit. Clearly the stronger the stimulus, the easier it will be for non-profits to cut through the 'clutter' of other charitable appeals. There is evidence that the strength of the stimulus is related to a number of variables. The first is the perceived urgency of the recipient situation. In general, high degrees of urgency would appear to engender high degrees of support (See e.g. Chierco *et al.* 1982, Farrington and Kidd 1977). It would also appear that approaches which build up the degree of personal responsibility on the part of the donor will be more effective at engendering a response (See e.g. Geer and Jermecky 1973). Other key variables warranting consideration under this general heading include the degree of personalization attained (Weldon 1984) and the clarity of the request. Personalized, clear and unambiguous requests for support are more likely to engender giving than those that are vague or general in nature.

SELECTION CRITERIA

In the modern era most individuals have the opportunity to support a wide variety of causes. In this section we consider how individuals decide between competing solicitations and select the specific organizations to which they will give. Notable here is the perceived performance of the non-profit organization. Donors will generally prefer to give to organizations that are both effective (in the sense that they do what they say they will do) and efficient (in the sense that they make the best possible use of the monies available to them).

A number of well-publicized abuses of donated monies have served to sensitize donors to these issues. In the USA, for example, the National Kids Day Foundation raised $4 million between 1948 and 1963 and spent the entire amount on fundraising and administrative costs (Cutlip 1980). When challenged, charity administrators said the Foundation's purpose was to promote the idea of needy children rather than actually providing aid. Similarly, the United Way suffered a dramatic fall-off in support following the Aramony scandal when its Chief Executive was accused of having misused the funds of the organization to pay for (among other things) business flights on Concord.

Glaser (1994:178) found that the variable 'an adequate amount spent per program' was the most important factor in the decision to contribute to specific charitable organizations. Donors appear to have a clear idea of what represents an acceptable percentage of income that may be applied to the cause as opposed to being 'squandered' on both administration and fundraising costs. Warwick (1994) identified that donors expect that the ratio between administration/ fundraising costs and so-called charitable expenditure would be 20:80. It is interesting to note that despite this expectation most donors believe that the actual ratio is closer to 50:50. Harvey and McCrohan (1988) found that 60 per cent was a significant threshold with charities spending at least 60 per cent of their donations on charitable programmes achieving significantly higher levels of donation. Steinberg (1986) suggests that this is something of an anomaly since fundraising costs are sunk (i.e. have already been incurred by the time the donor receives the solicitation), and should therefore not influence a donor's decision of whether or not to support a given charity.

On a related theme, perceived mismanagement by charity administrators and trustees can impact negatively on donations (Baily and Bruce 1992) with donors reportedly seeking a degree of professionalism from the organizations they support. There is also an interesting anomaly here, however, since while donors seem to want to see high-quality professional management, they appear to favour organizations that do not resemble business organizations and are actually 'amateurish but effective' (Nightingale 1973). Work by Sargeant *et al.* (2001) concludes that while donors may purport to demand professionalism they are in reality drawn to organizations that retain the ethos of voluntarism.

Work by Schervish and Havens (1997) suggests a range of other criteria that donors will use to select between non-profits to support:

- *Communities of participation*: Donors will frequently elect to support causes that are linked in some way to a donor's formal or informal networks. The authors argue that individuals enter into a variety of networks, either by choice or by circumstances that will bring them into contact with specific categories of need. They will thus have links to particular schools, colleges, football/baseball teams, churches/houses of worship and local community groups. The fact that specific causes are linked to a donor's network makes the likelihood of support all the more likely.
- *Frameworks of consciousness*: The authors argue that donors have ways of thinking and feeling that are rooted in their individual identity. Their particular ideologies, religious beliefs and social concerns will shape their pattern of thought and assist in developing the conviction to support particular patterns of cause.
- *Models and experiences from youth*: There may also be familial ties to certain categories of organization. As we grow up we may learn the attitude of our parents and other relatives to the support of specific causes. These, it is argued, may ultimately shape the donor's own views in respect of which organizations are worthy of support. The authors also note that 'models' can derive from adult exemplars in one or more of the communities of participation in which adults now find themselves.

Milne and Gordon (1993) recognize that donors are becoming more sophisticated, discriminating and selective, preferring to develop deeper relationships with those organizations they choose to support. Thus, once recruited to support a charity, a given donor will be significantly more likely to give again in the future. There is also evidence that once charitable giving is stimulated, an individual will be significantly more likely to give to other causes in the future. Once giving regularly it would appear that the norms attaching to the role of donor are strengthened and made personal (Callero *et al.* 1987).

Finally, it is worth noting in this section that where a donor has made a gift to a non-profit in the past, whether they will continue to give will depend to a great extent on the quality of the relationship the organization is able to maintain. In the context of direct mail fundraising, the quality of the service provided will be key. Non-profits need to respect the donor's right to privacy and, where appropriate, to select the pattern of future communications they receive. The organization also needs to be responsive to requests for information, and to deal with correspondence it receives efficiently and within a reasonable timeframe. All these factors have the potential to impact on future decisions in respect of whether to support the organization.

The same is also true in the case of major donors. Donors who value their relationship with the organization and feel valued by the fundraising team will also be far more likely to offer gifts in the future. While this sounds rather obvious, comparatively few organizations make an effort to measure the quality of the service that they provide to donors and to explore in appropriate detail how they can help donors to maximize the personal benefit they derive from the relationship. The importance of the effective stewardship of the donor cannot be over-emphasized and we discuss this in detail in Chapter 8.

WHY DO INDIVIDUALS STOP GIVING?

Sargeant (2001) conducted the first comprehensive study of why donors in both the UK and the USA stop giving to specific non-profits. In a large-scale survey of lapsed donors the author identified a remarkable degree of similarity between the feelings of donors in both countries. The results are given in Table 5.2. In interpreting the table it is important to recognize that donors could select as many reasons as they wished for the termination of their support. Thus the columns do not sum to 100 per cent.

As one would expect, it seems clear, that many donors lapse because of a change in their financial circumstances or because of a desire to allocate their resources elsewhere. It is important to note, however, that a good many donors appear to be simply switching their support to other organizations that they perceive as equally or more deserving. This is clearly good news for the non-profit sector, but bad news for the particular organization. Rather less encouragingly it seems that a number of donors quit because of poor-quality service from the organization. Many non-profits appear not to thank the donor adequately, inform them how their monies were spent, or offer them sufficient choice in communications.

Table 5.2 *Reasons why donors terminate their support in the USA and UK*

Reason	UK (%)	USA (%)
I can no longer afford to offer my support	22.3	54.0
I feel that other causes are more deserving	26.5	36.2
Death/relocation	23.1	16.0
No memory of ever supporting	11.4	18.4
X did not acknowledge my support	0.9	13.2
X did not inform me how my money had been used	1.7	8.1
X no longer needs my support	1.2	5.6
The quality of support provided by X was poor	0.9	5.1
X asked for inappropriate sums	3.1	4.3
I found X's communications inappropriate	3.6	3.8
X did not take account of my wishes	0.7	2.6
Staff at X were unhelpful	0.5	2.1

The study also examined the underlying reasons why donors quit, looking at the impact of a range of other determinants of giving. The following factors were identified as impacting on retention:

- *Recognition*: donors were significantly more likely to quit if the recognition offered to them was seen as being inappropriate or insufficient given the size and nature of the gift.
- *Personal benefit versus altruism*: Interestingly, donors motivated by a desire to attain some personal benefit in return from the gift were significantly more likely to lapse than those motivated by more altruistic concerns.
- *Pressure*: Those donors who felt under significant peer pressure to make a gift were more likely to lapse.
- *Impact*: Those donors who were reassured that previous donations had had the impact the non-profit had suggested were significantly less likely to lapse. This stresses the need for non-profits to provide adequate feedback when thanking donors and asking them for further resources.
- *Relationship*: The perceived strength of the relationship was also an issue, with donors who felt that they had genuinely been able to interact with the organization significantly more likely to remain loyal. Donors who felt that they had been able to shape the relationship, perhaps by exercising choice over the number and nature of communications received, or who felt that they had received a personalized service, tended to remain loyal.
- *Service quality*: The perception of the quality of service provided by the fundraising department to its donors impacted on retention. Donors who had more favourable perceptions in respect of the communications they received were significantly more likely to remain loyal. Indeed, donors who described themselves as 'very satisfied' with the quality of service were twice as likely to remain loyal as those who indicated that they were merely 'satisfied'. This highlights the need for non-profits to measure and reflect on the quality of service provided and is an issue that will be returned to in Chapter 7.

Further examination of the study data revealed a number of other interesting differences between certain categories of lapsed donor. In particular donors who lapsed after only one donation were significantly more likely to cite financial inability as the primary reason why they did not give again. Donors who had been giving for a period of some years were significantly more likely to lapse because they felt that other organizations were more or equally deserving. It thus appears that many donors prefer to continue their support unless or until they encounter a similarly worthy organization. This has clear implications for list swops or reciprocal mailings since, by sharing their donors with other non-profits, charities may well be encouraging loyal donors to quit their organization!

MODELLING GIVING BEHAVIOUR

Aside from the plethora of studies addressing specific aspects of charity giving, a few studies have also made attempts to synthesize the available literature and to develop a rather broader perspective on how and why individuals elect to give. Notable among these is the work by Sargeant (1999) and Burnett and Wood (1988). Their respective models are depicted in Figures 5.2 and 5.3.

Both Burnett and Wood (1988) and Sargeant (1999) developed what might be termed *process* models of giving behaviour in the sense that they attempted to synthesize the available literature

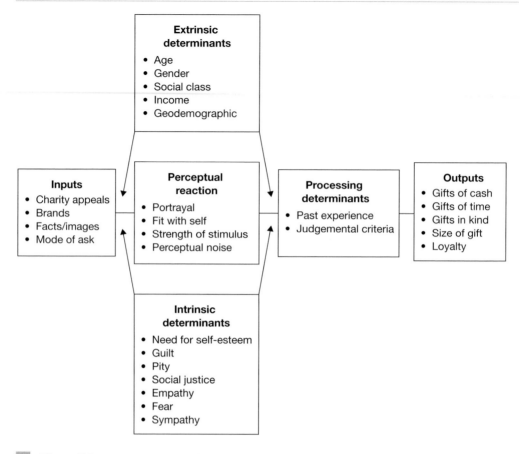

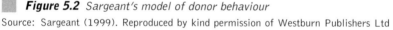

Figure 5.2 *Sargeant's model of donor behaviour*
Source: Sargeant (1999). Reproduced by kind permission of Westburn Publishers Ltd

by creating categories of constructs/variables that impact on giving and exploring their role in relation to the process of deciding whether a donation will be made. They consider a wide range of factors alluded to in our previous discussion. The primary difference between the perspectives lies in the concept of 'processing determinants' where Sargeant considers that donors develop criteria that may be used to identify which specific organizations will be supported, such as efficiency, effectiveness and the quality of service provided. There are also differences surrounding the handling of what Sargeant refers to as the intrinsic determinants of giving. While Burnett and Wood include the category 'personal traits' in their model this does not address the full range of intrinsic motives an individual may have for responding to a particular appeal (e.g. sympathy, empathy, belief in social justice).

Sargeant (1999) considers the capacity of a wide range of charity 'inputs' to the donor's decision-making process including brands, a variety of facts/images about the organization that may be attained from various media and the specific charitable appeal in question. Whether that appeal will be recognized as relevant to the donor will be a function of their perceptual reaction to the message. This in turn will depend on the manner in which recipients are portrayed, the perceived fit with the donor's self-image, the strength of the stimulus engendered and the extent to which other 'perceptual noise' might be present (e.g. other charity appeals, or other commercial marketing communications of various types). Those messages

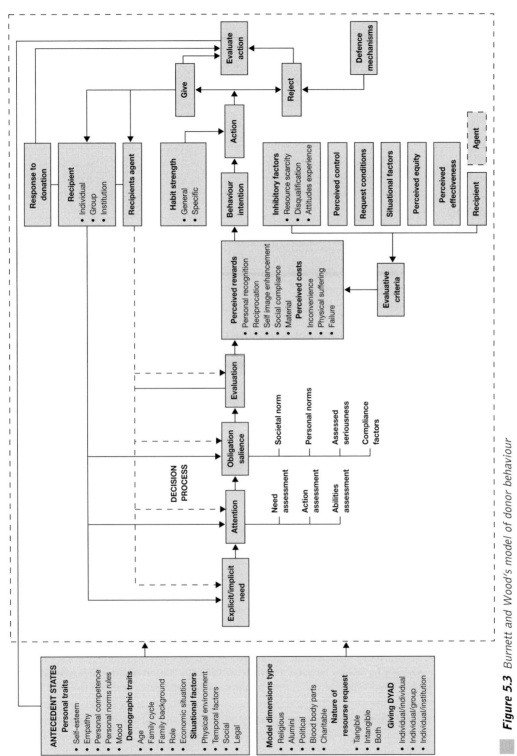

Figure 5.3 *Burnett and Wood's model of donor behaviour*

Source: Burnett and Wood (1988). Reproduced by kind permission of the authors

that are perceived as potentially relevant to the donor will be evaluated to determine whether support will be offered. Donors may look at the efficiency/effectiveness of the organization asking for support and, if they have past experience of dealing with the organization, the quality of service provided. Where a favourable view is formed a gift of cash, time or goods will be made. The more favourable the view the more likely a higher value gift will be made and the more likely it will be that the donor will remain loyal over time.

According to Sargeant (1999), however, there are two categories of construct/variable that can impinge on this process. First, some categories of individual as discussed above will be more likely to offer support to non-profits. Variables such as age, gender and social class will therefore influence whether the individual will elect to respond to a particular appeal. The author also argues that the extent to which a particular appeal is successful at arousing specific emotions will impact on the response. Those appeals that successfully engender feelings of sympathy, empathy, guilt or pity will therefore tend both to stimulate giving and to stimulate giving at higher levels.

Burnett and Wood (1988) acknowledge the impact of personality traits, demographic and situational factors on the donation-making process. They also acknowledge that their model will be applicable (with modification) to the context of various categories of giving, again in various contexts. Thereafter the authors postulate a complex process of decision-making beginning with the identification of need on the part of the non-profit. Donors will then evaluate the level of need, whether action is required, and their ability to make a difference. It is then necessary to determine whether the obligation to support the organization applies to them. They will decide whether this is the case by references to pertinent norms and the extent to which they believe the level of the need is urgent. The authors argue that where need is perceived as salient, they will then decide whether a gift should be offered by evaluating the costs and benefits of taking action. At this stage the donor will thus examine the rewards, either economic or psycho-social, that will accrue as a consequence of giving, and compare these with the economic costs of giving, the inconvenience of making a donation and the risk that their gift will not make the difference they believe it will. On the basis of this complex process donors will decide whether or not to offer their support. The authors argue that where the decision is taken to reject the appeal a number of defence mechanisms will be employed such as 'They don't really need the money', 'What possible difference could my money make?' or 'It's just not my responsibility'.

The final stage of the model is to evaluate the outcome, examining whether the rewards were as expected, whether the impact of the gift was as expected, whether the quality of service provided was as expected and so on. This final stage typically involves the assessment of intangibles and is thus highly subjective. Non-profits are advised to be aware of this process of evaluation and attempt to influence it by providing donors with explicit information to input to this evaluation process, perhaps through the nature of the thank you, data in respect of how the gift has been used and so on.

CHAPTER SUMMARY

In this chapter we have provided a summary of the extant research on donor-giving behaviour. We have reviewed a large number of studies examining specific aspects of giving and ended with a discussion of the merits of a number of composite models of giving behaviour. It seems clear that a variety of factors can shape giving, and non-profits would be well advised to review the fundraising activities they presently undertake in the light of these findings. Donor behaviour remains one of the most researched issues in the social sciences, drawing on work conducted in the disciplines of marketing, economics, clinical psychology, social psychology, anthropology and sociology. All have much to contribute to our knowledge of the topic and all have much to contribute to professional practice.

A greater degree of reflection on the needs of the donor and a greater degree of understanding of why donors behave as they do is long overdue in fundraising. Lee (1998) warns fundraisers that they risk becoming the 'used car salesmen' of the sector if they increasingly embrace 'techniques' and lose sight of the real reason for their existence. Future marketing activity must be based on a sound understanding of how and why donors elect to give and the practice of fundraising must reflect this. Ongoing market research would greatly assist fundraisers in enhancing the quality, precision and performance of their communications with donors and thereby ensure the future health and stability of the voluntary sector.

DISCUSSION QUESTIONS

1   In the light of your reading, critically appraise the fundraising practice of your own organization, or one with which you are familiar. Can you identify ways in which fundraising practice could be improved, taking account of the findings of the donor behaviour literature?

2   In your role as head of fundraising of a large national charity, prepare a report to your Chief Executive explaining how the organization might reduce its attrition rate (i.e. the percentage of donors it loses each year).

3   How do higher value givers differ from lower value givers? Consider demographic, lifestyle and behavioural differences.

4   You are head of fundraising for a small non-profit working to educate children with special needs. What are the issues you will have to deal with in developing a direct mail campaign to cover the running costs of the organization?

5   Compare and contrast the two composite models of giving behaviour. What do you see as the strengths and weaknesses of each? How might they be improved?

REFERENCES

AAFRC Trust (2002) *Giving USA*, Indianapolis, IN.

Adler, A.B., Wright, B.A. and Ulicny, G.R. (1991) 'Fundraising Portrayals Of People With Disabilities: Donations and Attitudes', *Rehabilitation Psychology*, 36(4): 231–240.

Andreoni, J. (2001) 'The Economics of Philanthropy', in N.J. Smelser and P.B. Baltes (eds) *International Encyclopedia of the Social and Behavioural Sciences*, Elsevier, London.

Atchley, R.C. (1987) *Ageing: Continuity and Change*, Wadsworth Publishing, Belmont, CA.

Baily, A. and Bruce, M. (1992) 'United Way: The Fallout After The Fall', *Chronicle of Philanthropy*, March: 2–6.

Banks, J. and Tanner, S. (1997) *The State of Donation*, IFS, London.

Batson, C.D. (1990) 'How Social An Animal? The Human Capacity For Caring', *American Psychologist*, 45: 336–346.

Becker, G.S. (1976) *The Economic Approach to Human Behavior*, University of Chicago Press, Chicago, IL.

Bendapudi, N. and Singh, S.N. (1996) 'Enhancing Helping Behavior: An Integrative Framework for Promotion Planning', *Journal of Marketing*, 60(3): 33–54.

Braus, P. (1994) 'Will Baby Boomers Give Generously?', *American Demographics*, 16(7): 48–52, 57.

Brehm, J.W. (1966) *A Theory of Psychological Reactance*, Academic Press, New York.

Brolley, D.Y. and Anderson, S.C. (1986) 'Advertising and Attitudes', *Rehabilitation Digest*, 17: 15–17.

Bryan, J.H. and Test, M.A. (1967) 'Models and Helping: Naturalistic Studies in Aiding Behaviour Of Crowding In On Others', *Journal of Applied Social Psychology*, 6: 95–104.

Burnett, J.J. and Wood, V.R. (1988) 'A Proposed Model of the Donation Process', *Research in Consumer Behaviour*, 3: 1–47.

Callero, O., Howard, J. and Piliavin, J.A. (1987) 'Helping Behaviour As Role Behaviour: Disclosing Social Structure and History in the Analysis of Prosocial Action', *Social Psychology Quarterly*, 50: 247–256.

Caplow, T. (1984) 'Rule Enforcement Without Visible Means: Christmas Gift Giving in Middletown', *American Journal of Sociology*, 80(6): 1306–1323.

Chierco, S., Rosa, C. and Kayson, W.A. (1982) 'Effects of Location Appearance and Monetary Value On Altruistic Behaviour', *Psychological Reports*, 51: 199–202.

Clark, R.D. and Word, L.E. (1972) 'Why Don't Bystanders Help? Because of Ambiguity?', *Journal of Personality and Social Psychology*, 24: 392–400.

Clary, E.G. and Snyder, M. (1991) 'A Functional Analysis Of Altruism and Prosocial Behaviour: The Case Of Volunteerism', In *Review of Personality and Social Psychology*, 12, London, Sage, pp.119–148.

Coliazzi, A., Williams, K.J. and Kayson, W.A. (1984) 'When Will People Help? The Effects Of Gender, Urgency and Location On Altruism', *Psychological Reports*, 55: 139–142.

Cutlip, S.M. (1980) *Fundraising in the United States: Its Role in America's Philanthropy*, Transaction Publishers, New Brunswick, NJ.

De Tocqueville, A. (1835/1966) *Democracy In America*, ed. G. Lawrence, trans. J.P. Mayer, Harper Collins, New York.

Dichter, E. (1972) 'Giving Blood or Lending Blood', presented before the Deutsche Gesellschaft für Bluttransfusion, Giesen, Germany.

Dixon, M. (1997) 'Small and Medium Sized Charities Need A Strong Brand Too: Crisis' Experience', *Journal of Nonprofit and Voluntary Sector Marketing*, 2(1): 52–57.

Douglas, J., Field, G.A. and Tarpey, L.X. (1967) *Human Behaviour in Marketing*, Charles E. Merrill, Columbus, OH.

Dowd, J.J. (1975) *Stratification Of The Aged*, Brooks Cole, Monterey, CA.

Eayrs, C.B. and Ellis, N. (1990) 'Charity Advertising. For or Against People With A Mental Handicap?', *British Journal of Social Psychology*, 29: 349–360.

Elliot, T.R. and Byrd, E.K. (1982) 'Media and Disability', *Rehabilitation Literature*, 43: 348–355.

Farrington, O.P. and Kidd, R.P. (1977) 'Is Financial Dishonesty A Rational Decision?', *British Journal of School and Clinical Psychology*, 16: 139–148.

Feinman, S. (1978) 'When Does Sex Affect Altruistic Behaviour?', *Psychological Reports*, 43: 12–18.

Feldman, D. and Feldman, B. (1985) 'The Effect of a Telethon on Attitudes Toward Disabled People and Financial Contributions', *Journal of Rehabilitation*, 51: 42–45.

Festinger, L. (1954) 'A Theory of Social Comparison Processes', *Human Relations*, 7: 117–140.

Fultz, J.C., Batson, D., Fortenbach, V.A., McCarthy, P. and Varney, L.L. (1986) 'Social Evaluation and the Empathy Altruism Hypothesis', *Journal of Personality and Social Psychology*, 50: 761–769.

Geer, J.H. and Jermecky, L. (1973) 'The Effect Of Being Responsible For Reducing Others' Pain On Subjects' Response and Arousal', *Journal of Personality and Social Psychology*, 27: 100–108.

Glaser, J.S. (1994) *The United Way Scandal – An Insider's Account of What Went Wrong and Why*, John Wiley & Sons, New York.

Gruder, C.L. and Cook, T.D. (1971) 'Sex Dependency and Helping', *Journal of Personality and Social Psychology*, 19: 290–294.

Guy, B.S. and Patton, W.E. (1989) 'The Marketing Of Altruistic Causes: Understanding Why People Help', *Journal of Services Marketing*, 2(1): 5–16.

Harris, R.M. (1975) *The Effect Of Perspective Taking, Similarity and Dependency On Raising Funds For Persons With Disabilities*, Unpublished Masters Thesis, University of Kansas, Lawrence, KS.

Harris, R.M. and Harris, A.C. (1977) 'Devaluation Of The Disabled In Fund Raising', *Rehabilitation Psychology*, 24: 69–78.

Harvey, J.W. and McCrohan, K.F. (1988) 'Fundraising Costs–Societal Implications for Philanthropies and Their Supporters', *Business and Society*, 27(1): 15–22.

Hogg, M.A. and Abrams, D. (1988) *Special Identifications: A Social Psychology of Intergroup Relations and Group Processes*, Routledge, London.

Kotler, P. (1991) *Marketing Management*, Prentice Hall, Englewood Cliffs, NJ.

Krebs, D. (1970) 'Altruism – A Rational Approach', in *The Development of Prosocial Behaviour*, ed. N. Eisenberg, Academic Press, New York (1982), pp. 53–77.

Krebs, D. and Whitten, P. (1972) 'Guilt Edged Giving – The Shame of it All', *Psychology Today*, January: 42.

Latane, B. and Nida, S. (1981) 'Ten Years Of Research on Group Size and Helping', *Psychological Bulletin*, 89(2): 308–324.

Lazer, W. (1963) 'Lifestyle Concepts and Marketing', in *Toward Scientific Marketing*, ed. S. Greyser, AMA, Chicago, IL.

Lee, S. (1998) 'What Goes In Must', *Third Sector*, 25 June: 14–15.

Marx, J.D. (2000) 'Women and Human Services Giving', *Social Work*, 45(1): 21–32.

Miller, D.T. (1977) 'Altruism and Threat to a Belief in a Just World', *Journal of Experimental Psychology*, 13: 113–124.

Millett, R. and Orosz, J.J. (2001) 'Understanding Giving Patterns in Communities of Color', *Fund Raising Management*, August: 25–27.

Milne, G.R. and Gordon, M.E. (1993) 'Direct Mail Privacy Efficiency Trade-offs Within an Implied Social Contract Framework', *Journal of Public Policy and Marketing*, 12 (autumn): 206–215.

Moschis, G.P. (1992) *Marketing to Older Consumers*, Quorum Books, Westport, CT.

Nightingale, B. (1973) *Charities*, Allen Lane, Sage.

Odendahl, T. (1987) *America's Wealthy and the Future of Foundations*, The Foundation Center, New York.

Ostrower, F. (1997) *Why the Wealthy Give*, Princeton University Press, Princeton, NJ.

Passey, A., Hems, L. and Jas, P. (2000) *The UK Voluntary Sector Almanac*, NCVO, London.

Penrod, S. (1983) *Social Psychology*, Prentice Hall, Englewood Cliffs, NJ.

Pharoah, C. (2002) 'How Much do People give to Charity and Who are the Donors?', in *A Lot of Give*, ed. C. Walker and C. Pharoah, Hodder & Stoughton, London, pp. 23–42.

Pieper, E. (1975) 'What Price Charity?', *Exceptional Parent*, 5(1): 35–40.

Piliavin, I.M., Piliavin, J.A. and Rodin, J. (1975) 'Costs of Diffusion and the Stigmatised Victim', *Journal of Personality and Social Psychology*, 32: 429–438.

Radley, A. and Kennedy, M. (1992) 'Reflections upon Charitable Giving: A Comparison of Individuals From Business "Manual" and Professional Backgrounds', *Journal of Community and Applied Social Psychology*, 2: 113–129.

Reed, D. (1998) 'Giving is Receiving', *Precision Marketing*, 9 February: 17–18.

Reingen, P.H. (1978) 'On Inducing Compliance With Requests', *Journal of Consumer Research*, 5: 96–102.

Reykowski, J. (1982) 'Development of Prosocial Motivation', in *The Development of Prosocial Behavior*, ed. N. Eisenberg, Academic Press, New York, pp. 377–393.

Roberts Wray, B. (1994) 'Branding, Product Development and Positioning the Charity', *Journal of Brand Management*, 1(6): 350–370.

Royer, M. (1989) 'Please Give Generously, Okay?', *NSFRE Journal*, summer: 17–20.

Sargeant, A. (1999) 'Charity Giving: Towards A Model of Donor Behaviour', *Journal of Marketing Management*, 15: 215–238.

Sargeant, A. (2001) 'Relationship Fundraising: How To Keep Donors Loyal', *Nonprofit Management and Leadership*, 12(2): 177–192.

Sargeant, A. and McKenzie, J. (1998) *A Lifetime Of Giving: An Analysis Of Donor Lifetime Value*, Charities Aid Foundation, West Malling.

Sargeant, A., West, D.C. and Ford, J.B. (2001) 'The Role of Perceptions in Predicting Donor Value', *Journal of Marketing Management*, 17: 407–428.

Saxton, J. (1995) 'A Strong Charity Brand Comes From Strong Beliefs and Values', *Journal of Brand Management*, 2(4): 211–220.

Schervish, P.G. and Havens, J.J. (1997) 'Social Participation and Charitable Giving: A Multivariate Analysis', *Voluntas*, 8(3): 235–260.

Schwartz, B. (1967) 'The Social Psychology Of The Gift', *American Journal of Sociology*, 73(1): 1–11.

Schwartz, S. (1977) 'Normative Influences On Altruism', in *Advances In Experimental Social Psychology*, 10, ed. L. Berkowitz, Academic Press, New York, pp.221–279.

Shelton, M. L. and Rogers, R.W. (1981) 'Fear Arousing and Empathy Arousing Appeals To Help: The Pathos of Persuasion', *Journal of Applied Psychology*, 11(4): 366–378.

Shurka, E., Siller, J. and Dvonch, P. (1982) 'Coping Behaviour and Personal Responsibility as Factors in the Perception of Disabled Persons by the Non Disabled', *Rehabilitation Psychology*, 27: 225–233.

Silver, M. (1980) *Affluence, Altruism and Atrophy*, New York University Press, New York.

Simmons, R.G. (1991) 'Presidential Address on Altruism and Sociology', *Sociological Quarterly*, 32: 1–22.

Simpson, J.C. (1986) 'Baby Boomers Have 60s Heritage, But Charities Say They're Cheap', *Wall Street Journal*, 11 September: 33.

Steinberg, R. (1986) 'Should Donors Care About Fundraising?', in *The Economics Of Nonprofit Institutions: Studies in Structure and Policy*, ed. S. Rose-Ackerman, Oxford University Press, New York, pp. 347–364.

Stirling, C. (2000) 'Gender Differences in Planned Giving: The Way Women Give', *Planned Giving Today*, December: 3

Tapp, A. (1996) 'Charity Brands: A Qualitative Study Of Current Practice', *Journal of Nonprofit and Voluntary Sector Marketing*, 1(4): 327–336.

Wagner, C. and Wheeler, L. (1969) 'Model Need and Cost Effects in Helping Behaviour', *Journal of Personality and Social Psychology*, 12: 111–116.

Ward, R.A. (1977) 'The Impact Of Subjective Age and Stigma On Older Persons', *Journal of Gerontology*, 32: 227–232.

Warwick, M. (1994) *Raising Money By Mail: Strategies For Growth and Financial Stability*, Strathmoor Press, Berkeley, CA.

Weisbrod, B.A. (1988) *The Nonprofit Economy*, Harvard University Press, Boston, MA.

Weldon, E. (1984) 'De-individualisation Interpersonal Affect and Productivity in Laboratory Task Groups', *Journal Of Applied Social Psychology*, 14: 469–485.

Wispe, L. (1978) *Altruism, Sympathy and Helping*, Academic Press, New York.

Yankelovich, D. (1981) *New Rule: Searching For Self Fulfillment In A World Turned Upside Down*, Random House Inc, New York.

Yavas, U., Riecken, G. and Parameswaran, R. (1980) 'Using Psychographics to Profile Potential Donors', *Business Atlanta*, 30(5): 41–45.

Chapter 6

Donor recruitment

LEARNING OBJECTIVES

By the end of this chapter you should be able to:

- Outline the key stages in donor recruitment planning.
- Develop customer acquisition objectives.
- Segment donor markets.
- Profile and target appropriate prospects
- Implement a customer acquisition campaign.
- Analyse and interpret the results.

INTRODUCTION

The recruitment of new individual donors at an acceptable cost is an increasingly challenging and complex activity.

It is widely accepted in fundraising, as in commercial marketing activity, that it costs five times as much to conduct business with a new customer than with an existing one. While fundraisers can expect to generate a return on investment (ROI) of up to 5:1 from a campaign targeting existing (warm) donors, acquisition campaigns are more likely to require an investment, or at the very best achieve break-even, than to generate a positive return. More enlightened and informed non-profits tend to be content with this scenario in the confidence that they will be able to cultivate profitable relationships with the donors they recruit over the full duration of their relationship with them. Less well-informed and experienced organizations frequently find it hard to justify and explain high recruitment costs to Board members.

> New donor acquisition efforts usually cost 75 to 150 percent of what they raise. The reality is that this has been the practice for decades. Many of the most prestigious and successful charities have developed very efficient multimillion-dollar appeals and major donor programs with donors originally acquired at 100 percent fund-raising costs.
>
> (Center on Philanthropy 1999: 16)

In terms of the balance of fundraising resource, it makes sense to target the majority of the resources available at those donors who will generate the highest levels of profitability. Typically, therefore, donor retention and development activity will account for 70 to 80 per cent of a fundraising budget. However, there will always be a need to recruit new donors to every organization. Even if relationships are excellent and levels of satisfaction high, some donors will terminate their relationship as interests and financial circumstances change, or they die or move away. Donor recruitment also provides an opportunity to refresh a database, as individuals often give most generously and demonstrate most enthusiasm for a cause during the 'honeymoon' period of the first few months of their relationship with a non-profit. The addition of new donors also allows an organization to grow and broaden its support base, test new fundraising offers and to attract new audiences and constituencies to the cause.

In recent years acquisition activity has been complicated by the introduction of new communication channels, new methods of giving, and increasing demands regarding transparency and privacy protection. Data profiling and research among givers and non-givers has indicated that non-profits are typically competing to recruit from an identical and diminishing pool of potential donors.

Against this background, careful acquisition planning is more essential than ever if donors are to be recruited successfully both in terms of the quantity of those recruited and of their quality and likely long-term value. This chapter will focus on 'mass' individual donor recruitment via direct marketing techniques. The recruitment of wealthy individuals through major gift and event recruitment is covered in Chapter 8.

RECRUITMENT PLANNING

In planning for donor recruitment, the initial 'macro' stages of the plan such as the audit and the development of overall fundraising objectives and strategies will be common to both acquisition and donor development activity (See Figure 6.1).

In implementing donor recruitment plans however, we are focusing primarily on the attraction of new supporters to an organization. Seven stages can be followed as a framework:

1 *Objectives* – identifying the objectives to be achieved.
2 *Segmentation and profiling* – research and analysis of the existing donor base to develop a broad profile to be used as a starting point in targeting recruitment efforts.
3 *Targeting* – having developed a detailed donor profile, the information may then be used to tailor the nature of the communication to be received and the channel through which it will be communicated.
4 *Media selection and planning* – allied to the above, media can be selected to reach the intended audience cost-effectively. Integration of the various media to be employed should also be considered at this stage.
5 *The nature of the fundraising message* – how best to communicate the fundraising 'ask' in line with the brand and mission of the organization. At this stage the parameters for the creative work and messages will be defined.
6 *Fulfilment* – how response to the campaign will be handled, followed up and the information stored on the fundraising database.
7 *Budgeting, control and evaluation* – testing, response analysis and tracking.

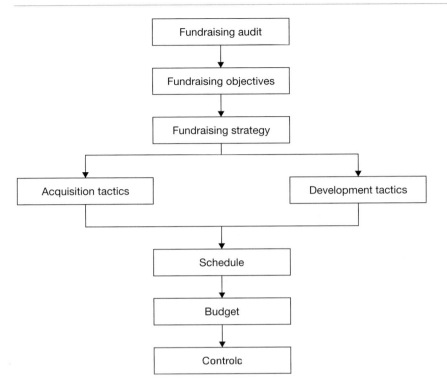

Figure 6.1 *Recruitment and development planning*

SETTING RECRUITMENT OBJECTIVES

The first step in developing a donor acquisition programme or campaign is to decide on the objectives the organization wishes to achieve, and by which the success of the activity will be measured. As with all fundraising activity, the objectives need to be SMART (See Chapter 4).

In donor recruitment the most common simple target set by fundraising managers is the recruitment of X new donors for Y cost, with overall levels of expenditure and investment set in accordance with a requirement to grow or to maintain the total size of the organization's individual donor database.

More valuable and thoughtful objectives and targets involve the consideration of the quality as well as the quantity of the donors to be gained, and are broken down further by segment and activity. Many organizations now recognize the long-term value of recruitment directly on to a regular gift, so additional objectives may involve the percentage of regular versus one-off givers to be acquired. The recruitment of 'fresh' audiences may be set as an objective (for example, an organization with an 'ageing' database may wish to recruit new donors from among younger age groups). In more sophisticated fundraising organizations where lifetime value is calculated, acquisition objectives will be set with the input of lifetime-value data. This may mean that certain media routes are favoured as tending to produce more valuable donors over time.

The distinction between regular and cash givers is important, particularly in the UK where each group may be defined as follows:

1   *One-off or cash givers* – individuals who do not commit to a regular gift, but who will typically respond to one or more direct mail asks in a given year by sending through a cheque.

2   *Committed givers* – individuals who sign up from the outset to give a regular monthly (or yearly) donation, direct from their bank account or credit card.

The economics of dealing with each group are quite different and separate objectives would therefore be derived. In the USA the need for the distinction may be less clear since fewer organizations are at present recruiting into regular or committed giving.

It is also essential that the objectives set for donor recruitment are tied into those set for the subsequent development of the donors. Many organizations make the mistake of viewing acquisition and development as separate entities, working to separate, unrelated and sometimes opposing targets. This can cause huge problems over time if the donors recruited are found subsequently to be unprofitable or problematic: they may be unresponsive, exhibit high attrition rates, or require a different programme of communication from the rest of the database in order to continue giving. For example, in recent years many UK non-profits have had great success in recruiting new donors with requests for a small regular monthly gift. These recruits tend to be much younger than the 'traditional' donor and to have very different lifestyles. While this may be seen as a success for the recruitment manager, these donors often prove difficult to retain and develop subsequently as they do not respond to direct mail, and prefer communication through alternative routes such as e-mail and text messaging – media which most non-profits have not yet developed cost-efficiently. The recruitment of younger donors is also likely in the longer term to work against the efforts of fundraisers promoting planned giving and bequest (legacy) fundraising. It is thus essential that recruitment and development targets are complementary and that planning for both is undertaken as a holistic exercise.

Finally, it is worth noting that many organizations develop objectives not only for 'cold' donor recruitment but also for the recruitment of those individuals who are 'warmer' to the organization. This category might include previously lapsed supporters whose giving the organization is looking to reactivate, previous enquirers who have not made a donation and other stakeholder groups who are linked to the cause in some way, such as service users.

SEGMENTATION

Having delineated recruitment objectives, the next stage is to determine which potential donors (or prospects) will be targeted. In essence there are two approaches, the appropriateness of which will be determined by the extent to which an organization has prior knowledge of its markets. These approaches may be categorized as being either a priori or *post hoc* (Green 1977). An a priori approach is based on the notion that fundraisers decide in advance of any research which categories of individual (perhaps by demographics or lifestyle) they intend to target. The fundraiser would then carry out market research to determine the attractiveness of each segment and make a decision on the basis of the results as to which target audience to pursue. *Post hoc* segmentation by contrast involves the fundraiser in carrying out research into the existing donor market. The research might highlight attributes, attitudes or benefits that relate to particular groups of donors. This information can often be obtained by profiling discrete groups of donors on the database (e.g. cash givers or committed givers). If a certain type of individual emerges as 'typical' this information can be used to refine the criteria for list selection and other similar individuals targeted. Non-profits commonly use geodemographic and/or lifestyle data for this purpose.

PROFILING

To inform the choice of segments to be targeted, those organizations who already hold a database of donors have a distinct advantage. Such organizations can profile their existing database to identify whether specific types of people seem to be:

- giving higher sums;
- giving in certain ways;
- responding to different media;
- responding to certain types of message.

This profile may then be used in the selection of prospects – in other words, list and media selection can be undertaken to ensure that individuals who match the profile of the required category of givers are targeted with appropriate recruitment messages. At best, profiling can serve to bring audiences to life by painting pictures of their main differentiating characteristics, thereby suggesting fundraising messages they are likely to find appealing.

In some instances this simple replication of the current donor profile may not be desirable, in which case the same techniques may be used instead to define a picture of alternative target audiences. If one of the objectives of a recruitment campaign is, for example, to recruit younger regular givers to supplement a database comprising older cash donors, a supplemental profile of the new target audience will have to be generated. Equally, higher value donors or those who have pledged a legacy may be profiled as a separate group if it is feasible to conduct a recruitment campaign to enlist high-value givers, perhaps through the promotion of a high-value or committed product such as a sponsorship package.

To work most effectively, the segments generated have to be:

- *Accessible*: It should be possible to access the segment cost-effectively. If communication media do not exist to reach the market without a high degree of wastage, attempts to access a segment could be costly and potentially unprofitable.
- *Substantial*: It should be cost-effective to market to the segment. Clearly the segment should be large enough in terms of the absolute number of donors to make it worthwhile targeting. It could also be small, but with the prospect of higher than normal gifts, again making it worthwhile to address.
- *Stable*: The segment's behaviour should be relatively stable over time to ensure that its future development may be predicted with a high degree of accuracy for planning purposes.
- *Appropriate*: It should be appropriate to target a particular segment given the organization's mission, resources, objectives and so on. While on the face of it, for example, it may seem appropriate to target sufferers of a particular condition to support a medical charity, the Board may well feel that this is inappropriate and that funding should be sought elsewhere.

TARGETING

Having developed a detailed prospect profile, the information may be used to tailor the nature of the communication to be received and to make decisions about the channel or channels through which it will most effectively be communicated. A picture of the individuals a non-profit is attempting to reach, even in outline or aggregate form, is an enormous advantage in designing recruitment materials, in deciding where such individuals are most likely to be reached, and what media and approach they are most likely to respond to. Targeting is the single most important consideration in cold recruitment campaigns. No matter how strong the creative treatment, if it does not reach the right people the campaign will fail. It is generally accepted in non-profit as in commercial direct marketing that the list is six times more important than the creative in the success of any campaign.

In seeking to reach prospect audiences to recruit new donors as cost-effectively as possible it makes sense to start by gathering prospect data from within the organization rather than embarking on the purchase of cold lists or other broadscale media immediately. While it may prove difficult to obtain the names of service users, enquirers, campaigners and so on from within an organization these are almost always the most worthwhile sources of new donors. Lapsed donors, volunteers and traders (catalogue buyers) should likewise be tested. These lists will be free (or low cost if the data needs to be captured) and the individuals appearing on them will almost certainly be more sympathetic to the needs of the organization, and therefore more responsive to a recruitment message, than individuals who may not have had any prior contact with or knowledge of the non-profit and its work. In planning a recruitment campaign, those prospects likely to be recruited at the lowest cost should be targeted first. Once the 'warmest' prospects have been identified the remainder of the budget can be allocated to 'colder' media.

An outline picture of the prospects being targeted will be of huge interest and utility to those designing recruitment materials. Information on the demographics and lifestyle of target audiences may be used to guide creative outputs generally (What sort of message is the audience most likely to respond to? What 'triggers' and cultural references are appropriate to the age/social group?) and practically – if an older audience is to be reached the typeface should be larger, for example, and copy may be written for male or female readers.

MEDIA SELECTION AND PLANNING

Once 'internal' warm lists of prospective donors have been assembled, the selection of external 'cold' media may begin. Media selection and planning is potentially one of the most complex areas of any tactical recruitment plan.

Even if the profiling process has been undertaken for the first time, or profiles have been revised or refreshed, part of this process will involve the review of past experience and results. Non-profits that are undertaking recruitment campaigns over time amass volumes of data on the response rates and profitability of certain recruitment routes, on response to a range of creative approaches and messages, and on the subsequent behaviour and lifetime value of the donors recruited. All this past history should be part of the planning process, though it is also important to rethink and review recruitment approaches regularly and to remain aware of new opportunities. In the non-profit sector peer networks may also be used to gather generic information on the likely performance of new routes and media, and to compare notes on the pitfalls associated with new recruitment ventures. In the commercial world such information sharing would be impossible under commercial confidentiality. Specialist agencies and consultants can also provide valuable insights into the likely performance of certain media and creative routes.

Some of the most commonly used recruitment media are discussed briefly here:

Direct mail

Cold mail remains the most common means of donor recruitment on both sides of the Atlantic, even though it has become far less cost-effective in recent years. Those charities using cold lists to recruit new donors would typically generate only 50 cents back for every dollar of investment. The organizations concerned would only make money on the second and subsequent gifts. Achieving break-even in donor recruitment activity would thus represent very high-quality performance indeed.

Thousands of mailing lists can be provided to facilitate donor recruitment, so navigating the range of alternatives may be problematic if an organization has no past experience on which to draw. List buying is an area where the services of a specialist adviser (list broker) are therefore essential. If you provide a list broker with the profile of the prospect audience, he or she will provide recommendations and advice on the lists which best meet those requirements. Lists can be rented for once-only use, for repeat use, or purchased outright (which is a much more expensive option).

Lists fall broadly into the categories of geodemographic and lifestyle, and some profiling will usually be required to refine the criteria that are eventually used in list selection. Lifestyle list providers will run a profile against their own base to find those names on their file that most closely resemble the target group. Other lists, typically generated through mail order product sales, will have less information available against which to select. Lists vary considerably in terms of the level of sophistication that can be offered. Some key checks to make when purchasing lists are:

- *What criteria may be used in selection and what are the cost and timing implications of selecting by multiple criteria?*
  Many list owners will, for example, offer the opportunity to select males only, or males who bought a product within the last six months, have bought previously, and where the last product purchased cost at least $50. Typically each overlay will incur an extra charge per thousand names selected. More complex selections will also take longer to process and output. Before running selections based on multiple criteria one needs to be confident that the uplift in response rates or donation levels is likely to justify the extra cost.

- *What is the roll-out potential of each list, or of each selection, and when and how is the list refreshed?*
  Any list should be tested initially. If the list performance is acceptable, the list can then be rolled out in a subsequent campaign. Those lists that can deliver large quantities of names are preferable to those that will be quickly exhausted as a source of new recruits. The tendency is to target with great care in the selection of the test quantity – if this selection is successful it is essential that the same selection can be used in pulling out a higher quantity of names for the roll-out. Recency is often key to list performance, so it is also important to be aware of when and how lists are refreshed and added to.

- *What is the history of non-profit usage?*
  List suppliers can give an idea of the response rates experienced by previous non-profit clients, and can provide data on how heavily the list has been employed by non-profits. This is key, as lists become 'tired' very quickly and assessing whether competitors have already used the list can be very significant. Before purchasing a commercially available list it is also imperative to check the 'cleanliness' of that list and to ensure that the relevant data protection or privacy legislation has been fully complied with.

A variety of opinions exist with regard to how intensively a cold mail programme should be run. At base, there is agreement that lists should be mailed only while doing so is profitable, and that every element of the list and the creative should be tested before it is rolled out or reused. Many organizations rent lists for once-only use, renting larger quantities later if the test meets the required standards. Some follow the advice of other experts such as James Greenfield and use lists far more intensively:

> A successful mail acquisition plan . . . should project a three-year, multimailing programme, a minimum of five to six mailings each year, and a total of between five and eighteen letter packages to be sent to substantially the same people.
>
> (Greenfield 1994: 85)

Cold direct mail has been used very creatively and to great effect by many thousands of non-profits worldwide. Examples of successful recruitment mailings are provided in Plates 6.1 and 6.2. When using direct mail for recruitment, non-profits over time identify mail packs that are particularly effective at recruiting donors and tend to stick with these until they are beaten in performance by other materials the non-profit is testing. This was the case with the Mothers Against Drunk Driving (MADD) mailing in Plate 6.1. The inclusion of the photo album, although adding to cost, proved worthwhile because of the heightened response rate and value of gifts.

The campaign pack illustrated in Plate 6.2 was developed by the Denver Rescue Mission. It was sent to prospective donors over a holiday period and comprised a brown paper lunch bag indicating that $1.79 would provide a full Thanksgiving meal or a night's shelter to a home-less person. The appeal generated $25,651 from 1,248 people.

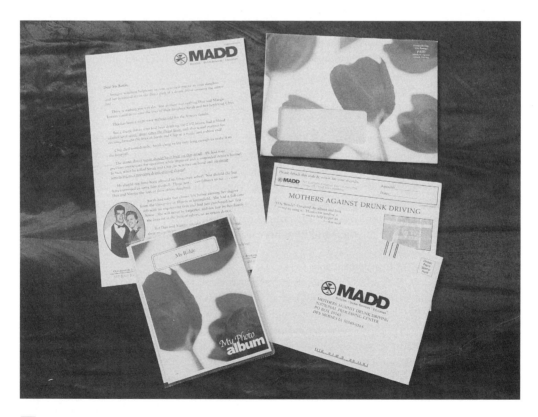

Plate 6.1 *MADD mailing*
Source: © MADD. Reproduced with kind permission

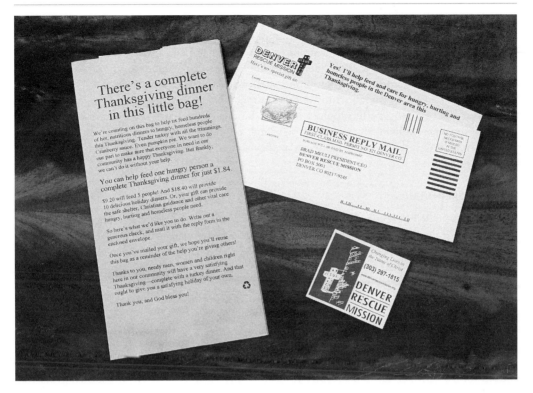

List swaps (reciprocals)

The non-profit sector is unusual in that organizations often exchange names of supporters for use in recruitment campaigns (again, exchanging customer names with competitors would be unheard of in the commercial world). These lists of known current givers are much more responsive than 'cold' lists, and are supplied free of charge by non-profits or at a nominal cost by agency intermediaries. They thus recruit new donors very cost-efficiently.

However, there are a number of negative points associated with this practice. Few non-profits monitor the subsequent giving patterns of donors whose details are supplied to competitor non-profits through list swaps. Research has shown that the response rate to development mailings can drop by 10 to 20 per cent among donors whose names have been included in reciprocal deals (Sargeant 1999). List swaps, though ostensibly an effective tool for recruitment managers, can prove to be damaging in the longer term. One of the most common complaints among donors is that they tend to be 'deluged' with non-profit direct mail appeals once they have given to one non-profit. In countries such as the UK with strict data protection legislation in place, names can be exchanged only if donors have had the opportunity to opt out of name exchanges.

Data processing and de-duplication

Every cold mail campaign will involve data processing, as the externally supplied lists will need to be run against the existing donor file to ensure that current givers are not mailed. This de-duplication (merge purge) process will also involve running the external lists against each other so that no individual (whose name may appear on several different lists) will receive more than one copy of the mailing. At this point any 'stop' list of people who have made it known that they do not wish to hear from the non-profit can also be excluded. On large campaigns this can become a complex, time-consuming and expensive exercise.

Valuable data can be gained from de-duplication reports. The degree of overlap between the 'house' file and externally supplied lists can be ascertained and used as a useful pointer, and 'multibuyers' (individuals appearing on a high number of lists) can be separated out and possibly treated differently (by remailing), as they should be the best prospects if the targeting has been effective.

Unaddressed mail

Mail can also be delivered unaddressed. These mailings are targeted by postcode/Zipcode, and are distributed via a number of suppliers, either through the mainstream postal service so that the packs arrive with the normal mail, or through specialist delivery companies. The response rates to unaddressed mail are considerably lower than those generated through personalized direct mail as the targeting is less sophisticated and the mailings less personal. However, the costs of distribution are also much lower as there is no list cost and no de-duplication, data processing or personalization involved. Unaddressed mail can reach individuals whose names do not appear on mailing lists and therefore may comprise a fresher audience.

Successful unaddressed mailings tend to be amended versions of a 'winning' cold mail pack. Some restrictions apply in terms of the delivery of bulky items or unusual sizes, so the creative options for this media tend to be slightly restricted in comparison with cold mail. Delivery can be arranged as either 'solus' or as a 'shared' delivery.

As the mailing piece does not carry personal details in this case, many non-profits find that up to 20 per cent of responses to unaddressed recruitment mailings are anonymous.

Telephone

In the USA outbound telephone calls are used in donor recruitment, often in conjunction with cold mailings. This is not the case in the UK, where the telephone is used only as an inbound response device in donor acquisition campaigns, and a Telephone Preference Service (Do Not Call) is in operation that makes cold calling very difficult and costly.

Telephone solicitation in enlisting new donors is used by US non-profits in a variety of ways. 'Phonathons' are used primarily by educational institutions and conducted by volunteers who contact researched lists of prospects, 'Telefund' uses paid callers through an agency, again using researched lists provided to the agency by the non-profit organization and 'Telemarketing' sales or cold calls are made by an agency through random calling from unresearched lists. Telemarketing is fast becoming unprofitable as response rates are low, and many states have now implemented 'Do Not Call' lists.

While the telephone can be used effectively in recruitment, especially where prospect lists are built of individuals known to be phone-responsive and/or where the use of the telephone is integrated with direct mail or other media, it often does not meet the minimum levels of cost-effectiveness required.

When integrated with other components of the campaign and particularly when offered as an inbound response mechanism (i.e. where the donor calls the organization), the use of the telephone can be highly profitable and creative. Donors, for example, wishing to donate money to the restoration fund for the Statue of Liberty in the early 1980s were invited to dial 1–800 THE LADY.

Press and magazine advertising

Press and magazine advertising is an expensive recruitment route, and press adverts tend to be cost-effective only if the non-profit is recruiting donors on to a high-value or regular gift, if the advert is soliciting funds against a high-profile emergency event, or if the newspaper or magazine is carrying a great deal of supporting editorial coverage of the event or cause.

Non-profit recruitment adverts tend to look very formulaic. This is partly because the cost of advertising space is prohibitive and non-profits therefore buy the cheapest standard ad sizes, and to buy at the last minute to keep costs down. Years of experience of press advertising have taught practitioners how best to use design and copy to maximize response. Headlines, coupons and response telephone numbers tend therefore to be of a certain size and prominence, with copy and images arranged in a certain way to ensure readability and impact within a small space and where the production values tend to be low. Best practice suggests that non-profits should provide the donor with both the problem and the solution within the copy of the ad. A recruitment ad from the World Society for the Protection of Animals is included in Plate 6.3. The figure contains three versions of an ad that were piloted by the charity. Advert A outperformed the others undoubtedly because it provides donors with a problem and an easy way in which they can resolve that problem: £10 buys a chaincutter!

As with all direct response recruitment, off-the-page advertising should be run over time as a series of tests; of copy and creative, of ad size, of media title, of placement of the ad within the publication, day of the week and so on.

Inserts

Some organizations use inserts in press and magazine titles in the recruitment of new donors. Like press advertising, there are a number of standard design and copy guidelines that should

Plate 6.3 *WSPA press advertisements*

Source: © WSPA. Reproduced with kind permission

Plate 6.4
Sightsavers' insert
Source: © Sightsavers.
Reproduced with kind
permission

be followed in the preparation of the inserts themselves. Again, the key point is to attract the eye, and as inserts can fall out of the publication, both sides of the insert should be arresting and attractive. Inserts can be successful, especially in specialist publications where the reader profile is a suitable match against the prospect profile. They typically achieve a response rate of six times that which would be generated by off-the-page advertising, but regrettably are substantially more costly. As with all direct marketing media they should thus be tested to ascertain the return on investment that will ultimately accrue.

When arranging inserts it is important to ensure that no non-profit competitors are placing inserts in the same publication on the same day, and to check the number of inserts that will be carried at any one time. As with cold lists, publications become 'tired' quickly, and may need to be 'rested' before another insertion is placed. It is possible to test a small number of inserts on a random basis initially before rolling out to the full run of any publication. Some publications can also offer segmentation by geographical area, or by subscribers versus news-stand copies.

Plate 6.4 contains an illustration of an insert developed by the charity Sightsavers. The insert, which has an involving message and illustration on both sides, pictures an individual's eyelids rimmed by barbed wire. This powerful image is still one of the best performing the charity has ever developed. When opened up, the insert explains how a small donation can restore someone's sight.

Plate 6.5
*Face-to-face
fundraising*

Direct dialogue and door-to-door

In Europe a high proportion of donors are now recruited via direct dialogue or face-to-face fundraising (see Plate 6.5). The initial impetus for this new development was the imposition of strict data protection legislation that made cold mail recruitment more difficult. In this form of recruitment trained recruiters stand in the street or in private sites such as shopping malls. Recruiters are clearly identified as representing a non-profit, as they wear a brightly coloured tabard featuring the non-profit logo. They approach passers-by and encourage them to sign up to support the non-profit through regular giving. While this approach has proved unpopular with some sections of the media in the UK, where it is now an important source of new donors, it is currently one of the most cost-effective recruitment routes on offer to UK fundraisers. Face-to-face recruits tend not to have given to any non-profit before, and to be much younger (80 per cent being under 30 years of age) than the 'typical' UK charity donor. It is impossible to undertake a great deal of targeting by this method as sites only work effectively if a high 'foot traffic' of passers-by is evident.

Face-to-face fundraising has recently transformed the finances of Action for Blind People, boosting its annual income from £2 million to £10 million in just over three years. The non-profit originally decided to test the new media when its fundraising department was restructured in 2000. Since its inception this new medium has generated £6 million and recruited 60,000 new supporters.

New donors are also solicited by trained recruiters going door-to-door in selected neighbourhoods, asking householders to consider signing up to support a non-profit with a regular gift. This activity is targeted by Zipcode/postcode. In door-to-door fundraising (which again is used mainly in the UK and Europe, but is also now working successfully in Canada), several non-profits may be represented in a 'basket' approach. Prospective donors are offered the opportunity to give to one of a selection of non-profits.

Direct response television (DRTV)

Direct response television advertising is an expensive media to enter, but can prove an effective means of donor recruitment. The cost of airtime has lessened considerably in recent years, while the number of channels available, and the number of niche specialist channels, have increased enormously, allowing non-profits to begin to target specific audiences through television.

However, production costs and the costs of telephone fulfilment still mean that DRTV is complex to manage, and tends to be used most successfully only by high-profile non-profits with a 'mass' appeal message. The most successful uses of DRTV have tended to be organizations asking for a low-value committed (regular) gift. It is also interesting to note in the UK that those charities asking for a direct debit which can be completed over the telephone, when the respondent calls, have tended to generate much higher returns than those that elect to send the user a standing order form through the post which must then be returned to the organization. The difference here is the number of stages that are required to complete the transaction and, if this can be limited to one, the return on investment will be substantially higher.

In the USA, some charities are able to take advantage of public service broadcasting slots and may thus acquire free airtime from the media owner. This can have a dramatic effect on the economics of DRTV and make it cost-effective for even smaller local non-profits to employ the medium. In the USA a number of non-profits also host their own television programmes on specialist channels. Life Outreach International is one of the most well known, offering *Life Today*. The programme has featured such celebrities as George W. Bush and Robert Duvall and is broadcast five times a week on cable stations, including Pax TV and Fox Family. It features topics such as health, grief and relationships, and also opportunities to buy products such as books and CDs alongside traditional fundraising appeals. Viewers of the show contributed $12 million in 2000 in response to appeals aired on the programme.

The Internet

In both the UK and the USA, web based fundraising has so far generally proved a disappointment. In the USA, some of those non-profits appealing for an emergency response to the September 11th tragedy reported receiving a relatively high proportion of donations over the web. It is hoped that this may mark a move towards the increased use of the Internet as a response mechanism, especially in connection with high-profile or emergency appeal drives.

Non-profit websites will eventually be key media in both donor recruitment and development, and a web element should be included in any integrated recruitment campaign. This is an issue that will be returned to in some depth in Chapter 14.

INTEGRATED CAMPAIGNS

It is now generally accepted that acquisition campaigns which use several media within the same time period, carrying a common message, and which combine awareness development with fundraising objectives, are more successful than single media campaigns. By integrating a message across different media streams a non-profit can build the momentum of a campaign. The promotion of the appeal or programme through public relations and communications work will likewise raise the profile of the campaign in the eyes of the public. Individuals who come across multiple messages are more likely to respond positively when afforded an opportunity to give.

Some media routes tend not to be successful when used alone, but can provide uplift when used in conjunction with other routes. The most effective integration employs each route or discipline to carry out the functions it does best, while pursuing a common communications objective – ensuring that each element reinforces the others without compromising its own effectiveness. Direct response radio advertising, for example, rarely delivers new donors profitably despite the relatively low costs of production and airtime. However, if radio ads are run at the same time as door drops or direct mail the response rates to the mail packs will increase.

Integrated multimedia campaigns, where the aim is to co-ordinate different channels in a cohesive and seamless way, can be extremely complex to schedule, manage and track, especially as awareness and direct response targets differ fundamentally and have to be measured very differently.

THE NATURE OF THE FUNDRAISING MESSAGE

In designing a case for support and producing the materials required for recruitment, both the target audiences and the position and brand of the non-profit organization have to be considered. There can be a tendency in recruitment creative to 'oversell' in order to recruit support. In the longer term this can lead to high rates of donor attrition and to donor dissatisfaction.

Recruitment communications need to be powerful in order to be seen and heard by the target audience – the strongest and most engaging message of the organization. Recruitment communications have by necessity to focus on and illustrate a limited part of the work of the organization, but that aspect should be representative, sustainable and should fit absolutely with the image and mission the organization wishes to project. For instance, it may be tempting for an art gallery or museum to tempt potential donors with a forthcoming blockbuster exhibition or exhibit and the benefits they receive should they become a donor, rather than focusing their recruitment message on the depth and strength of the permanent collection, and Third World development organizations find that they will attract a different (and often less committed) donor if they emphasize short-term emergency disaster relief efforts as opposed to longer term sustainable development projects.

Premiums, benefits and fundraising products

Many non-profits, especially in the USA, use premium offers in recruitment campaigns. These may be 'front end' such as name stickers, stamps and notecards, or 'back end' offers which may range from coffee mugs and certificates to plaques. Many UK and US fundraisers likewise use 'involvement devices' (such as pens or photographs) to increase response rates to cold mail. Plates 6.6 and 6.7 illustrate the use of involvement devices. The first example (Plate 6.6) illustrates the use of a 'survey pack' where prospective donors are asked to complete a survey and to return this with a donation. Charities that employ this device often find that the inclusion of a pen enhances the response rate and that surveys are more effective than other categories of pack. On the down side donors who respond to these packs tend to offer lower value gifts and tend not to remain loyal for extended periods of time. They should hence be used with care. Plate 6.7 depicts a pack employed by Marie Curie Cancer Care in which the charity sends prospective donors a single daffodil bulb to stimulate a response. The key with such involvement devices is relevance to the cause, in this case the fact that the recipient can grow the organization's emblem. It is absolutely critical that charities stimulate involvement with the cause in this way rather than with the selected device per se. Only the former strategy will result in an enhanced response rate.

While in many cases such devices guarantee an uplift in recruitment response rates, the longer term impact of their use should be considered carefully. In many cases, as with survey packs, the donors recruited through these routes are not of the highest quality, and may prove expensive to retain if they require the provision of premiums as a constant feature of the relationship. Any involvement device or premium gift must also fit with the image, mission and message of the organization, or damage will be done to the brand over time.

Some non-profits use benefit-led packages or donor products in the search for new fundraising supporters, such as membership schemes or sponsorship offers. Again, the costs of the maintenance of such schemes have to be monitored with great care, with thought given to how such relationships are to be maintained and grown over time.

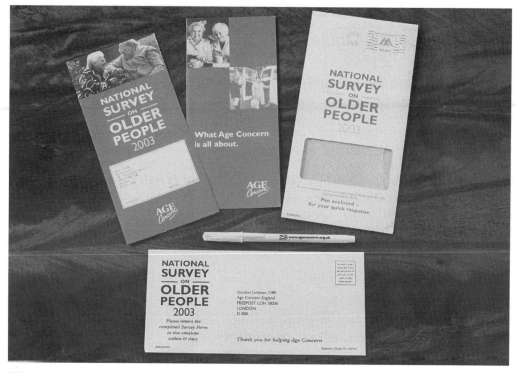

Plate 6.6 Survey pack

Source: © Age Concern. Reproduced with kind permission

Plate 6.7 Marie Curie Cancer Care recruitment pack

Source: © Marie Curie Cancer Care. Reproduced with kind permission

Methods of giving

In the UK the economics of donor recruitment and development have changed dramatically in recent years with the growth of regular giving vehicles. Banks have promoted the use of single-step electronic and automated banking and paperless payment schemes, which are now widely accepted and used throughout the population. These automated forms of banking put the control of the payments in the hands of the initiating organization rather than the bank, and do not attract high bank administration costs.

This has paved the way for non-profits to operate low-value monthly giving schemes, and to set up these regular giving arrangements electronically, without requiring the donor to sign any paperwork. New regular gifts can therefore be arranged over the phone in a single transaction rather than the previous two-stage arrangement whereby a new donor would have to phone in, pledge a regular gift, and then wait to receive the forms through the mail which would have to be completed and returned before the gift could be set up. These regular or monthly giving programmes are now also being used in the USA, where regular gifts can be set up through banks or credit cards.

Besides improving the profitability of media such as DRTV and the telephone, which were previously 'multi-step' media, UK fundraisers have found that regular giving schemes also broaden the 'traditional' prospect audience as younger sections of the population like to give in this way. The introduction of low-value monthly giving programmes has changed the nature of the supporter base for many UK non-profits, and are rapidly becoming more important in the US fundraising sector.

FULFILMENT

The 'back end' fulfilment of a recruitment campaign is a further key feature of donor acquisition work. The way that response to the campaign will be handled and followed up is often treated as something of an afterthought, but the treatment of new donors is hugely important in terms of building the image of the organization and beginning the relationship with the new recruit.

At base, fulfilment planning should ensure that systems and materials are in place to thank all new donors quickly, to deal with complaints and enquiries arising from the campaign, and to bank the cash donations and set up regular giving arrangements quickly and accurately. In many instances a great deal of time and thought is given to profiling, media selection, targeting and creative work on a campaign that then fails because the thought process was not carried through to the next stage. There are many case studies in existence of DRTV campaigns where the TV ad is hugely successful and generates a huge volume of calls, which cannot be handled by the telephone agency. Donors receiving an engaged tone or a holding message do not hold on or call back and the new recruits are lost.

Relationships can be made or broken with new donors during the initial or 'honeymoon' stage of the relationship with a non-profit, so the timing, accuracy and tone of the first 'thank you' or 'welcome' communication is extremely important. Fulfilment is a highly specialized operation and in many cases it is most cost-effective to outsource fulfilment to an external supplier rather than attempt to handle responses in-house. Where fulfilment is outsourced, careful and detailed briefing is essential, alongside the testing of systems and communications between the chosen supplier and the non-profit.

BUDGETING CONTROL AND EVALUATION

Testing

The control of donor acquisition campaigns initially involves the tracking and testing of pilots. The beauty of direct marketing techniques is that opportunities for testing abound, and therefore the risk of mistakes are lessened. Testing against controls is a way of life for direct marketing fundraisers, conducted on a cyclical basis as a source of continuous improvement. Creative, media, timing and response mechanism variants can be tracked and tested before any roll-out is arranged. The control of tests can become very complex and processes must be in place to ensure that only one variant is being tested at any time and that only significant variables are tested. Testing represents a sizeable investment of budget and always carries a risk of poor return on investment. For this reason test budgets are usually set as no more than 10 per cent of the total media budget. Sample sizes should likewise be limited to sufficient minimum quantities, so that the majority of the prospect base can be contacted with the most proven and cost-effective control communication.

Some direct marketing costs increase with quantity, while others, most notably the cost of printing, can be dramatically reduced at a unit level with increases in quantity. Straight-line extrapolation from test results can therefore distort the financial implications of a roll-out. Understanding the effects of quantity in each media stream is crucial if the correct inferences are to be drawn from a test campaign.

Control

Direct marketing works entirely through measurement, both during a campaign to monitor the success of the tactics selected and after a campaign to decide what succeeded and what failed. The information needed in monitoring tends to be fairly straightforward and to derive from the logical flow of a campaign. Information on, for example, the volumes actually despatched and the date of despatch, whether advertisements or inserts appeared according to schedule, and the availability of response packs, will be needed on a regular basis. Any suppliers should be briefed in detail on these requirements before a campaign is launched to ensure that the requisite statistics are always accurate and available.

Reporting and evaluation

In documenting and reporting on recruitment campaigns each medium necessitates slightly different controls and requirements. Each medium should be evaluated against as well as in conjunction with the other media employed. Some key performance measures used across a range of media are given below. These calculations should be performed across the campaign as a whole, and by each segment, medium and creative treatment.

- *Percentage response* – the response rate received to the original communication.
- *Cost per response* – the total cost of the campaign divided by the number of respondents.
- *Percentage conversion* – if the purpose of the original communication was merely to solicit enquiries it will also be necessary to examine the percentage of enquirers that ultimately offered a donation.
- *Cost per donor* – total cost of the campaign divided by the number of donors attracted.
- *Revenue per donor* – total value of donations divided by the number of donors attracted.
- *Profit per donor* – total profit from a campaign (if any) divided by the number of donors attracted.

- *Lifetime value per donor* – mean projected lifetime value for each donor recruited by a particular campaign.
- *Return on investment* – either calculated as an immediate return (i.e ROI for the recruitment campaign itself) or a projected return given the forecast lifetime value of the donors recruited.

Lifetime value is a topic to which we will return in detail in Chapter 7.

In reporting the success of any given segment or media route there are some standard pitfalls to avoid. One is the effect of extreme data or outliers – i.e. an exceptional result that can radically distort the true picture and lead to a false interpretation of the results. Outliers can occur by chance because of the extreme behaviour of one or two recruits, especially those giving very high-value initial gifts. Likewise, there is a danger in relying on average measurements – often the measurement of the median (or middle) value is more reliable, though more complex to calculate.

The costs of fulfilment should also be included and set against the income generated. It may not be possible to allocate such costs in detail to specific media or segments, but it is essential that they are allocated at least at the top level of the campaign.

A detailed assessment of the performance of any campaign is essential in building data over time and guiding future recruitment strategy and tactics. At this stage the results should be shared with those responsible for donor development to ensure that the whole process is managed holistically and that donor development and upgrade communications are appropriate for the newly recruited donors, and are likely to maintain and maximize their support over the full duration of their relationship with the non-profit organization.

SUPPLIER RELATIONSHIPS

Donor recruitment campaigns can involve a bewildering array of suppliers (an illustration of the potential range of suppliers is given in Table 6.1). Co-ordinating and briefing suppliers is a key skill in the management of recruitment campaigns, and harmonious relationships with suppliers are hugely important in avoiding problems and ensuring that things run as smoothly as possible. Suppliers should be respected, and should be involved as early as possible. They will be specialists and will be experienced in (often the least glamorous, but essential) aspects of the work. Communication channels should be kept open throughout the process with results and successes being shared. At some point there will be a need to 'lean' on a supplier for extra fast turnaround or to 'go the extra mile' in delivering a service – if the fundraiser has made an effort to understand the business of the supplier and to treat them as key and equal team members they are more likely to respond to calls for help with alacrity. A motivated supplier team is more likely to produce the extra effort required to solve your problems and prioritize your work.

CHAPTER SUMMARY

In this chapter we have drawn a critical distinction between donor acquisition and donor development activities. In respect of the former a planning process was delineated, including the derivation of objectives, segmentation and profiling, targeting, media planning, communication of the offer, fulfilment and response analysis. It is important to realize that this process does not occur in isolation and that in many ways it would be better regarded as a loop. Information about the performance of one recruitment campaign may be used to inform the development of those run subsequently and modifications to strategy can often result.

Table 6.1 *Donor recruitment suppliers*

Supplier	Function
List broker	Recommendation and purchase of mailing lists
Creative agency	Concepts, design and copy for packs, ads, scripts
Media buyers	Purchase of advertising space or airtime. Specialist media buyers may be used for DRTV and radio
Data-processing house	De-duplication and cleaning of mailing list data
Mailing house	Personalization of packs, insertion of involvement devices, collation and mailing of packs
Fulfilment house	Processing of response 'banking and thanking'
Telephone agency	Outbound calling or inbound call response
Product supply	Supply of premium gifts or involvement devices (e.g. pens)
Production studio	For TV ad production

DISCUSSION QUESTIONS

1   List and describe the main steps involved in planning a donor acquisition campaign.

2   How can you use profiling information about existing donors to inform a cold list mailing recruitment campaign? Is there any information that it would be inappropriate to use in this way?

3   As the fundraising manager of a small charity, prepare a presentation of the arguments for and against undertaking an extensive programme of list swops/reciprocals.

4   In your role as director of fundraising you have recently appointed three new staff who will undertake donor recruitment duties. Prepare a brief presentation to them explaining how the process works and the key points that should be borne in mind at each stage.

REFERENCES

Banks, J. and Tanner, S. (1997) *The State of Donation*, IFS, London.

Center on Philanthropy (1999) *Principles and Techniques of Fund-Raising*, Indiana University, IN.

Green, P.E. (1977) 'A New Approach to Market Segmentation', *Business Horizons*, 20(1): 61–73.

Greenfield, J.M. (1994) *Fund-raising Fundamentals: A Guide to Annual Giving for Fundraisers and Volunteers*, John Wiley and Sons, New York.

Kotler, P. (1991) *Marketing Management*, Prentice-Hall, Englewood Cliffs, NJ.

MacDonald, M.H.B. (1984) *Marketing Plans: How to Prepare Them, How to Use Them*, Heinemann, London.

Philips, L.W. and Sternthal, B. (1977) 'Age Differences in Information Processing: A Perspective on the Aged Consumer', *Journal of Marketing Research*, 14(4): 444–457.

Sargeant, A. (1999) 'Charity Giving: Towards A Model of Donor Behaviour', *Journal of Marketing Management*, 15: 215–238.

Chapter 7

Donor development

LEARNING OBJECTIVES

By the end of this chapter you should be able to:

- Outline the latest research on donor development and retention.
- Discuss the theory, practice and advantages of relationship fundraising.
- Understand how lifetime value, recency/frequency/value models and approaches such as the donor pyramid are used in donor development strategies.
- Discuss the optimum use of segmentation in donor development communication programmes.
- Isolate those issues that are critical to donor retention such as service quality, feedback and recognition.

INTRODUCTION

As we discussed in the previous chapter, the bulk of the income generated from donors comes through retention and development activity rather than at the point of recruitment. Non-profits tend to have to invest in the acquisition of new supporters. That initial investment is repaid and additional income is generated over time if the donor continues to give. Few would question that existing donors will always be the most cost-effective source of additional donations (Lindahl and Winship 1992). Donor development is thus the main income stream for non-profits, and as such should be the area in which the highest levels of investment are made.

Donor development techniques are used to maximize the profitability of every donor relationship. In practice this involves activity designed to retain donors over time and to develop and grow their giving to increased levels through the implementation of tailored fundraising communication and stewardship programmes. It should be recognized at the outset that not all donors are of the same worth to a fundraising organization. While the targeting and profiling work undertaken in the acquisition process should go some way to ensuring that newly recruited donors are all valuable additions to the supporter database, the identification of different types of donor, of their actual and potential value to the non-profit, and of the optimum levels of investment that should therefore be made in them, is vital to successful donor development.

The database, and the effective and efficient use of the information that the database can provide, is the key to this process. As with donor recruitment, a plethora of routes, options and models are available to fundraisers in devising development plans for existing donors. In this chapter we will look in detail at some of the most effective tools currently used in donor development segmentation and measurement, such as lifetime value, recency/frequency/value analyses, and relationship fundraising techniques. These should form the basis of donor development planning and strategy. We will also look at the available research on what drives donor loyalty and at what non-profits can do to encourage retention.

DONOR DEVELOPMENT PLANNING

Development objectives

Donor development objectives typically focus both on general measurements of retention and campaign-by-campaign evaluations. Many of the measures we described in the previous chapter, such as revenue, profit, campaign ROI and so on, would hence form the basis for donor development objectives. We may, however, add to this measurements such as:

- *Retention rate*: The percentage of current donors who will still be considered active donors at the end of the year (or planning cycle).
- *Attrition rate*: This is simply the converse of the retention rate and expresses the percentage of current donors who will lapse their support of the organization over the course of the year (or planning cycle).
- *Aggregate return on investment*: Non-profits need to set targets for the return on investment they achieve for donor development activities as a whole. This frequently sits alongside ROI objectives for specific donor development campaigns, but is an essential and more global measure of performance. This is simply because not all the communications donors will receive are designed to raise funds. Some may merely be imparting news and information about the work the organization undertakes. Since these are not 'campaigns' they would not be measured in the same way as other fundraising communications and are simply a facet of good donor stewardship. A global measure of ROI for development activities is therefore essential to ensure that in looking after existing donors a satisfactory level of performance is still being achieved.

Development strategy

Development planning usually involves the testing and adoption of a broad programme or annual plan of regular donor communications, which is then broken down by segment. Within this overall picture individual campaigns will be planned and targeted to achieve maximum effect. Some campaigns will be driven by clear income targets, while others will be designed as retention vehicles, and thus are not likely to be judged solely in terms of campaign profitability.

Discussions of donor development tend to be based on the belief that once supporters have been recruited, they can be cultivated over time and their contribution to the organization increased. Thus a new recruit who gives a small cash gift to an emergency appeal can be 'moved up' the scale of support to ultimately become a major giver or a legator. The development process also involves the 'cross selling' of other philanthropic 'products', so the one-off cash donor might also be introduced to retail trading goods, prize draws, membership or adoption schemes, or to volunteering or advocacy roles within the organization as a means of increasing the depth and profitability of the donor–non-profit relationship.

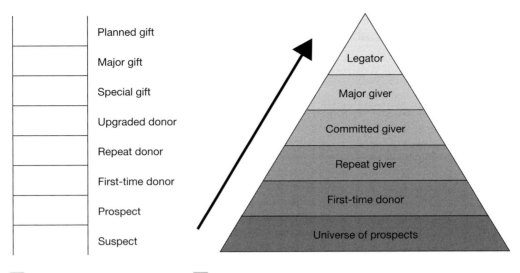

Figure 7.1 *The development ladder*

Figure 7.2 *The UK donor pyramid*

This process is often referred to visually as a 'Ladder' or 'Pyramid', as depicted in Figures 7.1 and 7.2. The 'Loyalty Ladder' was originated in principle by Raphel and Considine (1981). The 'Pyramid' model for donor development processes is intuitively attractive as it corresponds to the 'pyramid of giving', i.e. the observation that many small gifts are made, and fewer large gifts – so 80–90 per cent of the value of donations tends to come from just 10 to 20 per cent of the supporter base.

These models have been criticized in recent years as over-simplistic and static. Both assume a single route into a charity, the response to a first appeal at the base of the ladder or pyramid. In reality first donations can be a major or even planned gift, and major givers can 'descend' over time (if the relationship with them is not managed well) to lower value levels of support. Large legacy gifts are often received by UK charities from individuals who have never appeared on the charity's supporter database. Donor development planners must bear in mind that models are merely general guidelines, and that the reality is often more dynamic and less predictable than the theory would suggest.

Non-profits commonly refer to their core donor development 'programme' or 'cycle'. This is the regular pattern of communications and events for donors that form the central development process for that organization. The cycle may be very simple, based around a single annual fund drive or a membership renewal system, or it may be a complex system of timed communications. An example of a more complex cycle is provided in Figure 7.3.

Many organizations treat newly acquired donors differently during the first period of their support. We have seen that it is very difficult to persuade cash donors to give for a second time. It is therefore essential that the first stages of acknowledgement, welcome and re-solicitation are handled well, and that the first communications a new supporter receives are a logical development of the recruitment communication (in terms of both content and tone) that elicited their first gift. Special 'welcome' packages are often used, designed to thank new donors, to introduce them to the organization and to renew or deepen their interest. Some organizations then continue to treat new donors as a separate segment for a certain time period, targeting them with a special series of communications (usually by mail or phone) designed to foster interest and loyalty and to educate the donor about the organization and the ways in

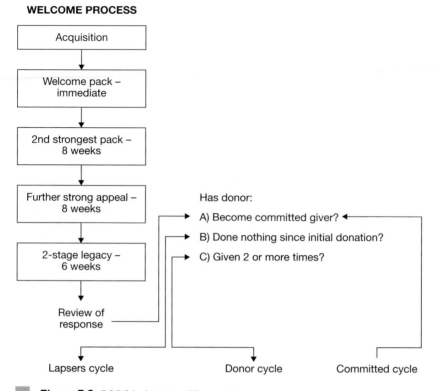

WELCOME PROCESS

Figure 7.3 *RSPCA donor mailing cycle*
Source: © RSPCA. Reproduced with kind permission

which they can become involved. After this set period the donor will be integrated into the main supporter base.

Donor development communications range from appeals for repeat support (by mail, phone or e-mail), updates and newsletter communications providing feedback and background information, through to events invitations and higher value appeal approaches which might involve video mailings and face-to-face visits. Donors may be invited to become members of clubs or schemes, to give regular gifts to the general fund or to sponsor an area of work or a beneficiary. Campaigning organizations might ask donors to take personal action through lobbying or protest activity. With such a plethora of options available, it is essential that fundraisers are equipped with information on the current and likely future value of individual donors, and with guidance on their likely future responses and behaviour. In the absence of this knowledge all donors will be treated the same, so some will not reach their full potential profitability while others will receive inappropriate levels of care and investment.

MEASURING DONOR VALUE

Relationship fundraising

Fundraising practice has undergone rapid change since the early 1980s and the dominant paradigm has shifted away from transactions to relationships. At the core of relationship fundraising is the development and maintenance of long-term relationships with donors, rather than simply a series of discrete transactions. Such a change in emphasis more accurately reflects real market behaviour, where few donation decisions are taken on a 'once only' basis. Real market behaviour consists of a series of exchanges rather than purely one-off transactions.

While the move from a transaction to a relationship approach to donor development fundraising may seem little more than a play on words, the differences in terms of the impact on strategy and performance are profound. In a transaction-based approach, development activity is driven by the need to maximize the returns generated by each individual campaign (except perhaps where a campaign has been jointly designed to achieve other goals such as awareness, participation or education). Strategy is based on achieving the highest possible return on investment (ROI) when the costs and revenues of a campaign are calculated.

Fundraisers following such a strategy tend to offer donors little choice. They cannot afford to – to do so would merely add to the cost. Little segmentation takes place and donors typically receive a standard pack. The emphasis of the content is usually on the immediacy of each appeal and donors are exalted to give 'now' because of the urgency of a specific situation. They may then be approached in a few weeks' or months' time with a further seemingly urgent issue the charity feels they should support. The donor thus receives a series of very similar communications, each designed with an eye to achieving the maximum possible ROI.

A relationship approach by contrast recognizes that it is not essential to break even on every communication with a donor. The relationship approach recognizes that if treated with respect donors will want to give again, and fundraisers are therefore content to live with somewhat lower rates of return in the early stages. They recognize that they will achieve a respectable ROI over the full duration of the relationship. At the heart of this approach is the concept of 'lifetime value' (LTV). Once fundraisers understand how much a given donor might be worth to the organization over time, they can tailor the offering to that donor according to the individual's needs/requirements, and yet still ensure an adequate lifetime ROI. These differences between the transaction and relational approaches to fundraising are summarized in Table 7.1.

Relationship fundraising may therefore be defined as: 'An approach to the management of the process of donor exchange based on the long-term value that can accrue to both parties.' From a donor's perspective, this style of approach addresses how an organization:

- finds you;
- gets to know you;
- keeps in touch with you;
- tries to ensure that you get what you want from it in every aspect of its dealings with you;
- checks that you are getting what it promised you.

Table 7.1 *Comparison of transaction and relational approaches*

Differences	Transaction-based fundraising	Relationship fundraising
Focus	Soliciting single donations	Donor retention
Key measures	Immediate ROI, amount of donation, response rate	Lifetime value
Orientation	Urgency of cause	Donor relationship
Time scale	Short	Long
Customer service	Little emphasis	Major emphasis

Naturally, as Stone *et al.* (1996: 676) point out, this depends on the effort being worthwhile to the organization concerned. This is clearly of paramount importance as donors themselves expect that the maximum possible percentage of their donation will be applied directly to the cause (Harvey and McCrohan 1988).

Burnett (1992: 48) was the first to recognize the need for what he termed 'relationship fundraising', which he defined as:

> an approach to the marketing of a cause which centres not around raising money but on developing to its full potential the unique and special relationship that exists between a charity and its supporter.

Burnett championed a move towards dealing with donors individually, recognizing each donor as unique in terms of their giving history, their motivation for giving and the overall standard of care that they expect to receive from the charities they support. The entire relationship with a donor, he argued, should be viewed holistically and fundraising decisions taken in the light of the perceived value of the overall relationship.

Relationship fundraising is characterized by donor choice. Recognizing the benefit of future income streams, fundraisers are not afraid to invest in their donors and to allow them greater flexibility over the content, nature and frequency of the communications they receive. As Jackson (1992) notes, this makes people feel important and thereby fulfils a basic human need. While the initial costs of implementing such a strategy are undoubtedly higher, the benefits in terms of enhanced patterns of donor loyalty – and therefore future revenue streams – far outweigh this investment.

Fundraising departments operating relationship fundraising therefore make every effort to segment their donor base and to develop a uniquely tailored service and, importantly, 'quality of service' for each of the segments they identify. At the core of this approach is the concept of lifetime value. It is this that drives the nature of the contact strategy and the dimensions of the relationship.

BOTTON VILLAGE – DONOR CHOICE AND SEGMENTATION

One of the most successful fundraising charities in the UK – Botton Village – had recently to write to all its donors asking them not to send any further monies. They had literally received all the funds they needed to sustain the Village into the medium term. Key to the charity's success was the concept of donor choice, and allowing donors to specify exactly what they wanted to receive from the charity and when. On the back of every communication donors received from the organization was a form inviting them to specify their individual choices. Donors could elect to receive only one mailing a year, to receive mailings, but not to be asked for money, to receive back editions of the newsletter, to receive information on how to make a legacy and, even, never to hear from the organization again. So successful has their fundraising been that their last Christmas mailing achieved a response rate of over 50 per cent – quite phenomenal in direct marketing terms and a testament to the move away from 'intrusion' in development activity to 'invitation'.

Let The Camphill Family help you

Your support means a great deal to us and we want to help you in return.
Please let us know your preferences by ticking the relevant boxes below.

Choose when you want to hear from us

1. **If you receive four issues of our newsletter each year:**
   ☐ *I would prefer to hear from you just once a year, at Christmas.*

2. **If you only receive a newsletter once a year, you may like us to contact you more often:**
   ☐ *I would like to receive Camphill Family Life four times a year.*

3. **If you would rather not receive appeals:**
   ☐ *I would like you to keep me up to date with news through Camphill Family Life, but I do not wish to receive appeals.*

4. **If you would rather not receive any further information from The Camphill Family:**
   ☐ *I would prefer you not to write to me again.*

To set up or change a regular gift

Giving The Camphill Family your regular financial support helps us to plan for the future. By setting up or amending a Banker's Order you'll continue giving our communities regular help, but your bank will be doing all the paperwork.

5. **If you would like to set up a regular gift:**
   ☐ *I would like to give to The Camphill Family on a regular basis – please send me a Banker's Order form.*

6. **If you would like to amend your existing regular gift:**
   ☐ *I already give regularly by Banker's Order and would like to amend it – please send me a form.*

Thank you.

Your guide to The Camphill Family

You can be sure of a warm welcome at any of the eleven communities supported by The Camphill Family. This guide gives you all the information you need to plan a visit, including our opening times.
☐ *Please send me a free copy of the guide.*

Do you want a word with someone?

Our office team of Kelly, Fran, Sue, Jackie and Joanne is here to help you. **Just ring our helpline 01287 661294 or our switchboard 01287 660871, 9am to 4pm weekdays,** and one of us will be pleased to talk to you. Do let us know if you have moved to a new address, if we are sending you more than one copy of our newsletter by mistake, or if there is anything else you would like to tell us.

Find out more about what life is like in The Camphill Family at Botton Village

7. **Our video of life in Botton**
   Botton Village: This is our home is set against the changing seasons in the rural beauty of Danby Dale and will help you to get to know us better. It tells the story of our community through the lives of our villagers and is a charming portrait of special people and the challenges they meet in sharing life together.
   ☐ *Please send me a complimentary copy of the video, Botton Village: This is our home.*

8. **The *Botton Village photo book***
   Featuring wonderful images of the people and places that make Botton special. Photographer Keith Allardyce used to live in the village and his close relationship with our community shines through.
   ☐ *Please send me a free copy of the Botton Village photo book.*

9. **Our *Sounds of Botton* audio tape**
   Our tape follows villager Jane Hill as she tours the village and meets her friends. It gives you a unique insight into life at Botton.
   ☐ *Please send me a free copy of the Sounds of Botton tape.*

10. **Visiting Botton Village**
    Visitors are always welcome at Botton. If you can, please ring us in advance on 01287 660871 and we can give you details of workshop opening times as well as directions.

11. **Sending you past issues of our newsletter**
    Interesting stories from the village's history feature in past issues of our newsletter, *Botton Village Life*. You may ask for any of the past issues you would like, or another copy of ones you may have mislaid.
    ☐ *Please send me issue no._____ (most issues are available).*

Plate 7.1 *Botton Village donor response form*
Source: © Camphill Village Trust Ltd. Reproduced with kind permission

Lifetime value (LTV)

Bitran and Mondschein (1997: 109) define lifetime value as 'the total net contribution that a customer generates during his/her lifetime on a house-list'. It is therefore a measure of the total net worth to a fundraising organization of its relationship with a particular donor. To calculate it one has to estimate the costs and revenues associated with managing the communication with that donor during each year of his or her relationship. If, for example, the relationship extends over a period of four years, one can subtract the costs of servicing the relationship with that donor from the revenue so generated. In essence the contribution each year to the organization's overheads and charitable appeals can be calculated. Of course there is a certain amount of crystal ball gazing involved since it becomes increasingly more difficult to predict costs and revenues the further one looks into the future. To take account of this uncertainty and to reflect the fact that a $20 donation in four years' time will be worth in real terms much less than it would today, it is also important to discount the value of the future revenue streams that will be generated. After all, instead of investing the money in donor acquisition activity the charity could simply elect to place the money concerned in an interest-bearing account. Unless the return from the fundraising activity can be expected to match, or hopefully exceed, what could be generated by an interest-bearing account, it will clearly not be worthwhile. If this analysis is conducted right across the database a key advantage accrues. Charities can employ an LTV analysis to increase their overall profitability by abandoning donors who will never be profitable and concentrating resources on recruiting and retaining those who will (See also Lindahl and Winship 1992).

There are two key decisions to be taken in this examination of donor value. First, nonprofits must choose between the uses of historic or projected future value. Second, they must elect to calculate value on either an individual basis or, more usually, on a segment-by-segment basis, examining specific groups of donors on the database.

The majority of voluntary organizations continue to equate lifetime value with 'total historic value' and thus to calculate lifetime value by conducting a simple historic analysis of their database. The question fundraisers are asking, by conducting their analysis in this way, is simply 'How much has this particular individual, or segment, been worth to my organization in the past?' However, lifetime value can and should be used as a projective measure, offering information in respect of how much a given donor or segment may be worth in the future.

Calculating the LTV of individual donors

The formula for calculating LTV in the case of an individual donor is as follows:

$$LTV = \sum_{i=1}^{n} C_i (1 + d)^{-i}$$

Where:

C = net contribution (i.e. revenue minus cost) from each year's fundraising activities
d = discount rate
n = the expected duration of the relationship (in years).

This somewhat complex-looking equation merely indicates that it is necessary to calculate the likely future contribution by a donor to each year's fundraising activities, discount these future contributions and then add them all together. The grand total is the LTV of a given donor.

It should be noted that in examining the contribution each year, an organization should subtract all the relevant costs of servicing the relationship with a given donor from the revenues so generated. The issue of what constitutes a relevant cost is driven by the purposes for which the analysis is being conducted. Thus it may be appropriate to include the costs of recruitment where the aim is to compare the performance of various recruitment media. If the aim is simply to apportion a donor to a given standard of care, these costs are sunk and therefore of no relevance. Similarly, a major issue for many organizations is the appropriate assignment of joint/overhead costs. There are many applications of lifetime value analysis where such costs are not of relevance (see e.g. Sargeant and MacKenzie 1999).

Of course the lifetime value of donors should take into consideration much more than just the revenue from their direct donations and the costs of the communications they receive. Donors are worth much more than this to an organization, because, for example, they often purchase goods from trading catalogues, sell raffle tickets, donate their time to fundraising events and so on. Each of these contributions needs to be accounted for in the equation. As an example, the net contribution figure for each year could therefore take account of the following costs and revenues.

Costs

- newsletters;
- appeal letters;
- acknowledgement/thank you letters;
- cost of promotional merchandise/donor gifts;
- cost of telemarketing activity, if any.

Revenues

- cash donations;
- tax reclaimed (in the case of tax-effective giving);
- cash value of donations in kind;
- cash value of any volunteering undertaken;
- cash value of referrals (i.e. introductions of other donors);
- revenue from sale of promotional merchandise.

Table 7.2 shows a worked example.

In this very simple example a donor has started her relationship with the charity as an uncommitted giver. Suppose for the sake of argument that this person is female, aged 45, lives in a certain type of accommodation (identifiable from her Zipcode information) and responded to a very specific type of appeal (e.g. famine relief) conveyed through an equally specific recruitment media – perhaps a list swop mailing. On the basis of a historical analysis of the database, the fundraiser understands that donors matching this profile would typically upgrade to committed giving in the third year of their relationship with the charity and would tend to be regular purchasers of raffle tickets. Indeed, it is not unusual for this type of person to persuade friends or relatives to also sell raffle tickets on the charity's behalf. On the basis of this information, coupled with forecast donation levels and projected costs, it is possible to produce the forecast given in Table 7.2 of the contributions that this donor will make to the organization over the duration of their predicted five-year relationship. As previously indicated, the value of future contributions must be discounted, and on this basis the predicted lifetime value of the donor is calculated to be $387. This information may then be used to assign the donor to an appropriate pattern of contact and quality of care.

Table 7.2 *An example LTV analysis for an individual donor ($)*

	Year 1	Year 2	Year 3	Year 4	Year 5	Total
Revenue						
Cash	50	50				100
Raffles	10	20	30	30	40	130
Covenants + tax refunded			100	100	100	90
Referrals				10	10	20
Total income	60	70	130	140	150	550
Costs						
Newsletters	2	2	2	2	3	11
Appeals	4	4	5	5	5	23
Thank yous	1	1	1	2	2	7
Raffles	2	2	2	3	3	12
Incentives				5	5	10
Total costs	9	9	10	17	18	63
Contribution	*51*	*61*	*120*	*123*	*132*	*487*
Discounted value	*51*	*55*	*99*	*92*	*90*	*387*

Discount rate of 10 per cent per annum

Major gifts

No mention has yet been made of major/estate gifts, or, in the case of the UK fundraising arena, legacies, which remain a major source of income for many voluntary organizations. The issue of whether or not to include an estimate of likely major gifts is one of predictability. In the UK it remains extremely difficult to predict legacy income, and organizations thus tend to exclude it from models used to shape day-to-day fundraising activity. In the USA where planned giving is a key facet of fundraising and where fundraisers have a much more detailed understanding of the incidence of this category of gift, it may well be appropriate to include variables pertaining to the costs and revenues associated with this form of giving.

Calculating the LTV of discrete donor segments

In the example quoted above we were concerned with how lifetime value might be calculated in the case of an individual donor. More usually, charities want to understand whether specific segments of their database exhibit higher lifetime values than others. This calls for a more sophisticated degree of analysis. In attempting to measure lifetime value the following process is recommended.

1   The first stage is to decide what the purpose of the analysis will be. Although this sounds rather obvious, many organizations are not clear from the outset exactly what they are hoping to gain from it. The technique typically employed is to determine whether specific segments of the database have a higher or lower value than others. Thus if female donors appear to be

worth more than male donors, or donors recruited by direct mail have a higher lifetime value than those recruited by press advertising, fundraising resources may be allocated accordingly. Not only can recruitment resources be more appropriately targeted, but contact strategies employing appropriate degrees of care can be developed to ensure the highest possible degrees of loyalty among those segments with the strongest lifetime values. Lifetime value analysis is therefore commonly employed to determine the LTV of donors who have specific character-istics. The nature of these characteristics needs to be determined from the outset. Clarity in respect of the purpose of the analysis can also guide the organization in assigning appropriate categories of cost for inclusion in the calculations.

2   The next stage is to decide the period of analysis to use. It is not essential here that the chosen time period selected is based on the longest standing donors (Carpenter 1995). Since predicting behaviour becomes progressively more difficult the further one looks into the future, and since contributions arising in the medium to long term will be heavily discounted, it is only important that the time period selected captures the majority of the contribution for a given segment of donors. Previous research in the commercial sector with similar value prod-ucts suggests that a time frame of five years might be most appropriate for application in the fundraising context (see e.g. Jackson 1992). The value of future contributions that occur beyond this period will be increasingly difficult to predict, as will the rates of donor attrition. In a sense therefore, the term 'lifetime' value is something of a misnomer. It is entirely up to the organization concerned to set a suitable time frame for the analysis and to look at the lifetime value of its donors over this very specific horizon.

3   The next step should be to segment the database into a manageable but distinct group of cells on the basis of the primary variable to be explored. Suppose one wishes to explore the LTV of donors who give their first donation at differing monetary values. To investigate this issue the database should be divided into a number of cells based on the level of the initial donation. In theory, the greater the number of cells the more accurate the predictive capa-bility of the eventual model. However, in practice, there is a trade-off between accuracy and simplicity; increasing the number of cells adds greatly to the complexity of the model. As a general rule, in the fundraising context, between ten and thirty cells are recommended. One might therefore allocate donors to cells on the basis that their initial donation was between:

- $1 and $5
- $6 and $10
- $11 and $15

and so on.

4   It is then necessary to establish the giving behaviour of each of the cells identified at (3) above. A historical analysis of donor behaviour for each level of donation should yield valuable information in respect of:

- *Attrition rate*. This will almost certainly vary from year to year. For example, comparatively few uncommitted givers will give a second donation. Those who do will probably exhibit a much reduced, but thereafter fairly even pattern of attrition. This information may be used to calculate the percentage of donors within the cell likely to be active in year 2, year 3 and so on.
- *Giving history*. It should be possible to calculate typical response rates for members of each value cell according to the type of donor development activity employed. It should also

be possible to track any trends in the actual amount donated in response to each campaign. Indeed, a number of donors will typically migrate from one cell to another as they decide to give more (or less), or upgrade, for example, to committed giving.

5   The final stage is to outline the intended development strategy, including, for example, the number of mailings and the projected costs thereof. This should include the costs of maintenance communications that a donor would typically receive (e.g. newsletters), even though they are not specifically aimed at raising funds.

6   The preceding information may then be employed to predict future value. Armed with information about likely attrition rates, the future costs of servicing donors, the predicted revenue streams and an appropriate discount rate, one may then proceed to make predictions about the projected lifetime value of each cell, or category of giver.

A LTV CASE

A LTV analysis employing the above methodology was conducted on behalf of a large international aid organization in the UK. The charity ranks among the Top 100 Fundraising Charities (as ranked by voluntary income) and is involved in a number of development projects worldwide. In the case of this analysis, the aim was to determine which recruitment medium generated the highest donor lifetime values. Only uncommitted giving (i.e. gifts from donors who give only a series of 'one-off' donations and do not commit themselves to future gifts) was considered. A random sample was therefore taken of 1,000 individuals who had been recruited from each of five primary recruitment media. This allowed the researcher to explore the behaviour of all the variables alluded to above and to build a model capable of predicting the lifetime value of donors who would be recruited by each method over the forthcoming recruitment campaign. The results of the analysis were employed to inform the allocation of recruitment resources between the various media available and to forecast the likely (lifetime) ROI of the campaign. A 10 per cent discount rate was employed and the duration of a donor lifetime was taken as five years. Since we are concerned here with the relative performance of each recruitment medium, the costs of recruitment have been included in the LTV calculation. The results obtained are presented in Table 7.3 and are similar to those reported by Sargeant (1998) for the sector as a whole.

Table 7.3 Forecast LTV by recruitment media

Medium	Mean LTV (£s)
Direct mail (cold mailing)	92.73
Direct mail (reciprocal mailing)	90.54
Door-to-door distribution	82.89
Direct response press advertising	75.78
Direct response television	56.76

The benefits of LTV analysis

Lifetime value may be used to drive four management decisions:

1 assigning acquisition allowances;
2 choosing media for initial donor acquisition;
3 setting selection criteria for donor marketing;
4 investing in the reactivation of lapsed donors.

1 Assigning acquisition allowances

An understanding of the lifetime value of a charity's donors can guide the determination of how much should be spent to recruit each new donor. Many charities conscientiously strive to achieve as close as possible a break-even position at the end of each of their recruitment campaigns. While commendable this is not necessary, so long as the future income stream from the donors being recruited is a healthy one. Charities employing the lifetime value concept would therefore tend to assign somewhat higher acquisition allowances than those which do not. In financial terms this is simply because a fundraiser employing a transaction-based approach will calculate campaign ROI thus:

$$\text{ROI} = \frac{\text{immediate revenue generated}}{\text{cost of acquisition campaign}}$$

A fundraiser adopting a relational approach based on lifetime value (LTV) would by contrast calculate ROI as:

$$\text{ROI} = \frac{\text{initial revenue} + (\text{sum of all future contributions less discount})}{\text{cost of acquisition campaign}}$$

Where

ROI = return on donor acquisition investment
Future contribution = estimated annual contribution to profit
Discount = reduction in value of future dollars to today's rate (discounted cashflow).

2 Choosing media for initial donor acquisition

Fundraisers engaged in the perennial problem of donor recruitment are well versed in the necessity of asking questions such as:

■ 'Which media should I be using for my recruitment activity?'
■ 'What balance should I adopt between the media options that are available?'

The traditional approach to answering these questions would have been to calculate the immediate ROI for each media and consider the response rates typically received from each media in the past. Such analyses suggest sub-optimal allocations of fundraising resource, because they ignore certain known donor behaviours. Donors recruited by one medium may never give again, while donors recruited by another medium exhibit much greater degrees of loyalty to the cause. The overall profitability from one relationship can therefore vary considerably from that of another. This is reflected in the results reported in Table 7.3.

3 Setting selection criteria for donor marketing

Lifetime value calculations can prove instructive for more than just recruitment planning. The information may be used to guide contact strategies for ongoing donor development. If a charity calculates a projected lifetime value for each donor on the database, donors can be assigned to specific segments, and contact strategies customized to build value. Initially, this may involve simply recognizing the difference in contribution, so as to offer particularly high-value donors a differentiated pattern of care that reflects their status. This might involve more detailed, higher quality mailings. As charities become more experienced in the use of LTV analysis, it would also be possible to associate the impact of differentiated standards of care, or forms of contact, upon the LTV for a given donor. In a sense, one then begins to model the optimal lifetime value. A simple example will illustrate this point.

Suppose a Third World charity has conducted a LTV analysis. The charity has divided donors into segments on the basis of projected LTV and decided to mail the highest value segments with an expensive mailshot designed to solicit funds to support Third World families. On the basis of the projected LTV the charity has calculated that sufficient funds exist to include a detailed case history of one family that warrants support, Polaroid photographs of each of the family members and a promotional video highlighting the work the organization could do with that family. While the LTV calculations suggest this is a very viable form of contact which will generate an acceptable rate of return, the charity has no way of knowing whether this is optimal. Through experience a charity can monitor the impact of different contact strategies on lifetime value (e.g. a standard mailshot, including/not including the Polaroid shots, including/not including the video). Contact strategies may then be selected which maximize the overall lifetime value of a given segment of donors. In our example, it may be that the inclusion of a video is perceived as wasteful and therefore lowers the value of subsequent donations, or it could have such an emotive and tangible feel that donors feel a greater sense of commitment and the longevity of their relationship is extended. As Peppers and Rogers (1995: 49) note:

> Instead of measuring the effectiveness of a marketing programme by how many sales transactions occur across an entire market during a particular period, the new marketer will gauge success by the projected increase or decrease in a customer's expected future value to the company.

4 Investing in the reactivation of lapsed donors

Few fundraisers would disagree with the notion that reactivating lapsed donors can be profitable. Having been sufficiently motivated to give at least once in the past, with proper encouragement it is eminently possible that donors will do so again. The problem, however, for many organizations lies in deciding which lapsed donors should be selected for contact. While one could do this easily on the basis of the total amount donated, the level of the last gift or the length of time since the last donation, it can be instructive to use projected lifetime value to inform the decision. With the right persuasion to respond, targeting those with a higher forecast LTV is likely to prove a most efficient use of resources. A 'reactivation allowance' may be built into the budget. How much an organization is prepared to commit to reactivating one donor would inform the nature and quality of the contact strategy employed.

Recency/frequency/value analysis (RFV)

An alternative to lifetime value analysis that is often available on database systems is recency, frequency and value (sometimes referred to as RFM – recency, frequency and monetary amount). Data on recency (i.e. the time since the last gift was given), frequency (i.e. the number of gifts that have been given) and value (i.e. the value of the gifts given) is calculated and used in segmentation or in the selection of data for a particular campaign. RFV data are often used in the generation of scores against each donor, assuming that:

- higher value donors are more attractive than lower value donors;
- donors who give frequently are statistically more likely to respond to a communication than those who do not;
- donors who have given in the last six months are more likely to give than those who have not given for the past two years.

RFV scoring can reflect the differences in individual donor behaviour and give the fundraiser considerable insight into who to target in a particular campaign.

Many charities use RFV scoring in conjunction with other forms of targeting in the selection of donors for development communications. Other targeting criteria might include donor communication preferences and ratings based on the sort of campaign approaches the donor has responded to, or rejected, in the past.

RFV may be used effectively in identifying those donors likely to lapse, and in patterns of lapsing. 'Pre-lapse' campaigns can be generated for those donors who have not given recently or where frequency and value patterns have been interrupted.

SEGMENTING FOR GROWTH

> You need to keep in mind that there are really many kinds of donors inside your donor base. This diversity is important to remember because in each case there are logical things to ask for and logical ways to make the request.
>
> (Squires 1994: 37)

As discussed above, effective segmentation is an essential part of successful donor development activity. Using the tools of LTV or RFV analysis, donors can be streamed into groups according to current or predicted value levels and communication programmes designed and implemented accordingly. In database selections for particular campaigns data may also be used on past response to similar appeal themes, or past patterns of communication preference. In the following section we run through some of the main definitions and development programmes that are commonly used in donor segmentation.

Major givers

The techniques involved in the generation of income from major givers are considered in detail in Chapter 8. Most US charities, and an increasing number in the UK, deal with potential and actual major donors through a discrete programme of personal contact, stewardship and events. This is often carried out by specially nominated staff and volunteers or by a separate department or division within the development function.

Ongoing RFV or LTV analysis will obviously identify donors who have already made a major gift, or where a number of high-value gifts have been made, indicating a propensity and ability to give at a higher level. These donors can then be flagged as such and provided with a personal level of stewardship and recognition. They can also be profiled to provide guidance for prospecting. The main donor base should also be 'trawled' for major donor prospects on a regular basis (this is described in more detail in Chapter 8).

The cultivation, retention and development of major givers is a very different process to that employed in the development of the bulk of the donor base. Much of the contact is on a personal, face-to-face basis. It is therefore unlikely that there will be a great deal of overlap in terms of the communications that are used for major givers and for the rest of the supporter base. Occasionally event invitations, feedback vehicles and special appeals may be sent to major givers and lower level donors, but even in these cases it is likely that the major givers will receive an enhanced version of the standard package, or a more highly personalized version of the communication.

Legacy/bequest prospects

Those donors who pledge to leave a bequest to a non-profit organization in their Will form a special supporter segment and should receive a tailored programme of development communications designed to retain their loyalty and interest, and to recognize that they have made a major commitment. Such donors do not necessarily possess high levels of disposable income in life, since the value of their estate may be in the form of property or other non-liquid assets.

Designing an optimum strategy for this segment of supporters can be challenging, since pledgers are likely to exhibit a wide variety of opinions as to how they feel they should be treated, and can be very demanding. Many prefer not to receive public recognition during their lifetime of their commitment to give after death (which they may see as highly confidential), while others expect regular and prominent acknowledgement of their pledger status. Any programme is therefore likely to be reliant on the accurate recording and use of individual preferences.

A typical programme for pledgers might involve a limited number of appeals, regular feedback and updates on the cause, plus courtesy communications such as invitations to special events and Christmas cards.

High-value donors

Many charities utilize a segment of 'high-value' donors. These are donors who have given at above-average levels, but where they have not given a major gift (non-profits use various definitions of the amount that qualifies as a major or high-value gift and these differ from one organization to the next. As an example, a major gift might be defined as £/$10,000, and a high-value gift as £/$250 to £/$9,999). High-value donors may be researched to see whether they are likely to become major donors in the future. They are valuable to the organization, and should receive an appropriate programme of communications.

High-value donors should be approached via appeals addressing areas in which they have demonstrated an interest, invitations to events, courtesy and feedback mailings. Mailing packages will tend to be of a higher production value than the 'standard', and may carry additional items. All communications should be highly personalized and should reference the previous giving history of donors and recognize the value of their contribution.

Committed giving

Donor development in the UK is largely based around the conversion of the maximum number of donors to committed giving through automated bank payments. As we discussed in Chapter 6, UK donors are often recruited directly on to a low-value monthly giving proposition. Where donors are introduced to the organization through a cash gift, they will be asked to change their giving method as early in the relationship as possible.

Monthly giving is increasingly being introduced in the USA (where the banking systems are less friendly to automated payments) as 'monthly sustainer' or pledge programmes (McKinnon 1999), and is prevalent in Canada.

UK charities have found that committed givers have a much higher LTV than one-off or cash givers. Maintaining relationships with regular givers is cost-effective, since the charity does not need to send out a new communication in order to obtain a gift each time. Donors who have committed to a regular payment tend not to cancel the arrangement, and so appear more loyal than cash donors (though this may be due as much to inertia as to a strong commitment). Monthly giving attracts a younger cohort of givers, and is also popular among those people who like to organize their giving and dislike receiving a high volume of repeat gift requests.

The development of committed givers is done most effectively via requests to increase the level of the monthly gift (upgrades). Regular givers will, however, on occasion also give additional cash donations (especially if the appeal request is in response to an emergency or a one-off opportunity for the charity; for example, a once-only chance for a heritage group to purchase a historical building and preserve it for posterity). UK charity experience indicates that requests to increase the regular gift level are often more effectively delivered by phone than by mail, as the donor base tends to be younger and the extra gift can be negotiated more flexibly in a conversation than on paper.

Much of the attraction for donors of a regular gift commitment is that this type of giving is cost-effective for non-profits to administer, ensuring that the bulk of the donation can be directed towards programmes, and in the fact that the donor need not 'be bombarded' with further fundraising appeals. Communication programmes for committed givers should therefore feature feedback and recognition vehicles, courtesy communications, an upgrade approach (perhaps once a year or every two years) and an occasional cash appeal if and when the theme appears appropriate. As with legacy pledgers, it is likely that committed givers will have a wide range of communication preferences, which should be respected wherever possible.

While committed givers tend to provide a very healthy ROI over the duration of their relationship with the charity, care should be taken in promoting the committed giving product to

EXHIBIT 7.1 THE IMPORTANCE OF COMMITTED GIVING

The Royal National Institute of the Blind (RNIB) had a successful donor recruitment programme through cold list mailings, but analysis showed that nearly 60 per cent of new recruits did not respond to subsequent mailings. The charity tested a new 'welcome pack' which went out immediately after the first gift was received. This pack thanked donors, told them more about the work of the charity, and informed them of other ways they could help and be helped. The pack explained the benefits to both the charity and the donor of signing up to a small regular payment through their bank. A few weeks after the welcome pack had been received a telephone call was made to the donor asking them to consider committing to a regular gift. The welcome pack and telephone call combined persuaded over 20 per cent of new donors to give on a regular basis.

A similar exercise, convincing donors of the merits of a regular gift, was then undertaken across the main RNIB supporter database. The charity now has a core of regular givers lending stability and predictability to the fundraising operation and substantially increasing the lifetime value of a significant cohort of donors.

certain audiences. High-value givers and major givers are obviously not good prospects for low-value monthly giving, as they would be of greater worth to the charity over time through gifts of occasional cash support. Committed giving programmes do tend to 'level' the base, which can mean that patterns and giving behaviours are harder to identify.

Low-value donors

One of the main advantages of LTV analysis is that low-value donors can be identified and a programme developed to ensure that the non-profit is not investing more in this cohort than is warranted by the level of income expected over time. Individuals who give regularly in small amounts can easily become a segment delivering a negative ROI. However, whereas in a commercial setting these 'customers' might be ignored or divested, in the non-profit scenario this is never advisable, as there is a great deal of anecdotal evidence to suggest that sizeable legacy bequests can come from donors who have given little during their lifetime.

Efforts should therefore be made to maintain a relationship and to retain low-value donors if possible, while also obtaining a positive ROI. Low-value donors may therefore receive a restricted number of appeal and update communications each year, and will also be approached to convert their giving to a regular commitment in order to reduce administration and retention costs.

Low-value donors may also be used in reciprocal mailings (list swops). As the least valuable donor segment, it may be considered worthwhile to use these donors (where data protection legislation permits) in exchanges with other non-profits in order to minimize recruitment costs. However, as we discussed in Chapter 6, reciprocal mailings are inherently risky ventures and should be used only with care.

Lapsed donors

We have discussed the worth of LTV analysis in assigning a potential value to lapsed donors and hence in guiding levels of investment and communication. Investment in lapsed donor reactivation is undoubtedly worthwhile, especially when the levels of ROI are compared with the costs of recruiting a new donor from a commercial list. However, as with low-value donors, it is easy to invest too high an amount in this group. When a lapsed donor is reactivated his or her subsequent giving history should be tracked carefully. In many instances reactivated donors lapse again, and the investment of the non-profit in keeping that donor on board is therefore not recouped.

KEEPING DONORS LOYAL

Why is loyalty important?

Loyal donors are those who give support time after time. While data analysis and segmentation exercises may indicate that certain types or groups of donors are not likely to be very profitable over time, and that little should therefore be invested in retaining and growing their support, there are very few instances where the loss of a supporter would be an optimum result. As has been noted above, major gifts, especially legacies or bequests, are highly unpredictable sources of charity income. There is much anecdotal evidence that even the lowest value giver in life can become a major benefactor after death. While segmentation based on profitability is essential, studies have shown that a small increase in customer retention can produce a significant impact on profitability (Reichheld and Sasser 1990).

As is the case in consumer marketing, it appears that there are several different levels of loyalty. Non-profits in the field of disaster relief, for instance, commonly find it extremely difficult to elicit repeat gifts from donors who give for the first time in response to an emergency appeal. In this instance, the giving of the gift has been motivated by the urgency of the cause or event and the perceived needs of the beneficiaries, while the identity of the facilitating non-profit agency has barely registered. The donor therefore feels no loyalty to the non-profit and he or she is unlikely to consider themselves to have any sort of relationship with the charity.

The donation of a second gift is always seen as a key point in the donor–non-profit relationship. As we have seen, most non-profits report that over half of new cash donors never give again. First gifts may be seen as a 'test', with donors (consciously or unconsciously) waiting to see what feedback they receive before going further.

In the 'middle' levels of loyalty a donor may give repeat gifts, but may also support other, similar causes and may not feel any great involvement with or preference for a particular organization. At the 'top' level donors feel that they have a strong relationship with a particular non-profit organization and will continue to support that organization even though competitors exist in the same field of work. At this level of loyalty the donor would be likely to be receptive to major gift or planned giving approaches, and would act as a strong advocate for the non-profit.

How can loyalty be increased?

In Chapter 5 we examined the reasons why donors stop giving to non-profits. The results of the research undertaken into reasons for quitting suggest a number of ways in which non-profits may seek to retain their donors. While there may be little that can be done to facilitate the retention of those donors who experience a change in their financial circumstances, there is much that can be done to deal with many of the other common causes of lapse.

The research indicated that only 22 per cent of donors appear to lapse because they can no longer afford to offer their support to the organization in question. Given that some of these donors may still be supporting other non-profits this result is encouraging, since it suggests that while a number of donors will be lost to a particular non-profit they may not be lost to the sector as a whole.

Indeed, the study suggested that over 26 per cent of lapsed donors typically quit because they perceive that other causes are more or perhaps equally deserving. If charities are to succeed in retaining this category of donor, the literature suggests that they need to find ways of improving satisfaction and deepening the bonds that exist between them and their supporters. Given that this study also highlighted the importance of feedback and perceived effectiveness, it seems that one way in which non-profits might achieve this goal lies in ensuring that they provide ongoing and specific feedback to donors in respect of the use to which their funds have been put and in particular the benefit that has resulted for the beneficiary group. If this feeling of impact on the cause is strengthened it seems less likely that donors will view other causes as being more deserving than those they already support.

Indeed, the feeling of identity or association with a given cause would seem to be a major cause for concern. One in ten of the lapsed supporters in the study reported that they had no memory of ever having supported the organization concerned.

Service quality was also identified as a key issue and would seem to be as much a prerequisite to non-profit customer retention as the literature suggests it is in the for-profit sector. Lapsed donors reported significantly poorer views of the quality of service they received than did active supporters, and in particular tended not to regard the organization as providing them with adequate feedback in respect of how their donation had been used. Donors viewing the communications they receive as informative, courteous, timely, appealing and convenient would appear to remain loyal for greater periods of time.

The issue then becomes one of how best to achieve this perception. The results of the study suggested that to engender loyalty, charities need to improve both the quality of their communications and the choice that they offer. The relationship fundraising approach, described earlier, would allow donors once recruited to select the pattern of communication they would wish to receive. A few charities, for example, currently offer donors the opportunity to specify how frequently they would like to hear from the organization, whether they would like news about how their gift has been employed, whether they would like such news but not additional letters asking for money and so on. The results of the research suggested that such practices would be likely to improve perceptions of the quality of communication received and thereby enhance loyalty. It is also worth noting that by taking the step of asking donors to specify how they would like to be treated, one is in effect engaging those donors with the organization and requiring them to think through the desired nature of the relationship. The donor thereby requests the communications he or she will subsequently receive, moving the organization's approach to marketing away from 'intrusion' towards 'invitation'. As the options for communication continue to increase, with e-mail likely to become a preferred route for many donors, offering choice will probably be all the more important in the future.

Given recent developments in database technology, there is no reason why even smaller charities cannot manage the requirements of their individual donors and ensure that each receives a pattern of communication identical to that specified. The results of this study suggest that this would enhance overall levels of satisfaction and ultimately, as a consequence, donor loyalty.

A further aspect of the study concerned donor expectations in respect of both the frequency of communication and the sums of money demanded. There was evidence that donor expectations in respect of these issues were currently not being met. It thus seems clear that charities could also offer donors some choice over whether or not they wish to be asked for specific sums. Some donors may well welcome guidance about the appropriateness of certain gift levels. Others may prefer to take such decisions themselves and not be prompted by the charity. Again, there is no reason why charities should not capture this information and use it to inform the communication strategy employed. Moreover, a consideration of relational issues, such as donor lifetime value, would ensure that, where specific sums are requested, these are appropriate to the financial ability of the donor.

Asking donors to specify what relationship (if any) they would prefer to have with an organization would therefore appear to offer considerable utility. Indeed, if donors are offered an additional opportunity to interact with their chosen charity, it would seem ultimately rather unlikely that they will lapse simply because they have no memory of ever having supported the organization.

The consequences of failing to embrace these relationship marketing techniques appear all too evident. Donors will be likely to increasingly complain that they are over-mailed and inundated with requests for inappropriate sums of money.

CHAPTER SUMMARY

This chapter has introduced and explained some of the latest research undertaken on what may be done to retain the support of donors over time and to develop their giving. The concept of relationship fundraising and the differences between this approach and the more traditional transactional route is explained, and the core measurement of lifetime value is introduced and investigated in some detail.

Segmentation is key to the implementation of successful donor development strategies, and we have examined some of the main donor categories and the sort of treatment each might receive in an optimal development plan. Finally, we have outlined some recent research on what causes donors to stop giving, and what organizations can do to retain their donors.

DISCUSSION QUESTIONS

1   List the reasons for donor lapse that can be effectively addressed by the fundraising function. How would you go about improving these areas in your own organization (or one that you know well)?

2   In your capacity as head of fundraising for an arts organization, make notes for a presentation to your CEO on the merits of undertaking a lifetime value analysis of your donor base.

3   Put yourself in the position of a donor who gives regularly to two non-profit organizations working in a similar field. One of the organizations has adopted relationship fundraising techniques while the other uses a transactional approach. How would your perceptions of the two non-profits differ?

REFERENCES

Bitran, G. and Mondschein, S. (1997) 'A Comparative Analysis Of Decision Making Procedures In the Catalog Sales Industry', *European Management Journal*, 15(2): 105–116.

Burnett, K. (1992) *Relationship Fundraising*, White Lion Press, London.

Carpenter, P. (1995) 'Customer Lifetime Value: Do the Math', *Marketing Computers*, January: 18–19.

Harvey, J.W. and McCrohan, K.F. (1988) 'Fund-raising Costs – Societal Implications for Philanthropies and Their Supporters.' *Business and Society*, 27 (spring): 15–22.

Jackson, D.R. (1992) 'In Quest Of The Grail: Breaking The Barriers To Customer Valuation', *Direct Marketing*, March: 44–47.

Lindahl, W.E. and Winship, C. (1992) 'Predictive Models for Annual Fundraising and Major Gift Fundraising', *Nonprofit Management and Leadership*, 3(1): 43–64.

McKinnon, H. (1999) *Hidden Gold*, Bonus Books Inc, Chicago, IL.

Peppers, D. and Rogers, M. (1995) 'A New Marketing Paradigm: Share Of Customer Not Market Share', *Managing Service Quality*, 5(3): 48–51.

Raphel, M. and Considine, R. (1981) *The Great Brain Robbery*, Business Tips Publications, New York.

Reichheld, F.F. and Sasser, W.E. (1990) 'Zero Defections: Quality Comes to Services', *Harvard Business Review*, September/October: 105–111.

Sargeant, A. (1998) 'Donor Lifetime Value: An Empirical Analysis', *Journal of Nonprofit and Voluntary Sector Marketing*, 3(4): 283–297.

Sargeant, A. and MacKenzie, J. (1999) *A Lifetime of Giving*, Charities Aid Foundation, West Malling, Kent.

Squires, C. (1994) 'Picking the Right Gift to Ask For: Donor Renewal and Upgrading', *Fund Raising Management*, 25(5): 37.

Stone, M., Woodcock, N. and Wilson, M. (1996) 'Managing the Change From Marketing Planning to Customer Relationship Management', *Long Range Planning*, 29(5): 675–683.

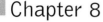

Chapter 8

Major gift fundraising

LEARNING OBJECTIVES

By the end of this chapter you should be able to:

■ Describe the extant research into major giving and the motives of major givers.
■ Explain the process of major donor recruitment and development.
■ Understand the concept of stewardship.
■ Provide an overview of the key tools and techniques used in major gift fundraising.
■ Discuss donor recognition and events management as part of major gift fundraising.

INTRODUCTION

Major gift solicitation is the most prominent and frequently discussed area of fundraising in the USA, while in the UK it is at an early stage of development. Differences in culture and in tax regimes are cited most often as the driving or limiting factors in the development and practice of major giving.

Major donors are individuals who make sizeable personal contributions. Major gifts are, broadly speaking, those that are large relative to the majority of the gifts the organization receives. The definition of a major giver thus varies from one organization to another, and donors will also have their own perspectives on what constitutes a significant gift for them personally at any time. In the USA it is now not unusual for 90 per cent or more of the money a non-profit raises from individuals to come from only 10 per cent of their donors.

Unlike companies and foundations, major donors are not regulated by time frames, restrictive giving policies or committee judgements. They can give as much as they wish, with few or no bureaucratic strings attached. As major donors will have extensive contacts in business, political or social circles, they are themselves vital sources of new prospects, and can be the most valuable of ambassadors. Major donor support can also have drawbacks – donors may exert excessive influence if they are major givers and are also members of the Board of Directors, for example, and may wish to influence programming in a way that compromises the mission of the organization. Despite this possibility, the pursuit of the major gift remains the holy grail of US fundraising.

158

The solicitation of major gifts is a very different process to that involved in the solicitation of small donations:

- it evolves over a lengthy period of time as the relationship with the prospect is cultivated;
- it involves face-to-face solicitation by peers who are often volunteers;
- throughout the process the donor is often encouraged to become involved personally in the work and running of the organization;
- major givers often require some form of acknowledgement or reward for their gift;
- major gifts may be paid immediately or pledged over time.

Major gifts may also come in the form of deferred or planned gifts through tax advantage investment vehicles and legacy bequests. This form of major giving is dealt with in Chapter 9.

In this chapter we will summarize the research that has been undertaken on the motivations that drive major giving and on what major givers look like. We will explain how the process works and the main techniques that are used in major gift solicitation, and discuss some of the concepts and experiences that lie behind this area of fundraising.

CHARACTERISTICS OF MAJOR GIVERS

Numerous US texts refer to the socio-demographic characteristics of big gift givers. They are likely to be people with a strong interest in and good knowledge of the charitable organization, are likely to have given in the past, and to have a personal contact within the organization at some level: 'They run the spectrum from a person who wants all the fame that money can buy to an anonymous donor' (Fredricks 2001: 34).

Practitioner guides thus recommend that when identifying and rating major gift prospects the key characteristics to look for are:

- *Linkage* – a strong connection between the prospect and the organization.
- *Ability* – the financial wherewithal to contribute a sizeable gift.
- *Interest* – belief in and passion for the cause or project (Irwin-Wells 2002).

Major donors usually have assets in mixed forms such as securities, real estate, retirement funds, insurance policies and savings. They are generally protective of these assets and cautious about giving them away. Some view the gift process as an investment and expect a return. They may involve lawyers and accountants in the process of giving, which can take years. Many support a range of non-profits, and most will expect a significant level of communication and feedback from a chosen non-profit.

Individuals with major gift potential are likely to demonstrate some of the following factors: Over 55 years of age, male, married, conservative, religious, approaching retirement, have a history of giving and involvement, hold mixed assets, a family foundation, a business and/or inherited wealth (Williams 1991). Research studies conducted by the Boston College Social Welfare Institute (Schervish and Havens 1995) have examined the connections between giving and wealth in the USA. One important contribution of the analysis was to correct the popular misconception that lower income US households were relatively more generous than upper income households. The research found that in fact lower and upper income households were equally generous, while very high-income households were markedly more generous. Among the wealthy:

virtually all the rich are contributors, they donate very large amounts to charity, and they give greater proportions of their income to charity than the poor or affluent. Fundraisers generally do not need to turn the rich into donors, usually that has already occurred.

(Schervish 1993: 87)

MOTIVES OF MAJOR GIVERS

It is generally accepted that the decision-making process associated with major gifts is far more complex than that entailed with the making of a small gift in response to a direct mail piece or telephone fundraising call. Major gifts are 'Stop and Think' gifts (Sturtevant 1996), and involve a complex and lengthy process. As the gift decision grows in magnitude the donor will require a stronger set of motives for giving. There are likely to be more influences and inputs into the gift decision, and while the decision is emotional the donor is more likely to express decision-making parameters in rational terms.

A major gift is not something that donors do on a whim or a lark, or on the spur of the moment. . . . They do not flow into an organization at the rate of one a week, and in all likelihood they do not materialize without a great deal of time, talent or effort attached.

(Fredricks 2001: 23)

Until recently, large-scale research among major donors was limited, despite their relative importance. This area is now beginning to receive increased attention from non-profit academics and researchers engaging in studies to establish the needs, motivations and strategies of major givers.

In a study of a sample of wealthy philanthropists, Teresa Odendahl (1990) used four broad philanthropic groupings in explaining key characteristics of major givers. The first of these, 'Dynasty and Philanthropy', concerns those families that maintain a prominent position in a community for a long period of time, with capital being accumulated, preserved and transmitted down several generations. Odendahl found that institutionalized philanthropy formed an important part of the formation of such dynasties, with the establishment of endowed foundations carrying on the family name.

'Lady Bountiful' is used to describe wealthy female major givers. Odendahl (1990: 100) explains that 'sexism is as prevalent among the rich as elsewhere in society', and that the wealthy women she interviewed tended to be active volunteers throughout life, having assumed the responsibility for the family's philanthropy alongside childrearing, household management and social and cultural activities. 'First Generation Man' is the term appended to elite givers who are self-made, the newly rich who have made money through the high-technology industries, manufacturing, real estate, oil or retail. These givers tend to take philanthropy seriously when their businesses are stable and mature and they feel less pressure to put profits back into the company, and therefore more comfortable about giving to charity. Odendahl's final category is 'Elite Jewish Givers'. While the history of Jewish charity in the USA parallels that of Protestant giving to a great extent, Jewish philanthropy is characterized particularly by the sympathy and kinship exhibited with Jews around the world, and the willingness to support them in times of hardship. The tradition of giving is an important aspect of the community life, ethnicity and religion for Jews of all classes, and hence wealthy Jewish people contribute to and lead non-profit enterprises across the USA.

The motives that lie behind major giving by the wealthy have been investigated at length by the Boston College Social Welfare Institute:

> What motivates the wealthy is very much what motivates someone at any point along the economic spectrum. Identify any motive that might inspire concern – from heart-felt empathy to self-promotion, from religious obligation to business networking, from passion to prestige, from political philosophy to tax incentives – and some million-aires will make it the cornerstone of their giving.
>
> (Schervish 1997: 70)

Those who hold great wealth and direct it to social purposes also invariably want to shape rather than just support a charitable cause. This tendency is summarized by labelling wealthy major givers 'hyperagents' – people capable of establishing the institutional framework in which they and others live. This research has also looked at the spiritual foundations of giving by the wealthy, and at the associations and identifications which motivate giving by this group. It was found that the level of contribution depends on the frequency and intensity of participation, volunteering and being asked to contribute, that larger gifts are generated from those already making substantial gifts, and that generally, charitable giving among the wealthy derives from the forging of associational and psychological connections between donors and recipients (Ostrander and Schervish 1990).

> Donors contribute the bulk of their charitable dollars to causes from whose services the donors directly benefit. It is not by coincidence that schools, health organizations and (especially) churches attract so much giving. It is here that donors, because they are also recipients, most identify with the individuals whose needs are being met by the contributions.
>
> (Schervish 1993: 87)

Hyperagency does not mean that all wealthy major givers achieve major innovative philan-thropic interventions, but they are more likely to do so than givers in general. Some become proactive producers of philanthropy rather than passive supporters of existing projects or causes – when a wealthy contributor provides a sizeable enough gift the whole agenda of a non-profit may be changed and the giver may become the director or architect of the work.

As well as the inclination to make a difference in a significant way, the top wealth holders also have the material wherewithal and the tax incentives to do so. There is clear evidence of a growth in wealth in the USA. There are now almost four million millionaires, and every indi-cation that the percentage of affluent and wealthy households will continue to grow, with increasingly larger numbers of American households achieving the resources for modest to substantial philanthropic giving:

> It is the first time in history that large proportions of a population can materially afford to consider charitable giving as a principal component of their financial strategy and moral agency.
>
> (Schervish 1997: 67)

Other literature on the reasons for donating major gifts applies classic theories of motivation to fundraising (Williams 1991), and maps out motivations as: religious belief, guilt, recognition, self-preservation and fear, tax benefits, obligation and pressure, with other factors listed as: acceptance, altruism, appreciation, enlightened self-interest, approval, being asked, belief in the cause, community interest, competition, gratitude, immortality and sympathy. The practitioner literature also promotes involvement as a primary motivator for major giving.

There is a debate around the importance of tax incentives in the donating of major gifts. It is agreed that tax is important, especially with regard to the timing and size of any gift. Practitioners appear to conclude that tax incentives are unlikely to 'spark' the giving of a gift, although they are important in enabling the donor to retain control of their money. As such, legal and financial advisers are seen as important players in the major gift scenario. Affluent people are accustomed to making financial decisions based on reason, so although the initial prompt to give may be emotional, a non-profit has to be prepared to provide a valid and fact-based rationale to affirm the initial emotional response (Goettler 1996).

> Major donors give because they are asked, they give to people, and they give to meet opportunities not to meet needs. They want to make an impact; they want to change the world.
>
> (Lawson 1998: 18)

Prince and File have undertaken an extensive programme of research to establish a donor-centred framework that can be used in 'understanding the concerns, needs, interests and motivations of individual affluent donors' (Prince and File 1994). Their work on the 'Seven Faces Framework' categorizes and segments wealthy donors into seven motivational philanthropic types:

1 *The communitarian* – (26 per cent) This is the largest segment. Communitarians give because 'it makes sense to do so . . . they believe in active philanthropy as they help their own communities prosper by supporting local charities'.
2 *The devout* – (21 per cent) This group is motivated to give for religious reasons, and channel almost all of their giving to religious organizations.
3 *The investor* – (15 per cent) Investors organize their giving to take advantage of tax and estate benefits. They are most likely to support 'umbrella' non-profits and to donate to a wide range of causes.
4 *The socialite* – (11 per cent) Members of local social networks who 'find social functions benefiting nonprofits an especially appealing way to help make a better world and have a good time doing it' (Prince and File 1994). They tend to support the arts, education and religious groups.
5 *The Altruist* – (9 per cent) 'Altruists embody the perception of the selfless donor – the donor who gives out of generosity and empathy to urgent causes and often modestly wishes to remain anonymous' (Prince and File 1994). Altruists tend to give to social causes and tend not to want active roles in the groups they support.
6 *The repayer* – (10.2 per cent) 'A typical Repayer has personally benefited from some institution . . . and now supports that institution from a feeling of loyalty or obligation' (Prince and File 1994).
7 *The dynast* – (8 per cent) Dynasts do good because it is a family tradition. Giving is something their family always stood for, and they believe it is expected of them to support non-profits. Dynasts support a wide range of non-profits, often selecting those that are not 'mainstream'.

These groupings may be used by practitioners in categorizing donors and prospects, in preparing solicitation presentations and responses to objections and questions that donors might have, and in planning recognition vehicles.

MAJOR DONOR RECRUITMENT

Major donor fundraisers use two key routes to the sourcing and development of prospects. The first is to draw prospects from among a non-profit's existing supporter base, the argument being that many major donors will begin their association with the cause through lower value giving. The second approach (often used simultaneously) begins with the identification of peer networks, with the address books of board members being a key source of potential contacts.

Major giver prospecting from the existing donor base

The theory behind this approach is that individual donors can be brought up through the ranks:

> The donor first gives through a small annual gift. Over time and based on capability, the donor is moved upward in gift size and type. Using this model, the development officer begins with the annual gift program and later introduces major and planned gift opportunities. It is assumed that major and planned gift prospects will thus emerge from the annual fund.
>
> (Dean 1996: 26)

This is often illustrated or explained in the US as a donor pyramid or ladder (see Figure 8.1).

Major gifts can appear at any stage, but are most likely to be generated once the donor is cultivated and approached through face-to-face personal methods rather than through direct mail or the telephone. In this system potential major givers are 'prospected' from the main donor file. Individuals who have made larger than average gifts or where a high degree of affluence is suspected will be drawn from the database to be researched, the theory being that some of these donors may have the financial capacity to make substantial gifts after appropriate involvement and cultivation:

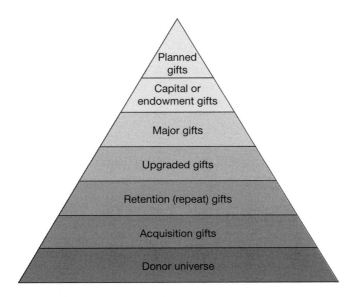

Figure 8.1 *The US donor development pyramid*

> A person may give ten times the amount they give through the mail if they're asked face to face. Gifts through the mail are impulse gifts – when asked in person the donor must give a major gift more serious consideration. You have potential major donors hiding on your donor base.
>
> (Reuther 1998: 46)

Major giver prospecting through peer contacts

This method of 'discovering' prospects starts from the premise that personal and peer contact with the prospect is all-important. Fundraisers will therefore require board members to provide details of qualified individual contacts through their own business and social networks, and will ask them to volunteer to make initial approaches to these contacts to introduce the cause and the appeal.

Indeed, major gift fundraising is unique in the degree to which the involvement of senior staff, trustees, high-level volunteers and executive board members is required at every stage of the process. The Board of Directors, trustees and the CEO are key in researching and providing links to high-level prospects, and in the solicitation and cultivation of their peers as both donors and volunteers. The creation of a major gift committee is widely recommended where committee members agree to represent the charity to the community, contribute a personal leadership gift and work to provide and cultivate potential major donor contacts. Such a committee may also be responsible for identifying and researching projects for big gift funding:

> Studies show that strong, committed, informed boards that are involved in resource building make for financially healthy and respected organizations. Weak, inactive boards make for financially troubled and short-lived organizations.
>
> (Maude 1997: 24)

Likewise, existing donors are used as advocates in major giving campaigns in recommending and introducing potentially wealthy friends and colleagues.

The recruitment process

The successful recruitment of major donors through either of the above routes requires access (you must know them personally or at least know someone who can make the introduction), belief (the prospect must believe in the organization's work) and ability (the financial ability to make the gift) (Reuther 1998).

This process of prospecting is often aided by the use of research agencies and specialist software providers that hold data on wealth, assets, family, business and community connections and on previous giving. The process of researching the background, connections and interests of prospective major givers is cited as absolutely key to successful solicitation. In this, US fundraisers have an advantage over their UK counterparts, since the stricter data protection legislation in the UK severely impacts on the type of data that can be held against an individual and on the format in which the data can be stored.

The many US practitioner texts available emphasize the need for a long period of research and cultivation prior to the 'ask' being made. Kotler and Scheff (1997) recommend a six-point plan for successful solicitation of major gifts: *Discover and qualify*, *Plan*, *Involve*, *Ask*, *Negotiate and close*, and *Thank and plan*. Fundraisers, through desk research, initially identify a sufficiently wealthy individual who might conceivably have a strong interest in the organization.

PETERBOROUGH CATHEDRAL

In the mid-1990s the cathedral administration recognized the need for major renovation work that would cost the organization £7.3 million to accomplish. To bring in the funds teams of volunteer fundraisers were established, each with their own speciality, ranging from business, music and local authorities to farming, parishes and major gifts/grants. The appeal treasurer recognized the need to bring in several large donations of over £100,000 if the target was ultimately to be met and sought to leverage the contacts of the volunteers and other friends of the cathedral to identify individuals with the ability and interest to make contributions at this level. Wherever possible the fundraising 'ask' was made by individuals who had themselves contributed to the restoration work so that they could have the highest possible credibility when approaching others. Ultimately £1.3 million was raised from private benefactors with a further £100,000 pledged in legacy gifts. The balance was funded by grants from government, business and grant-making trusts.

They then identify others who could supply information and arrange an introduction. They cultivate the person's interest in the organization without requesting a gift and evaluate his or her capacity for making a large gift. Eventually they make the 'ask'. Upon receiving a gift they express appreciation and lay the groundwork for establishing further involvement. Throughout the process approaches are made on a personal level through face-to-face contact.

In the early 1960s G.T. 'Buck' Smith developed a five-step process that has been described as the 'secret to securing major gifts' – *Identification, Information, Interest, Involvement,* and *Investment*. These steps should comprise a continuing cycle seeking to nurture and develop those people who are committed to the non-profit's mission. This has become known as the 'cultivation cycle' or 'moves management theory', and is still taught today as the route through which an individual can be 'moved' through a cycle until the relationship is developed to the point of investment (Smith 1997). The five 'Is' are actually the four 'Rs': Research, Romance, Request and Recognition according to Ernest Wood (1997), and the process parallels courtship and marriage.

MAJOR DONOR RETENTION AND DEVELOPMENT

While there is a vast array of practical 'how-to' guidance available from the USA on locating major donor prospects and on soliciting the first major gift, there is relatively little detailed information available on how to renew and develop major donors over time. Once a significant gift has been made it is recommended that an intensive and lengthy programme of thanking and recognition (if required by the donor) is undertaken. The donor then becomes part of the organization's stewardship programme.

Stewardship is a key current concept in US fundraising – the idea that, as best practice, fundraisers should become responsible guardians of donor assets that are held on trust for the public good. Stewardship is considered to be a guiding principle of philanthropic fundraising:

> The means by which an institution exercises ethical accountability in the use of contributed resources and the philosophy and means by which a donor exercises responsibility in the voluntary use of resources.
>
> (Tempel 2001: 34)

As such, stewardship focuses primarily on concern and respect for the needs and rights of those who give and of those who receive – the beneficiaries of the charity organization. The ultimate extension of stewardship would be a scenario whereby a fundraiser would be employed by donors rather than by non-profits.

Stemming from Judaeo-Christian tradition (Jeavons 1997), stewardship now implies a deep burden of trust, responsibility and accountability for the proper management and administration of the resources under the steward's care. Within the context of contemporary non-profit governance and management, the role of steward and its corresponding obligation of stewardship is used to apply to any person in a position to manage or account for financial resources: trustees, the CEO, the finance director, and fundraising staff.

Fundraising stewardship incorporates acknowledgement, recognition and gift management and is closely bound with ethical philanthropy practices: 'Stewardship is trust, responsibility, liability, accountability, integrity, faith and guardianship' (Conway 1997: 12). Planned and major giving sits particularly within this construct of stewardship, with estate and financial planning seen as an opportunity to service the needs of donors and to facilitate their philanthropy, requiring non-profits to look towards the longer term and to take an active role in the stewardship of the assets entrusted to them. Reports on asset management and investment performance are fed back to the donor as stewardship reports, increasing the confidence of the donor in the investment advice of the non-profit/the non-profit's financial representatives.

> Major gift stewardship is the continuous personal interaction and information exchange that you and others from your organization have with your donors. It paves the way for your donors to make repeat larger gifts. It is a form of cultivation.
>
> (Fredricks 2001: 23)

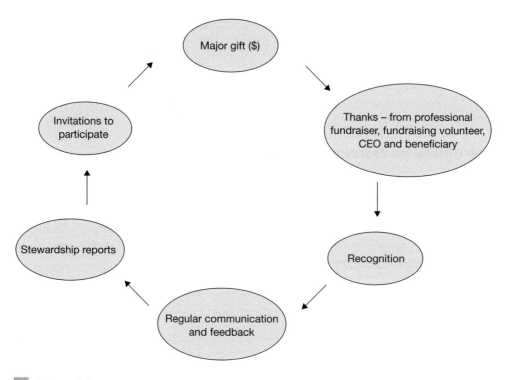

Figure 8.2 *Stewardship and major donor development cycle*

In practical terms, stewardship of major givers could include the provision of regular feedback on how the gift has been used and on the effect it has had, a regular programme of communications such as annual reports and newsletters, plus invitations to participate in a range of events both large scale and private. The solicitation, cultivation, development and stewardship of major donors works as a cycle (see Figure 8.2).

TOOLS AND TECHNIQUES

Capital campaigns

Capital campaigns can be considered as a subset of major gift fundraising. While it is not necessary to conduct a capital campaign to solicit major gifts the process of making the case for major giving tends to reveal special requirements and discrete needs that may be used to focus the fundraising effort and to provide indications of tangible outcomes for prospective donors. Institutions embark on a capital or endowment effort when they have a significant one-time need. These campaigns are intense, carefully organized and highly structured efforts to raise a large and specific amount of money over a finite period of time (typically three years). Outside consultants are often used to provide advice, and extra staff drafted in at every level. Various types of capital appeal are mounted:

- The 'Bricks and mortar' campaign – for new construction (or major renovation) of buildings or major new equipment purchases.
- The 'Endowment' campaign – where funds are raised to add to the organization's capital investment fund from which income is earned to support programmes.
- The 'Combined' campaign – where the campaign is targeted to raise funds for a mixture of capital and endowment needs. Current running costs may also be part of this sort of campaign.
- The 'Project' or 'Programme' campaign – where funds are to be raised to fund a specific project or area of programme activity that is packaged using a capital campaign model and where a tangible and specific outcome may be cited.

Capital campaigns typically employ a volunteer campaign chair and committee, who work through the operational side of the campaign and develop recognition and naming opportunities. Essentially the solicitation process is identical to that employed in all major gift work, the difference being that in a capital campaign a specific 'product' can be offered to the potential donor. The specific, often visually demonstrable nature of the need, and the time-limited nature of the campaign lend themselves to PR and events work – US capital campaigns are usually occasions for high-profile 'hoopla'.

Campaign structure and the use of volunteers

Major gift campaigns usually involve the setting up of a formal structure of campaign committees and subcommittees. These voluntary bodies serve to direct and steer the campaign, and, importantly, also undertake the bulk of the actual fundraising effort. Fundraising staff primarily service these committees, train and equip the volunteers, and facilitate the running, co-ordination and monitoring of the campaign. Committee members are also expected to be 'lead givers' themselves. Exhibit 8.1 details the role and responsibilities of major gift campaign chairs, honorary chairs and committee members.

EXHIBIT 8.1 KEY ROLES AND RESPONSIBILITIES OF COMMITTEE MEMBERS

Campaign chair

Primary role
To lead the fundraising effort

Responsibilities

- Identify and recruit volunteers.
- Hold regular committee meetings to steer and review the campaign as it progresses.
- Maintain contact with committee members and provide them with help and encouragement.
- Assist in identifying potential donors.
- Speak on behalf of the campaign.
- Host campaign events.
- Solicit key lead gifts.
- Make a generous personal gift.

Honorary co-chair

Primary role
To raise the public profile of the campaign

Responsibilities

- Facilitate the use of your name and photo in campaign promotional materials.
- Attend events.
- Assist in identifying volunteers and prospects.
- Make a generous personal gift.

Committee member

Primary role
To implement the campaign plan

Responsibilities

- Personally solicit gifts as per the campaign plan.
- Help plan solicitation strategies.
- Attend events.
- Make a generous personal gift.

Volunteers are thus used extensively in major gift fundraising, forming the main fundraising 'workforce', and delivering a high proportion of the income goal personally. There has been some debate in the USA about the role of volunteers in major gift fundraising and the degree to which campaigns can succeed without them. Some of the largest educational institutions in the USA are now extending their staff rather than relying on volunteers. However, volunteers are still widely thought to be essential to a successful campaign because:

- Organizations usually do not have sufficient staff to undertake face-to-face solicitation with a long list of prospects.
- The enthusiasm and motivation of a dedicated 'volunteer salesforce' is supremely effective.
- Fundraising staff do not usually have the right sort of contacts or background to solicit gifts from prospective major donors.
- When members of staff solicit gifts the prospect may feel that they are merely raising income to cover their own salaries rather than being able to inspire the giving of a gift to forward the mission of the organization.

Volunteers suitable for major gift campaign work are generally found among the 'inner circle' of an organization and already committed to the work the organization undertakes. As such, volunteers may be found from among current trustees and board members, former trustees and board members, programme volunteers, donors and service users. Volunteers are recruited best by their peers and, as with gift solicitation, they need to be motivated by the campaign vision and by the personal benefit that will accrue to them if they agree to help.

Once a volunteer has agreed to join the campaign committee he or she must receive a training programme to increase his or her levels of knowledge about the campaign and the work of the organization. Training should be prolonged, both formal and informal, with the aim of enabling the volunteer to speak confidently and accurately about the campaign. In many cases professional training agencies are employed at this stage to complement staff efforts, and a full 'tool kit' of information, solicitation and briefing materials is provided.

The case for support

The case for support document is a fundamental tool in major gift solicitation. At base, the case for support for major gift fundraising will rest on the mission statement formulated for the organization in the early stages of the fundraising planning process. However, the justification of why an organization is deserving of major gift support requires special treatment, especially in terms of an articulation of the benefits accruing to the donor, and of the impact a large gift may have on the community. A clear vision of the future is essential in major gift fundraising as donors are asked to consider the 'big picture' and will need to be inspired to invest significantly in the cause. 'People give to a vision rather than a need' (Matheny 1994: 12).

A draft case for support should be tested among a sample of potential major givers (this process in itself can be a useful donor cultivation tool). It should also be fully endorsed by senior staff, trustees, and all those staff and volunteers who will take part in solicitation and cultivation. Asking for input at this stage can increase the sense of ownership in a campaign and make these individuals more effective as representatives. Typically the document would cover:

- For what purpose will funds raised from major gifts be used?
- What need does this meet?

CHILDREN'S HOSPITAL, BOSTON

In 2000 the Children's Hospital saw big rises in its large donations, increasing the number of donors who gave between $100,000 and $500,000 from thirty-one to forty-six. In the $10,000 to $20,000 range numbers jumped from ninety-five to 157. The organization attributes its success to specialization, and trains nine senior major gift officers to become experts on two to five departments by shadowing nurses, doctors and researchers on the job. One major gift officer, for example, covers genetics, neurology and orthopaedics.

The hospital has also established philanthropic leadership councils, which bring together donors to raise funds for specific medical divisions of the hospital. By 2001 the hospital had established three such councils, comprising between ten and twenty-five members, each of whom has provided the hospital with $25,000 or more. Council members are able to bring in friends for tours and events or presentations by senior medical staff. The oldest of the three councils mails a biannual newsletter to 20,000 current and prospective donors and holds an annual Valentine's Day Dinner to recruit new donors.

- What happens if this need is not met?
- What benefits result from meeting this need?
- Why is this organization the best one to do this?
- Why should the prospective donor care?
- How does the donor benefit?

The case should be expressed throughout from the perspective of the donor rather than the organization:

> The solicitor should not say 'If you give us this money for a minority scholarship, we can attract more high-quality African-American and Hispanic applicants'. Rather the benefit should be stated in the donor's terms saying: 'If you give us money for a minority scholarship, you can feel that you are helping your alma mater increase the richness of the educational experience it can give future students like you'.
>
> (Kotler and Andreasen 1987)

The gift range chart

Major gift campaign fundraisers in the USA use gift range charts and tables of gift levels extensively in campaign planning and monitoring. These are statistical representations of patterns of giving generated through past experience of major giving campaigns and guide the fundraiser in terms of the numbers of gifts required of particular dollar levels if the campaign target is to be reached. An example is provided in Table 8.1. In this case the campaign target has been set at $100,000.

To prepare a gift range chart the following rules are applied:

1   the first two gifts of the campaign are set to equal 10 per cent of the goal (i.e. 5 per cent each);
2   the next four gifts are set to provide a further 10 per cent of the goal.

The remainder of the chart will be developed flexibly, taking account of the past experience of the non-profit in running such campaigns. The figures given in the example are not untypical and serve to illustrate that it would generally be expected that 60 per cent of the total would be provided by 10 per cent of the donors and that 80 per cent of the goal would be provided by 20 per cent of the donors. This pattern of performance is very common.

When developing the gift range chart it should be noted that the ratio of prospects to gifts tends to fall as one moves down the pyramid. It is typically necessary to identify five prospects to give at the highest level, to ultimately acquire one donor. At lower ends of the pyramid it will typically be necessary to name only two prospects to provide a gift of $60 for each eventual donation.

Of course, this example is only fictional and in reality the sums involved when addressing major donors will be substantially higher, but it serves to illustrate how the tool is employed in practice. The gift range chart can also be employed for the annual fund, but is most effective when goals of over $25,000 are set.

The construction of a gift range chart should allow the fundraiser to ensure that an adequate number of qualified prospects are available to meet the goal and that the overall financial goal is realistic. One of the most common causes of failure in major gift fundraising is the lack of adequate prospects.

The gift range chart is used throughout a campaign in monitoring and reporting progress and problems, and should be formally revised at intervals as prospects are solicited and actual results obtained.

Solicitation techniques

US practitioner texts offer a huge amount of practical advice on how to handle the solicitation (the 'ask') itself at a face-to-face meeting. This includes tips on listening and questioning skills,

Table 8.1 Gift range chart: $100,000 goal

Gift range ($)	Number of gifts	Cumulative number of gifts	Prospects required	Cumulative number of prospects	Per range ($)	Cumulative ($)
5,000	2	2	10 (5:1)	10	10,000	10,000
2,500	4	6	20 (5:1)	30	10,000	20,000
1,000	10	16	40 (4:1)	70	10,000	30,000
750	20	36	80 (4:1)	150	15,000	45,000
500	30	66	120 (4:1)	270	15,000	60,000
		10 per cent of donors			60 per cent of goal	
300	67	133	201 (3:1)	471	20,100	80,100
		20 per cent of donors			80 per cent of donors	
Under $300 average gift ($60)	333	466	666 (2:1)	1,137	19,900	100,000
		100 per cent of donors			100 per cent of goal	

sample solicitation scenarios and scripts, advice on body language and on how to handle objections (Irwin-Wells 2002, Williams 1991). Fundraisers are encouraged to view every solicitation as a separate campaign, with a distinct financial goal, set of strategies and timeline.

The case for support is used as the basis for the 'ask'. The Fund Raising School at the Indiana Center on Philanthropy (Seiler 2000) recommends that the case is made in a solicitation by:

- stating the need;
- documenting the need you are meeting;
- proposing strategies and tasks;
- identifying who will benefit;
- demonstrating organizational competency;
- specifying the resources required;
- stating how gifts can be made;
- communicating the benefits of making a gift.

The most effective 'askers' or advocates are volunteers who have a peer relationship with the prospect (i.e. they are of a similar economic status and move in the same social circles), as this tends to guarantee that the meeting takes place against a background of mutual respect. Ideally both parties should have similar levels of interest in and engagement with the fundraising organization, and the volunteer will have made a significant contribution in support of the campaign. 'They should not be put in the position of asking someone to do something they have not already done' (Irwin-Wells 2002).

If a high-level volunteer is not available a 'proportional giver/volunteer' can be employed, i.e. someone who would still engender mutual respect in the prospect but who may not be as closely matched in terms of economic or social status. In this case the solicitor will have donated a gift which is personally significant, but which may be much lower than that which is being asked of the prospect. The 'worst case' option is that a staff member is employed to make the ask. In this case the chance of success, and any amount donated, is likely to be much lower.

In every case the solicitation is unlikely to succeed if the person charged with making the ask is unknown to the prospect. Ideally they should be familiar with each other as friends or colleagues, but at the very least should have been introduced by someone known to the prospect, and to have been involved in cultivating a relationship with the prospect beforehand. Where the solicitor does not have a peer relationship with the prospect a team of two people should be involved in the solicitation process, such as a committee member and the development director, or the campaign chair and a committee member. 'Comfort, capacity and connections to the prospect are more important than job titles' (Irwin-Wells 2002).

DONOR RECOGNITION

While individuals offering small gifts in response to direct mail or telephone approaches are unlikely to expect a high level of recognition for their support, and often insist that the whole of their gift should go direct to the programmes they are supporting, people donating significant gifts are more likely to expect that this will be marked, and that they will receive something in return for their gift.

In theory the potential recognition need of a donor should be discussed as part of the donor cultivation process. By the time a gift is pledged the solicitor should have a good idea of what level and type of recognition might be appropriate. Recognition of the biggest gifts can involved the naming of buildings or projects, while devices such as framed certificates, citations in

Table 8.2 Donor recognition clubs

Environmental Health Foundation of Canada	New York General Hospital Foundation	Shriners Hospitals For Children	Luther College
Patron – Gift of $5,000 or more	*Cornerstone Society*: Friends who have donated a total of $250–$9,999 to the Foundation – receive a certificate recognizing their support, together with hospital publications	*The Gold Book Society* recognizes seven levels of giving from $2,000 to $25,000 and represents these in the form of one to seven states. Each donor may progress through all the awards, each of which attract distinctive statues made from materials such as brass, lucite and walnut	*The President's Council* honours donors giving personal gifts of $1,000 or more annually
Benefactor – Gift of $2,500 to $4,999			*President's Executive Cabinet*: Gifts of $50,000 or more
Advocate – Gift of $1,000 to $2,499	*Chairman's Circle*: Membership offered to those making a gift of $10,000 or more. Members' names are listed in the entry area and are honoured guests at the Chair's annual luncheon		*President's Associates*: $25,000 to $49,999
Supporter – Gift of $100 to $999		*Five-star, six-star and seven-star* donors are further honoured in their local Shriners Hospital on a 'Because We Care Givers' panel (and also at the Shriner Headquarters In Tampa)	*President's Academy*: $10,000 to $24,999
Donor – Gift of $25 to $99	*Heritage Circle*: Individuals committed to a future gift are invited to an annual luncheon to hear presentations from senior staff. They may also have their names placed in the main lobby and receive a regular newsletter		*President's Society*: $1,000 to $9,999
		Philanthropic Society – honours contributions in excess of £250,000 and provides additional recognition in a further four levels, culminating in the Spectrum Gold Philanthropic Society award for gifts exceeding £2 million	*The President's Circle* honours gifts at higher levels offering four different levels of status for gifts of over $100,000

publications and reports, and publicity through press announcements are also used. Special events may be appropriate either in recognition of a particularly significant contribution or of a group of contributors. Donor recognition events, societies and activities tend to focus on exclusivity and privileged access, whether to an event, to information and feedback or to senior staff. Table 8.2 provides some examples of four US donor recognition clubs.

EVENTS

Special events such as galas and benefits have been a popular fundraising aid for many years and are part of every major donor programme as a means of recognition and cultivation.

Special events are notoriously labour-intensive and can lose money because of the high costs involved. As with all US major gift work, the most effective events employ volunteers at every level of operation, and involve a group of 'leaders' in special event committees – prominent individuals with wide influence who will help generate funds through their prestige and encouragement of friends and colleagues to attend. Events are not commonly used as occasions to solicit funds directly, though they may well be the point at which agreement is reached that a further meeting can take place, and they are enormously valuable as networking opportunities when a prospective donor can be introduced to non-profit programme and fundraising staff.

THE UK EXPERIENCE

The biggest gifts from wealthy people in the UK over the past fifty years have gone to universities, and to museums, galleries and cultural organizations such as the Royal Opera House. The NSPCC Full Stop campaign, launched in 2000, is the first time a welfare charity in the UK has attempted to secure the very major sums previously only attracted for higher education and the arts.

Major gifts have been sought in the UK so far mainly through capital campaigns, using the US model. The Tate Gallery worked through a US-style fundraising development committee structure using high-level volunteers to introduce and cultivate prospects. Funding was attracted from individuals in the UK and overseas for capital projects to create the Tate Gallery of Modern Art and the Tate Gallery of British Art:

> The fundraising campaign was planned to follow the strategic model established by major fundraising campaigns in the US, the big gift pyramid. The focus was to begin with the biggest gifts and the supporters closest to the gallery, moving through to smaller gifts and donors who are not quite so warm and culminating with appeals to the Tate membership and general visitors.
>
> (Ballard 1999)

As in US campaigns, the main effort was expended in obtaining leadership gifts of £1 million and more. Gifts were solicited against named spaces in the gallery – many of the TGMA's individual galleries, education facilities and public spaces have been named after donors.

A case study from the British Museum Development Trust evidences the same influences and techniques (Marland 1999): 'Look to the US as a model and use periodic big pushes with capital campaigns', and warns that most UK organizations need to undergo a change of culture before they are ready to fundraise successfully in this way.

In the past two or three years more 'major gift' staff and departments have been set up among the larger UK fundraising organizations. While in many cases capital campaigns have been used, increasing numbers of UK charities are now introducing the technique as a permanent part of their fundraising effort.

In introducing major gift fundraising UK fundraisers have typically found certain areas particularly challenging:

Senior staff and trustee attitude

It is essential that trustees and senior staff 'buy in' to the concept of major giving, and that they take part in recommending contacts, making leadership contributions and actively 'making the ask' on occasion. Most UK trustees are extremely reluctant to make personal gifts, to surrender their address books and to ask directly for funding. In some cases this problem has been overcome by means of the creation of a separate high-level major gift committee, or a group of major gift advocates or representatives who are willing to take leadership roles in major gift fundraising initiatives.

Support systems

Most UK fundraising is undertaken through the encouragement of high volumes of donors giving small amounts. Database systems that efficiently support this type of fundraising tend not to be suitable in the support of major gift work, which requires the storage of a high level of detail against a low number of individual contacts. As mentioned above, the Data Protection Act also restricts the sort of data that may be held in the UK. As major giving is not well developed in the UK there also tends to be limited support and advice available in the form of consultants or agencies.

Cultural and fiscal barriers

Differences between the USA and the UK in terms of tax incentives for individual giving and cultural behaviours are often cited as the main reason why major giving 'will not work' in the UK. The tax changes introduced by the UK government in 2000 have gone a long way towards invalidating the 'tax barrier' argument, as individuals can now give very tax-effectively both in terms of cash and especially in the donation of stocks and shares, effectively lowering the cost of donating. Higher rate tax givers can also now benefit as they can claim back some of the tax they have paid on donations.

There is no doubt that cultural differences are still a factor in the translation of US practice into UK fundraising. However, those UK fundraising non-profits that are now implementing major gift fundraising are finding that the similarities far outweigh the differences and that the US model may be used as an effective template in developing major giving in the UK individual donor marketplace. Where research and anecdotal evidence is available, it appears that the motivations involved in major gift giving are the same in the UK as in the USA. The demographics of major givers in the UK is also similar to their US counterparts, with the majority of givers being male.

The wealth profile of Britain has changed over the past twenty years, and there are now many more people who have attained great wealth. These newly rich individuals are making gifts, sometimes in millions or tens of millions. A new intermediate group of prospects who are not 'rich' but who have significantly greater means than the majority is also evident. Like the rich, this new affluent group can be targeted to give large sums if they are sufficiently motivated, which is most likely to be through major giving or planned giving approaches.

CHAPTER SUMMARY

In this chapter we have summarized the research that is currently available on how and why individuals make major gifts to charity, and what is known about the key motives behind the donation of large gifts.

We have also worked through the major gift fundraising process to see how donors are recruited and developed, and to look at some of the main tools and techniques that have been developed to help in this form of fundraising. It is clear that major gift fundraising requires a very different approach and that fundraisers engaging in this process are required to think and work in a way that contrasts dramatically with the practices and techniques used, for example, in direct mail fundraising.

Major donor fundraising is a key route in the USA, but is relatively new, though growing, in the UK. It will be fascinating to see whether UK fundraisers succeed in growing major giving in the UK environment, and to what extent cultural and fiscal differences affect UK major giving practices. As we have seen, the concept of stewardship is all-important as a theory and ethical underpinning in major gift fundraising in the USA. In the next chapter we will look again at this idea in relation to planned and legacy giving.

DISCUSSION QUESTIONS

1 In your role as head of fundraising at a medium sized UK charity, prepare a report for your CEO arguing the case for the introduction of major giving techniques to run alongside existing direct mail fundraising.

2 Draft a template to be used in the gathering of information about major giving prospects. What information would be most important?

3 Draft a gift range chart for a capital campaign where the target is $500,000 over three years.

4 Using your own organization as an example (or one that you know well), outline the concept of stewardship and how it fits with your current practice.

REFERENCES

Ballard, F. (1999) 'The Balance of and Difference Between Revenue and Capital Campaigns', Presentation at 'Fundraising for Museums, the Arts and Heritage', Henry Stewart Conferences, June.

Conway, D. (1997) 'Interview with Henry Rosso on Stewardship and Fundraising', *New Directions for Philanthropic Fundraising*, Autumn: 11–22.

Dean, J. (1996) 'The Key to Major Gifts: Cooperative Relationships', *Fund Raising Management*, April: 26.

Fredricks, L. (2001) *Developing Major Gifts*, Aspen Publications, New York.

Goettler, R.H. (1996) 'Announcing the "Four Ws" of Major Gift Solicitation', *Fund Raising Management*, April: 40.

Irwin-Wells, S. (2002) *Planning and Implementing Your Major Gifts Campaign*, Jossey-Bass, New York.

Jeavons, T.H. (1997) 'Stewards for Whom? Problems with Stewardship as a Model for Fundraising', *New Directions for Philanthropic Fundraising*, 17 (autumn): 35–42.

Kotler, P. and Andreasen, A. (1987) *Strategic Marketing for Nonprofit Organisations*, Prentice-Hall, Englewood Cliffs, NJ.

Kotler, P. and Scheff, J. (1997) *Standing Room Only: Strategies for Marketing the Performing Arts*, Harvard Business School Press, Boston, MA.

Lawson, R. (1998) 'Involving the Board in Major Giving', *Fund Raising Management*, July: 18.

Marland, J. (1999) 'Developing Major Gift and Membership Programmes for the British Museum', Presentation at 'Fundraising for Museums, the Arts and Heritage' Henry Stewart Conferences, June.

Matheny, R.E. (1994) *Major Gift Solicitation Strategies*, Council for the Advance and Support of Education, Washington DC.

Maude, M. (1997) 'Catapult Your Development Efforts With an Advisory Council', *Fund Raising Management*, May: 24.

Odendahl, T. (1990) *Charity Begins at Home: Generosity and Self-Interest Among the Philanthropic Elite*, Basic Books, New York.

Ostrander, S. A. and Schervish, P G. (1990) 'Giving and Getting: Philanthropy as a Social Relation', in J. Van Til (ed.), *Critical Issues in American Philanthropy: Strengthening Theory and Practice*, Jossey Bass.

Prince, R.A and File, K.M (1994) 'The Seven Faces of Philanthropy: A New Approach to Cultivating Major Donors' Jossey-Bass, New York.

Reuther, V. (1998) 'Debunking the Myth of Bill Gates; Finding Major Donors', *Nonprofit World*, March/April: 46.

Schervish, P.G. (1993) 'Philanthropy as a Moral Identity of Caritas', in P.G. Schervish *et al.*, *Taking Giving Seriously*, Indiana University Center on Philanthropy.

Schervish, P.G. (1997) 'Inclination, Obligation and Association: What We Know and What We Need to Learn about Donor Motivation', in D.F. Burlingame (ed.), *Critical issues in Fund Raising*, John Wiley, New York.

Schervish, P.G. and Havens, J.J. (1995) 'Wherewithal and Beneficence: Charitable Giving by Income and Wealth', *New Directions for Philanthropic Fundraising*, 8 (summer): 67–82.

Seiler, T. (2000) *Developing Leadership for Major Gifts, The Fund Raising School*, Indiana University Center on Philanthropy, IN.

Smith, G.T. (1997) 'CEOs and Trustees: The Key Forces in Securing Major Gifts', in *Developing Major Gifts, New Directions for Philanthropic Fundraising*, Indiana University Center on Philanthropy, IN/Jossey-Bass, New York, pp. 123–128.

Sturtevant, W. T. (1996) 'The Artful Journey: Seeking the Major Gift', *Fund Raising Management*, April: 32.

Tempel, E. (2001) 'The Ethics of Major Giving', in *Developing Leadership for Major Gifts, The Fund Raising School*, Indiana University Center on Philanthropy, IN.

Williams, M.J. (1991) *Big Gifts*, Fund Raising Institute, The Taft Group.

Wood, E.W. (1997) '*The Four Rs of Major Gift Fundraising*', *Developing Major Gifts, New Directions for Philanthropic Fundraising*, Indiana University Center on Philanthropy, IN/Jossey-Bass, New York.

Chapter 9

Planned and legacy giving

LEARNING OBJECTIVES

By the end of this chapter you should be able to:

- Define planned giving and explain how it works in the USA.
- Outline the major planned giving vehicles currently used.
- Discuss the opportunities and barriers surrounding the possible extension of planned giving techniques into the UK donor marketplace.
- Discuss the importance of legacy or bequest gifts.
- Understand how legacy giving is currently promoted.
- Explain the likely challenges facing legacy fundraisers in the future.

INTRODUCTION

In the USA, gifts made by private individuals to 501(c)(3) organizations qualify for a tax deduction, the benefit accruing to the donor under the current tax legislation. In addition to this fundamental principle there are a number of tailored opportunities to give large 'planned' gifts through mechanisms that offer the donor a number of specific options and various degrees of control over his or her capital.

While still distinctive from the US fiscal system, the changes made to the tax system in 2000 in the UK have created a structure within which fundraisers (and financial institutions) now likewise have the chance to develop new, financially driven fundraising products designed to benefit both charity and donor. In this chapter we will explain how planned giving works in the USA, and discuss the possibility of the introduction of this form of giving to the UK.

The giving of bequests is an important part of planned giving in the USA, accounting for 7.7 per cent of total giving ($16.33 billion) in 2001. In the UK, legacy giving is a key income stream, with legacy income accounting for 28 per cent of the total voluntary income of the top 500 UK charities in 1999/2000 (Pharoah 2002). In this chapter we will examine what strategies are used in the promotion of legacy giving on both sides of the Atlantic and how demographic and cultural developments are likely to impact on this income stream in the future.

PLANNED GIVING IN THE USA

Planned giving: a definition

Also referred to as deferred giving, organized giving or charitable gift planning, planned giving is a process by which gifts are encouraged and produced where:

- The gift is legally provided for in the lifetime of the donor.
- The recipient organization has an interest in the gift, but full benefit is usually deferred until a point in the future (often the death of the donor). This date is specified in a legal agreement between the organization and the donor.
- The donor may receive tax benefits as a result of his or her gift provision.

Planned giving is thus a structured approach to planning a donor's long-term support of a non-profit involving the fundraiser in a detailed consideration of the financial affairs and aspirations of the donor, with the goal of offering a tax-efficient financial product that will meet the needs of the organization and donor alike. The sums of money and hence the size of the gift involved are often very large and the decision of which particular 'product' to invest in is inherently complex. Both the donor's cash and other assets may be involved. In taking such decisions donors will want to ensure that they and their families will be financially secure in their life-time and that on death the needs of any friends/family will also be adequately taken care of. Equally, in considering offering a planned gift, the donor is signalling that he or she has a passionate interest in the cause and cares deeply about the work that the non-profit is under-taking. Donors will thus be looking to manage their financial affairs in a way that can provide the maximum possible benefit to the non-profit too.

In attempting to reconcile these potentially conflicting needs, there is the additional consid-eration of tax. As we shall see below, there are a plethora of financial products that donors can invest in to both manage their finances and support good causes simultaneously. Each works in a slightly different way and offers different tax advantages to the donor, in essence lowering the cost of making a particular gift. Ensuring that donors optimize their position in respect of tax deductibility is therefore key and requires the input of skilled financial professionals. Indeed, the whole process of negotiating an appropriate planned gift is technical and complex, and both financial and legal professionals are required to input to the process.

The role of the fundraiser in all of this is to find prospective donors, interest them in the cause, involve them in the work of the organization and ultimately to ask for the gift. They may then facilitate the process that ensues and liaise with the legal/financial professionals to ensure that the donor's needs are met, but they would usually not be involved in offering finan-cial advice to donors.

History and growth

Tax policy in the USA has long been used to encourage giving to non-profit organizations. Personal contributions to non-profits became tax-deductible in the USA in 1917, shortly after the Federal Income Tax was established. The concept of life income gifts was established in 1927 with the formation of the Committee on Gift Annuities (renamed in 1994 the American Council on Gift Annuities). The Tax Reform Act of 1969 further encouraged planned giving as it created tax incentives for donors and spelt out the ways in which income trusts could be established so as to qualify for tax deductions (Fink and Metzler 1982, Harris 1999, White 1995).

Planned giving as a fundraising discipline began with the receipt and solicitation of bequests or legacies, which are both the simplest forms of planned giving, and also the basis of many of the other vehicles.

Initially, only the largest and most sophisticated fundraising non-profits promoted planned giving, and these were likely to allocate only a single staff member, or a proportion of a staff member's time to planned giving work. In recent years the popularity and importance of planned giving has increased enormously, and even small charities are now investing time and effort in this area of fundraising (Ashton 1991, Tueller 1994, White 1995). Meanwhile the larger charities have increased staff numbers and allocated more resources. A planned giving 'industry' now exists, with support networks, training opportunities, consultancy services and software available. The primary national association linking planned giving officers and allied professionals (the National Committee on Planned Giving) currently represents some 11,000 planned giving professionals across the USA.

As noted above, planned giving has always involved financial and legal professionals. In the past five years the financial community has woken up to the opportunities presented by charitable planned giving vehicles for their own industry, and has begun to actively promote planned giving products as tax shelters. This has changed the picture enormously.

Planned giving is a highly technical form of fundraising, and staff involved in planned giving require extensive training and continued study. However, they are not required to become experts in the intricacies of tax issues, financial products and the law. The role of the fundraiser is that of a knowledgeable facilitator/steward and motivator working with the donor, the non-profit and financial and legal professionals (both retained by the non-profit and/or the donor) to achieve the gift in the most advantageous form for both the donor and the recipient charity. Having said this, it appears that most planned giving directors in the USA are financial or legal professionals, with previous experience in the legal or financial field rather than in fundraising.

Planned giving is typically a fairly low-profile part of US fundraising, relying as it does on long-term development and a permanent presence. This category of gift cannot be solicited overnight! The nature of planned giving is thus that it works to projections rather than to rigidly enforced income goals. It is impossible to budget income with any precision – the process is characterized by patient long-term development and investment. Like major gift solicitation, planned giving is research-intensive and very time-consuming – desk research and face-to-face visits are used to gather data on the family circumstances, financial background and philanthropic ambitions of prospects.

From the point of view of the non-profit, planned giving can provide long-term finance and stability for the future. It is likely to be an area of fundraising with a very low cost/benefit ratio once an effective and professional programme is established. It is also a high-risk activity in some ways, as any mistakes are likely to be very costly and could potentially even involve the non-profit in litigation if bad advice or faulty administration can be proved.

The marketing of planned giving

Planned giving opportunities are marketed to existing donors and to other prospects primarily through face-to-face contact. Advertising is used to a limited extent, with creative executions commonly focusing on the financial advantages of a planned gift for the donor (see Plate 9.1). When looking at the solicitation of comparatively lower value gifts, direct mail and/or the telephone may be used in the initial stages to introduce a prospect to the concept of planned giving, and to set up appointments for face-to-face contact. Detailed literature can then be 'left behind' at the face-to-face meetings for the prospective donor to study at leisure after a visit. The contact can then be cultivated until the donor is willing to offer a gift.

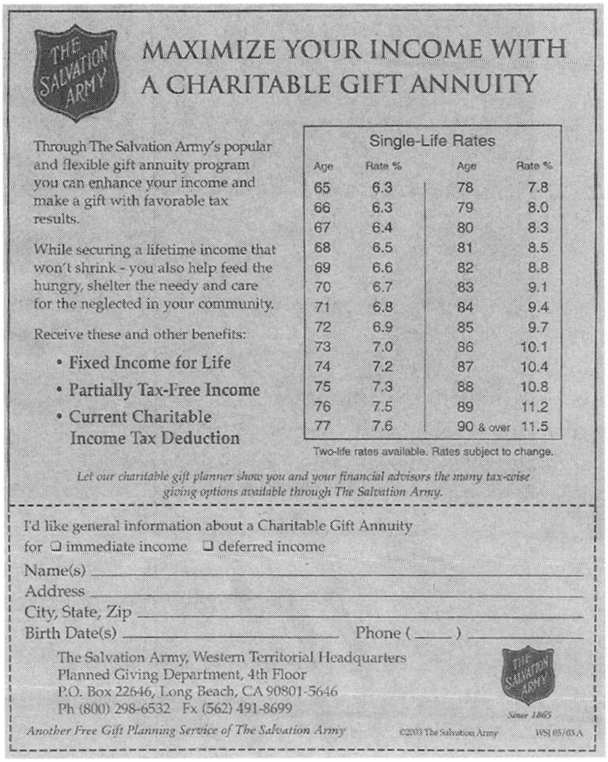

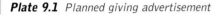

Plate 9.1 *Planned giving advertisement*
Source: © The Salvation Army. Reproduced with kind permission

Where larger gifts are concerned it is likely that the prospects will have come to the attention of the fundraiser by virtue of their contact with the cause, perhaps through one of its volunteers, employees or the board. They may also be individuals known to have an association with the cause and/or pertinent links demonstrating that some form of interest might exist.

In soliciting planned gifts the initial stages of research and cultivation are thus identical to those used in major gift work, discussed in Chapter 8. However, in planned giving, the process has to incorporate an element of education with reference to the financial products available to the giver. This is likely to happen in a face-to-face charitable financial planning interview, where the planned giving fundraiser/volunteer may be joined by the donor's financial adviser. When the time is judged to be right, the solicitation is made, often in the presence of a financial adviser. If a gift is made the last stage is a process of thanks and recognition, which is likely to be high level and perpetual, as a planned giving donor has in essence made a large investment in his or her chosen non-profit.

Planned giving fundraisers also promote their work to the financial/legal professional adviser community. This is undertaken through direct mail, advertising, via the setting up of committees and volunteer networks, and through the provision of seminars and events. It is assumed that many financial professionals themselves require training in the detail of some of the specialist products available.

Donor motivation

The bulk of the literature and support available to planned giving fundraisers concentrates on the technical aspects of that area of fundraising. Many texts point out that the 'human dynamic' is often missing – it seems that comparatively little is known about why donors choose to give in this way, and about the quality of the emotional commitment involved (Ashton 1991, White 1995).

However, it is generally recognized that donors may be attracted to planned giving because:

- There is a tax incentive. Planned giving vehicles are structured to be advantageous to the donor in terms of leveraging maximum tax deductions.
- They view it as pure philanthropy.
- It offers them a mechanism to express gratitude to the non-profit, perhaps because they or a family member have benefited from the work undertaken.
- Donors may be able to make a larger gift eventually than would be possible for them if they were to give an immediate and outright gift.
- It offers recognition/social standing – a large gift may be used to create a permanent memorial to the donor or to someone chosen by the donor.
- Gifts can be made where income is retained, providing secure income for donors and/or beneficiaries.
- Non-profits may be seen as providing free financial/estate planning/investment advice, and may manage assets at little or no cost to the donor.

The issue of whether tax avoidance is a motive is presently engendering some debate. While it is universally recognized that it is a key attraction, several surveys of planned givers, and of the largest givers in the USA, point to the fact that philanthropic intent, and the person who is asking, are far more important (Harris 1999). It should be remembered that, while conferring some tax advantages, planned gifts will never cheat the taxman totally or save the donor money – without making the gift the donor will always have more money in his or her pocket or estate. Tax considerations are likely to affect the timing and size of a gift even though they may not be the main prompt for the donation itself.

The issue of recognition as a motive is also somewhat clouded. While many donors undoubtedly use a planned gift to provide a memorial, and actively seek public recognition and reward, the literature also cites anonymity and control as reasons for considering some forms of planned gift. Planned gifts can be confidential, and certain types of gifts can be established and controlled by donors and their professional advisers up to the point of donation.

One of the reasons cited for the current growth in the appeal of planned giving is that many of the features of the donation mechanisms mesh well with the needs of a growing section of the US donor base. Planned giving vehicles are flexible; they allow donors to be creative in the way they choose to give. It tends to be a businesslike form of fundraising, involving a business relationship with the beneficiary non-profit. Wealthy people in particular tend to be comfortable and familiar with the notions of long-term capital investment and endowment – it is what they do with their own money. They may correspondingly be unhappy with the idea of outright cash gifts and with one-off donations being used for running costs. A section of US donors are increasingly referred to as 'sophisticated'; such donors are likely to require that planned giving options be made available to them as part of a portfolio of donation routes.

Future prospects for planned giving

The current and future prospects for planned giving in the USA appear very positive, with reasons for optimism cited as:

- *Availability of prospects* – planned givers tend to be older people. All demographic forecasting points to a huge increase in the numbers of 'seniors' in the US population. Younger audiences, especially the much discussed 'new breed' of wealthy young entrepreneurs, are likely to be as comfortable or more comfortable with notions of long-term investment and tax-effective large gifts than with annual fund support. There is a growing 'investor class' in the USA (Gray 1999) with almost 50 per cent of Americans owning stock. These people are likely to be at home with, and understand, the principles behind planned giving investments.
- *Increased wealth* – there are record numbers of wealthy people in the USA. Future decades will see a vast amount of wealth transferred between the generations.
- *Increased awareness* – planned giving is no longer the province of a small number of large non-profits. Most charities now have planned giving programmes, and many run co-operative ventures and generic educational promotions such as 'Leave a legacy' campaigns. The financial services sector has also started to promote and market charitable planned giving vehicles aggressively.
- *More planners* – as more non-profits initiate planned giving programmes the number of planned giving officer vacancies has grown sharply, as have the support and training resources available to them. Planned giving vacancies are drawing planners from other fundraising roles, and the number of professional advisers involved who are knowledgeable in gift planning is also growing (Schoenhals 1999).

The forecast growth in planned giving also presents potential problems for the sector. There is already vastly increased competition among non-profits for planned gifts, and this is likely to increase. Donors may find themselves bombarded with solicitations. Non-profits may react to this by increasing co-operation and joint ventures in the promotion of planned giving options.

The growth in competition in the for-profit financial sector is also increasing rapidly, and it is perceived that this carries with it a huge potential threat to the planned giving sector in undermining the integrity, tactfulness and philanthropic focus of planned giving solicitations. A survey of 700 financial planners carried out in 1999 found that 44 per cent were planning to emphasize charitable strategies. The market researcher who carried out the research concluded that: 'This market is going to explode, and financial advisors are going to drive it more than the nonprofits' (Novack and Saunders 1999: 180–188).

Forbes magazine recently ran a feature warning prospective donors about high commission rates paid to brokers in setting up planned giving arrangements. An advertisement in a broker's magazine is quoted as noting: 'Generosity has never been so profitable. With the American Gift Fund, not only do your clients do good; you, their advisor, will do very well' (*Forbes*, 2nd October 2000: 196–198).

Within the non-profit sector, the ethics of planned giving are well considered and regulated, with the National Committee on Planned Giving operating a code which requires full disclosure on the role (and compensation) of all parties involved in the planning process. There are signs, however, that with charitable planned giving entering the less genteel world of financial services, the achievement of ethical standards is likely to require more stringent policing:

183

Congress has always allowed generous tax breaks to encourage giving. But once upon a time, strategies were tailored to fit a wealthy donor's individual needs, usually by lawyers or by a charity's planned giving specialist. Now they are being packaged and sold like TV dinners. And where once charitable plans were primarily about giving, they are now being promoted as tax shelters and investment products – by insurance salesmen, stockbrokers, financial planners, lawyers and accountants.

(Novack and Saunders 1999: 180–188)

Increased scrutiny and regulation appears unavoidable, as non-profit boards and finance departments seek to avoid litigation and donors require clear reporting on the employment of their assets. State and Federal oversight is predicted to increase in order to curb abuses both in the non-profit and for-profit sectors.

Finally, increased initiative on the part of financial advisers is also likely to lead to an increasing number of instances where a planned gift is made without any involvement on the part of the non-profit beneficiary. Some law firms and trust companies are reported (Schoenhals 1999) to be creating their own gift planning officers, tasked with investigating potential charity recipients and presenting gift illustrations and proposals. If this proves to be the case, the non-profit sector is likely to be hard pressed to maintain the centrality of its philanthropic mission in planned giving.

PLANNED GIVING VEHICLES

The most common forms of planned giving vehicle are outlined below:

Wills

The most common form of planned giving involves the donor in leaving a charitable bequest or legacy in their Will. This is relatively easy to originate and administer for both the donor and the beneficiary. A bequest is revocable (i.e. donors can change their minds by amending

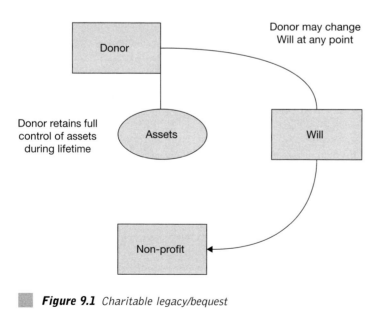

Figure 9.1 Charitable legacy/bequest

their Will), with the donor retaining complete control until death. If donors' estates are of taxable size, the estate may also deduct the amount of the bequest as a charitable donation.

As a legacy is revocable, no part of the income from a legacy gift is accessible to the non-profit before the death of the donor and the amount of legacy income is very unpredictable, bequests are often viewed by planned giving professionals as 'gifts of last resort' (Tueller 1994).

Charitable gift annuity

A charitable gift annuity is a contractual relationship between the donor and the charity. The donor agrees to donate a cash gift (or other asset) to the charity, which the charity invests. The charity then agrees to pay a life income to the donor (and/or to another named beneficiary). This annual income amount is fixed and cannot be changed.

When all the income beneficiaries have died, the charity receives the remainder of the donation. The payment to the donor is regulated and payment rates fixed by a national organization, the American Council on Gift Annuities, which calculates the amount payable based on the amount invested and the age of the donor.

For the donor, a gift annuity provides a secure, guaranteed and predictable income for life. A portion of the annual payment to the donor is tax exempt, and the donor can claim a charitable deduction against income tax. The donor may avoid capital gains tax, and as the assets have been transferred they would also avoid estate tax on the death of the donor.

Gift annuities involve the loss of control by the donor of the gifted assets entirely (this disadvantage applies to all irrevocable gifts).

Deferred payment gift annuity

A deferred payment gift annuity is the same as the charitable gift annuity, except that the payments to the donor are deferred, typically until retirement age (i.e. facilitating the use of the annuity as a retirement income plan). This arrangement can be of benefit to donors who do not require additional income at the time of the commitment – they can make the gift now and receive immediate income tax deductions while in a high tax bracket. Because payments are deferred, the payments will be higher when they come through (rates, again, are set by the American Council on Gift Annuities).

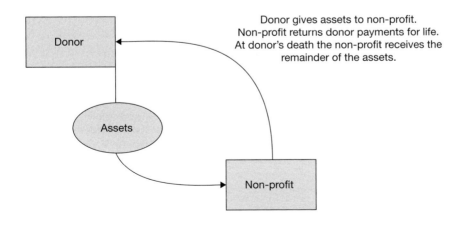

Figure 9.2 Charitable gift annuity

Pooled income fund

A pooled income fund is a trust (sometimes also called a charitable mutual fund). Multiple donors contribute assets to (i.e. buy shares in) the pooled fund of a specific charity. The assets are invested by fund managers (normally a financial institution is retained by the charity to manage the fund and organize the payments) and the resulting earnings are divided among the donors. The arrangement is irrevocable – donors cannot withdraw their assets from the fund.

The donor (and/or other beneficiaries stipulated by the donor) receives an annual payment for life, but this income will vary from year to year according to the performance of the fund. All earnings made are paid out each year, with beneficiaries' income calculated in proportion to their investment.

When a beneficiary dies, the shares are separated from the fund and delivered to the charity, or held as part of the fund with further annual payments going to the charity.

While no portion of the income from a pooled income fund is tax free, donors usually qualify for immediate income tax deductions for the present value of the amounts they give that the charity will receive eventually (the 'remainder interest').

By giving assets to a fund, the donor is reducing the value of his or her estate, thereby reducing estate tax and probate costs payable. The gifted assets can be sold by the fund without the requirement to pay capital gains tax on the sales.

As the fund is set up and administered by the non-profit and its retained financial institution, investing in a pooled income fund is a simple operation for the donor and probably requires no professional advice.

Pooled income funds are designed to enable relatively small donations to be contributed effectively – often minimum gift amounts are set for other planned giving vehicles.

Charitable remainder unitrust (CRUT)

The charitable remainder unitrust is the most versatile of the planned giving instruments. It has to meet strict Internal Revenue Code requirements in order to be tax exempt and achieve

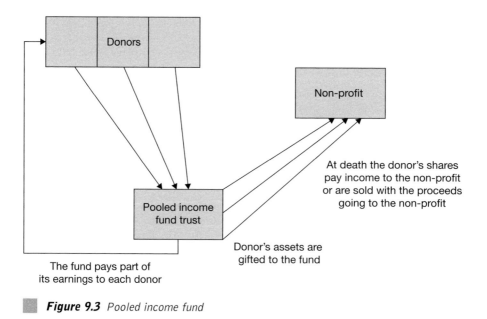

Figure 9.3 *Pooled income fund*

a charitable deduction. The charitable remainder unitrust is a stand-alone entity, an irrevocable trust that, once set up, cannot be changed by its donor or beneficiaries. The CRUT is established via a multiple agreement between the donor, the recipient charity and a third party, usually the donor's lawyer or bank.

The donor transfers assets to the trust. The use of this principal by the charity is deferred. The unitrust must make annual payments, equal to a fixed percentage (at least 5 per cent and not more than 50 per cent) of the trust's value each year, to one or more beneficiaries. The beneficiaries are usually the donors of the trust, or specified family members, or both. Charitable remainder unitrusts must last for as long as the beneficiaries live or for a set period of time (not more than twenty years).

A CRUT can take any one of three forms:

1 *Standard*: it must make annual payments of a fixed percentage of the trust's annual value, whether or not earnings from the trust's assets are sufficient to make the payments. If the earnings are insufficient, the difference would have to come from the trust's principal.
2 *Net income*: it must make annual payments of a fixed percentage of the trust's annual value, but never more than the amount earned by the trust in any given year.
3 *Net income with make-up provisions*: it must make annual payments as above, with an added provision: that in years when the trust's earnings exceed the percentage that must be paid, the excess earnings must be used to make up for any payments less than the fixed percentage in earlier years.

Donors can claim an income tax reduction for the present value of the assets they place in the trust. Assets placed in the trust are removed from the estate of the donor and hence avoid estate tax and probate costs. CRUTs can operate without incurring capital gains tax.

Charitable remainder unitrusts can be set up by donors in any of the three versions listed above, enabling them to invest many different types of assets. A CRUT established to pay net income with make-up provisions can effectively be set up as a retirement plan.

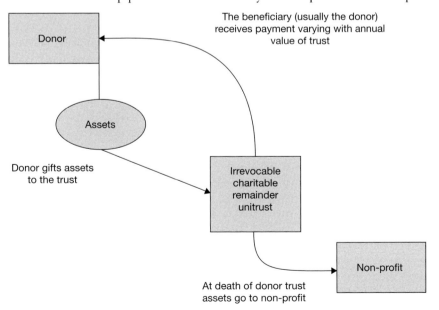

Figure 9.4 *Charitable remainder unitrust (CRUT)*

Donors can, if they choose, manage the trust themselves and retain complete control of investment decisions, and can establish trusts without involving non-profit beneficiaries – they do not even have to name the charity beneficiaries until the trust is about to terminate. Additional contributions may be made after the CRUT is established.

Charitable remainder annuity trusts

The charitable remainder annuity trust is the same as a charitable remainder unitrust, with the following exceptions:

- an annuity trust may take only one form;
- it must make annual payments, regardless of the trust's earnings in any given year;
- it must pay a fixed amount annually that is established at the inception of the trust and never varies;
- additional contributions cannot be accepted.

From the donor's perspective, a charitable remainder annuity trust carries the same advantages as a charitable remainder unitrust. In addition, as annual payments are fixed, they will receive a predictable income stream. The disadvantage of this vehicle for the donor is that, if necessary, the principal has to be used to meet the annual payment, so the principal may be eroded over time. If the trust should eventually lose all its assets the donor would receive nothing. In addition, the annual payment will not rise with inflation. A remainder annuity trust is a less flexible giving vehicle than the charitable remainder unitrust, facilitating the investment of a smaller range of asset types.

Charitable lead trusts

A charitable lead trust is, in essence, the opposite of a charitable remainder trust – whereby the annual payments of the trust (the 'lead' interest) are received by the charity, and the remainders (the assets) are received by the donor.

The payments of charitable lead trusts may be either unitrust payments or annuity payments. The donor makes an annual trust payment to the charity for a period of time specified by the

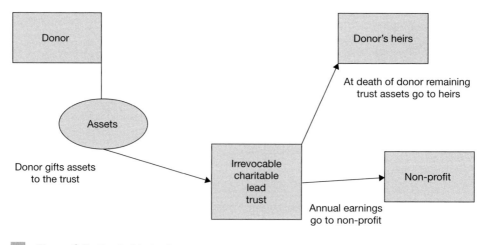

Figure 9.5 *Charitable lead trust*

donor. At the end of that period the assets return to the donor, or to another beneficiary named by the donor. The annual distributions to the charity are immediately tax deductible for the donor. The donor can stipulate the amount that the trust pays to the non-profit beneficiary – the trust must pay a fixed percentage of the annual value or a fixed amount.

Donors who wish to pass assets to heirs with reduced tax liabilities – for example, gift, estate and generation-skipping transfer taxes – commonly use a charitable lead trust. Donors can retain control of the trust – they can themselves be the trustee and can thereby administer and invest the assets they place in the trust themselves. Donors also have some flexibility in terms of the form that the trust takes (much like charitable remainder trusts).

The charitable lead trust feeds income to the beneficiary charity within a year of establishment – so donors can see the non-profit using their gift immediately.

Retained life interest/life estate gifts

A donor may transfer a property to a charity in return for a retained life estate contract, stipulating that the donor (or another named beneficiary) should remain in residence for life. This vehicle is similar to a charitable gift annuity in many ways, the income benefit being the right to enjoy the property for life (rather than the receipt of an annual payment). This giving vehicle may be referred to as a 'retained life interest', 'life estate', 'remainder estate' or 'remainder interest' gift.

Once the donor or other people named have died, the charity gains total control of the property. Such contributions are referred to as 'remainder' gifts because the non-profit gets the rights to the property that remains after the lifetime rights of the donors/other beneficiaries have expired. Life estate gifts can be made of any type of property, but a tax deduction may be claimed only if the property is a 'personal residence'. If this is the case, donors qualify for an immediate income tax deduction to the value of the charitable remainder interest. The donor's estate will be reduced by the gift, reducing estate tax and probate costs. The gift is irrevocable. This type of gift is relatively simple to set up and involves little in legal or advice costs.

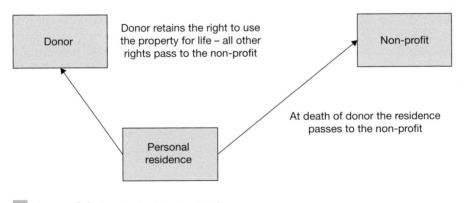

Figure 9.6 *Retained life interest gift*

Life insurance gifts

Life insurance policies can be contributed to a charity as a planned gift. Making the gift is a very simple process, essentially involving only one action: the naming of the non-profit as a beneficiary. The gift may be for part or all of the proceeds of the policy. Beneficiaries of

189

a life insurance policy can be primary (the first ones to receive benefits) or contingent or secondary (receiving benefits only if one or all primary beneficiaries cannot receive them; for example, if they have died).

A donor can also transfer ownership of the policy to the non-profit, in which case the gift becomes irrevocable. The non-profit must be the owner and beneficiary of a policy for the donor to be entitled to receive an income tax deduction against the gift.

When ownership of an existing paid policy is gifted, the donor can claim a tax deduction equal to the cash value of the policy. If the policy is an existing policy with premiums to be paid, the premiums are considered a deductible charitable gift. To obtain maximum tax benefit the donor should make the annual premium payment to the charity, which then makes the payment to the insurer.

The same arrangement may be used for the donation of retirement plan proceeds, though ownership of such plans cannot be gifted; donors can only make non-profits beneficiaries of their plan.

Trust savings account

An account held at a bank, credit union or savings and loan company may be held in the name of a depositor 'in trust for' someone else – a person or organization other than the depositor. This can be a non-profit. The beneficiary has no ownership or control of the account; the depositor has full ownership and control. The beneficiary receives the money in the account either when the depositor dies or when the depositor turns over the passbook.

Simple to set up and administer, requiring no professional advice, this sort of gift is completely revocable. Trust savings accounts are not subject to probate and, if the donor's estate is large enough to be taxable, the estate may deduct the amount of the account as a charitable deduction if the beneficiary is a charity.

Bargain sale

A bargain sale is just what its name implies: the sale of something for less than it is worth; for example, a donor may be willing to sell stocks or bonds to a non-profit for less than their real worth.

The amount that the non-profit pays is termed the 'sale' and the difference between the sale and the true purchase price is the 'bargain'. Donors may claim the bargain portion of their gift as a charitable deduction. Donors may reduce the value of their estate by the bargain portion of the gift. This type of gift can become complex depending on the amounts and types of assets being sold, how the non-profit pays the donor, and if the donor wishes to impose restrictions of any sort on the gift. In certain circumstances donors will incur income tax because of the sale (e.g. if the assets have appreciated they will be liable for a portion of the capital gains tax).

OPPORTUNITIES FOR PLANNED GIVING IN THE UK

Changes to the tax system

In 1999 the British government announced a campaign to engender a 'New Giving Age' (Brown 1999). This establishment of tax incentives to support the further development of giving builds upon a decade of cross-party governmental support for UK charity fundraising unprecedented elsewhere in history (Morgan 2000).

The primary changes to the tax regime were announced in the Budget Statement of March 2000. A new class of tax relief for the gift of certain shares and securities to charity was created and the Gift Aid scheme was extended. This scheme allows registered charities to reclaim the tax that would have been paid by donors on the income they gift to charity. In the case of lower rate taxpayers, the charity may claim back the lower rate tax that would have been paid on the gift and in the case of higher rate taxpayers the donor claims the balance between the higher and lower rates of tax paid on the gift.

As an example, consider the case of a higher rate taxpayer paying tax at the rate of 40 per cent and offering a gift to charity of £100. The charity may claim back £22 from the exchequer as the basic rate of tax (currently 22 per cent) that would have been paid by the donor on this sum. The donor may claim back a further £18 from the exchequer given that he or she would have been paying 40 per cent tax on the total donated (i.e. 40 − 22 = 18).

This change to Gift Aid now makes the UK taxation system resemble, at least for higher rate taxpayers, the system in the USA where the full value of charitable donations is tax deductible. The notion of a tangible tax advantage accruing from giving is thus very real and will genuinely lower the cost of giving from the perspective of many UK taxpayers.

These changes may also have the impact of making many of the planned giving products described above attractive to the UK market. To date there have been few attempts to stimulate planned giving in the UK and, as we suggest below, if a number of cultural and structural barriers may now be overcome, it could prove to be a significant growth area over the next five to ten years.

Product/marketing issues

There is a marked lack of product designed to promote philanthropic investment specifically to enable consumers to benefit particular charitable organizations in the UK. In addition, there appears to be a shortage of readily available specialist advice from the financial services sector targeted specifically towards individual investment for philanthropic purposes (Pharoah 1997).

Various schemes were introduced in the 1990s. However, as Worthington (1997: 4) points out:

> these attempts have almost always failed because insufficient attention has been paid to the product offered to ensure that all parties win. Usually it is an attempt to promote standard products to the charity supporter in exchange for a token contribution to the charity.

The few planned giving products that have been launched in the UK have not been marketed to prospective donors in a concerted manner. The charities concerned often formed an effective barrier to marketing activity, proving unwilling to open access to their databases, while the financial companies had insufficient confidence in the products to market direct to potential consumers. It is not clear therefore that if marketed differently, these products would not have been successful.

Ironically a plethora of ethical investment products are available, targeted at consumers in accord with general philanthropic intent. Evidence of such products covering pension planning, mortgages, Individual Savings Accounts, unit trusts and general personal banking may be found throughout the UK marketplace. However, few of these schemes directly promote philanthropic support to particular charitable organizations.

191

US/UK issues

Some of the differences between US and UK fundraising organizations in terms of practice and in organizational culture are relevant to discussions of the feasibility of introducing planned giving techniques to a UK or indeed any other setting. These include the following.

Board involvement

All the available texts underline the importance of board-level support in introducing and running a successful planned giving programme. As with major giving fundraising discussed earlier, board members are required to actively endorse and promote planned giving as a long-term investment for the non-profit, and are expected to take part themselves by making a 'leadership gift' and suggesting the names of prospects from among their own acquaintances and peers. Volunteers from board or committee level also constitute the main 'salesforce' in planned giving solicitation, going out 'on the road' to solicit planned gifts from prospects.

In the UK, charity trustees are seldom involved directly in fundraising, and very rarely to the extent that they take on prospect identification and solicitation themselves.

Departmental structures

In the USA, problems are reported in terms of different fundraising departments competing for access to the same donors. Generally the Annual Fund is the main means of short-term income generation, working through the solicitation of one-off gifts via the telephone and/or direct mail. Capital campaigns seek one-off large gifts and are run through fundraising volunteer committee structures, using events and reward schemes to reach a timetabled goal. Both these areas of fundraising target donors who may also be good prospects for planned giving. In the UK similar issues of donor 'ownership' would be likely to arise, and would perhaps be aggravated by the 'mass' contact strategy employed in most UK fundraising.

The US literature also alludes to some problems regarding the nature of the staff and systems employed in planned giving as opposed to the 'mainstream' fundraising staff. Planned giving staff are often ex-financial advisers or legally trained. Planned giving requires the recording of complex investment and legal data. Planned giving staff and processes may therefore appear to be concerned primarily or exclusively with financial/legal requirements rather than with mission-focused fundraising.

This issue already arises in many UK charities in the separation of the legacy marketing function from other fundraising sections, and in a corresponding lack of communication and data integration which is often to the detriment of the donor communication programme.

Stewardship

'Stewardship is the most important practice in the development process' (Sprinkel-Grace 1997). In the USA (as we saw in Chapter 8) stewardship is understood by fundraiser, donor and the personal financial services sector alike as integral to the fundraising process. It may be contended that this understanding lies at the heart of the success of US planned giving practice.

In the UK the majority of charities do not yet view themselves as being in the business of providing stewardship of their donors. The starting point for the donor, the charity and the financial services industry needs to be an explicit interest and concern for donors' ability to fulfil their moral or ethical needs in relation to the cause within the broader context of their financial well-being. The products that have been developed and targeted to customers in the UK thus far have not made this factor explicit either in product design or in the promotion to customers.

LEGACY GIVING

Background

Legacy or bequest gifts are an important source of income for non-profits on both sides of the Atlantic. In the UK legacies represent 28 per cent of voluntary income to the top 500 charities, and in some cases legacies account for 50 per cent or more of the voluntary income generated, with healthcare and animal charities benefiting in particular from this form of giving. Legacy income has continued to grow significantly for the larger UK fundraising charities in recent years.

In the USA, bequest income in 2001 represented 7.7 per cent of total contributions to non-profits. This represents a decline in bequest giving against the previous year, which is likely to be linked to fluctuations in the performance of the stock-market rather than being evidence of a general fall in popularity of the giving method. In the USA bequest giving is seen as part of planned giving, and may also lose popularity as demand for the other planned giving vehicles (that provide for the gift in the life of the donor) is stimulated.

In the UK, demographic movement means that legacy giving is about to enter a period of great change. The annual death rate in the UK has been relatively static for over 100 years at around 1 per cent of the population. This annual number of deaths is due to increase over the next forty years by 25 per cent or more due to the passing of the first 'baby boomer' generation. The number of people aged 65 plus will almost double. It is likely that the population will live longer, and that more people will need residential care.

This is also an era of rapid change in UK lifestyles and social values. Those generations holding 'traditional' values are passing, to be replaced by generations with very different approaches to consumerism, religious belief and civic society. The next generation to consider legacy giving will also feature large numbers of single households and will reflect an increasingly multi-ethnic and multicultural society.

Legacy fundraisers in the UK, under pressure to maintain or expand income from legacy giving, are evolving and developing strategies in response to actual and predicted changes in current and future audiences. Legacy communication routes have changed greatly over recent years, moving from low-profile communications to solicitors, through direct mail and press advertising to donors, to face-to-face legacy solicitation and events. The creative propositions, language and tone used in these communications have also altered radically over recent years in response to donor feedback, research and test results.

Demographic changes in the USA are likewise likely to have a tremendous impact on patterns and levels of bequest giving. Here an unprecedented transfer of wealth between generations is predicted which is universally cited as amounting to $10 trillion over fifty-five years, though this is said to be an underestimate by some commentators such as Schervish and Havens (2002), who predict that the wealth transfer will involve sums at least as large as $41 trillion ranging upwards to a possible $136 trillion over the period. Fundraisers are also acutely aware that changes in bequest giving are likely to arise as a result of the phasing out of the Estate Tax. President George W. Bush's legislation was passed in 2001. This raises the exemption to estate tax to $1 million and reduces the tax rate to 45 per cent by 2009, with an eventual repeal in 2010 but reinstatement thereafter. This has been claimed by both sides of the estate tax debate as a victory, and has left sector commentators unsure as to what the likely impact on charitable donations will be. The repeal of the tax is seen by some as likely to have a devastating negative impact on charitable giving, as tax avoidance is a key motivator in leaving charitable bequests. Others argue that the motivations behind bequest giving are more complex than this, that recent trends indicate wealth holders are increasingly likely to leave charitable bequests than to leave estates to family members, and that the underlying trends in bequest giving by the wealthy are likely to work against any short-term reduction in income.

Profiling legacy givers

Chang *et al.* (1999) analysed data from the 1992 US Gallup National Survey of National Giving and Volunteering to test some hypotheses on the importance of residence, tenure status, employment status and personal attributes in determining the likelihood of charitable bequests. These results are then used to develop a profile of the individuals likely to bequeath charitably. The donor model which results suggests that the individual most likely to leave a legacy bequest to a charity:

> has lived in the same residence for 2–9 years, is an unmarried, self-employed, non-Jewish white male, who believes strongly that charitable organizations are both needed and are unwasteful in funds; he also believes in a moral duty to help others and puts the goals of others before his.
>
> (Chang *et al.* 1999: 81)

Auten and Joulfaian (1996) used matched income tax records of older and wealthy parents and their children to analyse the effects of US bequest taxes and the children's income on the parents' lifetime charitable giving and on bequests upon death. Their results indicate that the higher the children's income, the more the parents donate to charity, and that a 1 per cent increase in the tax rate on taxable estates will reduce bequest donations by 2.5 per cent.

Other research has concentrated on bequest gifts to individuals rather than to charities. Laitner and Juster (1996) investigated the role of savings in household wealth accumulation and bequest decisions, finding that altruism towards one's children is not a major explanation of lifetime savings. Boskin (1976) hypothesized that the decision to bequeath was influenced by an individual's initial wealth, labour income, savings and the tax rules that affected the net cost of giving. Bequests have also been hypothesized to vary by state of residence, age, sex, marital status, number of dependents, form of bequest (i.e. cash versus fixed assets), non-charitable bequests and lifetime gift giving (Clotfelter 1985, McNees 1973).

Legacy fundraising

As noted earlier, in some non-profits, particularly in the USA, the solicitation of legacy gifts is a highly personal process and one typically administered by the planned giving department or fundraiser. For most non-profits, however, a significant amount of bequest funds may be raised from other sources, notably the general fundraising database and lists of other key stakeholders such as volunteers or service users. The volume of contacts here may be such that personal solicitation is not feasible or economic and where, as a consequence, the techniques of direct marketing may be more appropriate.

The gift of a legacy is generally seen as the peak of the giving pyramid in donor development, the theory being that a donor moves from initial low-value single gifts, through to repeat or committed gifts, on to gifts of an increased size, and, once committed to the aims of the charity and happy with the relationship, may pledge to leave that charity a gift in his or her Will. Legacy fundraisers therefore target committed donors from the base who have an established relationship with the charity. They may also target by age if the data is available, as individuals tend not to make a Will or to consider what their legacy gifts might be until they reach a certain lifestage.

Your passion for Art can inspire future generations...

...with a legacy to the Royal Academy

The RA receives no public funding, so the continuity and development of this exceptional institution is entirely in the hands of Friends like you who love the arts. A legacy will help us continue our unique contribution to cultural life which began over two hundred and thirty years ago. It will also help us maintain our high standards of creativity and excellence in all areas of our work, especially projects like these:

- Maintaining the quality and diversity of our exhibitions
- Supporting our education programme and students in the historic RA Schools
- Conserving and exhibiting the works in our Permanent Collections
- Preserving Burlington House and the Burlington Estate for the nation

Please contact us so that we may tell you more about how your legacy, large or small, can contribute to our plans for a creative future. We can offer advice on changing your will, inheritance tax and tell you how your gift will be remembered.

Please contact Sally Jones, Legacy Manager at the Royal Academy of Arts, FREEPOST 33 WD1057, Piccadilly, London W1E 6YZ or telephone her on 020 7300 5677 weekdays between 10am and 5pm.

Royal Academy Trust Charity number 1067270

Royal
Academy
of Arts

Plate 9.2 *Legacy appeal*

Source: © Royal Academy of Arts. Reproduced with kind permission

Direct mail has frequently been employed for the purposes of legacy fundraising. Donors are sent a personally addressed mail package that introduces the idea of legacy giving, explains the importance of legacies to the organization, talks about the importance of Will-making for the donor and provides information on how to go about leaving a legacy to the charity. Donors are then typically asked to send a response card or form to the charity to provide feedback on whether they have already made a legacy provision in favour of the organization, or will now do so. Within this outline, charities take many different creative approaches to asking for a legacy. An example is shown in Plate 9.2. If donors indicate that they have left a legacy to the charity, or plan to include one in their Will, they will be flagged on the charity database as legacy pledgers, and treated as a special group in terms of future communications, receiving, for example, special newsletters and Christmas cards.

In recent years, the tone of voice used in legacy communications to donors has changed greatly in response to research and feedback which has demonstrated that, while giving after death is of course a sensitive subject, donors are prepared in the main to take a rational and businesslike approach to the idea of Will-making, and think it entirely appropriate that a charity they support should approach them about this form of giving (Sargeant and Hilton 2003). As such the language used in legacy communications now mirrors the usual tone and style of the charity in question rather than, as had been the case formerly, tending to employ legalistic and flowery terminology. As legacies are such valuable gifts, legacy communications are often lavishly produced, with costly additional items such as Will advice booklets and videos.

The main barriers to Will-making (and therefore to the inclusion of a legacy to charity) in the UK have been found to be the cost of making a Will and the perceived complexity involved (Pidgeon 2001). Some charities have sought to combat these by offering free or reduced-price Will schemes in conjunction with solicitors (see Plate 9.3).

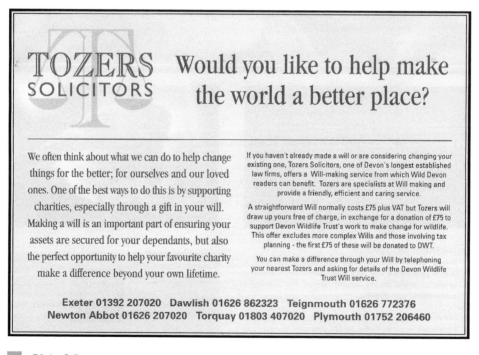

Plate 9.3 *Free Will offer*

Source: © Tozers Solicitors. Reproduced with kind permission

The promotion of legacies also tends to involve donor recognition schemes, which is an otherwise rare feature in UK fundraising practice. Incentive gifts such as pens, pins or prints are often offered in recognition of a legacy pledge, and on receipt of a legacy gift many charities offer the opportunity for the donor to be recognized (ultimately) through an entry in a Book of Remembrance, or, for larger gifts, a plaque, the planting of a tree or flower, or indeed the naming of a room or a building in the case of substantial legacies or 'in memoriam' gifts.

While direct mail is still the core of most legacy promotion strategies, an increasing number of UK charities are now also undertaking legacy fundraising through face-to-face solicitation. This is undertaken in much the same way as major gift solicitation in the USA, with legacy fundraisers or fundraising volunteers approaching donors in their own homes. This approach, while costly in terms of staff/volunteer time, enables charities to engage donors on a very personal level, and facilitates a dialogue during which many of the traditional barriers and concerns surrounding legacy giving can be addressed with sensitivity. Trained face-to-face legacy fundraisers also arrange group presentations to prospective legacy donors.

While the existing donor base tends to be the starting point for legacy promotion strategies, legacy giving is also promoted to other audiences, and through intermediaries. In some instances service users are an important source of legacy gifts to charity, and so are included in legacy solicitation planning. Some promotion is also undertaken to 'cold' audiences, mainly through two-stage press adverts which typically state the importance of Will-making and invite the reader to send in a coupon or call a telephone number to request a Will advice pack.

Charities also target solicitors who specialize in probate and estate planning through direct mail and through adverts in legal press titles. Solicitors are sent information on the charity and cause to encourage them to recommend the charity as deserving of support if clients ask for guidance, and to ensure that the correct charity registration details are to hand should the solicitor require these details in the making up of a Will.

Legacy marketing in the USA is handled much as in the UK, although US non-profits, better versed in 'Big gift' solicitation techniques, tend to use face-to-face contact more frequently, and have a greater range of resources available to them to support this approach. Often, as we have noted above, a legacy bequest is used as a starting point, with other planned gifts being suggested to donors after the bequest has been made. US bequest promotion tends not to involve high volumes of direct mail targeted at low-level direct mail givers, and thus bequests to US charities tend to be larger in size, but fewer in number than is the case in the UK.

Future challenges for legacy fundraisers

The legacy marketplace is set to change dramatically in the UK in the years to come. On one hand, the numbers of older people, and the numbers of individuals dying each year is set to rise dramatically. On the other, the generations reaching the age at which legacy gifts are traditionally made respond very differently to charity communications and have very different priorities and lifestyles. Legacy fundraisers will need to respond to these altered communication preferences and will need to reach and engage future potential legators in different ways if levels of legacy income are to be maintained or grown.

In the USA, the Estate Tax repeal and the forthcoming transfer of wealth between generations will pose huge challenges to bequest fundraisers as they track and respond to the likely changes in donor behaviour.

It would appear that, in legacy fundraising, the USA and UK would do well to exchange experiences. UK practitioners could learn a great deal from US experience in face-to-face legacy promotion, while their US counterparts might do well to test the direct mail approaches to lower value donors that have long been used in the UK in the solicitation of smaller bequest gifts.

197

CHAPTER SUMMARY

In this chapter we have provided some definitions of planned giving and have explained how this form of fundraising has developed in the USA. We have outlined the main giving vehicles employed by US fundraisers, and have looked at where planned giving fits in the US fundraising mix.

We have also reviewed the opportunities for the replication of this form of giving in the UK marketplace. As we have seen, recent fiscal changes have made this a real possibility, although some serious barriers remain to be tackled.

While UK charities are generally unfamiliar with planned giving techniques, the practice of legacy fundraising is well developed in the UK, where legacy income is a key fundraising stream. In this area it appears that a transatlantic exchange of ideas might be profitable, as US fundraisers are more experienced in face-to-face bequest promotion to major giving prospects, while their UK counterparts have successfully developed legacy marketing techniques delivered through direct mail and thus generate a large volume of smaller legacy gifts from less affluent sections of the donor base.

The value of legacies is closely tied to economic performance, fiscal change and the housing market. Legacy fundraisers thus need to be aware of changes in the external economic environment. They also need to be sensitive to the dramatic demographic shifts that are likely to impact on spending patterns and communication preferences in the decades to come.

DISCUSSION QUESTIONS

1   In your role as head of fundraising at a household name UK charity, prepare a presentation for your CEO explaining how planned giving works in the USA and why it would be worth further investigation in the case of your charity.

2   Prepare a draft argument to be used in face-to-face discussion with a major donor on what the advantages would be of a lifetime planned gift over the gift of a legacy.

3   Design a communication strategy for a group of donors who have recently pledged to leave a legacy gift to your organization. What sort of communications would you send them? How often would you contact them?

REFERENCES

Ashton, D. (1991) *The Complete Guide to Planned Giving: Everything You Need to Know to Compete Successfully for Major Gifts*, JLA Publications, MA.

Auten, G. and Joulfaian, D. (1996) 'Charitable Contributions and Intergenerational Transfers', *Journal of Public Economics*, 59 (January): 55–68.

Boskin, M.J. (1976) 'Estate Taxation and Charitable Bequests', *Journal of Public Economics*, 5: 27–56.

Brown, G. (1999) Pre-Budget Statement, House of Commons 9 November.

Chang, C.F., Okunade, A.A. and Kumar, N. (1999) 'Motives Behind Charitable Bequests', *Journal of Nonprofit and Public Sector Marketing*, 6(4): 69–83.

Clotfelter, C.T. (1985) *Federal Tax Policy and Charitable Giving*, University of Chicago Press, Chicago, IL.

Fink, F. and Metzler, H. (1982) *The Costs and Benefits of Deferred Giving*, Columbia University Press.

Gray, D. (1999) 'Charitable Gift Funds: A New Avenue for Philanthropy', *The Chronicle of Philanthropy*, 10 November.

Harris, T. (1999) *International Fundraising in Not for Profits*, John Wiley & Sons, New York.

Laitner, J. and Juster, F.T. (1996) 'New Evidence on Altruism: A Study of TIAA_CREFF Retirees', *American Economic Review*, 86 (September): 893–908.

McNees, S.K. (1973) 'Deductibility of Charitable Bequests', *National Tax Journal*, 26: 81–98.

Morgan, G. (2000) 'Changes in UK Tax-Effective Giving: Implications for Fundraising Strategies', *International Journal of Nonprofit and Voluntary Sector Marketing*, 5(1).

Novack, J. and Saunders, L. (1999) 'The New Giving Game', *Forbes Magazine*, 20 September.

Pharoah, C. (1997) 'Broad Trends – Sector Size, Scope, Income, and Expenditure', in C. Pharoah and M. Smerdon, *Dimensions of the Voluntary Sector*, Charities Aid Foundation, West Malling, Kent.

Pharoah, C. (2002) *Dimensions 2002*, Charities Aid Foundation, West Malling, Kent.

Pidgeon, S. (2001) Address to the ICFM Convention, July, UK.

Sargeant, A. and Hilton, T. (2003) *The Final Gift: Targeting the Potential Charity Legator*, Working Paper 01/03, University of the West of England.

Schervish, P.G. and Havens, J.J. (2002) 'The New Physics of Philanthropy: Part 2: The Spiritual Side of the Supply Side', *The Case International Journal of Educational Advancement*, 2(3): 221–241.

Schoenhals, G. (1999) 'Our Future in Planned Giving', *Planned Giving Today*, January.

Sprinkel-Grace, K. (1997) *Beyond Fund-raising: New Strategies for Nonprofit Innovation and Investment*, AFP/Wiley Fund Development Series, John Wiley, New York.

Tueller, A. (1994) *A Practical Guide to Planned Giving*, The Taft Group, Washington DC.

White, D. (1995) *The Art of Planned Giving: Understanding Donors and the Culture of Giving*, John Wiley & Sons, New York.

Worthington, S. (1997) 'Pennies From Heaven', *Charity Magazine*, CAF UK, February.

199

Chapter 10

Community fundraising

LEARNING OBJECTIVES

By the end of this chapter you should be able to:

- Discuss the range and types of activities commonly defined as community fundraising.
- Understand how community fundraising has changed in recent years.
- Outline the levels of return on investment that may be expected from this form of activity.
- Understand and manage the central role of the volunteer in community fundraising activity.

INTRODUCTION

Despite the increasingly professional stance of many non-profit operations and the widespread use of TV, direct mail, the Internet and the telephone in fundraising solicitation, community fundraising activities are still what most members of the public call to mind if they are asked to describe the ways that fundraising happens.

Community fundraising comprises a wide range of participative events and activities, all of which are visible within the local community, raise funds from individuals within that community and usually involve a volunteer workforce. Initiatives that would fall under the umbrella term 'community fundraising' would include the distribution of collection boxes to stores and businesses, cash collections in malls and on the street, local flag days, fêtes, yard sales, sponsored events in local schools and workplaces, and large-scale community events such as fun-runs or danceathons.

Community fundraising can be as much (or more) about raising awareness of a cause within a given community as about raising funds. Although there are exceptions to the rule, in general community fundraising is one of the least profitable forms of income generation for non-profits on both sides of the Atlantic. Given that it usually involves volunteers and apparently low-cost materials, this can be difficult to understand.

To an extent community fundraising is 'old-style' fundraising, and as such there are indications that it is becoming less effective and relevant as previous generations pass on and the demographics of giving and volunteering change. This is exacerbated by the fact that community fundraising is an area that is not easy to 'professionalize' in terms of centralizing, streamlining and controlling activities for maximum profitability.

In this chapter we will look at what community fundraising is, what rates of return may reasonably be generated by it and how it fits into the fundraising communications portfolio. We will also discuss the major trends affecting this area, including those impacting on volunteering and attitudes to volunteering.

COMMUNITY FUNDRAISING ACTIVITIES

Community fundraising works within the 'mass anonymous small gifts market' (Kotler and Andreasen 1991), generating a large number of small cash donations from individuals. This sort of fundraising is 'people intensive', involving the mobilization of large numbers of volunteers, often organized through committee structures.

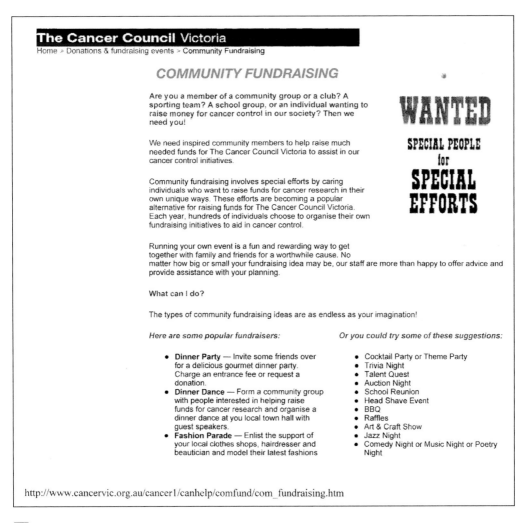

Plate 10.1 *Community fundraising ideas*

Source: © The Cancer Council. Reproduced with kind permission

The motives of donors in giving through community fundraising techniques are mixed. Some givers are no doubt motivated by 'pure' philanthropic motives, but community fundraising involves strong elements of exchange, whereby donors derive a benefit from the giving of the gift too. Community events provide opportunities for socializing, entertainment, competition, recognition and networking, while raffles, auctions and sales provide opportunities to win prizes or to buy and sell goods. Giving in response to community fundraising initiatives is 'low-impact', involving no great depth of thought and requiring little by way of knowledge of the specific work of the non-profit. The gifts are low value and impulsive, often triggered more by the person asking or by the event taking place than by the particular nature of the cause.

Participative community fundraising works by turning large numbers of people into agents on behalf of a non-profit, getting other people to do the asking and thereby enabling fundraisers to broaden their audience. It turns social networks into chains of agents and supporters. When a fundraiser persuades a school to run a sponsored activity, effectively a personal 'ask' is being made for that charity by the teachers, and then by the children. If guilt-tripped parents then seek sponsorship for their child's activity from work colleagues the net is widened still further. The best community fundraising offers several ways for individuals to contribute, by volunteering time and skills to organize and run events, by taking part and seeking sponsors, by suggesting other individuals, or by giving directly. Plate 10.1 provides some examples of community fundraising ideas from the Cancer Council of Victoria's website.

Community fundraising thus depends on networks and concentrations of people. Fundraisers either go to where people are already and work through schools, workplaces, clubs and societies, or create events in order to draw people to them. The second option is often necessary for unpopular or controversial causes, where it may be difficult to gain entry to existing mainstream institutions.

The sections below briefly outline some of the most common community fundraising routes:

Schools fundraising

Many non-profits seek to raise money through sponsored events in schools. In some cases the school allows children a 'non-uniform' day in return for a small donation to a cause, or distributes sponsorship forms to pupils. Children have been encouraged to seek sponsorship for a wide range of activities – from sports challenges through to sponsored silences, fasts, readathons and more. Most school fundraising has an educational aspect, whereby the children are provided with information on both the cause and the beneficiaries and are encouraged to discuss the issues raised as a class exercise.

As the number of non-profits approaching schools has increased, schools have reacted by organizing their giving and fundraising activity more formally, often supporting the same cause through the same event each year, or rotating their support to different organizations on a regular basis.

School pupils will seek sponsorship from their families and from friends of the family, and thus raise awareness and donations from among their own circle. Non-profits will also hope that support given by schoolchildren might be remembered fondly as the individuals grow to adulthood, providing a lasting sympathy and link to the work of the non-profit.

Fundraising within local organizations

Other local organizations are likewise employed by non-profits for fundraising activity. Masonic guilds, recreational clubs, guilds, rotary clubs and workplaces all provide networks of people who can be motivated to raise funds, especially where the organization itself is generally charitably inclined and is designed in part to advance the social good. Workplace fundraising is usually categorized as corporate philanthropy, though it can involve many of the same events and tools as community fundraising and is often best delivered on a local basis.

Street and house-to-house collections

Most non-profits have operated cash collections at some point, recruiting teams of volunteers prepared to collect with a bucket in the street or in a shopping mall; or going door-to-door in their own neighbourhoods and asking for small donations.

While these activities may appear to be fairly spontaneous, all cash collections are in fact carefully orchestrated. Permission for cash collections in malls or on the street has to be given by the mall owners or the local authority, who often enforce rigid guidelines as to how long the collections can continue, and on the positioning and behaviour of the collectors. Door-to-door collections are generally not subject to this sort of permission, but areas have to be allocated without overlap, and good practice guidelines carefully adhered to with reference to the safety of the volunteer collectors and the good name of the non-profit organization.

The recruitment, management and co-ordination of the large number of volunteers required for a large-scale collection campaign is also time-consuming and can be costly. The income generated has to be accounted for and banked. Volunteers will require recognition and thanks, and ideally will receive communications throughout the year in order to retain their goodwill and encourage them to repeat their involvement. Volunteers tend to be uncomfortable with making a direct request for gifts, which is why many organizations prefer to use collection envelopes, which are put into mailboxes and collected some days later. Raffle/lottery tickets may also be sold door-to-door, giving volunteers the opportunity to offer prospective supporters the chance to win a prize.

House-to-house collections have been badly hit by the diminishing pool and increased age of fundraising volunteers, plus an increase in fears for personal safety. This has reached the point where the co-ordination of house-to-house collecting is no longer profitable for some charities, even where a long history of the successful use of this method is established.

Fundraising events

Fundraising events range widely from fêtes and local galas through to sponsored sports events, challenge events, entertainments, yard sales and fashion shows. Events can involve anywhere from a dozen people through to thousands, and can require weeks, months or years of planning and co-ordination according to scale and complexity. There is a portfolio of 'standard' fundraising events available, tested and experienced over years of charity fundraising across the sector. These proven formulas may be run using documents such as sponsorship forms, raffle tickets and entry forms, which are simple and require minimal amounts of staff time in explanation and advice to volunteers.

However, those events that work best and remain successful over a longer duration are those where the core event has been creatively themed or given a new twist that makes it relevant to the particular cause or community. The community fundraising market is crowded and competitive, and new initiatives have to stand out in order to succeed.

Fundraising events and initiatives tend to have a lifecycle similar to that of a commercial product, whereby it takes time for the new product to become known and accepted, but once this happens sales rise rapidly and substantial profits can be made. In due course, however, the market becomes saturated, sales decline and, with many companies competing for business, profit margins fall sharply. This pattern may occur over a few years, or over decades as lifestyles and technology change. Many of the same factors such as novelty, costs and competition are at work in the charity events marketplace. Non-profits respond to this either by shoring up the success of community fundraising products through ensuring they are not overused, and by introducing new novelty elements to keep them fresh, or by regularly developing and testing new community fundraising products. This latter option can be high risk, as many new ventures are likely to fail, and it tends to take a long time to disseminate successful practice to volunteer community fundraising groups, which by their nature tend to be conservative and slow to embrace innovation.

The possibilities for fundraising events are endless, and non-profits are constantly devising new ideas. Some of the most well-tested sources of enjoyment and participation are listed below:

- *'Fun-raising'* – events involving humour, jokes, dressing up and fooling around. Many 'good cause' events give an opportunity for people to play the fool, receive attention and make people laugh.
- *Family events* – events or activities that families can undertake or attend together (see Plate 10.2).
- *Challenges* – events involving teams such as tug-of-war and quizzes provide a spectacle for others to watch and stimulate competition. Individual challenges such as bungee-jumping, parachuting and abseiling provide the chance to test yourself in front of your friends.

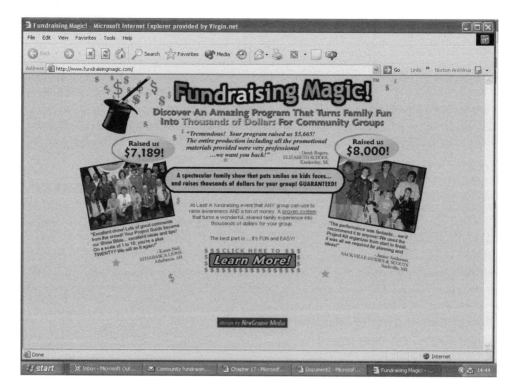

Plate 10.2 *Community fundraising events*

Source: © Fundraisingmagic.com. Reproduced with kind permission

■ *The chance to win a prize or secure a bargain* – often the fact that the proceeds are going to a 'good cause' enables people to justify participation in raffles, prize draws and similar activities that they usually would not consider or would disapprove of.

■ *Celebrities* – local events often offer the chance to see or meet a celebrity, or to buy or win items donated by celebrities.

■ *Fitness* – sponsored walks, cycle rides, aerobathons, swimming galas and the like all enable people to enjoy physical activities and to support a non-profit at the same time.

Community fundraising events require a great deal of organization and are extremely labour-intensive. Small events will take months to organize properly, while larger sponsored events can take over a year. Sites and facilities have to be booked long in advance, as do celebrities, while police and local amenity authorities require applications to be processed with long lead times. The design and production of publicity materials is a lengthy process, especially if recognition and inclusion of sponsors and supporters is involved, and the support and co-ordination of a wide range of other bodies may be required to help with arrangements on the day. Advance warning and a gradual buildup of publicity over time is virtually essential to ensure good attendance figures.

Event organizers therefore have to be well organized, and to plan through the production of detailed schedules and checklists. Public events require the organizer to be well aware of public health and safety regulations, and to be able to carry out risk-assessment exercises as part of the event planning cycle. Planning a successful community event requires a blend of creativity and calculation, blending the enthusiasm that will motivate volunteers with the detachment and analysis required to make the event smooth-running and profitable. Exhibit 10.1 provides an example of a schedule for an annual sponsored bike ride.

Centrally co-ordinated and integrated campaigns

In recent years a trend has emerged of fundraising organizations using more centralized methods to co-ordinate and promote community activities, in order to take advantage of participative fundraising while reducing the overhead costs involved in setting up, controlling and servicing local fundraising bodies. This might mean that a new fundraising idea or theme is developed and tested centrally, with generic materials produced by a headquarters team that can be used locally. At the most extreme, fundraising 'packs' are generated containing a complete set of materials, instructions and support, and are distributed to local groups. While this makes good sense in terms of co-ordination, control and cost, many volunteer groups would argue that it stifles local ideas, energy and creativity, and that the strength of local activity lies in its local flavour and originality.

The centralizing approach also helps to ensure that local fundraising activity is integrated with national campaigns, and that community fundraising can be co-ordinated with other fundraising activity to produce the maximum impact. A single campaign theme or message can be utilized across fundraising mailings, telemarketing, advertising, radio and DRTV, while at the same time volunteers are active in their local communities running events, sponsorship events, cash collections and flag days promoting the same central message and call for funds. Examples of this are the Christmas campaign in the USA by the Salvation Army, or in the UK, Christian Aid Week.

Church fundraising

Fundraising within religious congregations is an important community fundraising exercise. This activity can range from the standard collection plate through to the organization of activities in

EXHIBIT 10.1 SCHEDULE FOR ANNUAL SPONSORED BIKE RIDE

Month 1	Agree dates for next year's event with Head Office and local volunteer group.
Month 2	First event committee to debrief on this year and begin to plan for next year. Monthly meetings will be held from this point on.
Month 3	Identify top sponsorship fundraiser.
Month 4	Confirm sponsorship with local paper.
	Send sponsorship proposals to drinks manufacturer, paper cup makers, clothing suppliers. Identify likely suppliers of prizes and approach.
Month 5	Agree route.
	Prepare literature.
Month 6	Print literature.
	Plan launch event.
	Prepare administration systems and packs.
	Book site facilities, PA system, transport.
	Confirm booking of local celebrity.
Month 7	Hold publicity launch.
	Contact suppliers of first aid, marshals and refreshments.
Month 8	Meetings to plan detailed arrangements on the day. Prepare route signs and direction materials.
Month 9	Draft scripts for speakers and commentators.
	Draft press releases.
	Final arrangements with sponsors and volunteers.
Month 10	Event takes place.

which members of the congregation act as fundraising volunteers. Church fundraising may be undertaken by the church for the church, for related religious causes such as missionary activity, or for non-profits unconnected with religious activity. Individual church leaders may integrate the non-profit cause with education and information, providing displays or videos that present the background to the fundraising proposition, and featuring the appeal in church publications and communications. Individuals taking on sponsorship challenges in aid of good causes may also find potential sponsors from among members of their local religious community.

MANAGEMENT AND STRUCTURES

A community fundraiser requires skills primarily in organizing people and events. Success depends on the effective mobilization of supporters and resources. Many fundraising non-profits create a range of volunteer committees to facilitate this, or encourage the formation of local branches and fundraising groups affiliated to the organization. In some cases these groups are a constitutionally important part of the organization, electing members of advisory or governing bodies. Other non-profits opt for a less formal structure, working through other groups and organizations on a project or campaign basis rather than establishing permanent local committees.

Locally based committees or branches can be extremely effective, delivering funds, time and effort, and facilitating the organization of a demanding programme of fundraising events and activities. They can provide links into the social networks and institutions that make up the local community, and can add to the local credibility of a non-profit, effectively making the cause relevant and popular on a local basis. Over time, volunteer committees or branches can become extremely knowledgeable and experienced local fundraisers and effective representatives and advocates for the non-profit organization. That said, there are also significant costs and disadvantages associated with this type of structure.

Groups and committees have to be serviced. The members will expect to be kept informed, and to be supported with information, training, materials and advice. They will require recognition for their efforts. If they form part of the governance structure of the organization their decision-making bodies will require administrative support. Groups and committees also have to be controlled. They may want to undertake activities that the main organization considers inappropriate, or even damaging. Their work has to be carefully monitored to avoid the situation where key donors or potential donors are approached with multiple requests from local and head office sources, and become irritated by the evident lack of professionalism and co-ordination.

The servicing, control and co-ordination of local fundraising groups thus carries a substantial cost. When this is coupled with the fact that the fundraising activities they undertake bring in relatively limited levels of income, it will be appreciated that the costs of supporting community fundraising can easily begin to outweigh the income generated. Non-profits that make the decision to invest heavily in the creation of local fundraising offices and posts may therefore find that they fail to generate the requisite level of income to justify the infrastructure costs.

OUTCOMES AND PROFITABILITY

Despite the financial risks outlined above, many fundraising non-profits continue to support extensive community fundraising work. These organizations may recognize that community fundraising is far less profitable than other forms of fundraising activity, but also contend that community activity generates additional and different benefits to the non-profit, and hence that it should not be judged purely in terms of return on investment.

One of the main reasons for local fundraising is the publicity that can be generated for the organization, calling attention to the non-profit, its work and its needs. Publicity may be generated through local media coverage, and directly among individuals through the visibility that accrues. Such publicity will help the organization to reach out to supporters and potential supporters, many of whom would be unlikely to be aware of the non-profit otherwise.

Community fundraising events are also used to reward donors and to involve, thank and motivate volunteers, reinforcing their decision to support the organization and encouraging their renewed involvement and dedication. Many local initiatives also have an educational element, raising awareness of specific issues and providing information and advice. In making the organization visible at a local level, community fundraising activity can also have an impact on the levels of demand for the services that the non-profit provides. Recognition of the value of one-to-one contact with donor groups has made many organizations more aware of the value of a personal, local link to major donors, trusts and companies that may be located at a distance from the charity HQ.

Non-profit organizations therefore have to consider carefully the balance of costs and benefits prior to making any investment in community fundraising. This balance will vary according to the nature of the cause and the structure and needs of the particular organization, and will be impacted upon by the requirements of the organization to raise its profile locally, to campaign or to educate.

In the UK, one-third of the top 500 fundraising charities are estimated to engage in regional or 'local' fundraising activities. Recent research suggests that while a significant amount of income is typically generated, the returns from this form of activity are relatively poor. Across the Top 500 the mean income generated per £1 of expenditure has been shown to be £2.14. It is interesting to note that no significant size or category effects could be discerned in these figures, suggesting that charities of a different size and nature of activity will tend to achieve the same level of performance. Returns on community fundraising activity in the USA are hard to tease out from the available figures, but are likely to be of the same sort of order.

THE ROLE OF THE VOLUNTEER

Community fundraising relies on volunteers, who participate in fundraising activities that promote or advance some aspect of the common good without expectation of financial gain. According to Independent Sector polling studies, over 56 per cent of adult Americans volunteered in some capacity in 1998, with the average hours volunteered per week as 3.5. This represents a significant increase in numbers compared to previous years. Of this total, 16 per cent volunteered for fundraising activities.

In the UK in 1997 The National Survey of Volunteering cites 48 per cent of adults volunteering, at an average of four hours per week. This represents a small drop on previous volunteering levels.

Trends in volunteering

It is difficult to draw general conclusions, but it is clear that changes in lifestyle, in the numbers of women entering the workforce, and in working patterns have impacted on the nature of volunteer activity and on the demographic characteristics of the volunteer fundraising pool.

In the UK this volunteer pool appears to be shrinking. This is not the case in the USA, but the stated motives behind volunteering and the nature of volunteer involvement have altered.

Individuals take on volunteer work through:

- the desire to change society;
- the desire to obtain experiences that may be useful in paid employment;
- the desire to help a specific cause;
- the desire to meet others;
- the desire to prepare for a volunteer 'career' after retirement;
- the desire to get inside institutions and organizations and ensure that they are doing what they profess to be doing.

Other trends:

- A wider spectrum of people are now volunteering. Rather than just the healthy middle classes, many elderly and handicapped people now offer their services, as do increasing numbers of professionals. Surveys consistently show a marked drop in volunteering among young people aged 18 to 24.

- Volunteers are becoming more demanding. They want more input into what they are doing.
- In the USA, increased numbers of African-American and members of the Hispanic community are volunteering.
- The number of female volunteers aged 55 plus is dropping in both the USA and the UK. This group previously provided the main workforce for much local fundraising activity.

These trends are putting increasing pressure on non-profits to improve their systems for volunteer recruitment and management, while the potentially contracting pool of volunteers (at least from some sections of the population) points up the importance to non-profits of making every effort to retain volunteers for as long as possible once the investment has been made in recruiting and training them.

Recruiting fundraising volunteers

It tends to be more difficult to recruit volunteers prepared to undertake fundraising work than to attract voluntary help with programme work. For example, a group dealing with the welfare of domestic animals are likely to find it easier to recruit volunteers prepared to exercise dogs from the local animal refuge than to find volunteers to collect donations on the street. Fundraising (or 'asking for money') can be viewed as an unpleasant task, as well as being one step removed from the cause. Independent Sector surveys in the USA constantly evidence that 'direct service activity' is the most popular form of voluntary work, attracting nearly a quarter of all volunteers.

Generally, volunteers have to make a concrete connection with an organization before they will offer their time. This is often through being asked by a friend, through participation in the organization directly, or as a result of a friend or family member benefiting from the work of the organization. Volunteer recruitment thus operates primarily through 'word of mouth'.

As with donor recruitment, the profiles and sources of past volunteers will provide the best guidelines for locating and securing further recruits. The motivations of past and existing volunteer cohorts can be teased out and analysed to aid in presenting the offer that is made to volunteers. For many, the only 'payback' required is the knowledge that society is gaining from their efforts, or that they will get the opportunity to meet new people and make new friends. An increasing number, however, will be looking for specific experience that they can use later in the workplace, or will be looking to use specific skills in their volunteer work.

Retaining and managing fundraising volunteers

Recruiting and training new volunteers is expensive, and efforts are better placed in retaining and developing those volunteers who have already signed up to help. Surveys of lapsed volunteers, and of satisfaction and dissatisfaction among current volunteers, tend to yield the following issues:

- Unrealistic expectations when recruited. This can be the fault of the volunteer, who may have formed an inaccurate picture of what volunteering would be like. It is often, however, the fault of the non-profit, which may have 'oversold' the benefits of volunteering in its recruitment communications.
- Lack of appreciation from co-workers and beneficiaries.
- Lack of training and supervision.
- Feeling undervalued, especially by employed staff.
- Excessive demands on time.

Training is probably most commonly cited as a problem area, both in terms of a lack of training being offered and of the quality of training being perceived as poor and limited.

The use of volunteers can be problematic for a fundraising organization, and is certainly not an uncomplicated advantage for the non-profit sector. Some volunteers prove difficult to manage because they are of the opinion that since they are donating their time free of charge they do not work (as such) for the organization and should therefore be requested rather than directed to undertake tasks. Some feel that they should have the right to exercise a great deal of control and independence in their work, and some require continual expressions of appreciation for their generosity.

Other problems come through in mixing professional paid staff with volunteers. Staff are often critical of the attitude of volunteers, who can appear to be:

- short-term members of the team and therefore not likely to assume responsibility for the long-term repercussions of their activity;
- insufficiently aware of the workings and ethics of the organization and thus likely to make mistakes when representing it;
- unwilling to take direction or guidance.

The attitude of management with regard to volunteers may thus be seen to be absolutely key to the maintenance of good relations between paid and unpaid staff. The optimum attitude is to treat volunteers entirely straightforwardly and as much as possible like paid professional staff. This should encompass full training, job descriptions and the setting and monitoring of targets, benchmarks and goals. This 'professionalization' of volunteering is challenging for non-profits and carries significant costs, but experienced organizations maintain that it brings results. 'The steady transformation of the volunteer from well-meaning amateur to trained, professional unpaid staff member is the most significant development in the nonprofit sector' (Drucker 1989: 91).

THE FUTURE FOR COMMUNITY FUNDRAISING

Community and local fundraising is an area in which there is currently little agreement across the sector as to the optimum structure and reasonable expectations and measurements. It is also an area of great turbulence, with many major non-profits in both the UK and the USA reorganizing, restructuring and altering their local fundraising operations on a regular basis.

The key problems lie in the costs of maintaining an infrastructure to support community fundraising activity, and in making a local fundraising presence cost-effective in terms of a measurable ROI. Structurally the arrangements range from completely centralized non-profits with no local presence at all, through to federated structures where the local groups are separately registered legal entities and work independently of the central organization.

This situation is complicated by the other advantages of a local presence such as publicity and credibility, which are not easy to measure in balance-sheet terms but which undoubtedly have a value to non-profits in terms both of fundraising and service delivery.

Historically local and community fundraising has been heavily based on volunteer groups, and it is therefore an area in which changes in the demographics, motives and needs of volunteers impacts heavily. Competition in local fundraising is also fierce as both national and local charities compete in the arena.

If community fundraising is to be maintained as a viable part of the non-profit portfolio it would appear that its impact will have to be measured carefully, and not evaluated purely in terms of ROI. Those non-profits likely to develop local fundraising activity most effectively in the years to come will be those that can maintain a sensible balance of overheads and infrastructure, likely to arise from increased levels of central control and more integration of community fundraising activity with other fundraising routes.

CHAPTER SUMMARY

In this chapter we have discussed the wide-ranging fundraising activities that are undertaken within local communities. As we have seen, such activities generate relatively small gifts, and are labour- and people-intensive to organize and run. While reliant on volunteers to take on much of the workload, community fundraising carries substantial overhead costs and this, coupled with the relatively low income generated, means that the ROI across the activity is generally only of the order of $/£1:2.1.

However, local fundraising activity is also of value due to the publicity it generates, the credibility it may add to the non-profit and the increased accessibility it promotes in the local community. There is thus an argument for measuring its impact and value in terms beyond simple ROI.

Volunteers are key to local fundraising, and we have briefly discussed the levels of volunteering current in the USA and the UK, current trends in the volunteer market, and the likely impact of these trends on fundraising activity and profitability in the future.

DISCUSSION QUESTIONS

1   In your role as organizer of an annual sponsored walk, produce a timeline for the planning of the event. What documents and data would you look to gather from previous records?

2   Produce a job specification for a fundraising volunteer who will be expected to take part in a house-to-house raffle ticket sale.

3   Draft a projection of income and costs for a local fête event. What ROI would you expect from the event overall and how would you justify this to your fundraising director?

REFERENCES

Drucker, P. (1989) 'What Business Can Learn From Nonprofits', *Harvard Business Review*, July–August: 91.

Independent Sector (1999) *National Survey of Giving and Volunteering*, www.independentsector.org.

Institute for Volunteering Research (1997) *National Survey of Volunteering in the UK*, www.ivr.org.uk.

Kotler, P. and Andreasen, A.R. (1991) *Strategic Marketing for Nonprofit Organizations*, 4th edn, Prentice-Hall, Englewood Cliffs, NJ.

Part III

Corporate/trust fundraising

Chapter 11

Corporate fundraising

LEARNING OBJECTIVES

By the end of this chapter you should be able to:

■ Describe trends in the corporate fundraising market.

■ Assess the motives for corporate support of non-profits.

■ Develop a corporate fundraising plan

■ Develop an appropriate structure for corporate fundraising.

■ Quantify the impact of the fundraising approach adopted.

■ Develop plans for employee fundraising and payroll giving.

INTRODUCTION

US corporations and their associated foundations donated 4.3 per cent of the total income received by the non-profit sector (or $9.05 billion) in 2001. This total represents a 12.1 per cent decrease over the figure for 2000 (AAFRC Trust 2002), which is highly unusual in historic terms. Most years tend to see a modest increase in giving in line with inflation, but it is important to note that there is a strong link between corporate generosity and the perform-ance of the economy. Thus while corporate giving declined in this period it is against a backdrop of a fall in corporate profits of 17 per cent over the same period. This fall in giving also lowered the percentage of pre-tax profits that were donated to about 1 per cent. This again is lower than recent norms, which have been of the order of 1.1 to 1.3 per cent. In reality however, all these figures tend to underestimate corporate support of the non-profit sector since many companies support non-profits through marketing, public relations and advertising expendi-tures in addition to their charitable gifts.

The destination of corporate giving in the USA is depicted in Figure 11.1. As is the case in the UK, health, human services and education causes are those that derive the most benefit from corporate support. In the UK total corporate support stood at £111 million in 2000/1, an increase of 12 per cent on the previous year (Corporate Citizen 2002). This impressive figure was achieved in part by a significant growth in cause-related marketing schemes, which we discuss in detail below. As in the USA, the growth in corporate giving is generally linked

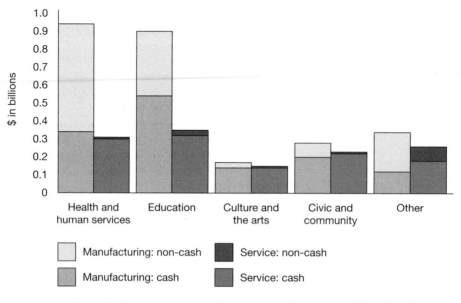

Data: The Conference Board, *Corporate Contributions in 2000*, tables 10–14

Figure 11.1 *Corporate giving by type of gift and type of recipient organization*

Source: © AAFRC Trust for Philanthropy. Based on original data supplied by the Conference Board. Corporate contributions in 2000 tables 10–14

to the health of the economy and has thus more typically reported very modest growth in line with inflation in recent years. It is fair to say though that UK corporates are not as generous as their American counterparts and the percentage of pre-tax profit donated to good causes each year is typically of the order of a mere 0.2 per cent.

While the aggregate value of corporate support represents a significant amount of income to the sector the percentage of corporate organizations that offer their support remains relatively small, the value of particular relationships will often be low, and these may be reduced further by the 'strings' attached to particular gifts by a corporate. Thus corporate fundraising should not be regarded as a panacea for cash-starved non-profits. Rather it is a highly complex form of relationship fundraising that will not suit either the needs or capabilities of every organization. The potential to truly make money from this market must be carefully evaluated and a strategy for entry developed only where there is a clear rationale for doing so.

In this chapter we will review a number of the important trends in corporate giving, explain why corporate support is offered, the forms that it might take and suggest a structured approach to corporate fundraising that can be adopted by non-profits looking to solicit funds from this sector.

WHY DO CORPORATES GIVE?

At the turn of the nineteenth century corporate philanthropy was little more than an extension of individual philanthropy. The large corporate organizations of the day supported the causes that the chairman or chief executive believed to be important – certainly within the UK. It is important to recognize that before 1950 in the USA corporate giving was legally restricted to non-profits that were in some way connected to the activities of the business. It was thus not uncommon for philanthropy to be targeted at local communities that served to attract and thereafter foster the general welfare of the workforce. Post-1950, when the American courts ruled that it was possible to give to any non-profit organization, corporate funding of the arts and education increased significantly.

However, the role of the chief executive should not be underestimated in the USA. Even in the early part of the twentieth century these individuals were still able to indulge their particular interests, directly through corporate giving, or indirectly through the personal wealth that had been accumulated through the business. High-profile individuals such as Andrew Carnegie and John D. Rockerfeller endowed institutions seemingly at random but in keeping with their own individual preferences and tastes. Indeed, up until the early 1980s corporate giving still owed much to the interests and concerns of chief executives who usually made the final decision in respect of the organizations they wished to support. Under this paradigm corporate giving could be viewed as a genuinely 'philanthropic' activity where the primary objective was for the business to give something back to the society in which it operated.

An alternative approach to corporate support first began to emerge in the late 1960s and early 1970s with a number of organizations beginning to look for benefits to accrue from their charitable giving. This 'opportunity'-based paradigm regarded a liaison with a non-profit as a means of attaining key business objectives.

Writers such as Mescon and Tilson (1987), Pifer (1987) or Wokutch and Spencer (1987) have identified a shift towards what they call 'dual agenda' giving whereby organizations will be predisposed to giving to charities that have a good fit with their own strategic objectives. As an example, Hunt (1986) points out that Hallmark (a greetings card manufacturer) chooses to support fine arts and design programmes in the hope that a supply of both employees and customers will be generated as a result. Similarly Chanel, when they wanted to launch an exclusive new fragrance to wealthy 'elite' consumers, sponsored the opening night dinner and fashion show connected with a performance at the Metropolitan Opera. The Met received $1.2 million in donations and Chanel was able to gain the exposure it required for its product.

In dual agenda giving the benefits sought by a business from its relationship with a non-profit might include: increased sales; brand differentiation; enhanced brand image; improved employee recruitment, morale and retention; demonstration of shared values with the target market; enhanced government relations; a broadened customer base, and the ability to reach new customer segments (See e.g. Andreasen 1996, Sagawa 2001, Wymer and Samu 2003). Authors such as Shell (1989) have, in addition, emphasized the benefits of giving in relation to strengthening ties to the local community and offering companies an opportunity to express corporate values in the public arena.

Putting aside the philanthropic and opportunity-based paradigms Himmelstein (1997) argues that in some communities where philanthropy thrives out of proportion to per capita income (e.g. Minneapolis/St Paul), there are further reasons why corporate philanthropy is stimulated. He argues that corporate leaders with strong links to the philanthropic community effectively set the agenda for their peers and encourage others to give by example. The more ties a given CEO has to these leaders the more that particular corporation will give away. It is interesting to note that so pervasive is this culture of giving in these communities that for a manager to succeed in business and to become a powerful figure in the business life of that community he or she must publicly demonstrate their generosity and have a proven track record as a philanthropist.

Norms are enormously important. Where organizations collaborate on other business matters it would appear that they begin to develop very similar patterns of corporate giving. While it may not be possible for a business to share all the aspects of the corporate strategy it is adopting, those aspects that pertain to giving are not regarded as sensitive and are significantly more likely to be shared and perhaps copied by others. Extant research has identified that the more 'professional' an organization's approach to managing giving, the more likely its pattern of support is to resemble that of the corporate sector as a whole. Where managers have a strong tie to their professional community, they share their experiences of philanthropy through that community and thereby establish norms of support.

FORMS OF BUSINESS SUPPORT

Overview

Whatever the initial motive for engaging with a non-profit there are a variety of different forms of corporate support that can be solicited. A selection of the most common are as follows:

- *Cash donations*: this remains the most common form of corporate support of non-profits and is popular in many countries partly because there are corporation tax benefits that can accrue as a consequence of the gift.
- *Donations of stocks/shares*: In some countries corporates can also elect to give stocks and shares to a non-profit of their choice. Again, this is typically tax efficient since the gift accrues a tax deduction equal to the value of those shares at the time of donation.
- *Publicity*: Non-profits can gain from the association with a business since that business may promote its link to the cause and thereby heighten public awareness of the organization. The relationship in the early 1980s, for example, between American Express and a little-known charity 'Share Our Strength' served to greatly increase the standing of this organization (Himmelstein 1997). This enhanced awareness has been shown to lead to greater success in attracting public donations, members, volunteers, advocacy support and community understanding of the goals of the non-profit (Bragdon 1985, Wagner and Thompson 1994). An example of a case where an organization was able to donate publicity to a non-profit is provided in Exhibit 11.1.
- *Gifts of products/services* (also known as gifts-in-kind): Frequently the goods or services produced by a corporate can be of value to the beneficiaries of a charity. The donation of food at or near its 'sell-by' or 'expiry date' to soup kitchens is one such example. The donation of computer equipment to schools and colleges is also common, and gifts of office equipment, furniture, computer supplies or even photocopying facilities have been reported. In both the USA and the UK there are now specialist charities that encourage corporates to provide gifts of this type and act as a clearing house for organizations that wish to find appropriate recipients (Elischer 2002). Such gifts can also be tax effective in some countries with the current value of those goods (i.e. not their full sale value) typically being tax deductible. Finally, it is important to recognize the public relations value to some companies of this form of gift. If a clothing company disposes of 500 coats with slight imperfections at the local dump while inner-city children are freezing in the cold it could very well end up facing a major public relations challenge. Such gifts can therefore benefit both parties.
- *Staff time*: Some corporates will agree to second staff to a non-profit where specific expertise is being sought. This may be management expertise or perhaps technical expertise where this would assist in improving the service provision to beneficiaries. Other corporates are willing to release staff who can act as volunteers to work with the non-profit in whatever way desired (Sagawa and Segal 2000, Smith 1994). Indeed, some companies have even created their own volunteer departments, complete with their own budget and staff. The most successful employee volunteer programmes have several

EXHIBIT 11.1 SHOES FOR ORPHAN SOULS

One of the key needs for children in orphanages around the world is shoes and socks. In 1999 Buckner Orphan Care International (an international relief organization) took over a programme designed to meet part of this need, known as Shoes for Orphan Souls. The organization solicited the interest of the Mall operator Macerich in Dallas and worked in partnership with the Mall owner to create a test market shoe drive at Macerich's Dallas property – Valley View. The programme was timed to coincide with the back to school season since shopping for children's shoes is high on the priority list of many families at this time.

With the combined promotional support of both the Mall owner and the non-profit – fifty other organizations were persuaded to hold drives of their own and sixty individual volunteers were recruited to distribute promotional fliers and shopper incentives to collect shoes. As a consequence 20,000 pairs of shoes and socks were collected (double the programme's target) and $60,000 in cash donations. The media also promoted the drive, giving exposure to both partners over eight radio slots, ten television slots and thirteen stories in local and national print media. The pilot was thus highly successful, and for the Mall owner the benefits in enhanced publicity, greater shopper traffic and regard as a local community partner created much goodwill.

Of course these benefits accrue not only for the Mall owner but also for the stores represented on the Mall. Merchants were invited to participate in the programme by giving discounts and/or coupons to shoppers buying one or more pairs of shoes. Some merchants also agreed to donate a pair of shoes for each that was purchased in their store.

The Mall has been keen to continue its support as a consequence of this interest, and in 2000 Macerich Malls collected 52,000 pairs of shoes, 30,000 pairs of socks, thousands of shoelaces and over $200,000 in cash donations in the back-to-school period alone. The total value of aid over the whole of 2000 was estimated to be over $2,000,000, and for the Mall owner the programme obtained eleven local and fifteen national television slots, fourteen local and seven national radio spots and forty-three stories in the print media.

Source. Lovell 2001

---

elements in common. First, employees drive the effort, and those doing the volunteering are allowed to select the causes they support. In addition, successful programmes are vigorously supported by the company with volunteers being featured in the corporate newsletter and being recognized in other ways by management.

- *Sponsorship*: Corporates are often willing to sponsor a particular aspect of a non-profits service provision in return for an acknowledgement, or perhaps placement of the organization's name or logo. Organizations may also sponsor events or gala dinners that offer brand enhancement to the corporate while at the same time facilitating fundraising for the non-profit from those present (Mescon and Tilson 1987).

- *Fundraising from staff*: A number of corporates are prepared to open up access to their workforce. Rather than give as an organization, such businesses will allow a fundraising team to solicit donations from their staff, perhaps through a simple monetary collection or by facilitating payroll giving. These are topics we will return to in detail below.

- *Fundraising from customers*: Finally, some corporates make it possible for non-profits to fundraise from their customers. This may be either direct or indirect. In the case of the

NATIONAL PUBLIC RADIO

National Public Radio (NPR) provides high-quality, informative and frequently challenging broadcasting across the USA. Unlike the UK's Radio 4, which is probably the closest equivalent, the station is not funded by licence payers, but is entirely free to those who use the service. Indeed, NPR is prohibited by its by-laws from directly soliciting contributions from listeners. Instead the organization must rely on unsolicited donations, foundations and corporations.

The corporate underwriting of the service doubled in 2000 to $32 million when research showed that 67 per cent of listeners reported that their opinion of a company improved when they heard that the company had supported NPR. Corporations are reported as particularly keen to sponsor broadcasts at key times of the day such as the morning 'drive-time' slot where audiences are high.

former, non-profits can solicit funds directly from customers – as in the 'Change For Good' case below – perhaps collecting money on a business premises or placing a collection box in a retail outlet. In the case of the latter the arrangement is more complex and would involve either collecting a donation from customers when they pay their bill, or making a donation on customers' behalf when purchase of a product/service has been made. This final category of arrangement is known as cause-related marketing, which we will consider in further detail below.

Cause-related marketing

McDonald's in the USA was the first organization to develop cause-related marketing, linking the purchase of their products to the Ronald McDonald House Charities. It was not until 1981 however that the term was coined for the first time by American Express who introduced the phrase 'Cause-related marketing' (CRM) to define a new form of corporate 'giving'. Under CRM the link with a non-profit is used to assist the business in increasing sales of its product. Its motivation is thus not philanthropic since such arrangements often make considerably more money for the corporate partner than they do for the non-profit. As the Senior Vice-President of American Express noted in 1984: 'if your primary goal is to make money for a worthy cause, stay away from it. It's not meant to be philanthropy. Its objective is to make money for your business' (Josephson 1984: 10).

BRITISH AIRWAYS – CHANGE FOR GOOD

UNICEF and British Airways have been working in partnership since 1994, creating the ground-breaking Change For Good programme. Passengers on all British Airways flights are invited to donate any unwanted foreign currency to UNICEF using envelopes stowed in their seat pocket, or available from the flight crew. Change For Good has supported UNICEF's work in fifty countries and made significant contributions to programmes in Zambia and Nigeria in 2002.

Varadarajan and Menon (1988: 60) define cause-related marketing as:

> A process of formulating and implementing marketing activities that are characterized
> by an offer from the firm to contribute a specified amount to a designated cause when
> customers engage in revenue providing exchanges that satisfy organizational and indi-
> vidual objectives.

The exact form that the relationship takes varies considerably, but classically what this means
in practice is that in return for using the non-profit's brand name on a particular product (or
service) the business will make a donation to the non-profit every time a purchase is made.
From its humble beginnings, work conducted by the PMA/Gable Group in 2000 identified
that 85 per cent of US corporations and 65 per cent of non-profit organizations now report
participation in some form of cause-related marketing scheme (see also Basil 2002). In the UK,
participation rates are similar, with CRM experiencing 52 per cent growth between 2000 and

Plate 11.2 *Cause-related marketing examples*

2001 (Corporate Citizen 2002). This rapid growth appears to have been driven by a recognition that consumers generally favour organizations which have demonstrable links to good causes (Farquarson 2000). Examples are illustrated in Plate 11.2.

Large-scale surveys in both the UK and the USA have consistently shown that if key factors such as price and quality are equivalent, consumers are willing to break a previous tie with a product in favour of an alternative identified with supporting a particular cause (Cone Inc 2002). In the UK Farquarson (2000) reports that consumers feel that companies supporting causes are more trustworthy and innovative than other companies. The study also reports that 77 per cent of consumers are positively influenced in their buying decisions by CRM programmes. It is interesting to note that this seems particularly true of female customers. Authors such as Ross *et al.* (1991) have consistently shown that females are more favourably disposed to pro-social appeals and hence are more receptive to CRM appeals. Women also develop more favourable attitudes towards both the cause and the sponsoring company (See also Kropp *et al.* 1999). On balance the evidence thus suggests that there may be very real advantages for a business in developing a CRM scheme, particularly where a substantial proportion of its customer base is female.

Before leaving the topic of CRM it is important to note that such schemes are not without their critics. A number of writers have argued that CRM can deflect corporate attention away from genuine philanthropy and mislead consumers. He has also argued that CRM tends to generate funds for those causes that are least likely to require such funding and thus acts to concentrate corporate support in the hands of only a few organizations.

Work by Webb and Mohr (1998) has further identified that some segments of individual consumers are highly sceptical of CRM activities, and writers such as Corkery (1989) and Levine (1989) regard CRM as little more than a shallow sales ploy that will leave consumers largely unimpressed. More recent empirical work suggests that the feelings consumers have about a particular scheme are likely to be a function of the degree of benefit that accrues to the non-profit. Where only paltry sums are donated relative to the value of the product/service, consumers are significantly more likely to react negatively to the scheme. There is thus a strong case for both partners to a CRM initiative to sit down together to work out a mutually beneficial arrangement. There is nothing to be gained on the part of the business by being seen to exploit the non-profit partner.

Where CRM schemes do work well they can raise significant sums. Johnson and Johnson, for example, raised $1.5 million in 1987 for Shelter Aid (a charity which runs shelters for battered women), and the link between Share Our Strength and Evian resulted in 20 per cent more sales of the one-litre bottles of water produced by the company and $30,000 per annum for the charity (Shore 2001).

Payroll giving

In both the USA and the UK it is possible to make a donation direct from an individual's payroll to particular non-profits. To facilitate this form of giving it is normally necessary for the non-profit to seek permission to address groups of employees at the place of business either directly or through the use of a fundraising agent/intermediary.

In the UK, payroll giving was first introduced in 1990 when Barnardo's pioneered work in this area. The present operation of the scheme in the UK is depicted in Figure 11.2. Employers willing to offer payroll giving as a service to their employees (there remains no statutory requirement for them to do so) must make their staff aware that the facility is available. Employees wishing to participate then authorize their employer to deduct a regular donation from their pay. This donation may be made to any registered charity currently in existence. There is presently no minimum or maximum limit for donations. Since the donations are deducted before PAYE (Pay As You Earn) tax, employees receive all the tax relief for the donation at their top rate of tax. Therefore, for a basic-rate taxpayer wanting to make a £10 donation, it will cost (at the time of writing) £7.80 or just £6 for higher rate taxpayers. Currently, the UK government offers an additional 10 per cent top-up incentive on every donation, greatly enhancing the real value of this form of giving. In our example above the £10 gift then becomes £11 for the charity. This is illustrated as follows. It is unclear at present whether this additional incentive will be continued.

Pledge	Value to charity	Cost to donor (paying 22% tax)	Cost to donor (paying 40% tax)
£10	£11	£7.80	£6

It is also important to recognize that some employers value the scheme as a means of fostering the retention of their staff and can offer a system of matching, or part-matching the donations made by their employees. This can clearly increase the value of the donation still further.

Once an employee has notified the employer of his or her intention to donate through payroll giving, the employer then makes the deduction and passes the donation to an 'agency charity' (which must be approved by the Inland Revenue). The agency charity claims the tax relief to which the recipient charity is entitled and then passes the donation to the organization concerned. In return for a 5 per cent commission these agency charities typically assist an employer in creating a scheme, encourage internal promotion of the scheme and provide information and statistics in respect of how the scheme is progressing. The agency system is also helpful as it makes it possible for employees to give, quite literally, to any charity of their choice. It was originally felt that the cost of dealing directly with all the charities which their employees might choose to support could otherwise prove prohibitive for many employers.

British payroll giving has grown only slowly since its introduction, and £32 million was donated in 1998 to 1999 through the payroll (Romney-Alexander 2001). By 2001 over 5,000

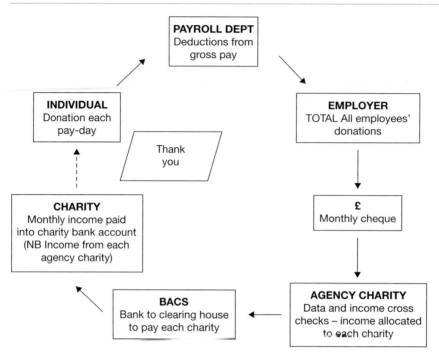

Figure 11.2 *Payroll giving scheme*

or 2 per cent of employers and 500,000 participating employees were enrolled. Impressive though these figures are, they compare unfavourably with the USA, where payroll giving has been available since 1943 and over 35 per cent of employees currently participate (Hall 1999).

In the USA the operation of payroll-giving schemes is much more straightforward than in the UK. Umbrella charities (or larger non-profits) will typically work with local employers to persuade them to establish a workplace-giving scheme. The gifts from participating individuals are tax deductible in the same way that all gifts are tax deductible in the USA, and the non-profit establishing the scheme draws the benefit of the support. The choice available to employees is thus more limited than is the case in the UK with big organizations such as the United Way typically accepting the lion's share of donations.

Employee fundraising

As we noted above, corporates can sometimes open up access to their workforce for other forms of fundraising. In such cases there are a variety of activities that may typically be organized to solicit funds from members of the workforce. Each of these may be established either as a stand-alone programme or as part of an integrated pattern of corporate support where the organization will also participate in giving, perhaps through a variety of the methods alluded to above.

Employee fundraising may either be initiated by a corporate opening up access for a non-profit to its workforce, or it may be initiated by individual members of the workforce who put pressure on the employer to support the philanthropic activity with which they are already involved. Both forms are common and there are a variety of activities that come under this general heading:

- *Events*: The employer may donate time or space for the hosting of a charity event in which members of staff may participate. This may be a social gathering or dinner, but it may equally be an 'activity' such as a sponsored walk, golf, tennis, swimming or challenge event. While it is the employees themselves who fundraise, it is often the case that an employer will also donate funds, perhaps matching the funds generated by the employees.
- *Workplace collections*: Often where particular members of staff have a link or commitment to a particular cause they will raise funds simply by collecting cash donations from their peers. Typically, permission would be sought from the employer for this to happen on work premises and/or the employer's time.
- *Sales of merchandise and raffles*: Some corporates will permit members of staff to distribute the trading catalogues of non-profits they are involved with and for purchased goods to be held on the premises for collection by members of staff who have made a purchase, or to sell raffle tickets.
- *Group activities*: A further common form of employee fundraising involves the non-profit in making a presentation to groups of staff who have expressed an interest in the cause. The goal here is to explain to members of staff how they can get involved with the work of the organization or in fundraising for it and to suggest activities that these groups of individuals may engage in. Such presentations are usually made on the company's premises and/or on company time.
- *Charity of the Year*: The final category of activity is really only an amalgam of those noted above. Some businesses will focus attention in a given year on one specific cause or organization. Usually the corporate will offer a donation of cash, time or gifts in kind and take steps to encourage the employees to conduct additional fundraising of their own. The result is an overall commitment on the part of everyone within the organization to provide meaningful support to one particular non-profit. Indeed, several large corporations now have 'Charity of the Year' schemes and, since the value of support can in aggregate be very substantial, the competition among non-profits to achieve this status is intense.

TRANSCO

Transco provides and maintains gas pipelines and has an ambitious commitment to an 'injury-free' working environment. In the mid-1990s despite increasingly high-profile campaigns within the organization, the number of accidents taking place at work had not reduced according to the company's plan. In 1998 Transco took the radical step of creating a new initiative – the so-called Safety Charity Challenge.

Under this initiative, employees are asked to identify, report and remove hazards they encounter at work. For each hazard that is spotted, the company donates $6 to a learning disability charity. If more serious hazards are identified a larger donation is offered to the non-profit.

After only eighteen months the number of lost time incidents at Transco fell by 33 per cent, saving 2,521 working days and resulting in donations of £1 million from 14,000 eliminated hazards. The improvements in safety are described by the community affairs manager as 'almost unimaginable'.

WHO TO ASK?

Selecting the right organization

Pick up any good practitioner 'How-to' guide on corporate fundraising and it will be guaranteed to exalt the need for a careful process of research to identify suitable corporate partners. Scrutiny of the local/national press, business directories and online data from websites and so on is suggested as a means of identifying the interests of particular organizations and thus the likelihood that they might be willing to support the fundraiser's non-profit.

While this process may well yield results, research into corporate fundraising has suggested a number of ways in which fundraisers can focus their prospecting efforts. These are summarized below.

Profitability

Profitability is key to whether donations will be offered and the level of such donations. Less profitable organizations are less likely to engage in philanthropy (McGuire *et al.* 1988). The fundraiser may thus find it useful to look at the recent financial performance of potential supporters and to use this data to narrow the list of potential prospects.

Turnover

Turnover is also key. Larger organizations are significantly more likely both to participate in giving and to offer higher value support (Adams and Hardwick 1998). Writers such as Watts and Zimmerman (1978) and Lenway and Rehbein (1991) have argued that this is because larger companies are likely to be more visible in their communities and also to government. Support of the non-profit community may thus serve to enhance their reputation and mitigate any risk that the government might intervene in their sector with higher taxes or compliance costs. There are many advantages to being seen as a responsible corporate citizen.

Longevity

The longevity of both the non-profit and corporate partners is positively related to donations. In other words, firms that were created some decades ago are significantly more likely to offer support to non-profits than firms created more recently. It also appears that non-profits which have been around for a while are more likely to attract support. While it would be wrong to speculate in the absence of research it does seem likely that these older non-profits have had longer to establish a reputation/brand and may thus have more to offer any potential corporate partner.

Business sector/country of ownership

Adams and Hardwick (1998) have identified that participation in and the level of giving varies considerably depending on the sector of business a particular firm might be operating in and the country of origin of its ownership. We have already seen in Figure 11.1 differences in giving between the manufacturing and service sectors, but patterns of support also vary within these broad headings, reflecting the various needs of different sectors and subsectors. Firms that are owned by others in countries with a strong tradition of corporate support also tend to be more generous than those without such links.

Nature of the shareholding

It is interesting to note that those firms with widely dispersed shareholdings are also felt to be more likely to donate money to non-profits. The rationale here is that managers will often give, not for business reasons, but rather to enhance their own standing and influence in the community. A non-profit association can enhance its reputation capital in both internal and external labour markets (Haley 1991). As Hart (1993: 16) notes, 'it is not clear that [donations] . . . are made with the consent of the firm's owners or whether they are a form of self-aggrandizing, or self promoting behavior by management'. Companies with dispersed shareholdings present managers with more power in this regard than in circumstances of concentrated ownership (Grossman and Hart 1980). When stockholding is concentrated, managers are unlikely to pursue strategies inconsistent with shareholders' direct interests (Hill and Snell 1989). Similarly, Ullman (1985) has argued that diverse ownership may act to increase the pressure for socially responsible behaviour since a breadth of shareholders increases the possibility that one or more of them will have a philanthropic motivation. It should be noted that while intuitive, no empirical support has yet been provided in support of these assertions.

Potential fit

Non-profits may well attempt, quite rationally, to identify potential partners based on simple accounting data as alluded to above. However, the concept of 'fit' is also highlighted in the literature and on many occasions. The idea here is that an organization ought to look for certain characteristics in a potential partner, leading to a higher probability of successful outcomes. Samu and Wymer (2002) describe fit in terms of the degree of congruence between a cause and a business's product/service. For example, Gerber (baby food/products) would have a higher level of fit with the March of Dimes (cause: preventing birth disabilities) than Exxon (petroleum products). We develop this theme in more detail below.

The concept of fit

Drumwright (1996) views fit between a business and a cause as a type of affinity, in which supporters of a cause feel the business partner's core business has some relationship to that cause. More recent work by Drumwright *et al.* (2000) has operationalized this notion of fit by looking at seven distinctive dimensions:

- *Mission fit*: The fit between a partner's mission and the purpose of the relationship formed.
- *Management fit*: The level of interpersonal compatibility between partner managers.
- *Workforce fit*: The fit between a company's workforce and the cause the company is supporting.
- *Target market fit*: The fit between the company's target market and the cause.
- *Product/cause fit*: The degree of congruence between the company's product and the cause.
- *Cycle fit*: The degree of synchronization between operational events in the collaborating organizations.
- *Cultural fit*: Similarities among partners regarding norms, behaviours and attitudes.

It is interesting to compare this list developed by an academic team with one developed by a non-profit professional. Elischer (2001) suggests that fit should be evaluated by examining:

- *Values*: Do the non-profit and corporate partners share the same values base? Does the corporate respect the same issues as the non-profit? Does the corporate take a strong (and compatible) stand in relation to business ethics?

- *Brand*: What will be the impact of a partnership on the brands of both organizations? How will this work, look and feel? How will stakeholders respond to this?

- *Objectives*: Is there a clear fit between the objectives of both parties? What do both organizations want to achieve? Can both sets of objectives be met?

- *Structure/geography*: In seeking to build a relationship with a corporate it will be necessary to assess the fit between the structure/geography of both organizations. Are they located in the same city? If they are both international, do they operate in the same countries? Most corporates will expect to engage with a non-profit that can adequately match their needs and respond at an appropriately local level. In the UK, for example, UNICEF has a strong relationship with the soccer team Manchester United, even though the charity is based in London. The relationship works because the charity has been able to offer a dedicated (and local) member of the regional fundraising team to manage the relationship and to respond to the needs of the corporate partner (UNICEF 2002).

The central idea running throughout these two lists is that the greater the degree of fit between the non-profit and corporate the stronger will be the resultant relationship and the more likely it will be to succeed. This presupposes, however, that both parties do want a 'relationship', and in fact many forms of corporate support, as we established earlier, do not require this level of engagement.

It is also important to note that although these lists have been offered as a means of appraising potential partnerships, many of the points made by both authors are difficult to appraise a priori. While they can certainly be appraised in the course of discussions it is doubtful whether they could genuinely be used to shortlist potential partners for support. Drawing from Drumwright *et al.* (2000), issues of management fit, cycle fit and cultural fit, for example, would be difficult to research in advance as would Elischer's notion of 'values' fit. Thus while some of these criteria could be used for the purposes of targeting potential new partners, the real utility of these lists probably lies in reflecting on the strengths and weaknesses of various relationships and fostering an understanding of when and why things may go wrong. They are thus most useful as a framework once discussions are under way and should be borne in mind as a check-list of points to consider before any form of contract is eventually signed.

Selecting the right level of contact

The starting point for many corporate fundraisers will be the Board. In essence the Board of a company exists to serve the shareholders' interests and to monitor the way in which the organization is being managed. The composition of the Board is often quite diverse, with individuals being drawn from many different walks of life. From a fundraising perspective it may well be the Board that drives the philanthropic involvement of an organization or perhaps sanctions the suggestions offered by management. It is possible in both the UK and the USA to research Board composition, and non-profits would typically look to identify whether anyone within their organization has a personal contact on the Board who could be approached to act as a 'champion'. The key here lies in building up the network of contacts and relationships a non-profit has, particularly given that many Board members are in fact members of more than one Board.

Reporting to the Board is the executive management of the organization, most significantly the chairman, chief executive officer or managing director. This individual would typically wield the most influence over the direction the organization might take and in some, particularly smaller organizations, any corporate philanthropy is likely to reflect their personal interests. Sadly, these individuals are easy for charities to target with solicitations and they are frequently bombarded with 'asks' from a plethora of causes. As Elischer (2002) has noted, many have thus developed sophisticated 'defence shields' to protect them from this blanket solicitation. It should also be noted that in medium and larger sized organizations, the decision over which non-profit will be supported will frequently be taken lower down the organizational hierarchy, drawing on one of a number of departmental budgets. Contact with the CEO may therefore be neither desirable nor necessary.

The most notable of these budgets will be the marketing budget. Where a strong business case can be made to a director of marketing for increasing sales, it may well be most appropriate for a non-profit to target this part of the organization first. Where the benefits are likely to accrue to the company as a whole, perhaps through building the overall brand image or reputation of the organization, it may be more appropriate to approach the public relations function, perhaps in tandem with an approach to the director of marketing.

If the non-profit believes that the benefit to the corporate will lie primarily in the enhancing of its relationships with its workforce or local community, it may be preferable to target the personnel or human relations (HR) department. Some organizations house their corporate giving budgets here, particularly after the introduction of payroll giving initiatives, which tend to impact on the organization most within this particular function. It is also important to recognize that many forms of corporate support, such as staff secondments, the facilitation of volunteering, the provision of training and so on, will all typically be controlled by the HR department.

Of course a typical business contains a number of other departments such as finance, corporate affairs, research and development, and sales. It may be possible for a non-profit to tap into one of these budgets with a particular approach, but which ever department is approached the rationale must be clear and the non-profit should give adequate thought to the case for support, what this may be able to deliver in terms of benefits to the business and who within the business would be most affected. This should then suggest both the level at which contact should be initiated and, in the case of lower level contacts, the particular departments that might be most interested in the opportunity presented.

It is also worth noting that many, particularly larger corporations establish a charity committee, which typically comprises representatives from both management and the workforce and will distribute the donation budget that many firms still have (Elischer 2002). The activities of these committees are generally well known in the non-profit sector and the competition for their funds is intense. Non-profits seeking to raise funds from this source must have a strong case for support and accept that the ultimate decision may well be something of a lottery, as the individual interests and biases of the members of the committee may be difficult to predict.

Finally, as Sargeant (1999) notes, too many non-profits neglect the role individuals can play in facilitating corporate fundraising. While a non-profit might lack a network of contacts that extends to Board members or even to individual managers of an organization, they may well find within their volunteer or donor base that there are individuals who work for the organization concerned. It may be appropriate to ask these individuals to take the lead in approaching the corporate, since an approach from an employee can be an excellent way of cutting through the clutter of fundraising solicitations that businesses receive. Fundamentally, if the business believes its staff are interested in the cause it may well wish to demonstrate an interest too.

FOSTERING RELATIONSHIPS

Having selected and approached an appropriate corporate supporter, the non-profit is then faced with the task of managing the relationship and, where possible, ensuring that the pattern of support becomes ongoing. Some non-profits will find that the corporate dictates in fine detail the nature of the relationship the two organizations will have. Others, by contrast, may find that they can exert more influence and thus begin to 'tie in' the corporate partner to the cause.

Academic writers such as Austin (2000, 2003) view non-profit and business relationships as progressing through a series of three distinct stages, namely:

1   *Philanthropic stage*: In this stage the business is viewed by the non-profit as a source of potential resources and primarily as a benefactor. The business views the non-profit as a charity, and hence communication and interpersonal contact between the organizations is limited. There is no need for greater involvement.
2   *Transactional stage*: In this stage the business and non-profit begin to look for benefits from the association. The relationship moves towards one based on exchange, where both parties recognize that they have something to offer the other and a dialogue opens accordingly.
3   *Integrative stage*: In the final stage, both partners seek to deepen their relationship. They find common values and overlapping missions, eventually blurring the identity boundaries of their own organizations as the two parties define themselves partially from their relationship with the other. The integrative stage approaches a merger between the organizations. Austin acknowledges that all non-profit–business associations do not evolve to the integrative stage, but he offers this stage as the ideal.

While there are clear benefits that may accrue from this approach, some authors have expressed concern about the loss of a distinctive non-profit identity that might result from an excess of corporate influence on an organization (Bruce 2000, Sargeant 1999). Such prescriptive approaches may also be criticized for failing to take account of the diverse and multiple relationships that often exist between a non-profit and various ongoing supporters. While some might benefit from an integrative approach, this is clearly not appropriate for all the organizations working with a given non-profit.

Where closer relationships are sought however, there are a variety of issues that must be managed to facilitate this growth. Among these the issue of effective communication is paramount. Academic research into such relationships has shown consistently that open and regular communication among partners is highly important, since it acts to build trust and can be an enabler for effective problem-solving (Austin 2000, Berger *et al.* 1999). In building effective relationships partners need to develop multiple communication channels, both formal and informal, at different organizational levels (Austin 1999, Sagawa 2001).

Sagawa (2001) argues that the primary forms of communication in business–non-profit relationships are:

- *Joint planning*: This form of communication involves various levels of the organizations in face-to-face interactions deciding jointly on the nature of the relationship and how it will develop. Joint plans are typically produced as a consequence, and these may or may not form the basis of an agreed contract. Sagawa argues that joint planning with teams drawn from both organizations can facilitate problem-solving and reduce conflict.
- *Ongoing communication*: Once established, a variety of forms and channels of communication, both written and oral, will be initiated. To be effective these should be regular, candid and a balanced two-way flow of ideas and information.

■ *Internal communication*: While communications between the two organizations are significant, it is also important to recognize the necessity of communicating with internal constituencies (e.g. employees, volunteers, board members, sponsors) about the relationship and its benefits.

■ *Intimacy*: Intimacy is perhaps the most difficult to define of these dimensions. Sagawa's view on intimacy is that it refers to the 'closeness' which develops between the two partners and thus the degree to which a strongly shared sense of vision and/or purpose emerges. The greater the extent to which this is present, the stronger and more enduring will be the relationship.

Other relationship variables are highlighted in the literature such as the need for a balance of power in the relationship and a sense of equality among the partners (Drumwright *et al.* 2000, Sagawa 2001). The notion of shared vision and goals (Austin 2000, Sagawa 2001) is also highlighted and, allied to this, Drumwright *et al.* (2000) add that relationships can fail because each category of organization can use different jargon to the other, fail to adequately understand the objectives of the other, and, in the case of businesses, fail to understand the complicated politics typically operating within the non-profit.

OUTCOMES

When a relationship is initiated it is important to determine from the outset how that relationship will be assessed and measured by both parties. This not only serves to reduce the capacity for conflict later, but it can act as an aid to the retention of corporate support. A very high number of businesses do not assess the relationships they have with non-profits even though these relationships may be entered into for clear business reasons. While this may be good for benefiting non-profits in the short term, since they are freed from stringent evaluation, there is a danger that support will be abandoned in times of economic downturn, since no clear business case will ever have been established and any expenditure thus rendered impossible to justify. Steckel and Simmons (1992) suggest that businesses should use the following criteria to assess their relationships with non-profits:

■ impact on sales;
■ target market results;
■ retailer and distributor activity and response;
■ scope and timing of publicity;
■ employee involvement and attitudes;
■ managerial support and attitudes;
■ public reaction to partnership choice;
■ revenue and expense results;
■ the quality of the working relationships with partners.

Non-profits should also assess the quality of any relationship from their perspective and consider factors such as the value of monetary and other support received, the exposure and media coverage generated, the public response to the partnership and the increased public awareness of the cause.

Literature on the financial outcomes of business–non-profit relationships is sparse. Work by Sargeant and Kaehler (1998) and the Centre for Interfirm Comparisons (2001) suggests that for the non-profit, an association with a corporate can be a highly lucrative venture. Sargeant and Kaehler (1998), for example, report that the mean revenue generated per $1 of fundraising expenditure in this area was found to be $6.62, noting a correlation between the size of a non-profit and the rate of return it was able to generate. This was felt to reflect the fact that many large corporate donors wished to associate themselves with a top charity brand. The study by the Centre for Interfirm Comparisons (2001), based on a much smaller sample, reported a somewhat lower rate of return from this activity at only $4.67 per $1 invested.

It is interesting to note that while data are available on the sums donated to good causes by business organizations, there has to date been no empirical study of the benefits that accrue to the business organization. This may be due in part to a reluctance on the part of business organizations to be seen to have exploited good causes, yet it remains a significant gap since better quality information may well serve to enhance corporate interest in this area.

THE PITFALLS

While we have painted a somewhat rosy picture of corporate–non-profit relationships to date, it is important to note that from the business perspective these frequently fail as the result of unrealistic expectations, inappropriate implementation of marketing tactics, or a flawed partnership or programme (Barnes and Fitzgibbons 1992). Relationships can also fail because businesses may be perceived by the public to be exploitative. As noted above, relationships that are perceived as being exploitative can actually have a harmful effect on businesses' sales. There is also risk inherent in the planned longevity of a relationship. If a non-profit decides to pull out early as a consequence of some unfavourable action on the part of the corporate partner, the resultant publicity could disproportionately damage the reputation of the organization.

Of course the risk accruing to a relationship can also affect the non-profit partner. While the for-profit's brand may benefit from the values imbued, the non-profit's brand may suffer disproportionately if negative publicity accrues to a partner (Andreasen 1996, Donlan 1998). A non-profit may be viewed as being guilty by association and even accused by other non-profits of 'selling out' (Charter 1994). This proved to be a particular issue recently for the British Red Cross, which was criticized for its relationship with Nestlé by Baby Milk Action and the Save The Children Fund. These charities felt that Nestlé was breaching World Health regulations in respect of its handling of the promotion of its baby milk formula in the developing world and that the Red Cross should not be accepting significant donations from an organization which, in their view, engaged in dubious and harmful business practices.

Non-profits can also be accused of turning away from their core values, or somehow becoming more commercial in the minds of supporters (Caesar 1986). Indeed, there is a danger that traditional supporters may elect to offer their support elsewhere when they learn of the corporate support. They may either not agree that monies from a particular corporate should have been accepted, or they could decide in the light of the additional sums being donated that their own support is no longer needed (Andreasen 1996, Caesar 1986). A further risk for the non-profit is the potential for wasted resources. If the alliance does not work out, the non-profit may have committed scarce resources and staff to the alliance that could have been used in other areas. Some corporate partners may seek to place restrictions on non-profits which may limit their ability to criticize their partner should the need arise. This is of particular relevance in respect of alliances between environmental protection non-profits and the corporate sector (Andreasen 1996).

CORPORATE FUNDRAISING PLANNING

So far in this chapter we have dealt with a range of corporate fundraising issues. In this section it is our intention to draw these various strands together and to posit a framework for corporate fundraising planning. The model we propose is depicted in Figure 11.3.

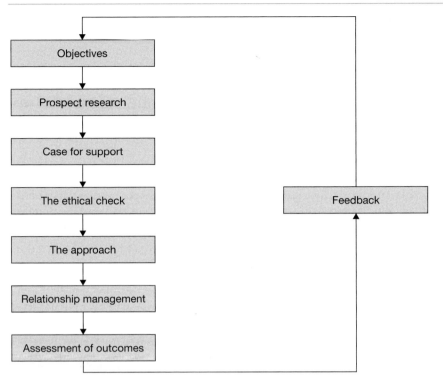

Figure 11.3 *Planning for corporate fundraising*

Objectives

As with all other forms of fundraising the first stage in the process will be for the organization to set the objectives to be achieved by the corporate fundraiser or team. These objectives will undoubtedly emerge from the detailed fundraising audit we proposed in Chapter 2 and may be couched in terms of income targets, numbers of volunteers attracted, or volume in respect of various categories of goods in kind. Some organizations will set only overall targets while others will set targets for the development of both new and existing business.

Prospect research

If one of the objectives is to generate new corporate business the organization has then to decide which organizations it should target with the fundraising resources available to it. For larger non-profits this may involve profiling past corporate supporters to see whether certain categories of business have a propensity to support the cause. This information may then be used to try and identify other, similar businesses that might have an interest.

Smaller organizations, or those without a track record in this area, will be forced to begin by examining trade and press reports of the corporate support that has accrued to other, similar non-profit organizations. This will give them a sense of the kind of organization that may also wish to support them.

Similarly organizations of every size could begin by looking at what they have to offer a business and work up from this list of capabilities to those businesses that may have the required 'fit' with this profile. Again data may be gleaned from the trade media, public media and business directories and journals. The Internet also offers considerable utility in researching potential corporate partners.

In the USA the Foundation Center in New York produces *The National Guide to Corporate Giving and Corporate Source Profiles*. The Taft Group (Rockville Maryland) produces *The Taft Corporate Giving Directory* and *The Taft Guide To Corporate Giving Contacts*. The *Chronicle of Philanthropy* is also a key source of data and in particular its annual review of corporate giving activities. In the UK the Directory of Social Change produces *The Guide to UK Company Giving* in book and CD-Rom formats, plus a magazine, *Funding for Change*, which provides updates on corporate and trust donors, activities and policies.

We highlighted earlier that many good leads could be generated from existing supporters, staff and/or volunteers. Many individuals connected with the non-profit may already have strong links to a corporate, or even be working currently for a potential partner. These links need to be identified and examined to see whether potentially useful partnerships or other forms of support might accrue.

Case for support

Once a list of potential supporters has been assembled an appropriate case for support can be generated. This requires the non-profit to consider carefully what it can offer a corporate, what the interests of the corporate are likely to be, the nature of the support the non-profit will be looking for and the nature of the relationship, if any, it is looking to establish. It is the marriage of these factors that together combine to form the case for support. It should offer a business a strong, clear and highly attractive set of reasons for why corporate support should be offered.

The ethical check

Having delineated a list of prospects and specified appropriate cases for support many non-profits then proceed to the solicitation stage. However, non-profits rushing into relationships with corporate partners have frequently had occasion to regret this decision as it can subsequently become clear that some relationships are wholly inappropriate. This is frequently because the organization is involved in something that is directly or indirectly at odds with the non-profit's cause. A children's charity, for example, can find that its corporate partner in the USA owns a toy manufacturer in Asia that employs large numbers of children in its workforce. Similarly an environmental charity in the UK may find that it is accepting donations from a company which is actually pumping lethal gases into the atmosphere in one of its chemical plants in Africa. In both cases, should these facts become public knowledge, significant and very damaging publicity could accrue for both the non-profit and corporate partners.

It is for this reason that many non-profits have now generated ethical policies which map out the kinds of organization the non-profit will work with, the standards of behaviour that are expected and the consequences of any breach (e.g. immediate termination of the partnership). Such policies make it clear to fundraisers which organizations they can work with and in effect pre-empt problems by ensuring that the non-profit only works with enterprises compatible with its own mission. An example of an ethical policy is provided in Exhibit 11.2.

Of course, life is rarely this neat and when one attempts to apply an ethical policy a number of issues commonly arise:

■ *Chain of command*: While it may be relatively easy to research the activities of a corporate partner directly, it is less easy to research the activities of the companies that might own this partner or be owned by it, particularly in Third World countries. Indeed, it is legitimate to ask: At what point should this research cease? Is it only the partner organization, its parent company, its subsidiaries that should be addressed by the ethical policy, or literally every business that is owned or part-owned by the partner? The wider the scope of enquiry, the more difficult the task, and thus the more time-consuming and expensive it will be.

- *Polluter pays?* It is no accident that many major oil companies are keen to invest in environmental charities. When a major oil spill occurs or a tanker sinks on the high seas, unimaginable damage can be done to wildlife and the environment. Some might therefore argue that it would be obscene to allow oil companies to fund the charities that may have to engage in the clean-up, or who exist to put pressure on companies to enhance their safety procedures. They argue that such non-profits need their independence and must be free of 'tainted money' to have the maximum possible impact. There is also the opposite view that this work would have to be undertaken anyway and thus why shouldn't the oil companies foot the bill for this kind of work? After all, they create the problem, so is it not right that they should also contribute to its resolution? There is no 'right' answer to questions of this type; it really depends on one's ethical perspective, and a non-profit needs to take a clear stance and to be ready to defend that stance when necessary.
- *History*: When does a tainted supplier become untainted? In other words, when a corporate previously engaging in unacceptable behaviours ceases those behaviours, at what point may donations be accepted by the non-profit? Does this happen immediately on cessation of these behaviours, or at some future date?

None of these issues are straightforward and a good ethical policy will help fundraisers to decide what is and what is not appropriate. Relationships should be sought only with corporates that meet the requirements of the ethical policy. Similarly, unsolicited donations must only be accepted from those companies who meet the requirements of the ethical policy. Both dimensions are of equal importance.

The approach

The non-profit must then decide how to approach potential corporate supporters. At its simplest level this will usually be a decision about whether to deal directly or indirectly with the organization. What we mean here is that if the non-profit has only very limited resources and a large number of corporate prospects with only a weak case for support, it may be appropriate to simply initiate an approach through direct mail. Where a non-profit has a corporate fundraising team, significant numbers of volunteers, a strong case for support and highly qualified prospects, it will be more appropriate to focus on a more personal approach involving site visits from the fundraising team.

The complexity of the issue is such that it is impossible to be prescriptive, but the form the approach will take will be a function of the likely value of the support, the degree to which the prospects are qualified, the strength/relevance to the corporate of the case for support, the availability of volunteers, the fundraising resources available and so on.

Relationship management

Once a relationship is established the non-profit needs to create a plan for administering and managing that relationship. This will have two key components to it. The first is the delivery of an appropriate quality of service to the corporate supporter. For some kinds of relationship this may only be as simple as a timely and personalized acknowledgement of a gift. For other

EXHIBIT 11.2 CORPORATE CONTRIBUTIONS POLICY

Introduction

Under no circumstances will policy or programme decisions be affected by the companies that donate to support the work of Breast Cancer Action. BCA cannot be bought, influenced or discouraged from our mission to eradicate breast cancer. Throughout our history, Breast Cancer Action has relied primarily upon the financial support and generosity of our individual members. Nevertheless, financial realities dictate that Breast Cancer Action also seek funding from other sources such as foundations and corporations.

BCA recognizes, however, that the effectiveness of our work in public education, advocacy and coalition-building depends on the organization's credibility, particularly in the eyes of our members and the people we serve. The funding sources of any advocacy organization can appear to affect its political legitimacy, particularly in situations where corporate support raises the possibility of inference or perception of a conflict of interest.

BCA's corporate contributions policy aims to reconcile the need to ensure the long-term financial health and longevity of the organization with the desire to avoid potentially real or perceived conflicts of interest related to corporate giving.

Guiding principles

The following principles guide BCA's corporate fundraising strategy:

1   Providing unbiased information about breast cancer diagnosis and treatment necessitates that Breast Cancer Action be free of any appearance of conflict of interest. Accordingly, BCA will not accept financial support from corporate entities whose products or services BCA knows include cancer diagnosis or treatment.

2   BCA advocates the precautionary principle of public heath that calls for acting on the weight of the evidence that links environmental carcinogens to breast cancer and other cancers, rather than waiting for absolute proof of cause and effect. Consistent with this position, Breast Cancer Action will not knowingly accept funding from corporate entities whose products or manufacturing processes directly endanger environmental and/or occupational health or may possibly contribute to cancer incidence, nor will BCA knowingly accept donations from corporate entities that work to weaken or circumvent environmental and occupational regulations that would protect the public health and might decrease cancer incidence.

Unacceptable corporate contributions

Based on these guiding principles as well as BCA's mission and operating principles, BCA will not knowingly accept funding from the following categories of corporations (the following list is not necessarily exhaustive):

- Pharmaceutical companies
- Chemical manufacturers
- Oil companies

- Tobacco companies
- Health insurance organizations
- Cancer treatment facilities

This policy is intended to ensure that BCA is independent from outside influences in the pursuit of our mission and to avoid potential or perceived conflicts of interest. While we understand the impact of global capitalism and the structures of multinational corporations, this policy does not require BCA to engage in exhaustive review of every corporation to trace the sources of income. BCA does recognize that the activities of many corporations change rapidly, and that we will periodically need to evaluate new information about corporate donors and the implications of that information in light of this policy. We encourage our members and others to provide information about corporate activities that they believe has bearing on this policy.

Potential corporate contributions that may be problematic but are not adequately addressed by this policy will be evaluated by the Executive Director, and, if necessary, by the Board of Directors. In addition, as questions arise, an ad hoc committee comprised of staff, board and outside participants may be formed to recommend refinements of this policy.

This corporate contributions policy will be used as a guide for BCA's Executive Director and Board of Directors to inform the organization's fundraising activities. BCA will continue to focus our fundraising efforts on individual giving, either through direct contributions or through workplace giving programs. This policy shall not be construed to prohibit BCA from accepting matching gifts from corporations that are initiated by donations from individual corporate employees.

Adopted August 1998

Source: © Breast Cancer Action. Reproduced with kind permission

categories of relationship the non-profit needs to ensure that it is honouring its obligations and that any objectives the corporate might have are likely to be met. If not, this needs to be recognized as soon as possible and corrective action initiated.

The second key component is a plan for developing and taking forward the relationship in the way that the non-profit would prefer. This might include plans to deepen the relationship, cross-sell other fundraising products or increase the organization's share of the donation income available. In cases where the relationship is not working out as envisaged, this may also be a plan for withdrawal from, or the ultimate cessation of, the relationship.

Both components of a relationship management plan must be carefully integrated.

Assessment of outcomes

As we noted above, the non-profit should seek to evaluate its relationships with corporate partners on an ongoing basis. This is essential to ensure that the quality of such relationships is developed and/or maintained. It is also essential to ensure that the relationship remains appropriate and that the costs/benefits of involvement are as envisaged.

It is also important that the corporate be invited (in all but the cases of philanthropic donations) to appraise the effectiveness of its non-profit involvement. A clear rationale for support and demonstration of the achievement of corporate objectives will substantially increase the likelihood of future support.

Feedback

Finally, the non-profit should reflect on the outcomes obtained and use these data to inform subsequent corporate fundraising planning. At the very least a knowledge of the characteristics of successful relationships can greatly assist in prioritizing the recruitment resource available for subsequent year's activities. Fundamentally, however, all knowledge gained from the market will have value in informing subsequent planning.

STRUCTURES

Thus far in this chapter we have largely ignored the issue of organizational structure. While we noted that it may be appropriate to seek corporate partners who 'fit' with the non-profits' existing structure, this matter was not elaborated on in depth. In this section it is our intention to return to this issue and to explore how non-profits typically structure their approach to corporate fundraising and the alternatives available.

Non-profits serving a large geographic area such as a country or state have to decide whether to focus their corporate fundraising activity around their headquarters, or whether to attempt to fundraise across the whole of the geographic coverage of the organization. Where the non-profit is based in a large city, there may well be a plethora of contacts that can be followed up locally which could result in corporate support. If it is based in a more rural location, this is likely to be more problematic, and it may be better to focus attention on businesses operating near the programmes the organization is involved in running.

Focusing effort around the organization's base has the advantage that control can be retained centrally, ensuring that only appropriate relationships are entered into and that the quality of these relationships is maintained. Proximity also makes it easier to package the kind of benefits a business may be seeking, such as access to celebrities, leveraging the brand and so on. Where appropriate, volunteers can also be easily recruited in centres of population and again trained by head office staff to ensure a consistent quality of skills.

The downside of this degree of centralization is that the organization may be missing out on significant opportunities in other parts of the country where businesses may very well wish to support the organization and often with large sums of money. The difficulty with fundraising in other regions is that it then becomes necessary to create regional teams of corporate fundraisers, either on a paid or volunteer basis. The distance can make it difficult to achieve appropriate recruitment, retention and supervision of the work undertaken. Unless these individuals work from home, overhead costs may also become an issue and the costs of corporate fundraising can spiral.

Sadly there is no one right approach. Many organizations struggle to find the optimal approach for them and there is frequently an element of 'trial and error' until the appropriate structure is identified. The best advice that may be offered is simply to:

- Appraise the scale of the opportunity for corporate fundraising in each of the regions in which the organization operates.
- These opportunities should then be banded, indicating the likely financial worth of each region.
- In those areas with the greatest potential, a regional office may be created, including salaried corporate fundraisers and/or volunteers. If particularly large corporate accounts exist, one or more dedicated staff may be appointed to liaise with particular clients.
- In those regions with only minimal potential, the overheads associated with an office can be avoided by individual members of staff working from home in that region, possibly soliciting volunteer support and involvement to assist them in their task.

■ Where the greatest potential is concentrated around the headquarters of the non-profit, the temptation to expand wastefully into other regions should be avoided, unless it is possible to 'piggy-back' corporate fundraising on other forms of fundraising that are being undertaken in these areas. The temptation for too many organizations is simply to attempt to chase every corporate donation that might potentially exist. This is not only an approach that is doomed to failure from the outset, it may very well achieve a highly negative return on investment and lose the non-profit cash it has worked hard to earn from other sources.

CHAPTER SUMMARY

In this chapter we have provided a framework that may be used by non-profits to consider the planning of their corporate fundraising activity. We have also conducted a review of the available research into this form of fundraising, delineating what is known about the kinds of businesses that support non-profits, their motives for such support, what they look for in a partner and how such relationships might be managed.

In reviewing this chapter, however, it is important to retain a sense of perspective. The significance of the corporate sector as a source of income should not be overstated. Businesses provide only a very small percentage (typically well under 10 per cent) of the income accruing to the non-profit sector in most major Western countries. Businesses are also notoriously ungenerous and offer only a small fraction of their pre-tax profits to good causes.

We have also noted how the trend in recent years has been away from philanthropy and towards dual agenda giving, where businesses expect to see very real returns for their investment. Perhaps inevitably it is not every non-profit that is in a position to be able to deliver this return and, as a consequence, corporate giving tends to be concentrated in the hands of a few large non-profits with equally large and established brands.

Of course, there are exceptions to this – but in deciding whether to engage in corporate fundraising for the first time it is important to recognize that a large number of organizations either lose money on this activity or achieve returns that are little above break-even. When the opportunity costs of not being able to use fundraising resources elsewhere are taken into consideration, corporate fundraising can become a 'blind alley' that wastes significant time and monetary resources. It should thus not be entered into lightly.

DISCUSSION QUESTIONS

1 Explain the difference between dual agenda and philanthropic giving.

2 In your role as a fundraising consultant you have been invited to make a presentation to the Board of a non-profit new to corporate fundraising. The Board has asked you to explain the process that the non-profit might establish to raise this category of funds.

3 What is CRM? What are the advantages and disadvantages of soliciting this form of funding?

4 Explain how the approach to soliciting payroll gifts differs between the USA and the UK.

5 Why should a non-profit engaging in corporate fundraising require an ethical policy? Explain the significance and utility of this document.

6 Why may corporate fundraising not be appropriate for every non-profit to engage in?

REFERENCES

AAFRC Trust (2002) *Giving USA*, AAFRC Trust For Philanthropy, Indianapolis, IN.

Adams, M. and Hardwick, P. (1998) 'An Analysis of Corporate Donations: United Kingdom Evidence', *Journal of Management Studies*, 35(5): 641–654.

Andreasen, A.R. (1996) 'Profits for Nonprofits: Find a Corporate Partner', *Harvard Business Review*, 74 (November/December): 47–59.

Austin, J.E. (1999) 'Strategic Collaboration between Nonprofits and Businesses', *Nonprofit & Voluntary Sector Quarterly*, 29 (supplement): 69–97.

Austin, J.E. (2000) *The Collaborative Challenge: How Nonprofits and Businesses Succeed Through Strategic Alliances*, Jossey-Bass, San Francisco, CA.

Austin, J.E. (2003) 'Marketing's Role in Cross-Sector Collaboration', *Journal of Nonprofit & Public Sector Marketing*, 11(1): 23–41.

Barnes, N.G. and Fitzgibbons, D.A. (1992) 'Strategic Marketing for Charitable Organizations', *Health Marketing Quarterly*, 9(3/4): 103–114.

Basil, D.Z. (2002) 'Cause-Related Marketing and Consumer Attitudes: The Effects of Balance and Fit on Cognitive Processing', Ph.D. dissertation, University of Colorado.

Berger, I.E., Cunningham, P.H. and Drumwright, M.E. (1999) 'Social Alliances: Company/Nonprofit Collaboration', *Social Marketing Quarterly*, 5(3): 49–53.

Bragdon, F.J. (1985) 'Cause Related Marketing: Cases To Not Leave Home Without', *Fund Raising Management*, 16(1): 42–47, 67.

Bruce, I. (2000) *Marketing Need*, ICSA Publishing, London.

Caesar, P. (1986) 'Cause-Related Marketing: The New Face of Corporate Philanthropy', *Business and Society Review*, 59 (autumn): 15–19.

Centre for Interfirm Comparisons (2001) *Fundratios 2000/2001*, Centre for Interfirm Comparisons, Winchester, Hants.

Charter, M. (1994) *Greener Marketing*, Greenleaf Publishing, Sheffield.

Cone Inc (2002) *Our Research. Cone, Inc*, available online 11 March at http://www.conenet.com/Pages/research.html.

Corkery, P.J. (1989) 'What's In It For Me?' *Business Month*, 34 (November): 46–47.

Corporate Citizen (2002) 'Major Charities' Corporate Income', *Professional Fundraising*, January: 14–18.

Donlan, J.P. (1998) 'Zen and the Art of Cause-Related Marketing', *Chief Executive*, 138 (October): 51–57.

Drumwright, M.E. (1996) 'Company Advertising with a Social Dimension: The Role of Noneconomic Criteria', *Journal of Marketing*, 60 (October): 71–88.

Drumwright, M.E., Cunningham, P.H. and Berger, I.E. (2000) 'Social Alliances: Company/Nonprofit Collaboration', *Marketing Science Institute Working Paper Report*, No. 100–101.

Elischer, T. (2001) 'Two's Company', *Professional Fundraising*, July.

Elischer, T. (2002) *Corporate Fundraising*, Directory Of Social Change, London.

Farquarson, A. (2000) 'Marketing Campaigns Impact on Consumer Habits', *Guardian*, 15 November, available online 25 February 2002 at http://society.guardian.co.uk/voluntary/story/0,7890,397881,00.html.

Grossman, S. and Hart, O. (1980) 'Takeover Bids, The Free-rider Problem and the Theory of the Corporation', *Bell Journal of Economics*, 11(1): 42–64.

Haley, U.C. (1991) 'Corporate Contributions as Managerial Masques: Reframing Corporate Contributions as Strategies to Influence Society', *Journal of Management Studies*, 28(5): 485–509.

Hall, H. (1999) 'Fundraising Trends and Ideas', *Chronicle of Philanthropy*, 26 August: 25–29.

Hart, O. (1993) 'An Economist's View of Fiduciary Duty', LSE Financial Markets Group Discussion Paper, No. 157, London School of Economics, London.

Hill, C.W.L. and Snell, S.A. (1989) 'Effects of Ownership Structure and Control on Corporate Productivity', *Academy of Management Review*, 32(1): 25–46.

Himmelstein, J.L. (1997) *Looking Good and Doing Good: Corporate Philanthropy and Corporate Power*, Indiana University Press, Indianapolis, IN.

Hunt, A. (1986) 'Strategic Philanthropy', *Across The Board*, 23, (July/August): 23–30.

Josephson, N. (1984) 'AmEx Raises Corporate Giving To Market Art', *Advertising Age*, 23 January: 10.

Kropp, F., Holden, S.J.S. and Lavack, A.M. (1999) 'Cause Related Marketing and Values In Australia', *Journal of Nonprofit and Voluntary Sector Marketing*, 4(1): 69–80.

Lenway, S.A. and Rehbein, K. (1991) 'Leaders, Followers and Free Riders: An Empirical Test of Variation in Corporate Political Involvement', *Academy of Management Review*, 34(4): 893–905.

Levine, J. (1989) 'I Gave At The Supermarket', *Forbes*, 144 (December): 138–140.

Lovell, B.A. (2001) 'Cause Marketing That Touches The Heart', *Fund Raising Management*, September: 22–25.

McGuire, J.B., Sundgren, A. and Schneeweis, T. (1988) 'Corporate Social Responsibility and Firm Financial Performance', *Academy of Management Journal*, 31(4): 854–872.

Mescon, T.S. and Tilson, D.J. (1987) 'Corporate Philanthropy: A Strategic Approach to the Bottom Line', *California Management Review*, 29 (winter): 49–61.

Pifer, A. (1987) 'Philanthropy, Voluntarism and Changing Times', *Journal of the American Academy of Arts and Sciences*, Winter: 119–131.

PMA & Gable Group (2000) 'Survey of Cause Marketing,' available online on 4 March 2002 at http://www.pmalink.org/causemarketing2000/index.html.

Romney-Alexander, D. (2001) 'Payroll Giving in the UK: Donor Incentives and Influences on Giving Behavior', *International Journal of Nonprofit and Voluntary Sector Marketing*, 7(1): 84–92.

Ross, J.K. III, Stutts, M.A. and Patterson, L. (1991) 'Tactical Considerations for The Effective Use of Cause-Related Marketing', *Journal of Applied Business Research*, 7(2): 58–65.

Sagawa, S. (2001) 'New Value Partnerships: The Lessons of Denny's/Save the Children Partnership for Building High-Yielding Cross-Sector Alliances', *International Journal of Nonprofit & Voluntary Sector Marketing*, 6(3): 199–214.

Sagawa, S. and Segal, E. (2000) *Common Interest, Common Good: Creating Value Through Business and Social Sector Partnerships*, Harvard Business School Press, Boston, MA.

Samu, S. and Wymer, W.W. Jr. (2002) 'Social Advertising: Effects of Dominance and Fit on Attitudes and Behavioral Intentions', 2002 Academy of Marketing Science Conference, 29 May to 1 June, Sanibel Island, Florida.

Sargeant, A. (1999) *Marketing Management for Nonprofit Organizations*, Oxford University Press, Oxford.

Sargeant, A. and Kaehler, J. (1998) *Benchmarking Charity Costs*, Charities Aid Foundation, West Malling, Kent.

Shell, A. (1989) 'Cause Related Marketing: Big Risks, Big Potential', *Public Relations Journal*, 45(7): 8, 13.

Shore, B. (2001) 'Companies and Communities Sharing A Message', *New Century Philanthropy*, 11(2): 3.

Smith, C. (1994) 'The New Corporate Philanthropy', *Harvard Business Review*, 72 (May–June): 105–116.

Ullman, A.A. (1985) 'Data in Search of a Theory: A Critical Examination of the Relationship Among Social Performance, Social Disclosure and Economic Performance', *Academy of Management Review*, 10(1–2): 540–557.

UNICEF (2002) *Annual Report and Accounts 2000/01*.

Varadarajan, P.R. and Menon, A. (1988) 'Cause-Related Marketing: A Coalignment of Marketing Strategy and Corporate Philanthropy', *Journal of Marketing*, 52 (July): 58–74.

Wagner, L. and Thompson, R.L. (1994) 'Cause-Related Marketing', *Nonprofit World*, 12(6): 9–13.

Watts, R.L. and Zimmerman, J.L. (1978) 'Towards a Positive Theory of the Determination of Accounting Standards', *The Accounting Review*, 53(1): 112–134.

Webb, D.J. and Mohr, L.A. (1998) 'A Typology of Consumer Responses to Cause-Related Marketing: From Skeptics to Socially Concerned', *Journal of Public Policy & Marketing*, 17(2): 226–238.

Wokutch, R.E. and Spencer, B.A. (1987) 'Corporate Saints and Sinners', *California Management Review*, 29 (winter): 72.

Wymer, W.W. Jr and Samu, S. (2003) 'Dimensions of Business and Nonprofit Collaborative Relationships', *Journal of Nonprofit & Public Sector Marketing*, 11(1): 3–23.

Chapter 12

Trust and foundation fundraising

LEARNING OBJECTIVES

By the end of this chapter you should be able to:

■ Outline the charitable Trust and Foundation marketplace.

■ Describe the main processes used in fundraising from Trusts and Foundations.

■ Describe the 'grant cycle' and the importance of feedback and reporting in this form of fundraising.

■ Discuss the reasons applications to Trusts and Foundations might fail.

INTRODUCTION

A Charitable Trust or Foundation is a body set up privately to make grants for charitable purposes. There are about 10,000 Charitable Trusts and Foundations in the UK and they give in the region of £2 billion in grants each year, which makes them as important an income source as local authorities or central government departments. Data suggests that grant-making trusts are responsible for supplying approximately 13 per cent of an 'average' UK charity's income. In the UK, grant-making Trusts and Foundations are regulated under the same laws as other charities, being required to register with the Charity Commission in England and Wales (the law is slightly different in Scotland and Northern Ireland) and to publish an annual report and accounts giving information about their grants. They are thus required to be transparent, though as independent bodies they are not publicly accountable. UK grant-making Trusts have been classified (Clay 1999) into the following groups:

1 *Institutional* – Set up with a number of trustees. Institutional Trusts tend to make grants according to detailed procedures, have established criteria and guidelines on which to base their decision-making, and employ professional staff.

2 *Private* – Set up by a single individual who takes most of the grant-making decisions alone or after discussion with a spouse.

3 *Family* – Often set up by one individual, in memory of an earlier family member or as a result of a discretionary form of Will, with trustees who are related or at least closely connected to each other. Decisions tend to be taken collectively but informally.

4   *Corporate* – These are Trusts where the income of the Trust is dependent upon the profits of a company or group of companies. Decisions tend to be made by committees and ratified by directors of the company. These Trusts now increasingly take account of the views and interests of employees.

In the USA a clearer distinction is made between public charities, which are those with multiple sources of income and exist mainly to carry out charitable work themselves, and Foundations, which are usually funded by one (or a few) benefactors and exist to give money away to good causes. Different rules apply to these two types of organizations, and Foundations are required by law to distribute at least 5 per cent of their assets each year to other non-profits.
   In the USA a Foundation is defined as:

- a non-profit, nongovernmental organization with a principal fund or endowment of its own;
- an organization which maintains or aids charitable, educational, religious or other activities serving the public good, primarily by making grants;
- an organization created and organized as a corporation or charitable trust under state laws and which receives federal tax-exempt status from the Internal Revenue Code.

There are four types of Foundations in the USA:

1   *Independent* – A fund or endowment, designated by the IRS as a private Foundation, the primary function of which is to make grants. Assets are most commonly derived from the gifts of an individual or of a family. Governance and management vary widely.
2   *Company sponsored* – A private Foundation, set up to make grants, which derives its funds from a profit-making business, which often works to reflect corporate policies and interests. Governance may include company employees and non-employees.
3   *Community* – Usually classified as a public charity rather than a Foundation, Community Foundations derive their funds from many donors, but in other ways function much like an independent Foundation. They are often established to service the needs of a specific geographical area.
4   *Operating* – A private Foundation that conducts research, promotes social welfare and engages in programmes determined by a governing body or a charter, and rarely makes grants. Operating Foundations are required by the IRS to spend 85 per cent of their income on their own activities. Examples include the Getty Trust and the Amherst Wilder Foundation.

According to The Foundation Center, there are nearly 62,000 grant-making Foundations in the USA, and they gave approximately $30.3 billion in 2002. This represents about 12 per cent of the total given to non-profits.
   Given the importance of Trusts and Foundations as a funding source, comparatively little research has been undertaken in this area, and the decision-making process followed in awarding grants remains obscure in many cases. The basic tools and methods employed in raising funds from Trusts and Foundations have remained the same over many years, though technological developments have facilitated some advances (as well as an increase in competition for grant income). If it is managed well, Trust and Foundation fundraising can be creative, deliver high returns and produce lasting, profitable relationships with important funders.

GIVING PATTERNS AND PREFERENCES OF TRUSTS AND FOUNDATIONS

Most Trusts and Foundations derive their income from an endowment: a capital sum given by a wealthy individual, family or company. The endowment may take the form of cash, stocks, shares or land. It provides a tax-exempt income that funds grant giving. Some Trusts derive income from other sources, such as gifts from a company's current profits, or from a regular public appeal (e.g. Comic Relief or Children in Need).

Overall, Trust and Foundation giving levels are closely tied to the performance of the stock market as most assets are held in the form of stocks and shares. In the late 1990s the market rose quickly and Foundation giving rose alongside. With market drops in recent years, Trust and Foundation grant-making has been sustained by the formation of new Trusts and Foundations (both individual and corporate), by continued payments against multi-year commitments and by some large gifts of assets to existing Foundations. In future years it is thought that the Trusts and Foundations marketplace will continue to grow as an increasingly popular method of giving for individuals with significant personal wealth.

Trusts and Foundation giving decisions reflect individual and often idiosyncratic preferences and styles. These will depend on the history of the Trust, on its stated policies and priorities, and also on the personalities and preferences of individual trustees at any given time. Many Trusts are set up to give grants for 'general charitable purposes', while others have narrowly defined objects, and most fall somewhere in between. Trustees have to bear the origin and ethos of the Trust in mind when allocating grants, but are also duty-bound not to ignore external changes in social, economic and political conditions. Where Trusts date from previous centuries their objects sometimes have to be reinterpreted by trustees to reflect current circumstances. All Trusts and Foundations are different, and they range from those where a single trustee makes giving decisions on an informal basis to those with a professional secretariat and formal application, selection and decision-making processes and materials in place. Within the terms of their Trust, trustees can be creative, unorthodox and independent in the decisions that they reach on the awarding of grants.

In the UK there are little data available on patterns of Trust giving by charitable cause. Generally, Trusts and Foundations like to fund areas that do not attract government funding. According to the Association of Charitable Foundations, key preferences include:

- new methods of tackling problems;
- disadvantaged and minority groups which have inadequate access to services;
- responses to new or recently discovered needs and problems;
- work which is hard to finance through conventional fundraising;
- one-off purchases or projects;
- short- and medium-term work which is likely to bring a long-term benefit and/or to attract long-term funding from elsewhere.

Twenty-five per cent of grant expenditure in the UK is made by a very few large scientific and academic research-oriented Trusts, which hold 44 per cent of the assets of the Trust sector. These Trusts make an important contribution to activity in their areas of interest.

In the USA approximately a quarter of all Foundation grants go to the education subsector. Giving priorities differ greatly between independent and community Foundations in other areas of giving, as Table 12.1 demonstrates.

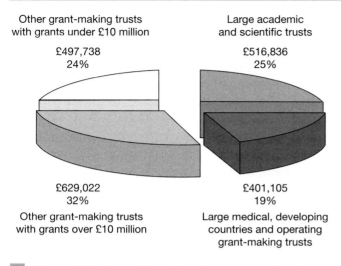

Other grant-making trusts
with grants under £10 million

£497,738
24%

Large academic
and scientific trusts

£516,836
25%

£629,022
32%

Other grant-making trusts
with grants over £10 million

£401,105
19%

Large medical, developing
countries and operating
grant-making trusts

Figure 12.1 *Composition of total grant expenditure (£000s), 2001–2002 (UK)*
Source: © Charities Aid Foundation and Caritas Data Ltd. Reproduced with kind permission

Table 12.1 *Percentage of total Foundation grants given by subsector in 2000 (USA)*

Subsector	Independent Foundations	Community Foundations
Arts, culture and humanities	11	14
Education	25	27
Environment/animals	7	4
Health	23	12
Human services	13	24
International	3	1
Public/society benefit	10	11
Religion	2	5

Source: The Foundation Center (2002) *Foundation Giving Trends: Update on Funding Priorities*, p. 66

All forms of US Foundation tend to allocate the largest share of their grant giving to programme support as opposed to capital funding, equipment purchase or general operating support. In the USA and the UK their preference is usually for one-off or time-limited grants rather than for the provision of long-term funding.

RAISING FUNDS FROM TRUSTS AND FOUNDATIONS

As discussed above, Trusts and Foundations cover a huge range; from the small, informal personal Trust, operating on a voluntary basis from a home address, through to the large, professionally run concern. The first category of Trust seldom has the capacity to communicate with applicants and is unlikely to acknowledge applications or reply to organizations that have been unsuccessful. In some cases the information available on the previous giving history

EXHIBIT 12.1 STRENGTHS AND WEAKNESSES OF GRANT-MAKING TRUSTS AND FOUNDATIONS AS A FUNDRAISING SOURCE

Strengths

- availability of information. Online resources are multiplying and it is easy to obtain core information;
- many Trusts will fund over a three-year period, providing stability and the potential for planning;
- trusts exist to give money away;
- trusts will often fund projects or areas which are not attractive to other sorts of funders;
- applying to Trusts is relatively easy and inexpensive.

Weaknesses

- lack of in-depth information on giving patterns;
- lack of feedback, especially in the case of smaller Trusts;
- tend to fund only short-term projects, and not to fund overhead or staff costs;
- difficult to build relationships;
- high levels of competition for funding.

and founding objectives of such Trusts is scant. Larger Trusts and Foundations by contrast are likely to have a professional staff, a range of printed information materials and a website (some US Foundations now encourage online applications) and will issue formal application forms or guidelines, deadline dates for submissions, requirements for supporting information and full details of previous grants given.

In seeking to raise funds from Trusts and Foundations each Trust should therefore be approached as a unique organization. As with the other forms of fundraising discussed in this book, there are essential stages that can be followed in the preparation and submission of any funding request to a grant-making Trust or Foundation, of whatever size and level of professionalism. Exhibit 12.1 outlines some of the strengths and weaknesses of Trusts and Foundations as a fundraising source.

TRUST/FOUNDATION RESEARCH

Directories and databases of grant-making Trusts and Foundations are available, and are increasingly kept updated with information. In both the UK and the USA these data are now available online. The Directory of Social Change and CAF in the UK and the Foundation Center in the USA provide the core services in this area. A sample entry from the DSC/CAF online directory is provided as Figure 12.2.

While such entries provide the basic information required to make an application, more can often be gleaned from the Internet, or through enquiries to previous grant recipients. Trustees may also be researched as individuals — as in major gift prospecting — to ascertain whether any links between the individual and the charity requesting funding can be made or any further information about the interests of individual trustees can be gathered.

The Tilda Foundation

Grant total £25,000 (1998/99)
Beneficial area UK and Asia.

Health, education, Asian charities, general

The trust makes grants towards health, education, Asian charities and for other purposes.

In 1998/99 the Trust had assets of £112,000 and made 14 grants totalling £25,000.

Grants for the year included £15,700 to Sarvoday Yuvak Mandal, £5,000 to The Gujarat Hindu Society, £2,500 to Bharatiya Vidya Bhavan, £500 each to CYANA: Cancer – You Are Not Alone and Alzheimer's Disease Society, £200 each to Muscular Dystrophy Group and Age Concern, £100 each to Leukaemia Research Fund, Whizz–Kid, Saint Francis Hospice and The Children's Care Challenge and other smaller donations.

Applications In writing to the correspondent.

Contact details and other information

c/o Tilda Limited
Coldharbour Lane
Rainham
Essex
RM13 9YQ
Tel 01708 717777
Fax 01708 717700

Correspondent Shilen Thakrar, Trustee

Trustees S Thakrar; R Thakrar; V Thakrar; R Samani

Figure 12.2 *Sample entry for the DSC/CAF online directory*
Source: © Charities Aid Foundation and Directory of Social Change. Reproduced with kind permission

Most Trusts and Foundations are hugely over-subscribed with applications. It is therefore essential that approaches are directed only at those grant givers with a clear mandate to support the area of charitable activity the non-profit organization is engaged in. Application guidelines should always be respected, as Trusts and Foundations receive a high level of misdirected applications and will screen out any that are not presented in the required way, clearly fall outside their area of interest or where deadlines have not been adhered to. Research is also essential on the level and type of grant that tends to be given to ensure that any application made is for a suitable gift amount. Many Trusts stipulate that grants will not be given for certain types of cost such as staff or overheads, and again, given the level of competition for Trust funding, there is little point in ignoring such guidance.

THE APPLICATION/PROPOSAL

Some Trusts and Foundations require an initial outline letter of enquiry to be sent for consideration prior to a full application. If this is the case, the letter should be very concise, providing initial information about the non-profit, the project and the way a grant would be used. If this is seen to fall within their guidelines and current priorities, clearance will be given for a full application to be submitted.

APPLICATION FORM

Please complete this form in the spaces provided (please do not attach any supplemental pages). **Please ensure that you do not exceed the specified word limits, or we will be unable to process your application.**

Please send your completed application form, together with a copy of the **latest audited or independently examined accounts (as applicable) of your charity and a recent bank statement,** to:

Catherine Small
The Tubney Charitable Trust
c/o Nabarro Nathanson
The Anchorage
34 Bridge Street
Reading RG1 2LU

Telephone: 0118 925 4662
Fax: 0118 950 5640

Further copies of this application form can be downloaded from www.tubney.org.uk

CHARITY DETAILS

1. Name of charity

2. Charity address:

3. UK Registered charity number
    (if applicable)

4. Website address:

5. Contact's name:

6. Contact's position
    (e.g. Trustee, Senior Manager):

7. Telephone number:

8. Fax number:

9. E-mail address:

CHARITY BACKGROUND

10. Charity's objectives:

11. Activities: **in no more than 50 words**
    please provide a brief description of the
    activities carried out by your charity.

DETAILS OF APPLICATION

12. In no more than 50 words please describe
    the purpose for which funds are sought.

13. The Trustees as a matter of policy intend only to fund projects
    which provide a significant degree of outward provision and
    benefit to the community. Please therefore explain **in no
    more than 50 words** how you intend this to be achieved.

14. Amount requested:
    *(please note the minimum grant level of £30,000 and the
    maximum grant level of £250,000 per annum)*

Figure 12.3 *Tubney Trust application form*

Source: © The Tubney Trust. Reproduced with kind permission

15. When would you like to receive the funds
    (indicate if in instalments):

16. (a) Indicate the overall total needed for the project;
    (b) Indicate how much money you have raised so
        far towards the project, and where this funding has
        come from;
    (c) Indicate how you are intending to raise the balance of
        funds and from what sources. If known, indicate when
        funding decisions will be made.

17. Have you applied to us before for funding, whether
    successfully or not?

    If yes, please give brief details including the date(s) of the
    application(s), the amount(s) applied for/awarded and what
    the funding was for.

18. Further Information:
    Please list any relevant additional documentation which is
    available. Any further information will be requested only if
    required.

19. How would you like to receive payment: Cheque
    tick as appropriate
                                               Made
                                               payable to:

                                               or

                                               Bank account:

If you would like funds paid directly into your charity's bank   Bank Name:
account, please provide details:

                                               Sort code:

                                               Bank address:

                                               Account name:

                                               Account No.

20. I enclose a copy of the charity's latest audited or   ☐
    independently examined accounts (as applicable).
    (Please note that we will not be able to process your
    application without this)

21. I enclose a copy of the charity's entry from the Register   ☐
    of Charities or proof of the charity's exempt/excepted status.
    (Please note that we will not be able to process your
    application without this)

22. I enclose a copy of a recent bank statement for the charity ☐
    (Please note that we will not be able to process your
    application without this)

I confirm that the details given above are correct and I acknowledge that these details may be provided to a third party individual or
organization for the purpose of processing the application, including peer review of the application.

Signed: ....
             Trustee/Senior Manager

Name: ....

Position: ....

Date: ....

Applications should be as concise as possible. Those Trusts and Foundations that issue application forms often severely restrict the word length, as all trustees are required to read and consider a high number of applications (see Figure 12.3).

The application should include a short opening paragraph on the fundraising organization, its history, mission and objectives. This should be followed by more specific information relating to the nature and size of the need to be addressed, a more detailed description of the project or part of the organization for which funds are being sought and an indication of the impact a grant would have. Innovative or unique features of the proposal that may set it apart from others should be clearly featured.

The full cost of the project should be stated, and an itemized budget presented. A realistic time scale should be included, plus information on what other fundraising is being undertaken to resource the project, including the names of other Foundations being approached, or from whom funding has already been secured. If the project is long term, information should be provided on how the work is likely to be sustained after the grant income is exhausted. Every application should include an outline of how the success of the work will be judged and monitored.

In terms of presentation, applications to Trusts should be personalized and professional, attractively presented but not produced to such high standards that profligate spending on fundraising might be suggested. Where photographs are included they should be carefully chosen and limited in number. Clarity and simplicity is key.

If specific forms of supporting information are requested in Trust application guidelines (such as supporting letters from beneficiary groups or letters of reference from partnership agencies), these, and nothing extra, should be submitted. Where no specific guidance is given, Trusts and Foundations should always be provided with evidence of the legal standing of the non-profit, its governance structures, senior trustees and personnel, and of its current financial situation. The latest annual report and accounts of the non-profit usually serve these purposes.

In some cases, often with larger Trust and Foundations, a visit will be arranged by an assessor as part of the decision-making process. If this is the case, the Trust representative is usually there to assess the need for the project and the extent to which the applicants have found a good and workable solution. They may also be looking for reassurance that the applicants are able to deliver what they promise. This is the chance for the non-profit to bring the project to life, so the assessor should meet individuals who know about the project and are passionate about it. If the application is for a capital project it may be necessary for the potential funder to request technical plans, equipment specifications and specialist assessments to ensure that they understand what is intended and that the project is viable and well planned.

When UK Trusts were asked to rank the criteria they used to evaluate applications, the data in Table 12.2 were obtained.

INTERNAL PROCEDURES AND TOOLS

To fundraise successfully from Trusts and Foundations a non-profit needs to have certain internal procedures in place. It is essential that programmes and support requirements are costed and packaged into discrete units, and that budgetary procedures enable support services and overhead costs to be allocated to these units. Trusts and Foundations will consider covering these essential costs only if they are presented to them as part of a fundable unit or project.

Procedures must also be in place to facilitate financial management and accountability of grant funds received. Grant funders differ widely in the sort of feedback and reporting they require, but all non-profits applying for such funding must be able to offer transparency in grant allocation and to ensure that where restrictions are imposed these are honoured.

Table 12.2 *Criteria used by Trusts in evaluating applications*

Factor	Ranking
Strategic fit with Trust's mission	1
Figures requested realistic	3
Amount requested within acceptable parameters	4
Past experience of applicant	5
Amount of benefit to accrue to society	5
Evidence of support from other Trusts	6
Evidence of applicant's own efforts to raise funds	4

Source: © *International Journal of Nonprofit and Voluntary Sector Marketing.* Reproduced with kind permission

Tailored database applications relating to Trust and Foundation fundraising are available. These enable fundraisers to record details of Trusts approached, their basic grant criteria, the size of grants given and application requirements and deadlines. All correspondence between the non-profit and the grant-making Trust can be recorded, alongside grants given and reporting required.

Whether a database or a less sophisticated system is in place for recording Trust approaches and relationships, the Trusts and Foundations marketplace should be segmented and targeted for best effect, with larger Trusts prioritized over smaller ones, and those with remits closely matching the non-profit organization prioritized over those with wider or less closely matching objects.

BUILDING RELATIONSHIPS WITH TRUSTS AND FOUNDATIONS

Once a grant has been obtained, a letter of thanks should be dispatched immediately, and any requirements for reporting, recognition, anonymity or feedback clarified. These should be recorded and adhered to strictly. Where no specific guidance is issued, reports on progress should be submitted every six months.

Designing a suitable 'stewardship' or relationship-building process for Trust and Foundation funders can be problematic, as they vary widely in the way they are structured, and in what they deem suitable in terms of levels of communication from grant recipients. In most cases trustees and Trust administrators will not wish to be added to general mailing lists or given subscriptions to magazines or newsletters, as this would add to the deluge of mail and information they receive. They may, however, respond positively to invitations to events, and often request that new annual reports and accounts should be sent to them.

In each case the best rule for the fundraiser is to treat every instance as a separate and unique relationship. Table 12.3 reports on what feedback is preferred by UK Trusts (Sargeant and Pole 1998).

It is also interesting to note that while 26.9 per cent of Trusts welcomed invitations to visit the project, when probed further only 11.5 per cent of Trusts said they would actually attend, with over 48 per cent saying that they would appreciate being asked but would be unlikely to attend!

Once a grant has been given, a non-profit can consider that a relationship of some sort exists, and that prospects for further support are positive if the non-profit proves responsible, communicative and respectful of the Trust funder. Research should be a continuous process, and

Table 12.3 *Additional feedback preferred by Trusts*

Additional feedback welcomed	Percentage of respondents indicating
Financial information about how the grant was used	51.1
Invitations to visit the project	26.9
Requirements for likely future funding	26.7
Number of eventual beneficiaries	24.4
Nature/profile of eventual benefactors	22.2
Problems encountered with the project	20.0

Source: © *International Journal of Nonprofit and Voluntary Sector Marketing*. Reproduced with kind permission

should build a comprehensive picture of the requirements and preferences of all the Trusts and Foundations that fund an organization. This ongoing research should include the tracing of any personal links between trustees of charitable Trusts and individuals involved in the beneficiary charity, as any such personal links can be invaluable in fostering the relationship and enabling more direct and individual approaches to be made. However, it should also be noted that many Trusts and Foundations deliberately maintain an impersonal and strictly businesslike approach and discourage unnecessary 'familiarity'.

THE GRANT CYCLE

Grant-making Trusts and Foundations differ greatly in relation to how often they will accept applications from an individual charity, and how long they will take to consider and make a decision on any application.

Figure 12.4 represents this as a cycle taking place over a one-year period. Many Trusts will not consider submissions from a charity that has been given a grant more than once a year, though in special cases additional funding may be given before this date if a good relationship has been built and the charity can present a sufficiently urgent and impressive case for support. In the case of some larger Trusts and Foundations a three-year period is stipulated as a mandatory 'gap' between grants. Some Trusts prefer to allocate the bulk of their funds each year to an established cohort of charities they have selected for ongoing support, while others will adhere to a policy that a proportion of all gifts given each year should go to new recipients. The fundraiser must be responsible for researching the grant cycle in the case of each Trust or Foundation to ensure that applications adhere to the correct timings.

Why applications fail

Research undertaken among UK Trusts (Sargeant and Pole 1998) provides useful information on why applications for Trust funding fail. Table 12.4 provides data on key mistakes made by applicants. Respondents in the research project were also asked what areas required most additional research by fundraisers. Table 12.5 records the findings.

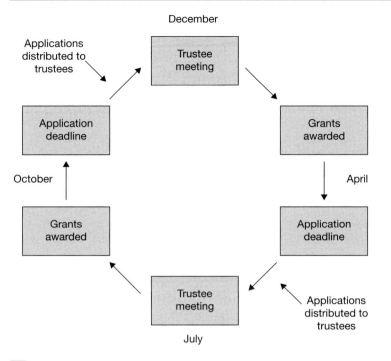

Figure 12.4 *The grant cycle*

Table 12.4 *Reasons for declining grant applications*

Category	Percentage of respondents identifying
Applicant did not read requirements	55.3
Applicant sent large amounts of unnecessary information	23.4
Application poorly presented	19.2
Applicant did not state how funds would be used	14.9
Applicant did not read the instructions for making an application	14.9
Applicant did not send a copy of accounts	14.9
Applicant did not make it clear that it was a charity	12.8
The application was impersonal and mass produced	12.8
No stamped addressed envelope was enclosed	10.6
Applicant was 'over-friendly' either in postal or telephone communications	8.5
Applicant sent insufficient information for a decision to be made	8.5
Applicant did not state the amount of funding that was sought	6.4
Application was too 'plush'	6.4
Other	8.6

Source: © *International Journal of Nonprofit and Voluntary Sector Marketing.* Reproduced with kind permission

Table 12.5 *Additional research suggested by Trusts*

Additional research	Percentage of respondents
Nature of causes supported	58.9
Past record of giving	30.6
Interests of Trustees	14.6
Submission dates	14.3

Source: © *International Journal of Nonprofit and Voluntary Sector Marketing*. Reproduced with kind permission

In the USA, similar findings are reported on why proposals are declined. The Fund Raising School at the Indiana University Center on Philanthropy provides the following list:

- the project has not been documented properly;
- the project does not strike the reviewer as significant; the statement of the project does not interest him or her;
- prospective client groups appear not to have been involved in planning and determining project goals;
- the proposal is poorly written and hard to understand;
- proposal objectives do not meet objectives of funding source;
- the proposal budget is not within the range of funding available through the funding agency;
- the proposed project has not been co-ordinated with other individuals and organizations working in the same area;
- the funding source has not been made aware that those individuals submitting the proposal are able to carry out what is proposed. Not enough substantiating evidence is provided;
- project objectives are too ambitious in scope;
- the proposal writer did not follow guidelines provided by funding agency;
- there is insufficient evidence that the project can sustain itself beyond the life of the grant;
- the evaluation procedure is inadequate.

It would seem that the availability of information on Trusts and Foundations, and the increased ease with which non-profits can produce application materials, is leading to an increase in the number of applications and a decrease in their quality. While fundraising from Trusts and Foundations is always a 'hit-or-miss' activity at times, it remains profitable if fundraisers undertake research, tailor funding proposals with care, and adhere to the guidelines and requests issued by Trust funders. With levels of competition increasing, there is little point in pursuing Trust and Foundation funding in any other way.

CHAPTER SUMMARY

Charitable Trusts and Foundations are an important source of funding for both US and UK non-profits across a range of subsectors. Trusts and Foundations range from small private funds run on a very part-time and voluntary basis by one person who may be both chief administrator and sole decision-maker, to the huge Foundations run by paid full-time staff and featuring formal application and decision-making procedures.

As such, it is important that non-profits research potential Trust and Foundation funders with great care, gathering all the available information before making any request for funding. Building relationships with Trust and Foundation funders is a mixture of the personal and the professional. Where personal links can be made or built the non-profit will undoubtedly be at a great advantage, but many Trusts operate on an impersonal, businesslike basis and state their preference for a formal and distanced relationship with the organizations they choose to fund. In both instances the Trust and Foundation fundraiser bears the responsibility of researching these communication preferences and reacting accordingly in order to build the most appropriate relationship.

While every Trust requires individual attention, the core 'rules' of a good application should be laid down and followed. Non-profits engaging in fundraising from Trusts and Foundations need to have systems in place to record and segment, and the financial controls in place to enable the packaging of requirements including staff and overhead costs into 'projects' that can be presented as fundable units. Trust and Foundation fundraising can be one of the most profitable sources of income generation in terms of the return on investment produced, but fundraisers will be required to reach and maintain high standards to ensure continued success in an increasingly well-resourced and competitive fundraising marketplace.

DISCUSSION QUESTIONS

1   Explain the differences and similarities in the ways Trusts and Foundations are categorized in the USA and the UK.

2   In your capacity as head of fundraising, draft the headings you would use to structure a grant application for a capital project to restore an Edwardian theatre in London.

3   Draft a question guide for use in telephoning charitable trust administrators to gather information from them prior to submitting an application. What key information would you wish to gather?

4   Trustees of Trusts and Foundations may also appear on a charity database in another guise. Make a list of the overlaps you might find.

REFERENCES

Clay, A. (ed.) (1999) *Trust Fundraising*, Charities Aid Foundation, West Malling, Kent.

Sargeant, A. and Pole, K. (1998) 'Trust Fundraising – Learning To Say Thank You', *Journal of Non-profit and Voluntary Sector Marketing*, 3(2): 122–135.

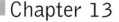

Chapter 13

Branding and campaign integration

LEARNING OBJECTIVES

By the end of this chapter you should be able to:
■ Define branding and describe a number of models of 'brand'.
■ Explain the various approaches to brand management an organization may adopt.
■ Explain the role of branding in fundraising activity.
■ Delineate brand values.
■ Understand the importance of integrating fundraising campaigns with other non-profit communications.

INTRODUCTION

The topic of branding is generating ever more interest in non-profit circles, and with good reason. A strong and effective brand offers a non-profit a number of distinctive advantages that can greatly enhance the efficiency of both its fundraising operations and charitable service provision.

Roberts Wray (1994) was one of the first to explicitly debate the relevance of branding to the charity sector, arguing that one could brand charities in the same way as corporate organizations or their products. There is evidence that this may indeed be true – at least in part – and that although as Tapp (1996: 335) notes,

> charities do not describe much of what they do as 'branding', but organizations have long been concerned with maintaining a consistent style and tone of voice and conducting periodic reviews of both policies and actions to ensure that a consistent personality is projected.

Such practices are the very essence of brand management, irrespective of whether the organization's management might regard it as such.

It is interesting to reflect on how times have changed. Until recently branding was regarded as something of a 'dirty' word by non-profit managers afraid of being seen to grasp at some of the most 'disreputable' elements of for-profit marketing practice. There was a fear that in

Plate 13.1 *RSPCA fundraising materials*
Source: © RSPCA. Reproduced with kind permission

giving active consideration to branding, non-profit organizations would somehow lose a sense of what made them distinctive (Ritchie and Swami 1998).

In reality nothing could be further from the truth; attempts to manage an organization's brand should actually enhance the character of the non-profit, emphasizing its strengths and achievements alongside its *modus operandi*. Saxton (1995) suggests that the practice of branding in this context should differ from commercial practice insofar as it should both draw on, and project, the beliefs and values of its various stakeholders. This leads to what Hankinson (2000) regards as the greater complexity associated with managing charity brands. She argues that charity brands require a different approach that distinguishes between the 'functional attributes of the brands – their causes – and the symbolic values of the brand – their beliefs' (Hankinson 2001a: 233). Hankinson (2001b) cites the example of the RSPCA whose cause is preventing cruelty to animals, while its values are 'caring', 'responsible', 'authoritative' and 'effective'. Both dimensions pervade its communications (see Plate 13.1).

In this chapter we examine the concept of 'brand' and explore what it can offer a non-profit. We also discuss a number of models of brand and the implications for brand strategy and campaign integration.

WHAT IS A BRAND?

The American Marketing Association defines a brand as follows:

> A brand is a name, term, sign, symbol or design, or a combination of them, intended to identify the goods or services of one seller or group of sellers and to differentiate them from those of competitors.

257

In the non-profit context a brand is thus a device to allow members of the public to recognize a particular non-profit that may take the form of a name, trademark or logo. Legislation in Northern Europe and North America provides protection to the owners of these devices which ensures that no other organization can impinge on their intellectual property. Brands may not be borrowed or copied without permission.

This degree of protection is important since brands are in essence a promise to the public that an organization possesses certain features, or will behave in certain ways. Aaker (1997) argues that in fact brands can convey up to six levels of meaning to a consumer:

1   *Attributes*: Brands can suggest certain attributes the organization may possess. These attributes may include the size of the non-profit, the scope of its activities, the nature of the work undertaken and so on. In short, the brand can act as a vehicle for summarizing what the organization does and how it does it.

2   *Benefits*: Brands also offer a series of functional and emotional benefits. From donors' perspective when they elect to associate themselves with a particular brand by offering their support they are buying a distinct set of functional benefits either for themselves, or more likely for the beneficiary group. By giving to a branded organization that they already know by virtue of the non-profit's general communications, they will already be aware of the impact their gift may have long before a fundraising solicitation is actually made.

Benefits can also accrue to the donor and these again could be functional in nature. As we discussed in Chapter 5, some donors may be motivated to give because of the status their association with the organization will confer. They may also wish to attract the awards on offer through a donor recognition programme. However, donors may also gain emotional benefits from their association with a brand. Wearing the logo or symbol of a non-profit organization might confer an identity to the donor, just as in the commercial world wearing a brand such as Nike conveys an identity to the young people that sport their shoes. Of course in the non-profit context this process may be a little more thoughtful and may often involve a desire to express a sense of solidarity with the cause. A powerful UK example of this would be the Royal British Legion's Poppy Appeal, where many millions of small gifts are solicited in return for the token of a poppy that may then be worn in public from the time of purchase until Remembrance Sunday when the nation acknowledges the sacrifice of its armed forces (see Plate 13.2). It is interesting to note how many public figures elect to wear their poppy in the run-up to the commemoration and that over thirty-three million poppies are produced in total.

3   *Values*: The brand can also convey something of the organization's values, not only what it stands for, but also the way in which it will approach key issues related to the cause. A non-profit, for example, may have bold, authoritative and challenging values, while another may be helpful, sympathetic and caring. The values of an organization will often be derived from the passion of the founders of the organization, from religious associations or from the nature of the work undertaken. What is actually happening here is that the values of the various stakeholders to the organization are being projected into how the organization communicates with the outside world. When the charity Botton Village, for example, began fundraising for the first time, it was keen to imbue its communications with the ethos of the Steiner philosophy that drives the organization forward. Fundraisers were thus keen to bring donors inside the organization and to make them feel a genuine and valued part of their community.

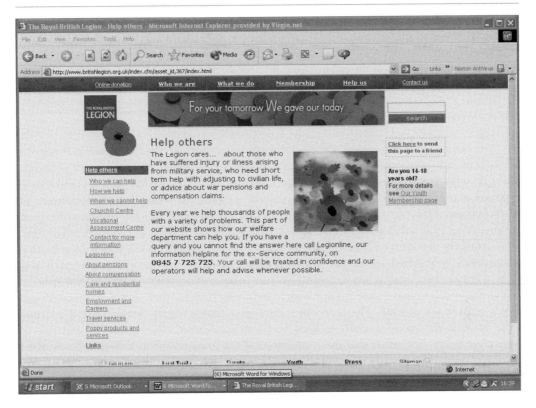

Plate 13.2 *Royal British Legion Poppy Appeal*
Source: © Royal British Legion. Reproduced with kind permission

Using brands to convey the values and beliefs of stakeholders can greatly aid a donor's understanding of the charity concerned and suggest very potent reasons why it might be worthy of support (Dixon 1996). This latter point is of particular significance since authors such as Dixon (1996), Kennedy (1998) and Denney (1998) have noted that an increased focus on branding, or indeed a complete rebranding exercise, will often be precipitated by a crisis in income generation.

4   *Culture*: In the non-profit context this element is hard to differentiate from values. In the commercial sector an individual brand may have distinctive values, but it will also communicate something of the corporate culture of the parent organization (i.e. the way it does business). For non-profits, the culture of the organization will be driven in large measure by the values of the various stakeholder groups. Indeed, a non-profit organization is often a melting-pot of such values, which in turn drive how the organization will behave. Greenpeace's culture, for example, has historically been very confrontational, since the non-profit seeks to put pressure on commercial organizations it sees as damaging the environment.

5   *Personality*: Aaker argues that some brands can convey a distinctive personality. In the case of commercial sector marketing, the Fosters lager brand drew heavily on the character of the Australian comic Paul Hogan in the late 1980s. Non-profit brands can also convey a distinctive

personality and there are often personal characteristics that accrue to the image of an organization. This may occur because of the activities of a particularly flamboyant founder whose own personality becomes indelibly stamped on the organization's brand, but equally it can simply develop over time as the public come to view the non-profit more as a personality than an organization per se. The charity Comic Relief is an excellent example of this. Grounds and Harkness (1998) have argued that the clarity with which this personality is projected will have a direct impact on an organization's ability to fundraise.

6   *User*: Many brands also convey a sense of the nature of the user. Charity brands may suggest the kind of individual who will either donate to the cause, benefit from the work it undertakes, or some combination of the two. Age Concern, for example, has built a brand that is regarded as responding to the needs of the elderly, tackling the issues that are of concern to this group and attracting funding not only from this age category but also from caregivers in the preceding generation who will be facing these issues themselves in ten to twenty years' time. Similarly the charity ENABLE uses its brand to good effect. It is the largest membership organization in Scotland for people with learning disabilities and family caregivers. It was formed in 1954 by a small group of parents because many families with a child who had learning disabilities felt alone and isolated. They wanted better services for their sons and daughters and better support for parents. The brand they have now built over the years conveys a strong sense of what the group is really looking for from supporters. The message is not one of sympathy or pity, but rather that the organization seeks to empower its beneficiaries to make a real change in their lives. The brand conveys to donors that this is what they are 'buying' by making a donation.

Of course there is more to branding than the mere selection of an appropriate name. All the communications the organization creates, both in character and style, should reinforce the brand image that the non-profit is trying to project. The focus should thus be not only on what is said but how it is said, and this should pervade all the communications channels employed. Thus all direct mail, press, TV, radio, Internet and outdoor advertising should reflect the brand, but so too should the manner in which the organization responds to telephone enquiries, interacts with all its beneficiary groups and even presents required statutory data such as annual accounts.

WHY BRAND?

There are a number of reasons why an organization should consider branding.

Organizations that develop brands are simply more successful at fundraising than those that do not. Frumkin and Kim (2001) found that non-profit organizations which spent more on marketing themselves and branding their organization to the general public did better at raising contributed income. Regardless of the field in which non-profit organizations serve, positioning around mission and using this to drive the brand positively influenced the flow of contributions. Why should this be?

First, brands are an aid to learning. If branding has been used as a tool to educate members of the public over time there is no need for a fundraiser to begin from a 'zero base' in his or her fundraising communications. There will be a baseline of understanding about the work the organization undertakes and its values in the minds of potential supporters. This makes the fundraising task a lot easier. Harvey (1990), for example, identified that the most familiar non-profits tended to generate greater levels of both help and giving, reinforcing the notion that branding may play a key role in 'drip feeding' potential donors with a knowledge of various facets of the organization's role, values and work. This is highly significant since, as Bendapudi and Singh (1986) note, where a knowledge of the charity's image is lacking, donors may either ignore a communications message or 'distort' it to excuse themselves from making a gift.

Branding is also of relevance since the learning imparted to potential donors through the brand can serve to reduce the risk to them in offering a donation. Agency theory is key in relation to this issue, since in making donations donors are in effect requiring non-profits to act as their agents in disbursing funds. The brand image of a non-profit will provide numerous clues as to how well a particular non-profit will perform in this capacity. This is particularly the case in impersonal forms of fundraising such as direct mail, press or radio advertising, where donors may be entirely reliant on their *perceptions* of the organization in deciding to offer a donation. On a related theme Tapp (1996) argues that brands can serve to enhance trust between a non-profit and its donors/potential donors. Brands provide assurance that an organization is worthy of trust and that funds donated will be used in a manner consistent with standards that have been established over time (Ritchie and Swami 1998).

A further key benefit that branding can offer is differentiation (i.e. making it clear how an organization differs from its competitors). It conveys what is distinctive about the range of activities undertaken, or the manner in which these are approached. It is absolutely essential that the concept of differentiation is understood and fully integrated into brand strategy, or a non-profit's communication budget may actually benefit other organizations in the sector which the donor may support in the mistaken belief that they are supporting the focal organization. Research has shown consistently that organizations with similar brand names, values or personalities can quickly become confused in the minds of donors to the point where a regular payment is offered to one organization while the donor believes they are supporting another (Sargeant and Jay 2003).

It is also worth noting that the sheer number of non-profit organizations that are currently seeking funds can easily confuse even the most diligent of donors. Branding can help reduce this clutter, make it clear why a particular organization is deserving and thus make it easier to raise funds (Hankinson 2000).

Successful branding can also have a dramatic impact on the bottom line by opening up opportunities to offer the brand to appropriate third parties, as is the case with cause-related marketing (see Chapter 11). In the USA a number of large charities have even introduced their own branded products, earning substantial sums of revenue as a consequence. The Children's Television Workshop has been highly successful in its licensing arrangements for some 1,600 Sesame Street products, ranging from a Big Bird battery-operated toothbrush to a Cookie Monster Bulldozer, to thirty companies, including J.C. Penny and Hasbro (Meyers 1985). Commercial endeavours of the Children's Television Workshop with its brands were estimated to generate $70.3 million in 1995. Other examples include Girl Scout Cookies, a first-aid kit developed by the Red Cross, and the best-selling software in American schools by the Bank Street College of Education in New York.

Branding can also offer a form of reputation insurance to a non-profit. Having built up a consistent image over time that becomes trusted and increasingly well understood by donors and other stakeholders, short-term crises can be survived. The Aramony scandal rocked the United Way in the USA when the Chief Executive was accused of wasting donated funds by building up expenses such as unnecessary flights on Concord. This had a dramatic impact on donations in the short term; however, the reputation of the organization was such that in the medium term the organization was able to regain its share of gifts and relative position in the market. Thus while one would hope that scandals as acrimonious as the Aramony affair would be relatively rare, non-profits will inevitably find that they will make mistakes on occasion. A strong brand makes it considerably more likely that such mistakes will be forgiven or even overlooked.

261

Finally, branding is an aid to loyalty, particularly where the benefits we discussed above accrue in part to the donor. As donors are rewarded for their association with the brand and begin to learn more about the activities it undertakes, the brand begins to serve as a tool for building a closer relationship with the donor. Polonsky and Macdonald (2000) thus argue that organizations with an established brand can leverage this to build donor loyalty and protect themselves from competitive pressures. Indeed, empirical support for this proposition is provided by Sargeant *et al.* (2001).

BRAND STRATEGY

Having discussed the concept of branding and how it may be of relevance to non-profits, we will move on to consider how a brand strategy is developed.

Brand relationships

Thus far in the text we have implicitly assumed that it is only the non-profit as a whole that will be branded. This need not be the case. While the non-profit's name may constitute one level of branding it is quite possible that distinct fundraising products could be branded, or even discrete components of the service the organization provides to beneficiaries. A number of approaches are thus possible.

1   *Corporate umbrella brand* – Where the organization itself is branded. There are numerous examples of this as it is by far the most common non-profit practice. The United Way, Red Cross, UNICEF and the World Wildlife Fund all have strong and in some cases international corporate brands.
2   *Family brand* – Non-profits may elect to have separate brands for their fundraising and service provision products. Schemes such as Adopt A Dog or Sponsor a Granny have been branded by their respective non-profits as distinctive fundraising vehicles. These may well be subdivided to send a different message to distinct donor segments. Similarly, there may be branded components of service provision such as Talking Books or Lifeline, which could in turn have sub-brands for specific categories of service user.
3   *Individual branding* – Finally, an organization can simply elect to brand aspects of its service provision or fundraising with separate and entirely unrelated brands. Such a strategy may be appropriate where the donor or service user population is diverse and/or where service provision is complex with may different components. In such circumstances it is unlikely that a family or umbrella brand could be developed coherently and where, as a consequence, it would be more practical to simply look to brand each product.

In taking such decisions it is important to bear in mind that there may be risks in relying too heavily on only one brand. While we have noted that a strong brand can help mitigate the risk of unfavourable publicity should something go wrong, weaker brands may not weather the storm and any ill-performance or dissatisfaction may directly reflect on the organization. When an organization develops multiple brands this risk is mitigated since, if the public trust in one is damaged, there are other opportunities to regain this through the work of the other brands in the portfolio. By developing multiple brands and a leadership in multiple target markets, the organization increases its chances for survival (Kotler and Andreason 1996).

Of course, no brand strategy is carved in stone and multiple brands must be managed in exactly the same way as multiple products. Gallagher and Weinberg (1991), for example, suggest employing the matrix depicted in Figure 13.1. Here each brand is evaluated for its

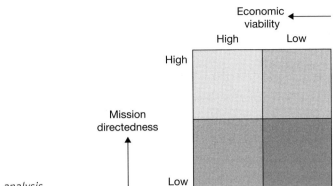

Figure 13.1 Brand portfolio analysis

contribution to the mission and contribution to the economic viability of the organization. As with other models of portfolio, those brands in the lower right-hand corner of the matrix would be clear candidates for divestment, while those in the top left-hand corner would be clear candidates for investment. Those on the diagonal would require further evaluation to determine an appropriate strategy to adopt.

Differentiation

Whatever approach is ultimately adopted, each brand must be carefully differentiated from those of the competition. We discussed in Chapter 4 the concept of positioning, and it is positioning that forms the basis for shaping an appropriately differentiated approach.

To achieve this an organization must undertake a detailed analysis of the other provision in the market and identify in particular those organizations with similar names, brands, values, activities and stakeholder groups. In the case of each brand the organization should look at how it compares with the nature of other provision and what, if anything, is genuinely distinctive about it.

In seeking to achieve this, organizations frequently employ a model such as that depicted in Figure 13.2. There are notable similarities between this and Aaker's six categories of meaning discussed above. It is simply a further way of conceptualizing a brand and thus seeking to identify components that either are, or could be, genuinely distinctive. It also draws a helpful distinction between the rational components of a brand, where perhaps donors are consciously aware of the rationale for their support and the emotional aspects of a brand, which may impact at a more subconscious level.

It comprises:

1   *Brand essence* – The core of what the brand will stand for.
2   *Source of authority and support* – The brand may be differentiated on the basis of the quality of the organization's authority (i.e. those whose views are expressed). A number of the large cancer research charities, for example, can draw on the authority of the medical staff and researchers they represent.
3   *Attributes*.
4   *Physical benefits* – To the donor or beneficiary.
5   *Personality* – The human attributes of the brand.
6   *How it makes the donor feel* – Does the brand offer any emotional benefits to the donor as a reward for their support?

263

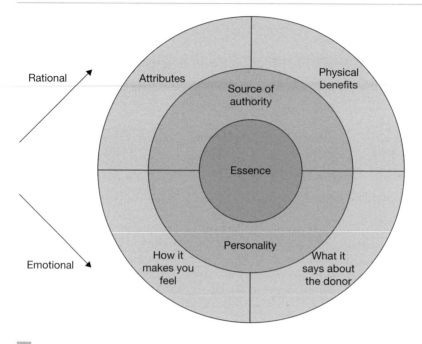

Figure 13.2 *A model of brand*

7 *What it says about the donor* – Does the brand convey an identity to donors by virtue of their support?

Brands may be differentiated by one or more of the above components. The strongest brands tend to be those that can offer a powerful sense of differentiation on all seven components, but this is often very difficult to achieve on a practical level.

Brand partnerships

The majority of the largest non-profit organizations in both the USA or the UK have developed strong brands, either by the conscious evolution of strategy, or by default where, whether the organization likes it or not, a brand has evolved by virtue of the organization's presence in a given market. In the past too many organizations have assumed that because they did not regard branding as appropriate or desirable that they would not have a brand. It is actually the perception of donors and other stakeholders that matters.

Other brands have been built through collaboration with for-profit commercial organizations. There are numerous examples of small non-profits which have been helped to become household names by virtue of their association with a large corporate partner. American Express, in particular, has been very helpful to a number of fledgling non-profits.

Equally, many non-profits will elect to develop brand partnerships with corporates in return for a fee or some form of cause-related marketing agreement. In such circumstances the non-profit brand is very much a partner in the agreement and may indeed have more to offer the corporate by way of meaning and values than could ever be offered in return. Whether an agreement is worth entering into will be a function of the following advantages and disadvantages.

Advantages

- The relationship can generate considerable income for little financial or human cost on the part of the non-profit.
- The positive brand images of the for-profit can be transferred, at least in part, to the non-profit.

Disadvantages

- A non-profit organization will probably have little say in how the branding process will evolve, since the branding strategies will typically be developed by the commercial partner to ensure that their specific objectives are met.
- There are very real risks that the image of the non-profit could be damaged if the commercial partner is later found to be behaving inappropriately in some aspect of its operations. This can be particularly damaging where these activities are at odds with the mission of the non-profit.

EXPLORING BRAND VALUES

Given that many non-profit brands pertain to the organization as a whole and that a key component of such brands is the value they project, it is worth exploring briefly what is meant by the term 'organizational value' and how this may be reflected in a charity brand.

Dose (1997: 227–228) defines organizational values as 'evaluative standards relating to work or the work environment by which individuals discern what is "right" or assess the importance of preferences'.

Similarly, Van Rekom (1997) refers to an organization's 'central value orientations' as pervading its overall behaviour, and Collins and Porras (1996: 66) regard values as a set of 'timeless guiding principles' which require no external justification. This latter point is expanded by Saviour and Scott (1997), who argue that while values are highly important in explaining the behaviour of individuals and groups within organizations, they are often unperceived, unspoken and taken for granted. Organizational values are 'common sense' and thus require no explanation.

Academic interest in organizational values has been frequently focused on the relationship between specific values, or forms of values and organizational performance. Authors such as Deal and Kennedy (1982) and Collins and Porras (1996), for example, have identified a link between 'strong' organizational values and corporate success. The authors argue that the difference between good and visionary companies is that the latter have a stronger sense of their core values. Companies that enjoy enduring success have a set of core values that are not compromised by the vagaries of the marketplace but remain fixed, and that many of these values have a 'likeable' or 'humanist' dimension. This point is particularly key for non-profits, many of whose brands reflect these very dimensions. The lesson is that successful brands convey a consistent and strongly differentiated message over time.

Practitioners in the non-profit sector often claim that being value(s)-based is one of the features that distinguishes their organizations from those in the public or private sectors (Aiken 2001). The distinctive way in which non-profits manage and organize themselves is viewed as due in part to organizational values, and writers such as Batsleer *et al.* (1991) argue that without these values some non-profits would simply not exist. Although it is recognized that charity values are difficult to identify, their maintenance and development is seen as being crucial to the distinctive identity of the sector and important for the wider health of society as a whole (Korten 1998, Putman and Feldstein 1993).

EXHIBIT 13.1 BRITISH CHARITY BRAND VALUES

- Accountable
- Ambitious
- Approachable
- Authoritative
- Bold
- Boring
- Caring
- Cautious
- Challenging
- Complacent
- Compassionate
- Conservative
- Determined
- Dedicated
- Direct
- Dynamic

- Effective
- Engaging
- Established
- Exciting
- Exclusive
- Fair
- Focused
- Friendly
- Generous
- Greedy
- Helpful
- Heroic
- Inclusive
- Independent
- Informative
- Innovative

- Inspiring
- Outspoken
- Passionate
- Practical
- Professional
- Reputable
- Responsive
- Rich
- Supportive
- Sympathetic
- Traditional
- Trustworthy
- Visionary
- Welcoming

Source: Saxton *et al.* (2002)

Charity values appear not only to drive the organization but also to have an ethical or moral dimension. Hankinson (2000) argues that a charity's symbolic values relate to its beliefs, for example, being passionate, caring and innovative. This is supported by Malloy and Agarwal (2001), who argue that the dominant climate in non-profits is based on an individual caring or 'feminine' model. Saxton (2002) deepens our understanding by suggesting forty-six distinctive values that may be associated with British charities. These are listed in Exhibit 13.1.

CAMPAIGN INTEGRATION

While we have stressed throughout this chapter the need for all communications to reflect the nature of the brand, we have as yet not focused on the increasingly important topic of campaign integration. The brand has a key role to play in this, since all forms of non-profit communication should be true to the brand or brands it adopts. Too many non-profits assume that they are dealing with discrete groups of stakeholders who will not have access to other communications that the organization might generate for other stakeholder groups. They do not as a consequence see the need to be consistent from one form of communication to another. To be successful, however, the whole organization has to 'live the brand' and to reflect its various dimensions in literally every form of communication that leaves the organization.

Many non-profits produce 'style guides' that stipulate how letterhead, compliment slips and other communications will be laid out. Others focus on the use of the logo, its colours, where it should be positioned on a page and the variants that are acceptable. It must be realized that this is only a small part of brand management and should not be regarded as a satisfactory approach in isolation.

It is rather more important to manage the tone of communication, both written and verbal, to ensure that this reflects the brand's values and personality. It is all too easy to be regarded as uncaring and arrogant when a fundraiser fashions a hurried reply to a donor enquiry, or provides faulty information to an enquiring journalist.

Of course achieving consistency in approach is not easy and some organizations have taken steps to produce a brand book that stipulates not only the details of the logo and presentation, but also how the organization should convey its core values. This type of publication specifies in great detail the content of the brand and how an appropriate style of communication may be fostered. It also provides information as to where individual members of staff can turn to for advice if they are unsure how to implement any aspect of the guidelines.

MANAGING MULTIPLE COMMUNICATIONS

Of course there is more to campaign integration than just consistency of brand message. A non-profit organization will be involved in sending many different communication messages over the course of a typical year and almost certainly involving a variety of media. The difficulty here is that many different departments will also be involved. Fundraisers, trading staff, service providers and corporate branders will all be striving to convey often very disparate messages over the course of the year.

In many cases this diversity in communications may not matter, particularly if they are strongly branded and directed to very distinct stakeholder groups. More often than not, however, an individual may be subject to a variety of different communications and, in the case of donors (with whom we are primarily concerned here), it will be important to ensure that the overall pattern of what they receive is appropriate and timely. To achieve this it is absolutely essential that all departments and functions with responsibility for external communications meet at regular intervals to plan the nature of the communications that will be dispatched. It is also essential that this is done by looking at distinct categories of donor (e.g. legacy pledger, direct mail donor, major donor, trust donor).

A view should be taken on the volume of communication that any one individual should receive, to ensure that they are not bombarded by the organization. Care should also be taken to ensure that the order in which these communications are received is appropriate, and that in aggregate the communications paint a consistent picture of a relationship with the donor evolving over time.

Many non-profits achieve this by a high degree of interactive planning between departments and then control the process by seeding an address of a staff member in each segment of the fundraising database. This individual then takes responsibility for recording everything that he or she receives which in turn is fed back to planners to ensure that any inconsistencies identified are avoided in the future. From our own experience this can be something of an eye-opener. While a fundraiser may assume that the only communications donors receive are the quarterly appeals it dispatches, they may also be being asked for planned gifts, legacy gifts, to buy goods from a catalogue, to engage in proactive campaigning on behalf of the organization and to volunteer to assist in local service provision. They may also receive an annual report and a regular service provision newsletter. Of course, some of this overlap may be appropriate, but for some segments of donors it may well be appropriate for the organization to initiate this volume or even all these categories of communication.

CHAPTER SUMMARY

In this chapter we have examined the contribution that successful branding can make to fundraising practice. We have outlined some of the key benefits the development of a branding strategy can offer and discussed a number of key branding decisions currently facing non-profits.

In doing so we have perhaps painted a rather rosy picture of what branding can offer, but it is important to understand that despite the advantages, some constituencies, including donors, may be antagonistic towards the organization spending monies on branding. Indeed, a number of major charities have recently been criticized openly in the press for spending on this rather than on service activities per se. While this may just be a matter of reassuring the public of the benefits, there are a number of legitimate criticisms of branding expenditure that can be raised.

First, Spruill (2001) argues that branding can create barriers that prevent non-profits from building collaborative partnerships with each other for either service delivery or fundraising. Managers are understandably reticent about diluting their brand and thus unwilling to develop partnerships as a consequence. Spruill also argues that branding can develop a spirit of 'unhealthy competition' for visibility, prompting others to undertake similar expenditure, none of which will directly benefit beneficiaries. There may also be a sense that the voice of smaller causes is buried under the noise created by high-profile 'names'. Meyers (1985) notes that such concerns prompted Planned Parenthood to drop the idea of licensing condoms, which could have earned about $300,000 a year in royalties.

Of course such objections assume that it is possible for a non-profit not to brand. Regrettably as noted above, many non-profits have brands whether or not they choose to call them that. The issue is rather whether an organization should take steps to manage its brands and it would be puerile to suggest that this would be in some sense inappropriate. That is not to say that organizations should simply plough ever greater sums into brand building communications without giving a second thought to the impact on others; merely that the development of effective brand management is a matter that deserves serious management attention and thought. In an era when consumers and hence donors are becoming increasingly sophisticated, their expectations of non-profits are becoming similarly enhanced, and modern fundraising and non-profit marketing practice needs to reflect this change.

DISCUSSION QUESTIONS

1   Your non-profit is considering a change of name. What impact might this have on fundraising?

2   Select a well-known non-profit and illustrate the components of its brand diagrammatically.

3   As a fundraising director, you have been responsible for creating a committed giving product that is now better known than your organization's name. Prepare a presentation for your CEO explaining how and why this has happened, what the impact might be and what actions you would recommend the organization to take.

4   Select a recent high-profile non-profit campaign and evaluate critically the extent to which the various aspects of the campaign were integrated. Suggest how this might have been improved.

REFERENCES

Aaker, D.A. (1995) *Building Strong Brands*, Free Press, New York.

Aaker, J.L. (1997) 'Dimensions of Brand Personality', *Journal of Marketing Research*, August: 347–356.

Aiken, M. (2001) *Keeping Close to Your Values: Lessons From a Study Examining How Voluntary and Co-operative Organisations Reproduce their Organisational Values*, Open University Press, Milton Keynes.

Batsleer, J., Cornforth, C. and Paton, R. (1991) *Issues in Voluntary and Non-profit Management*, Addison Wesley, Wokingham.

Bendapudi, N. and Singh, S.N. (1996) 'Enhancing Helping Behavior: An Integrative Framework for Promotion Planning', *Journal of Marketing*, 60(3): 33–54.

Collins, J.C. and Porras, J.I. (1996) 'Building Your Company's Vision', *Harvard Business Review*, (September–October): 65–77.

Deal, T.E. and Kennedy, A.A. (1982) *Corporate Cultures*. Penguin Books, Harmondsworth.

Denney, F. (1998) 'Not-For-Profit Marketing in the Real World: An Evaluation of Barnardo's 1995 Promotional Campaign', *International Journal of Nonprofit and Voluntary Sector Marketing*, 4(2): 153–162.

Dixon, M. (1996) 'Small and Medium Sized Charities Need A Strong Brand Too: Crisis' Experience', *Journal of Nonprofit and Voluntary Sector Marketing*, 2(1): 52–57.

Dose, J.J. (1997) 'Work Values: An Integrative Framework and Illustrative Application to Organizational Socialization', *Journal of Occupational and Organizational Psychology*, 70(3): 219–240.

Finegan, J.E. (2000) 'The Impact of Person and Organizational Values on Organizational Commitment', *Journal of Occupational and Organizational Psychology*, 73(2): 149–169.

Frumkin, P. and Kim, M.T. (2001) 'Strategic Positioning and The Financing of Nonprofit Organizations: Is Efficiency Rewarded In The Contributions Marketplace?', *Public Administration Review*, 61 (May/June): 266–275.

Gallagher, K. and Weinberg, C.B. (1991) 'Coping With Success: New Challenges For Nonprofit Marketing', *Sloan Management Review*, 33 (autumn): 27–42.

Grounds, J. and Harkness, J. (1998) 'Developing A Brand From Within: Involving Employees and Volunteers When Developing A New Brand Position', *Journal of Nonprofit and Voluntary Sector Marketing*, 3(2): 179–184.

Hankinson, P. (2000) 'Brand Orientation in Charity Organizations: Qualitative Research into Key Charity Sectors', *International Journal of Nonprofit and Voluntary Sector Marketing*, 5: 207–219.

Hankinson, P. (2001a) 'Brand Orientation in the Charity Sector: A Framework for Discussion and Research', *International Journal of Nonprofit and Voluntary Sector Marketing*, 6(3): 231–242.

Hankinson, P. (2001b) 'The Impact of Brand Orientation on Managerial Practice: A Quantitative Study of the UK's Top 500 Fundraising Managers', *International Journal of Nonprofit and Voluntary Sector Marketing*, 7(1): 30–44.

Harvey, J. (1990) 'Benefit Segmentation for Fundraisers', *Journal of the Academy of Marketing Science*, 18(1): 77–86.

Kennedy, S. (1998) 'The Power of Positioning: A Case History From The Children's Society', *Journal of Nonprofit and Voluntary Sector Marketing*, 3(3): 224–230.

Korten, D.C. (1998) *Globalizing Civil Society: Reclaiming Our Right to Power*, Seven Stories Press, New York.

Kotler, P. and Andreasen, A. (1996) *Strategic Marketing For Nonprofit Organisations* (5th edn), Prentice Hall, Englewood Cliffs, NJ.

Malloy, D.C. and Agarwal, J. (2001) 'Ethical Climate in Nonprofit Organizations: Propositions and Implications', *Nonprofit Management and Leadership*, 12(1): 39–54.

Meyers, W. (1985) 'The Nonprofits Drop The "Non"', *New York Times*, 24 November.

Polonsky, M.J. and Macdonald, E.N. (2000) 'Exploring the Link Between Cause Related Marketing and Brand Building', *International Journal of Nonprofit and Voluntary Sector Marketing*, 5(1): 46–57.

Putnam, R.D. and Feldstein, L. (2003) *Better Together: Restoring the American Community*, Simon & Schuster, New York.

Ritchie, R.J.B. and Swami, S. (1998) 'A Brand New World', *International Journal of Nonprofit and Voluntary Sector Marketing*, 4: 26–42.

Roberts Wray, B. (1994) 'Branding, Product Development and Positioning the Charity', *Journal of Brand Management*, 1(6): 350–370.

Sargeant, A., West, D.C. and Ford, J.B. (2001) 'The Role of Perceptions in Predicting Donor Value', *Journal of Marketing Management*, 17: 407–428.

Saviour, L.N. and Scott, J.V.J. (1997) 'The Influence of Corporate Culture on Managerial Ethical Judgments', *Journal of Business Ethics*, 16(8): 757–776.

Saxton, J. (1995) 'A Strong Charity Brand Comes from Strong Beliefs and Values', *Journal of Brand Management*, 2(4): 211–220.

Saxton, J. (2002) *Polishing The Diamond*, The Future Foundation, London.

Spruill, V. (2001) 'Build Brand Identity For Causes, Not Groups', *Chronicle of Philanthropy*, 13 (June): 45.

Sternberg, P. (1998) 'The Third Way: The Repositioning of the Voluntary Sector', *Journal of Nonprofit and Voluntary Sector Marketing*, 3(3): 209–217.

Tapp, A. (1996) 'Charity Brands: A Qualitative Study of Current Practice', *Journal of Nonprofit and Voluntary Sector Marketing*, 1: 327–336.

Van Rekom, J. (1997) 'Deriving an Operational Measure of Corporate Identity', *European Journal of Marketing*, 31(5–6): 412–424.

Part IV

Critical issues in fundraising

Chapter 14

The rise of new electronic channels

INTRODUCTION

No text on fundraising would be complete without a consideration of the opportunities offered by the Internet. Since its introduction in 1991, the use of the Internet has grown faster than any other electronic medium, including, historically, the telegraph. In 1993 when the first web browser became available, only 140 websites existed and only 1 per cent of these were commercial (or '. com') sites. By 1996, almost 75 per cent of the then 610,000 sites were .com in nature. By the turn of the millennium the number of organizations trading online numbered in the millions with many times that number of consumers seeking to do business. At the time of writing, growth rates are still so rapid that quoting more specific statistics is fraught with difficulty. They would almost certainly be out of date by the time the data were published.

Of course the current growth rates are not sustainable. It seems likely that the exponential growth currently being recorded will reach a plateau within the next decade as the numbers of consumers and organizations likely to benefit from a web presence begin to reach the optimum. Indeed, it seems likely that the most significant growth over the next few years will occur in Asia where countries such as China are opening up web access for the first time.

The current statistics on Internet growth are astounding. The US Internet Council estimates that the capacity of the Internet to handle traffic is doubling every 100 days. With over twenty million unique domain names (e.g. Amazon.com) registered worldwide at the end of 2001, the number continues to grow by 500,000 per week. There are currently 2.2 billion pages of data, 500 million images and 35.6. trillion bytes of text. What is all the more amazing is that a typical webpage remains current for around only forty-four days (The Censoware Project, 26 January 1999). This means that to keep up with all the changes taking place it would be necessary for a user to download 873,000,000,000 bytes of information per day and have a connection capable of downloading over ten million bytes per second!

In the USA there are estimated to be over 159 million computer users, 145 million in the EU and 116 million in the Asia Pacific region. Some 80 per cent of these individuals go online. However, despite the scale of the opportunity the non-profit sector has been relatively slow to capitalize on the new technology on both sides of the Atlantic. Despite the reticence, examples of good and creative practice abound and the Internet is now being used effectively by a number of 'household name' non-profits for the purposes of fundraising, communication, information provision, branding, advocacy, selling products and building relationships.

In both the USA and the UK, pioneer non-profit organizations are testing new routes to raising funds online. Oxfam GB (www.oxfam.org.uk) and Breast Cancer Care (www.breast-cancercare.org.uk) have both, for example, run successful fundraising auctions online, and many non-profits have teamed up with established web partners such as Amazon.com in affiliate schemes.

In the UK, the most frequently quoted online success story is Comic Relief (www.comic relief.com) which received £1.75 million in six hours on the night of its recent Telethon representing 8 per cent of the total for its appeal. The National Society for the Prevention of Cruelty to Children (www.nspcc.org.uk) claims considerable success from offering password-protected access to regular donors who can enter a privileged section of the NSPCC website and alter their mailing preferences, view their giving history, change their address details and make a donation (See Plate 14.1). UNICEF UK (www.unicef.org.uk) offers a similar service for major donors, and ActionAid (www.actionaid.org) has pioneered a number of special sites in its youth marketing and child sponsorship campaigns.

Campaigning groups such as Greenpeace (www.greenpeace.org.uk) and Amnesty International have also been notable in using e-mail alerts in their lobbying campaigns, and employ their websites extensively in supporter communication. In the USA the World Wildlife Fund offer a much-cited interactive site at www.panda.org, where users can collect 'stamps' for their 'Panda Passport' as they engage in a variety of activities (including campaigning and offering funds) to support the organization. The Environmental Protection Fund (www.edf.org) also offers a highly interactive site (www.scorecard.org) which allows users to identify the companies that are polluting the air, land and water in their specific Zip code, and e-mail or fax them to complain (see Plate 14.2).

In this chapter it is our intention to explore how fundraising over the web and other emerging media is best conducted and to learn from these examples of best practice. We begin however by examining the nature of the opportunity and in particular the profile of a typical web user.

CHANGING USER PROFILES

In total, 41 per cent of adults in Europe and the USA are estimated to use the Internet. In only a few years, the profile of a typical user has shifted from a white middle-class, educated male, aged 29 to 34, to become gradually more representative of society as a whole. As Figure 14.1 illustrates, a wider spread of ages is now represented by web users with more recent growth accounted for by both younger and older individuals. As the costs of access continue to decrease it seems likely that this trend will continue.

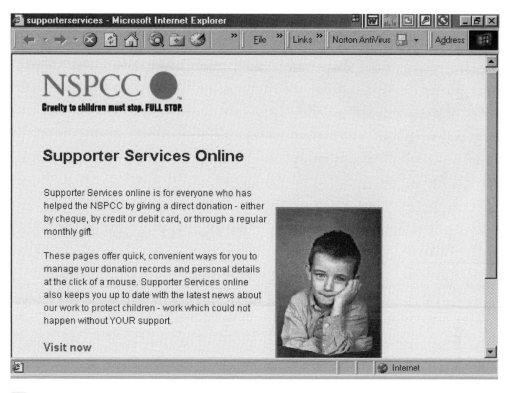

Plate 14.1 *NSPCC website*

Source: © NSPCC. Reproduced with kind permission

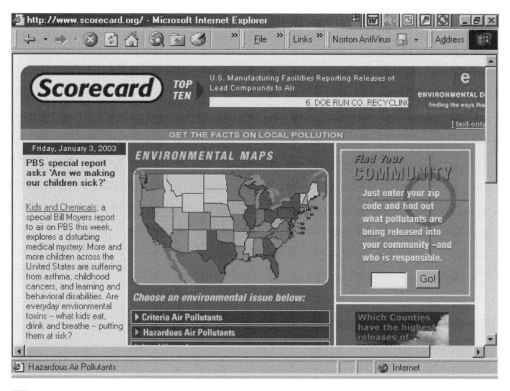

Plate 14.2 *EDF Scorecard website*

Source: © EDF (www.scorecard.org). Reproduced with kind permission

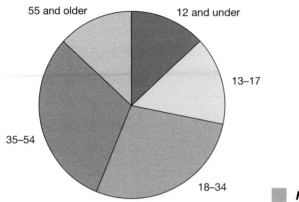

Figure 14.1 *Age profile of Internet users*

The demographic is also softening by gender. There has been a particularly sharp increase in recent years in the numbers of females using the Internet with the balance now only marginally in favour of males. There has also been a rise in the number of lower income or more poorly educated families connecting to the Web for the first time and a sharp increase in the number of connections established purely for pleasure usage. Table 14.1 illustrates these differences.

It is interesting to note that some differences in behaviour have been reported between new and existing users. Those individuals who connected to the Internet two years ago or more, tend to spend longer online than those who have connected only recently. The former tend to spend 10.5 hours per week online, while the latter spend only 6.6 hours (NUA/Roper Starch, November 1999).

BARRIERS TO USAGE

Despite the almost exponential growth in the number of consumers going online, fewer than 40 per cent of web users are estimated to have actually made a purchase online and fewer than 1 per cent a donation. Key barriers to online purchasing and donations would appear to be concerns over the security of credit cards, privacy issues and the perceived problem of returning defective or inappropriate merchandise. Consumer concerns in respect of security, in particular, have received considerable publicity in recent years, although the incidence of actual credit card theft over the Internet is estimated to be minimal and many times smaller than would occur in a traditional retail environment. As always, however, it is the perception that matters, and many sites now go to great lengths to offer consumers secure connections, in some cases achieving accreditation by organizations such as Verisign, TRUSTe or BBBOnline.

Another major concern is privacy. Many consumers worry that by sharing information with a site perhaps to receive acknowledgement of a donation, or a more tailored environment when they next visit the site, they will as a consequence receive a high volume of unsolicited mail or e-mail. They also worry that their personal data might be shared with other organizations without their consent being sought. For many individuals the issue of privacy is thus a major concern and sites are increasingly compelled to offer some reassurance in this regard, by posting an easily accessible privacy statement which maps out exactly how personal information will be used (if at all).

Central to the issue of privacy is the cookie. A cookie is a small, encrypted data string that website servers write to the hard drive of a user's computer. It contains the user's unique ID

Table 14.1 *Changes in profile of Internet users*

	Started using in the past year (per cent)	Used more than a year ago (per cent)
Percentage of all Internet users	46	53
Gender		
Male	48	55
Female	52	45
Age		
18–29	25	30
30–49	52	50
50–64	16	15
65+	4	4
Income		
$50,000+	35	45
$30,000–$49,000	23	22
Under $30,000	23	16
Education		
University	29	46
Some university	32	30
High school	33	19
< High school	6	3
Usage		
Work	24	30
Pleasure	52	39
Mix	22	31

for the website. It can be accessed on subsequent visits to a site by the host computer and interrogated to eliminate the need for a user to log on. In effect the cookie allows a site to recognize a returning visitor and, if appropriate, to tailor the environment to suit their needs. Cookies can thus be used to deliver web content specific to visitor interests, keep track of orders and control access to premium content. Cookies cannot be used to access or otherwise compromise the data on a user's hard drive.

Many users object to sites storing data on their hard drive and consider the practice an invasion of their privacy. The use of such mechanisms can therefore deter many potential visitors from returning once they discover the practice is in operation. For this reason many privacy statements make it clear whether cookies will be used and the aims of so doing. The American Cancer Society, for example, includes the planned use of cookies in its privacy statement.

SITE DESIGN

The costs of setting up a website for the first time can vary considerably. Such costs are clearly a function of the complexity of the site, the number of pages, the amount of information that will be posted and the degree of interaction that will be offered to visitors. Costs can also be a function of the quality of design undertaken and the degree of integration that will take place with other existing computer systems such as the donor database and financial management systems.

Smaller non-profits can find the costs of start-up considerably lower, with a number of Internet service providers (ISPs) now offering flexible design and hosting packages for only a few hundred dollars. For most non-profits, however, the costs associated with establishing an Internet operation for the first time can be considerable. It is therefore important that the design be carefully thought through to achieve its stated objectives.

In designing a site the following points should be considered:

Determine precise goals

The organization should be clear from the outset what the specific goals of the website will be. Is it designed to raise funds, provide information, co-ordinate volunteers, provide non-profit services, or more likely some combination of the same? Whatever the purpose, this needs to be agreed up-front since the costs of 'bolting-on' additional functionality at a later date are likely to be considerable.

If the purpose is to raise funds it is important for the organization to realize that very few organizations are able to generate acceptable returns from their presence on the web. Only those with high-quality content that attracts traffic from the major search engines are at present raising money successfully. For those organizations whose cause makes it difficult to provide attractive/informative site content, there may still be good reasons for going online, but the organization needs to be clear from the outset what these might be, and to be realistic in respect of the fundraising goals (if any)

Keep the site simple

While it might be tempting to adopt the most modern up-to-date graphic presentations and to offer users complex levels of interaction and routes through the site, the most successful sites are undoubtedly those that are simple and easy to use. Many consumers who access a site for the first time will leave the site again after only a few seconds if it is not immediately apparent that the site will both meet their needs and be easy to navigate. If it takes an age to download complex graphics, potential visitors may be deterred and simply move on to the next site before the process is completed. Similarly, if a complex path must be navigated to find the pages that are of most interest, many users will lose interest before reaching their desired target. For this reason many homepages contain a simple navigation guide. Plate 14.3 illustrates an example – the American Cancer Society homepage. The right-hand side of the screen contains a menu offering each class of user their own unique gateway into the site.

Striving for simplicity in use should therefore be an overriding design specification and it would not be unusual for site designers to develop a series of flow charts that illustrate the route proposed for various classes of users to take through the site. These can subsequently be edited to ensure that navigation is as smooth, direct and simple as possible.

Develop content that is both beneficial and pertinent to visitors

Great care should be taken to ensure that the needs of various stakeholders are reflected in the site. Of particular relevance here would be a consideration of the specific benefits that will be sought by each category of potential users. In designing the site it will be important to seek the views of each key grouping and to ensure that not only is pertinent material provided, but anything not of direct relevance is dropped. Peripheral information (particularly if it contains graphics) serves only to lengthen download times and slow down access to the site. At a simple level one should therefore be asking, 'What information do potential users really need?'

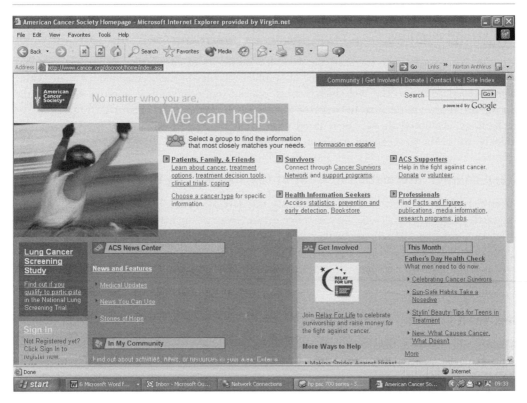

Plate 14.3 *American Cancer Society website*

Source: © American Cancer Society. Reproduced with kind permission

Use caution in developing links to other sites

There are two primary reasons for offering this caveat. First, organizations can find themselves in considerable legal difficulty if they suggest to those visiting their site that the site is in some way endorsed by a third party. Establishing links from a host site to another organization is therefore something that should be undertaken with considerable care. Indeed it is good practice to seek the permission of any organization to which it is proposed to forge a link.

Aside from the legal difficulties that might be encountered in including links, a second major concern is the degree of encouragement that might be offered users to exit. Internet research has shown consistently that there are two major types of readers inhabiting the web: browsers and seekers. Seekers are those who have a specific information need in mind and work their way methodically through sites to achieve their goal. Browsers, by contrast, are using the web almost as one might drive a car for recreational purposes. They move from place to place looking for the next exciting experience or tranche of useful information. They keep one hand on the virtual door (Johnston 1999) and pay more attention to hyperlinked text on a page than to any other.

In attempting to retain this second category of user it is therefore somewhat ironic that many organizations are intent on providing as many possible exits as they can on a given screen. Clearly one would wish to provide as friendly and useful an environment as possible for users, but providing higher numbers of links merely increases the likelihood that someone will be tempted away even before they have glanced at the content of the host organization's site.

Aim for a middle ground between quick intelligible communication and strong graphics

Mention has already been made of the need for simplicity in site design. It is worth emphasizing, however, the role that the choice of graphics can play in the accessibility of a site. Until higher speed access to the web such as that offered by broadband technology becomes the norm, site designers need to be wary of the lowest common denominator in Internet access technology. As noted above, users faced with a lengthy time to download a given site will quickly tire of the process and move on.

Keep contact information in front of the visitor at all times

At any stage in visiting a website or perusing the data available, visitors may identify a need for further information. Users may also decide part-way through visiting a site that they wish to make a donation, or request further information. Not all users of a site will wish to do this online and it is thus good practice to ensure that the contact information for an organization is available at all times, perhaps following a convention such as providing it at the bottom of each page.

Ask for a donation on every page

Allied to the above, if one of the purposes of the site is to raise funds, the site should ask for a gift on every page. It is not enough for a non-profit to assume that potential donors will navigate their way through the site to find the requisite donation page. Many gifts are made on impulse and it should be made as easy as possible to make a donation. An 'ask' or a link to the fundraising section of the website must therefore be provided on every page.

Fulfil promises in a timely manner

When a donation has been made, any promises that have been made in respect of recognition for that gift need to be honoured as quickly as possible. Similarly, requests for literature, further information, or contact with specific individuals should be met in a timely manner. As was explained in Chapter 7 the quality of service provided will be a key determinant of how well an organization can retain its donors.

Publicize your site in every medium possible

Designing an attractive and user-friendly site will not in itself guarantee success. Potential customers and users still need to be made aware of the online presence. The launch and ongoing operation of a website should therefore be reflected in other forms of marketing communication which an organization might generate. Business cards, letterheads, advertising and other forms of direct marketing communications should all feature the web address and seek to make it available at times when potential customers might require it for access.

Test and measure results

Once operational, it is essential that an organization review the performance of its site. There are a variety of different measures that may be employed for this purpose and an equal variety of measurement tools, each with slightly different outputs and *modus operandi*. Some of the more common measurements undertaken are provided below:

- *Ad views (or impressions)*: The number of times a www ad banner is downloaded by visitors.
- *Reach*: The total number of users a vehicle reaches – calculated by deriving the number of persistent, unique cookies present in a site's log files over a period of time.
- *Frequency*: A measure of how often a unique user interacts with a site over a period of time – calculated as a series of requests by a unique visitor without thirty consecutive minutes of inactivity.
- *Visit*: User's interaction with a site within a specified time period. The visit includes all the pages seen on the same site during one session. It is now common practice to consider a visit terminated when new pages are not consulted for more than fifteen to thirty minutes depending on the country in which the website is located.
- *Visit duration*: The period over which a visit is undertaken. Most measurement software provides a range of data on this variable including mean, median and modal durations.
- *Visitors*: The number of individuals consulting the same site in a given period. The total number of visitors thus takes account of visit duplication. It should be noted that some systems refer to visitors as users.

Measurement software is also capable of tracking movement through a particular site. By tagging each webpage with a unique identification number it is possible to trace the typical way in which visitors, or specific segments of visitors, interact with the material presented. It can also track the typical duration that visitors spend viewing each individual page.

Clearly all these data may be used to great effect in refining ineffectual aspects of the site and improving the quality of a visitor's experience.

Finally, it is important to note that many organizations will simply assess the performance of the website by the trading income it has been able to generate and/or the fundraising income that may be attributed to it. At the time of writing, average gifts through the Internet are impressive and compare very favourably with those from other direct marketing media. The National Council of La Raza, for example, currently achieves an average gift of $60, while in 2000 the American Red Cross was achieving $141 (Warwick *et al.* 2002).

In the vast majority of cases, however, the volume of donors giving online has been comparatively small and the income accruing to a typical non-profit in a given year is a mere $12,000 in both the UK and the USA (Sargeant and Jay 2003). Given the costs of initial development it can take a period of several years for some non-profits to achieve break-even on this activity and it is thus important to have reasonable expectations from the outset as to performance.

Adhere to the spirit as well as the letter of all professional codes of conduct, laws and regulations

While thirty-nine US states currently have legislation governing charitable solicitations, the majority of this focuses on direct mail and telemarketing. Some states have attempted to apply the same rules to the Internet, but the picture is confusing, and many freely admit that the legislation is not proving adequate. One of the notable complexities is the requirement in many states for a charity to register if it wishes to operate within that state to raise funds. While prior to the development of the Internet this was relatively easy to assess and enforce, those organizations now operating online can easily find themselves either soliciting donations from other states, or receiving unsolicited gifts therefrom. In an attempt to deal with this additional complexity the National Association of State Charity Officials (NASCO) has created a set of guidelines, now known as the Charleston Principles, to offer guidance to non-profits (see www.nasconet.org to view the principles online).

The Charleston Principles indicate that if a non-profit actively solicits donations from individuals (perhaps through e-mail) in a state requiring registration, it must register there. If the organization only receives passive donations from individuals in that state, without having actively solicited the gift, then the charity need not register there. Of course if the number of donors from that state rises to a significant level this may no longer apply and the charity may be obliged to register anyway. The regulations suggest that a cut-off point of 100 donors or $25,000 in donations would trigger the need for registration.

It should however be noted that the regulation governing this arena is highly fluid, and fundraisers are well advised to seek legal advice on a frequent basis to stay within the law.

WRITING ONLINE

Before a webpage can be satisfactorily created a number of issues must be considered.

Flow chart/site map

When organizations prepare off-the-page advertising, or put together a fundraising appeal mailing, information is laid out in a linear format. Each paragraph of the text leads logically to another. In essence the designers have provided a logical sequence that guides the reader through each section of the information presented.

When writing for the Web, however, a complex non-linear format replaces this simplistic framework. Websites generally consist of a maze of interlocking decisions and directions. For larger sites the easiest way of opening up access for visitors to the site is to consider offering a flow chart or site map which makes it very clear how the material within the site will be divided.

A map such as the one in Plate 14.4 performs a number of functions. It:

- gives the users the freedom to create their own experience rather than be guided through pages that the organization feels may be appropriate;
- can highlight those aspects of the site that are most important and likely to be visited regularly;
- provides a useful pictorial overview of the information that the site contains.

Inclusion of links

Links move the user to a new webpage. In most versions of browser the cursor is pointing at a link when the arrow changes to a pointing finger. Almost any object can be designed as a link, but the five more common types are described below.

Text-based links – hypertext links

These are usually very easy to identify as they appear in a different colour to the rest of the text and are often underlined. The webpage illustrated has a number of these links and they helpfully change colour after a visit to remind users that they have already explored that link.

Most common browsers can also be set to remember pages the users have visited. Microsoft Explorer, for example, allows users to set the colours of visited and unvisited links by accessing the View menu and clicking on Options. They then click the General tab and on the right of the screen will view a box illustrating the colour of visited and unvisited links. A colour palette allows users to choose the colour they prefer in each case.

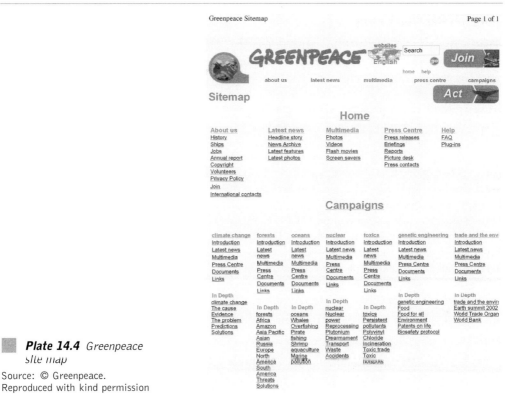

Plate 14.4 *Greenpeace site map*

Source: © Greenpeace.
Reproduced with kind permission

Images

Links can also be created by graphics, icons or photographs. As is usual with a link, the cursor will change to a hand and pointed finger when directed at such an image. Clicking on the image will transfer the user to the new site or page.

Image maps

Some of the more complex sites on the web have a number of different links embedded in a single picture or map. Such maps can be a very powerful way of illustrating the design and layout of the site. The links are usually obvious and users will see the cursor change into a hand as they move over various aspects of the map. A glance at the bottom of the browser will confirm that the destination URL changes as each part of the image is run over with the mouse. Clicking on any one item will move the user to that part of the site.

Blind links

Blind links are becoming increasingly common on the web. They are a somewhat devious attempt to bring additional users into a site. Users could, for example, be invited to click on an icon suggesting a free picture or download. Rather than either of these they are immediately directed to a new site. Unscrupulous webmasters have employed this technique to great effect in uplifting traffic to particular sites. Of course consumers have a habit of remembering such devious behaviour and it seems likely that they will avoid offending sites in the future.

283

Long versus short copy

When writing for the Web many writers feel that long copy should be avoided. As direct marketers know all too well from their experience with direct mail this is not necessarily the case. The test is always whether the text is relevant and whether all the key information and arguments are included. If extraneous information is provided, the text is too long; if it covers the key essentials it is probably about right.

It should be remembered that many visitors will have 'self-selected' their visit. They will have determined that the site has relevance to their needs and will not necessarily be put off by longer copy. The key in writing text for the Web, however, lies in breaking it up into manageable chunks. Copy should not fill one long page. If individuals have to continue scrolling down one page to reach the desired information, they are considerably more likely to tire of the experience and leave.

Instead, web authors can compact the text by using a series of hypertext links. This allows the user to skip those sections of the text that are of no relevance and to jump immediately to those that are. Her Majesty's Stationery Office (hmso.govt.uk), for example, makes many statutes such as the Data Protection Act available online. Rather than present the whole document as an extended page, the table of contents is offered as a menu and users can jump through a hypertext link to those sections of the Act that are of most interest.

Bullets

While few organizations would choose to make an extensive use of bullet points in most of their corporate communications, bullet points and the Internet are a match made in heaven. Not only are they a convenient means of summarizing information, bullet points can also be authored as hypertext links steering users from one section of the site to another. Bullet points can also be made an attractive feature of a given page.

The power of words

In designing copy for a webpage many of the same rules apply as would be the case in direct mail, direct response press advertising, or indeed any other direct marketing media.

Use short sentences and vary the length

In writing copy nothing matters except the meaning. Short sentences are fine. Verbs are not necessarily required. Not really. Nor is it necessary to create long, verbose sentences that simply demonstrate one's dexterity in the use of punctuation. To quote George Smith (1996: 87):

> A [sentence] need not be long, need not defer to the Johnsonian tradition of the periodic sentence that ran to perhaps 200 words complete with subclauses and the full complement of colons and semi-colons to separate the various constructs; a tradition that continues to this day in the hands of writers such as Bernard Levin a journalist who rarely deploys 20 words when 200 can fulfil his sense of personal grandeur, a quality that some may admire but which most would resist on the basis that there are only so many hours a day in which one can read a newspaper.

As Smith later notes – hands up those who fell asleep during that last sentence!

Use short paragraphs and vary the length

Paragraphs can consist of only one sentence.
There is nothing wrong with that.
But if a writer consistently engages that technique it can become boring.

Far better to group the ideas and ensure that the length of paragraphs is varied. This will not only look more visually appealing, but the text should be easier to read.

Use 'I' and 'you' not 'we' and 'one'

The difficulty in using words such as 'we' is that text can quickly appear very pompous. A phrase such as 'we at Routledge' conveys a certain arrogance, whereas the use of 'I' makes the text more intimate, personal and unassuming.

It is also good practice in the context of trading to allow potential buyers to 'rehearse' the benefits of ownership through the text. Phrases such as 'you will experience' put the buyer in the position of already owning the product and suggest to them how they will feel thereafter.

Avoid clichés

While the Internet is still comparatively new there are already words that are suffering from overuse. Words or phrases such as

Cutting edge
Check it out
Cool
Hot

are not particularly helpful and will serve only to irritate the reader. Sites with original language stimulate the eye and gain additional attention.

Avoid polysyllables

Long words are rarely more impressive than shorter ones. They create the impression of a bureaucratic, inhuman organization that is distant from the needs of its customers. Smith (1996: 89) uses the following examples to make the point.

Approximately	About
Participate	Take part
Establish	Set up
Utilize	Use

MARKETING ONLINE

Of course authoring and presenting a site is only one way in which an organization might use the web for the purposes of marketing and fundraising. A number of other opportunities are presented by this new medium. These include Web rings, reciprocal links, e-mail and news groups.

Web rings

These are a comparatively recent phenomenon and are in essence an association of related sites. They are designed to link together in a way that creates the impression of a single community, with a single focus in mind. There are many thousands of these now in existence and the number continues to grow daily. Non-profit organizations could thus consider joining a currently established ring or to form one of their own. Thus in consumer markets it may make sense for organizations offering products/services pertinent to one lifestyle category or interest group to get together and form an alliance in this way. Ring World is a helpful central index of such rings and information in respect of starting up a new Web ring may be found at www.webring.com.

Reciprocal links

Even if it does not prove possible to establish the more formal exchange that would typically be a feature of a Web ring, it may still be possible to forge alliances with specific individual organizations which offer related services to those of a given organization. Links could be provided to the website of this complementary organization in return for them providing a similar link offering customers a route in the opposite direction.

This is by far the most common kind of web marketing strategy. Almost all websites now contain some kind of reciprocal link to other organizations. These may be to sites offering related information or services, or to sites that the host believes will be of wider interest.

To encourage such links it would be normal for webmasters from non-profit sites to talk to those responsible for the management of other sites to see whether some form of collaboration might be possible. If agreement can be reached it would be usual for a short description of the site to be provided, together with an icon or graphics that may be inserted into the reciprocating site, containing a hyperlink that will then direct the user to the new site. This site would reciprocate by having a similar link to the partnering site.

Those organizations wishing to maximize the opportunity for reciprocal links would be advised to maintain a short description of this site and an icon that may be used for the purpose of developing a link on their site. Interested parties could then copy this and provide a link.

Of course, while this may maximize links, there is also the danger that links will appear on inappropriate sites, suggesting an arrangement that does not in fact exist. The webmaster responsible for a site therefore needs to be clear up front in respect of the degree to which the creation of links will be encouraged.

There are ways to identify whether any reciprocal links may already be in place. You need only visit www.altavista.com and search for your own site at: www.your.domain. The results of the search will then reveal those organizations that have already established a link to the site.

Link exchanges

Small organizations, or those operating on limited web budgets, may draw some benefit from another comparatively recent phenomenon – the link exchange. These are similar to co-operatives, in that organizations join a number of other link members in promoting each other's sites. Members must prepare a graphic banner containing their link for display on other sites, and agree to display the links of partner organizations. A monitoring system for each link exchange keeps track of how often a banner appears on member sites and how often that particular member shows the banners of other members. The number should roughly equate, to ensure a fair distribution of benefit. There are a number of companies that specialize in fostering this kind of link exchange – the most obvious being http://www.linkexchange.com.

E-mail

E-mail can be a very cost-effective tool for marketing over the Web. In 1998 Stanford University began sending a monthly newsletter by e-mail to alumni and others associated with the University (see Plate 14.5). Stanford research demonstrated that those people who receive @Stanford have a higher propensity to give. Specifically, about half (49 per cent) of the recipients made a gift in financial year 2000 compared to only one-third of non recipients. Indeed, e-mail can be particularly effective where a relationship already exists between a donor and non-profit and where as a consequence permission will have been given for the organization to make contact in this way. More thoughtful users of e-mail communications attempt to tailor the content of the communications to the specific needs of the individual and offer a very clear 'opt-out' facility where donors can delete themselves from the list and hence decline to receive subsequent communications.

Some use has also been made of 'cold' e-mail lists, particularly in the realm of environmental causes, or those involved with advocacy. Here it is relatively easy to purchase a list of potential supporters, but the cost of the list is typically three to five times more expensive than for an equivalent direct mail list. This simply reflects the costs associated with collecting e-mail addresses online and securing opt-in from the individuals concerned to certain forms of communication. This latter feature is important because reputable list suppliers will always have secured the permission of the members of the list to receive communications, thus differentiating the practice from 'spamming' where literally thousands of e-mail addresses are

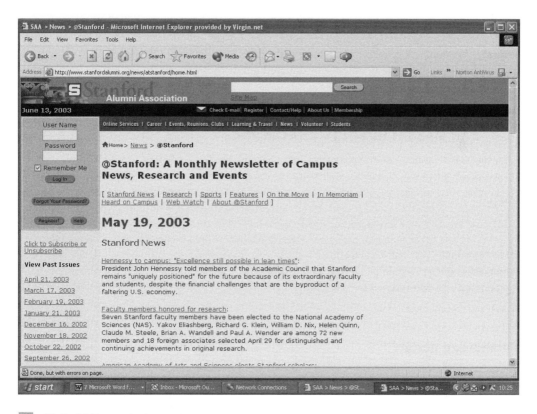

Plate 14.5 *Stanford e-mail newsletter*

Source: http://www.stanford.edu/~jpearson/@stanford.pdf. Reproduced with kind permission bombarded at random with unwanted 'junk' mail. Response rates from professionally compiled lists are reported as being of the order of 1 per cent.

Of course, it is possible for a non-profit to compile its own e-mail list. The best way to accomplish this is to:

- offer users the facility to sign up to a free electronic newsletter. Importantly this offer should be made in all the communications media employed;
- offer e-mail action alerts that provide donors with the opportunity to act on their beliefs, perhaps by engaging in campaigning;
- include a request for an e-mail address in the response forms used in traditional media;
- consider offering a prize draw which requires individuals to supply only their e-mail address to enter;
- offer discounts on events or membership for online completion.

While e-mail communication is likely to become an increasingly important communication medium for non-profits and donors, and therefore the collection of e-mail addresses should be prioritized, it should also be recognized that individuals tend to change their e-mail addresses very frequently, so any listing is likely to become quickly outdated.

Online events

A further good way of marketing a site and generating interest in its content is to consider hosting an event online. Those non-profits with access to celebrities or individuals with distinctive expertise or knowledge could consider running an online event. Typically this might comprise an online discussion of a cause-related issue, a 'surgery' session where individuals could ask advice, or even an auction of donated goods or services.

PAN MASSACHUSETTS CHALLENGE

A successful variation on this theme was developed by the Dana-Farber Cancer Institute which organized a two-day charity Bikeathon to raise money for the organization. Riders who sign up must raise at least $1,000 for cancer care and research. To assist them in this, organizers sent riders a twenty-second e-mail advertisement about the challenge that combined images of past events with stirring music. Riders were then invited to forward the e-mail to friends, relatives and other potential sponsors. These individuals could then click on a link contained in the e-mail, visit the organization's website and make an online contribution to the rider's fundraising goal. Within just one week of the original dispatch of the e-mail, donors had made gifts of $137,000 through the website.

Fundraising portals

There are three types of portal that are of relevance to fundraising, namely:

1 *Giving portals* – Such as helping.org supported by the AOL TimeWarner Foundation. These organizations allow non-profits to be added to their list of supported organizations and donors visiting the site can elect to make a donation to their chosen causes.

Helping.org is reported as raising £3 million for good causes in early 2001 and donations for all categories of cause are supported. In the UK the Charities Aid Foundation has launched 'Givenow' in partnership with AOL which will perform a similar function, allowing individuals to send donations to a wide range of non-profit organizations. It is important to recognize that while these general sites exist, some have a more limited geographic focus or are limited to only one category of organization. Some, for example, focus on animal rights (e.g. animalfunds.org). It is usually free for a non-profit to register with these portals and some, including helping.org, will provide software for the non-profit to provide a branded click-through link on its website.

2   *Affinity shopping portals* – There are a number of virtual shopping malls on line that support the non-profit community. In such cases the mall charges commission to the stores that populate it and then shares a percentage of this commission with non-profits. In many cases non-profits need only register for shoppers to have them as an option of designated recipient charity.

3   *Online charity auctions* – A number of commercial organizations such as eBay or specialized organizations such as allstarcharity.com auction items donated by celebrities and donate the funds generated to good causes.

News groups

There may be some occasions when an organization is engaged in activities, or presenting ideas that may in some sense be newsworthy. If this is the case it may be worth an organization considering the use of Internet news groups. There are many thousands of these, each of which is focused on a specific issue or topic. Online press releases can be targeted at any news groups it is felt may have an interest in the subject matter of the item. Infinite Ink offers a useful service for locating news groups on specific issues: http://www.ii.com/Internet/messaging/newsgroups/.

Announcement sites

With so many new sites appearing on the web every day, a new category of web directory has appeared – that of the announcement site. Such sites provide links to the newest additions to the Web. Unlike search engines they do not have robots searching for data and thus rely on manual postings. Listings are typically only for a short period and usually a maximum of two to four weeks. Some announcement sites focus exclusively on new sites, while others are more flexible and willing to consider new additions to an existing site. Submit-it has a useful directory that might be helpful in identifying appropriate announcement sites. It may be found at www.directoryguide.com.

Viral marketing

The term 'viral marketing' refers to marketing undertaken on the back of communications sent by individuals to other individuals over the web. The earliest commercial example was the growth of Hotmail, where recipients of e-mail sent from that organization would be invited to open their own account, through advertising placed at the bottom of each e-mail transmitted.

A number of non-profits have now made use of the medium, most notably Barnardo's in the UK, which created an 'e-baby' which was dispatched to all members of staff, who were in turn encouraged to share it with their own friends and relatives. The e-mail contained a programme for an e-baby which the recipient would have to look after – or when not available deposit with an e-creche. When tired of the baby it could be returned to Barnardo's when the individual would be invited to make a donation.

In the US viral marketing has also been employed by organizations such as Bet Tzedek-The House of Justice, which is based in Los Angeles and exists to help the local poor. A viral e-mail was sent out to a group of under-35s who were then invited to share it with their friends and acquaintances. The e-mail promoted a gala event that was ultimately successful in gaining 1,000 new donors.

SEARCH ENGINES

Table 14.2 presents a summary of the parent companies of the most visited sites (from the USA) on the Web. It is no accident that a number of search engines make it on to this list. A search engine is in essence a site that provides a gateway for users to those sites on the Web most likely to match their interests or information needs. The user simply types in keywords or phrases that reflect their needs and the search engine searches the Web (or rather its memory of the Web) to retrieve page listings that are normally sorted by relevance.

From a non-profit's perspective there are three ways of generating traffic from a search engine: (1) achieving click-throughs from searches undertaken, (2) from advertising with banner ads on selected pages of the search engine, and (3) by purchasing a favourable placement in the listing for each pertinent category – although it should be noted that this service is not available from every search engine on the web.

No one search engine yet covers the whole web, but a large number of sites are typically recorded in the search engine's database. The task for an Internet fundraiser is to ensure that its site is listed on as many search engines as possible and that the listing adequately reflects the content of the site. Position Agent (http://www.positionagent.com) allows users to identify what each search engine has as a listing for their organization. Various combinations of keywords that researchers might use can be input and the site will then report back and tell the enquirer on what page and in what position its URL occurs in each category in each of the major search engines. If the site is not listed on the first page in a given category the chances

Table 14.2 Top online sites (April 2003)

Parent	Unique audience (000)
Microsoft	76,531
AOL Time Warner	74,880
Yahoo	65,451
Google	33,177
United States Government	28,078
eBay	26,546
About-Primedia	22,864
Amazon	22,806
Real Networks	21,291
Terra Lycos	20,413

Source: Nielsen/NetRatings

of a user actually accessing the site through the search engine rapidly diminish. Few users scan beyond three or four pages of URL listings before choosing to open a site.

So how do search engines gather data about sites on the web? They actually run software programs called robots or spiders that continually crawl around the web looking for new pages. They record information about every new page they encounter and add it to the engine's database. The robot records all the text on the page and the search engine then analyses it ready to include it in its index.

Thus one really need do nothing to have a website recorded on a search engine. However, in practice, the robots spend a lot of time crawling around sites they have already visited updating the material on file by looking for changes. It could thus take considerable time for a new site to be identified. It is therefore better for a fundraiser to be proactive, approach the engines directly and give them the information firsthand.

There are many search engines on the web. The most common are listed in Exhibit 14.1. On each of the sites hosted by these engines, it should be possible to find a link entitled ADD A SITE or ADD YOUR URL. The webmaster responsible for a particular site could therefore visit the key search engines and rapidly update them in respect of their site's existence. What happens from there is that the website is added to the list of sites for a robot to visit. The site will be added to the search engine's database only after it has been visited by a robot. Manual registration along the lines described merely allows the organization concerned to queue jump.

Of course visiting all the key search engines can be somewhat tedious. The reader will therefore not be surprised to learn that there are a number of specialist companies that will undertake this work on behalf of an organization. The fee is usually under $100, and for this sum the company will usually register the site with over 200 search engines, directories and announcement pages on the Web. Examples of companies offering this service are submit-it.com and acclaimweb.com.

The search engines will not treat all the content of a webpage as being equally significant. Certain sections of the page receive more weight than others. It is therefore essential that webpages are designed to maximize the opportunity to achieve a good listing.

<TITLE> keywords

Each webpage should be given a title. By title, we do not mean the section of bold text that appears across a visitor's screen. Rather we mean a specific chunk of hidden code that helps to identify the page, but which visitors are unaware of. The <HEAD> section of each page should contain a <TITLE> section that in turn contains a description of the content of the page. Search engine robots will scan the data stored in the <TITLE> section. This is the text that is displayed by the search engine, when it generates its list of 'hits' for the user.

<META> tags

Meta tags are also codes that the user will not be aware of. They can be read by special programs however, and in particular by robots as they attempt to refine the profile of each page in their respective database. Information in the META tags will be used to inform the way in which a particular page is indexed.

<ALT> image tags

Organizations employing a lot of images on their site may well make the site attractive to visitors, but they can also make them invisible to search engines. Organizations, for example,

EXHIBIT 14.1 MAJOR INTERNET SEARCH ENGINES

Infoseek	http://www.infoseek.com
AltaVista	http://altavista.com
LiveLink Pinstripe	http://pinstripe.opentext.com
Excite Search	http://www.excite.com
Google	http://google.com
HotBot	http://hotbot.com
Microsoft Network Search	http://www.msn.com
Webcrawler	http://www.webcrawler.com
Lycos	http://www.lycos.com
Yahoo	http://www.yahoo.com
Magellan	http://www.magellan.com
DogPile	http://www.dogpile.com
Highway 61 Multi Search	http://www.highway61.com
Mamma Mother of all Search Engines	http://www.mamma.com
Web Search Meta Search	http://www.web-search.com
CNET's Search	http://search.cnet.com
Edirectory	http://www.edirectory.com
International Regional Search Engines	http://searchenginewatch.com/regional/
Inquiry Com Information Technology Search	http://inquiry.com
Mediafinder	http://www.mediafinder.com
NameSpace Whose Domain Information	http://whois.namespace.org
Study Web Research Site	http://www.studyweb.com
Library of Congress Search	http://lcweb.loc.gov/harvest
InfoMine Government Info Search	http://lib-www.ucr.edu/search/ucrgivsearch.html
MedScape	http://www.medscape.com
Medical Matrix Medline Search	http://www.medmatrix.org/info/medlinetable.html
Liszt Mailing Lists	http://www.liszt.com
Companies	http://www.companiesonline.com
Galaxy Professional Directory	http://www.einet.net
Lycos A2Z Internet Directory	http://a2z.lycos.com
Nerd World Subject Index	http://www.nerdworld.com
Starting Point	http://www.stpt.com
Suite 101	http://www.suite101.com
Brint: A Business Researchers Interest	http://www.brint.com/interest.html
About.com	http://www.about.com
Netguide Live	http://www.netguide.com
Digital Librarian Best of the Web	http://www.servtech.com/public/mvail/home.html

depicting their logo or name in a fancy graphic may well find that the name is invisible to robots since they search text not graphics. The way around this problem is for the webpage designer to use image tags that contain a brief description of each of the pictures on a page. These are again invisible to a standard browser, but they can be read by robots, making the listing of a site all the more effective.

WEB DIRECTORIES

The search engines listed in Exhibit 14.1 have an enormous task: they attempt to list every site on the web. Users visiting a search engine can therefore quickly find themselves swamped with masses of relevant and less relevant material. For this reason a site that would actually be of great interest to a user can be buried under a list of spurious citations of only limited appeal. To get around this problem some users now employ the services of a web directory. These consist of nothing more than a list of sites known to be of relevance to a particular topic. Web directories can be very general (e.g. medical) or highly focused (e.g. cancer research). Many of the larger directories, which will often contain the details of many thousands of sites, are divided into subcategories and are designed to be searched by keyword.

Web directories rely on manual submission, as they do not run robots to collect site data. The owners of such sites review paper or electronic notifications of new sites and then decide for themselves whether it is appropriate to forge an additional link to this site. Anyone new to the task of 'hunting down' new directories may find the site (//ds.internic.net/ds/dsdirofdirs.html) helpful. It is a Directory of Directories and users can use the site to identify those that are likely to be of relevance to their product or service category.

RELATIONSHIP MARKETING ON THE WEB

Writers such as diGrazia *et al.* (2000) advocate that good websites should treat different constituents differently. They suggest that websites should identify, differentiate, interact and customize if they are to successfully build relationships with visitors. Each of the facets they suggest is described briefly below.

Identify

Websites should capture information in respect of users. This involves much more than simply gathering the names and addresses of visitors, but rather gathering information about their habits, preferences and interests. Of course, there is a trade-off here. Web users are increasingly being asked for their details when they visit specific sites. The most effective way to encourage completion appears to be in tying it to specific benefits such as a tailored environment or homepage, or specific promotional offers.

Some sites have recognized user reticence to supply information and have adopted a 'build' policy in the sense that only a few details are recorded each time a user visits a site. A detailed profile is built up over time, yet users perceive that the data-collection process is minimal and inoffensive. The method is known as 'drip irrigation' dialogue.

Differentiate

To build a relationship strategy in the web one needs to understand the relative worth of each user. In some circumstances it may be appropriate thereafter to tailor the content to reflect relative worth. At its most simple level this may involve prioritizing the effort of designers to offer the greatest utility to higher value donors.

It is also possible to differentiate content by the needs of particular users, using a technique known as 'collaborative filtering'. This involves comparing the interests of a specific user with those of a larger cohort of visitors with a similar profile. In essence the organization can demonstrate to a user that it knows what he or she might be interested in and offer a list of pertinent suggestions for reading and/or support. Aside from engendering a feeling of relationship this technique can also provide substantial added value, by suggesting resources that the user might not otherwise have been aware of.

Interact

The most effective websites engage the potential donor in a dialogue and add value by being seen to interact with the user. Many examples of successful interaction abound. The Dana-Farber Cancer Center (www.danafarber.org) for example has almost 600 easily searchable articles on cancer that may also be downloaded. The Virtual Wall created by the Vietnam Veterans Memorial Foundation (www.thevirtualwall.org) provides a database of 58,000 soldiers who were killed in action and users can post messages, create remembrances for individual soldiers and participate in chats. The Moratorium Campaign also has a highly interactive site (www.moratoriumcampaign.org) where users who want to end the death penalty can provide their 'signature' on a virtual petition (see Plate 14.6).

Customize

The final aspect of implementing a relationship strategy lies in customizing some aspect of the service based on a particular user's needs. Many of the newer sites allow users to visit a site and to tailor that site to their own specific requirements. In many ways, this fourth dimension follows from the first. Having gathered information about users it is important that the organization then uses that knowledge to add value for consumers, by customizing the offering as a result. The World Wildlife Fund, for example, sends out regular updates on specific issues that it knows a number of visitors to the site will find of interest.

In using the Internet as a relationship-building tool, therefore, organizations should pay particular attention to the four dimensions listed above and perhaps appraise their performance against the best performing sites on the web. They may also find it instructive to conduct an analysis of the performance of related sites (perhaps those of similar causes) to develop a benchmark of their own performance and delineate scope for potential improvement.

INTERACTIVE TELEVISION

Interactive television has been offered since 1999 in the UK and for a similar period of time in selected pilots in the USA. It represents the first real attempt to engage viewers equipped with modern digital technology in a two-way conversation with advertisers and/or programme makers. The earliest attempts to offer interactive TV (iTV) linked the digital decoder (which unscrambled satellite or cable broadcasts) to the subscriber's own telephone line. The use of a modem allowed the box to communicate with the system operator when subscribers wished to make a purchase/donation, request additional information or access an interactive service, such as e-mail.

Most early systems allowed the viewer to enter the interactive section of their channel package by selecting it just as they would any of the traditional viewing channels. They were then faced with a menu very similar to that which they might encounter on the Internet. By highlighting and clicking on a range of icons, the user could very quickly enter and play a range

Home > State Signature Counts

>> Sign the petition | View the petition

Last updated 2/01/2003

Alabama	2,852
Alaska	782
Arizona	3,514
Arkansas	1,222
California	138,721
Colorado	3,131
Connecticut	4,565
Delaware	998
DC	2,259
Florida	26,224
Georgia	12,607
Hawaii	683
Idaho	528
Illinois	11,241
Indiana	10,012
Iowa	5,532
Kansas	3,277
Kentucky	2,596
Louisiana	7,096
Maine	1,258
Maryland	5,501
Massachusetts	7,463
Michigan	9,900
Minnesota	7,530
Mississippi	931
Missouri	8,116
Montana	552
Nebraska	1,100
Nevada	487
New Hampshire	1,146
New Jersey	11,576
New Mexico	2,765
New York	35,288
North Carolina	29,788
North Dakota	468
Ohio	9,789
Oklahoma	3,328
Oregon	2,784
Pennsylvania	16,902
Rhode Island	820
South Carolina	3,551
South Dakota	1,674
Tennessee	2,280
Texas	13,491
Utah	853
Vermont	1,428
Virginia	7,962
Washington	6,407
West Virginia	727
Wisconsin	6,960
Wyoming	184

http://www.moratoriumcampaign.org/statecounts/index.lasso   13/06/2003

Plate 14.6 *Moratorium Campaign petition*

Source: © Moratorium Campaign. Reproduced with kind permission

of computer games, or look to make a purchase from one of a number of online stores. In these early pilots, however, the interactive environment was held largely separate from the 'normal' television environment and the opportunity to interact directly with specific broadcasts was very limited. Early versions of iTV were very limited and offered access to only a small range of goods and services. Only a small number of non-profits have as yet elected to make use of the medium and the full potential has yet to be realized. As the technology improves and begins to offer full integration with normal television viewing, radical changes to the way in which television is enjoyed will shortly be forthcoming.

eTV

Many organizations are now beginning to recognize the potential of an emerging medium termed 'Enhanced TV' (eTV). It is really an advanced form of interactive television and looks set to transform traditional mass media such as broadcast television and the Internet by merging the two.

eTV allows certain technologies to deliver graphics and information content to the same screen as a video programme. These elements thus appear on top of video programming viewed on traditional television sets. The additional elements can be opaque or transparent or semi-transparent. They tend to be icons, banners, labels, menus, information about the programme, data that may be printed, open text fields (e.g. for a user to send an e-mail address), or even forms that may be completed in order to buy a product or send a donation.

Swedlow (2000) argues that 'what was once . . . a passive, linear, absorbing-only, viewing experience for millions of people around the world can now become a participatory, non-linear viewing and communications medium as well'. People will be empowered to develop a dialogue with the producers and/or characters of shows and to e-mail their friends/relatives immediately about a particular channel's content.

For non-profits this will allow individuals watching a DRTV commercial to click away to the organization's website, make a donation, take part in online discussion, or sign up for an advocacy programme. Links could also be provided from pertinent news items, something that will appeal particularly to emergency/disaster relief organizations, or from programmes specializing in specific issues. The capability to merge the characteristics of the Internet with traditional broadcast medium therefore holds particular potential.

DIGITAL RADIO

Just as television is currently undergoing a revolution, so too is radio. In the UK it was as long ago as 1995 that the BBC began offering its first digital broadcasting. In 1999 the corporation offered its first digital-only radio service, although consumer awareness of the new medium is still relatively low. This has been due largely to the fact that digital radio cannot be received on traditional radio receivers.

When radio made the quantum leap from AM to FM over a generation ago, listeners were offered a revolution in the quality of the broadcasts they could receive. Gone were the hisses and crackles of medium and long wave. In came the stereo sound and greater bandwidth afforded by frequency modulation. Digital radio will offer a similar quantum leap offering listeners a completely interference-free environment, a facet that should prove particularly attractive to listeners on the move in cars and so on. It will also offer CD quality sound for a much wider choice of programmes and ultimately, text and data services.

In the future radio will thus be capable of offering interactive services much in the same way as television, alluded to above. This represents a significant opportunity given that in the UK, the radio audience measurement organization (RADAR) estimates that 91 per cent of the population listen to the radio at least once a week. Radio is felt to be particularly pervasive since it can be regarded as a secondary medium (i.e. it is usually consumed while the listener is doing something else).

The ability to broadcast scrolling text alongside the programme content is already exciting some advertisers. It may be used to cite dedications, the details of competitions, or even to provide additional information to supplement advertising or programme sponsorship.

The contemporary hit station Core, for example, offers listeners an enhanced range of services. 'Core Control' allows listeners to pick a song and dedicate it to someone they know.

The system then informs the user exactly when it will run and illustrates the dedication in text. The station has also run a promotion with Warner Music to run a text line credit informing users when a track is featured on a new CD.

It should also be possible to arrange the content of digital radio broadcasting like a website in the sense that users enjoying a particular track may be afforded the opportunity to hear news and/or an interview with the pertinent artist purely by clicking an icon or pressing a particular button. Doubtless the accompanying text will appraise future listeners of these opportunities.

Of course, all these applications do not presently offer a return path. It does seem likely, however, that PC manufacturers will shortly offer a digital radio facility, thereby facilitating the development of an appropriate return path. The manufacturer Psion, for example, launched its first digital radio 'Wavefinder' device for connection to a PC in October 2000. It seems likely that such digital technology will also be included in mobile phones in the near future. It is particularly interesting to note that digital radio is an 'addressable' technology, allowing stations to target specific content to specific users. One can therefore easily imagine a scenario in which lifestyle information is collected in respect of new subscribers and then used to drive the specific nature of the advertising they receive. The adaptive nature of the technology would also make it possible to improve the nature of this targeting as the user's pattern of response is recorded and analysed.

At the time of writing, digital radio is not available in the USA.

SMS TEXT MESSAGING

The final digital revolution worthy of note is that taking place in the mobile telephony market. The ability to send text messages from one phone to another has been popular among the young since its inception in the late 1990s. Text messaging is now becoming a mainstream use of the mobile phone, however, and adults of all ages now routinely send and receive text messages using their mobile. In the UK, for example, the Mobile Data Association reports that the daily average text messaging figures leapt from 28.8 million in February 2001 to 44 million in late 2002.

Text messages can contain standard text, or they may also contain graphics, or small software packages such as ring tones for the mobile phone, should the recipient wish to use them. In the commercial sector, organizations provide links that take users into a mobile friendly (i.e. simple) version of their website, where information may be sought or a purchase initiated. Indeed, some shopping malls such as Bluewater allow mobile users to subscribe to a free service, whereby text messages pertaining to special offers are delivered as the user passes the store in question. It is a simple matter to triangulate position in the context of the mall and it may ultimately be possible to triangulate position on a standard high street, so that timely text messages may be delivered. Some UK theatres use a similar system to send out offers of last-minute reduced price ticket availability to individuals who have subscribed to a free alert service.

A final development worthy of note is the capability to link mobile communications to other forms of technology. A number of suppliers (e.g. Vodaphone) are currently looking to work with financial service providers so that the mobile may be used as a psuedo credit card. Users subscribing to the technology will be able to visit a store, scan their own merchandise using a scanner built into the phone and avoid checkout queues by paying for the goods when they receive their mobile phone bill.

The implications for non-profits are profound if this technology continues to gain acceptance. Amongst the range of options available, non-profits will be able to:

- Send text messages to potential shoppers/supporters as they approach their store or location.
- Send text message updates in respect of the progress of a campaign, or perhaps an alert warning of the emergence of an issue, such as a disaster in the Third World.
- Warn individuals of forthcoming events and link to an ability to purchase tickets or get involved. Oxfam GB, for example, used text messaging as part of its 'maketradefair' campaign.
- Recruit new donors by partnering with other media. A number of charities have used text messaging in partnership with ticket media. The back of each (train/theatre/airline) ticket contains a number that the user can text to make a donation and/or keep in touch with the work of the charity. It should ultimately be possible for the simple transmission of a text message to trigger a donation as the links between financial service providers and mobile operators, alluded to above, are strengthened. In the UK UNICEF recently printed a number on the back of one million bus tickets and invited individuals to text in to request a copy of its Christmas trading catalogue.

At the time of writing, the use of text messaging in the USA is still in its infancy. Problems securing agreements between the mobile telephony companies to exchange text messages between networks greatly delayed the introduction of the facility. It remains to be seen whether texting will become as popular in the USA as it has in Europe and elsewhere.

SPORT RELIEF

Sport Relief, a joint venture between BBC Sport and the charity Comic Relief, was among the first organizations in the UK to employ SMS text messaging for fundraising. In a campaign timed to coincide with the soccer World Cup there were three opportunities to give, highlighted on air on BBC Sport television programmes. Viewers could enter the Total Ticket sports quiz, guess the year of TV tennis footage shown during Wimbledon and receive updates on the soccer World Cup. To take part, viewers had to text into the BBC. Each text message cost £1 of which 60p was donated to Sports Relief. Over £100,000 was raised.

CHAPTER SUMMARY

In this chapter we have briefly reviewed a number of the new e-media that may be employed for the purposes of marketing and fundraising. In particular we have examined the role of the Internet, the opportunities created by the medium and a number of the key facets of raising funds in this arena. It was argued that a sequential development process be adopted and that, at the page level, many of the same design concerns arise as would be the case with traditional print media. We have suggested how some of these issues might best be dealt with. We have also reviewed the techniques that can be employed to promote a site and encourage visits. Of particular note was the use of search engines and the techniques that could be employed to attract the attention of their spiders to new sites or the amended pages of existing ones.

It seems clear that the use of electronic channels for fundraising will continue to grow over the next decade. The pace of technological change makes it essential that organizations continue to appraise themselves of the opportunities available and to plan innovative new ways of developing the level of interaction and customization they offer to customers as a consequence.

DISCUSSION QUESTIONS

1   You are the fundraising manager of Cancer Research UK. Suggest how the Internet could be used by the organization to raise funds.

2   How might a small non-profit organization setting up a web presence for the first time publicize the existence of its site?

3   You work for a large animal rights charity. Your CEO believes that interactive TV might offer your non-profit a new and exciting channel for acquiring donations. She has asked you for some guidance in a report outlining what you consider to be the key advantages and disadvantages of the medium.

4   In your role as the fundraising manager of a large national charity you are preparing a presentation to a visiting group of students about recent developments in e-media. Outline the points you would cover in this presentation.

REFERENCES

http://www.netnames.com/template.cfm?page=statistics&advert=yes

http://www.censorware.org/web_size/

http://www.aeanet.org/aeanet/research/ordercybernation.asp

http://www.emarketer.com/ereports/econsumer/welcome.html

http://strategis.commnow.com/

http://gartner11.gartnerweb.com/dq/static/dq.html

http://www.durlacher.com/fr-pub.htm

http://www.nua.ie/surveys/

Johnston, M. (1999) The Fund Raisers Guide to the Internet, NSFRE/Wiley, New York.

Sargeant, A. and Jay, E. (2003) 'The Fundraising Performance of Charity Websites; A US/UK Comparison', Interactive Marketing, 4(4): 330–342.

Smith, G. (1996) Asking Properly: The Art of Creative Fundraising, White Lion Press, London.

Swedlow, T. (2000) http://www.itvt.com/etvwhitepaper.html, Interactive TV Today.

Warwick, M., Hart, T. and Allen, N. (2002) Fundraising on the Internet: The Philanthropy Foundation Organization's Guide to Success Online, Jossey-Bass, New York.

Chapter 15

Benchmarking fundraising performance

LEARNING OBJECTIVES

By the end of this chapter you should be able to:
- Explain the need for effective benchmarking of fundraising performance.
- Understand the drawbacks of using published accounts for the purposes of comparison.
- Describe a process by which the benchmarking of fundraising costs may be accomplished.
- Explain typical patterns of performance experienced in modern fundraising practice.

INTRODUCTION

The issue of cost has long been a subject of concern to charity managers, not only so that individual managers can ensure the most appropriate use is made of their organization's resources, but also to ensure that this is seen to be the case by those who support the organization. Non-charitable expenditures are unpopular with the majority of donors, and it is not unusual for charities to be criticized by either the media or the general public for what are seen as 'wasteful' expenditures.

As a consequence, Hind (1995) notes that a certain 'paranoia' has gripped the management of many charities, characterized by an anxiety to avoid such 'unnecessary' expenditures. Non-profit managers are now keen to use every means at their disposal to present their performance in the most positive light possible and in some cases have undoubtedly reapportioned cost accordingly.

This has been something of a problem on both sides of the Atlantic, particularly where published accounts have been used by the media as the basis for analysis and comparison. As we shall show in this chapter, it is relatively easy to manipulate patterns of performance and there is little doubt that a number of non-profits lie outright on their returns.

Putting aside the public interest in fundraising cost and the call for fair and accurate reporting, the need for effective benchmarking to guide organizational management should not be underestimated. Every non-profit, no matter how large or small, should be aware of its performance and how this might compare to other, similar organizations in the sector.

Only by conducting this form of analysis can non-profits ensure that they continue to provide value for money to donors and that they are operating within acceptable boundaries of efficiency.

In this chapter it is our intention to review what is known about the behaviour of charity and fundraising costs, illustrating typical patterns of performance for each form of fundraising undertaken. We will also examine how benchmarking should be undertaken and explore current issues that must be tackled to ensure that the process is as accurate as possible.

NON-PROFIT PERFORMANCE

A non-profit organization is in essence one that is barred from distributing its net earnings to those who exert control over it, including, for example, shareholders, members, governors, directors and so on. (Hansmann 1980). It therefore exists with the sole purpose of satisfying one or more identified societal needs. The generation of profit by such enterprises is, however, not banned per se. Some non-profits can and do earn a healthy operating surplus; it is only the distribution of this surplus that is limited. Indeed, it must be retained and reinvested in the production/supply of ever-greater amounts of the goods/services the non-profit was originally constituted to provide. In the case of most non-profits this process is not problematic since demand usually far exceeds supply.

As Hansmann (1980) points out, however, the non-profit is far from being an ideal organizational form. The removal of the profit incentive can give rise to a number of potential problems. Non-profits could, for example, be slow to respond to the demands made of them and there is perhaps a greater potential for non-profits to be wasteful of valuable resources than their for-profit counterparts. Less scrupulous organizations may also find ways of distributing their operating surplus in the form of enhanced staff salaries, or other perks and benefits. Hence, as Henke (1972: 51) notes, 'as (nonprofits) increase in size and influence, it becomes increasingly important (to find some way) to measure their performance'.

Regrettably there have been a number of well-publicized instances where this would appear to be a genuine cause for concern. Baily and Millar (1992) cite the example of the United Way and the damage that was done to the organization by revelations about the unnecessary expenditures incurred by its incumbent CEO. In a further example Cutlip (1990) reports that the National Kids Day Foundation raised $4 million between 1948 and 1963 and managed to spend the entire amount on fundraising and administration costs. In response to the inevitable criticism, the organization attempted to argue that its aim was to promote the idea of aiding needy children rather than actually providing services.

Historically the accountancy profession has always been more concerned with the measurement and control of for-profit enterprise. As Henke (1972: 51) notes, 'the profession has never really faced up to the problem of trying to convey to the constituent groups of (nonprofit) organizations the data which would disclose the operational stewardship of the management of these entities'. This is due partly to the fact that there is seldom any real measure of operational efficiency for these organizations. While in the for-profit sector, loss-making organizations are soon forced out of existence, in the case of non-profits, an operating deficit could easily indicate to donors an organization worthy of additional support. Inefficient organizations can potentially survive as the donor has no way of distinguishing those that are efficiently meeting the needs of their recipient group(s) from those that expend needless sums of money on administration and management. Inevitably because of their ease of calculation, simple financial ratios have been used to discern between these two groups.

Of course it is not entirely legitimate to use ratios to draw direct comparisons between one charity and another (Rooney 1999), particularly where this comparison is based on published accounts. This is simply because the manner in which these accounts are prepared does not lend itself to this purpose.

Public reporting of performance

In the USA, non-profits above a certain size must file a Form 990 return with the IRS. This simple form (see Figure 15.1) contains only modest amounts of information and a high proportion of non-profits elect to show no fundraising cost at all, even where they show high levels of income from donors. Research by Cordes and Wilson (2000) identified that 59 per cent of non-profits receiving direct public contributions did not report any fundraising expenses at all, including nearly a quarter of those receiving more than $5 million in contributions! This seems quite remarkable, and of course a cynic may wonder how such sums of money were raised in the absence of individuals being asked and, moreover, how the gifts were collected, paid in and acknowledged with absolutely no staff time (and hence cost) being involved. Form 990 and hence studies based on its data are therefore of severely limited use and should be interpreted with caution.

The picture in the UK is sadly no better. While registered charities must file detailed annual accounts with the Charity Commission, such accounts are prepared in accordance with the most recent accounting SORP (Statement of Recommended Practice). While at face value one might presume that this would provide a reasonable basis for comparison between organizations there are a number of reasons why this is not the case.

The first contains the manner in which charity accounts are presented. Unlike business organizations, the accounts are compiled following the principles of 'fund accounting' (i.e. one organization may comprise a number of funds), making the application of a standard ratio analysis problematic (Palmer and Randall 2002).

There are also issues of variation in accounting policies and the definitions of key categories. Hyndman and McKillop (1999) argue that these problems are so acute that the use of ratio analysis based on financial accounting data is a nonsense. As Pharoah (1997) notes, accounting practices can vary substantially from one organization to another, and what may be classified as fundraising expenditure for one organization may be classified as charitable expenditure by another.

> Feasibility work (for example), carried out as part of the preparation for bids for large capital grants can be considered as direct charitable expenditure and not as a fund-raising cost.
>
> (Pharoah 1997: 168)

Similarly, many organizations have a mission which requires them to involve themselves not only in benefiting the members of a certain target group, but also in educating the general public about the very particular needs thereof. Thus a charity such as the Terrence Higgins Trust will not only endeavour to alleviate the suffering of those with HIV infection or Aids, it will also seek to raise the public awareness of Aids and to eliminate many of the common misconceptions associated with the illness. Those organizations that feel it important to develop such a role face a dilemma in accounting terms over the manner in which they report the costs of awareness generation or educational activity. Since there are often substantial benefits to be gained by combining such activities with those designed specifically to raise funds it often becomes impossible to distinguish between them. In these circumstances charities must decide quite arbitrarily whether to show the costs against fundraising or as direct charitable expenditure, a decision that will obviously have profound implications for the subsequent calculation of fundraising ratios.

Allied to this, many charities now adopt the practice of 'awareness recharging' where a proportion of the cost of fundraising (typically 10 to 20 per cent) is taken out of funds and shown as a direct charitable expenditure, since it is argued that one of the purposes of fundraising communications is to raise an awareness of the cause. This, they would argue, is a legitimate goal of the organization and hence it is appropriate to make this adjustment.

Form **990**

Return of Organization Exempt From Income Tax

Under section 501(c), 527, or 4947(a)(1) of the Internal Revenue Code (except black lung benefit trust or private foundation)

▶ The organization may have to use a copy of this return to satisfy state reporting requirements.

OMB No. 1545-0047

2002

Open to Public Inspection

Department of the Treasury
Internal Revenue Service

A For the 2002 calendar year, or tax year beginning _____, 2002, and ending _____, 20 ___

B Check if applicable:
- ☐ Address change
- ☐ Name change
- ☐ Initial return
- ☐ Final return
- ☐ Amended return
- ☐ Application pending

Please use IRS label or print or type. See Specific Instructions.

C Name of organization

Number and street (or P.O. box if mail is not delivered to street address) Room/suite

City or town, state or country, and ZIP + 4

D Employer identification number

E Telephone number ( )

F Accounting method: ☐ Cash ☐ Accrual ☐ Other (specify) ▶

● Section 501(c)(3) organizations and 4947(a)(1) nonexempt charitable trusts must attach a completed Schedule A (Form 990 or 990-EZ).

G Web site: ▶

J Organization type (check only one) ▶ ☐ 501(c) ( ) ◀ (insert no.) ☐ 4947(a)(1) or ☐ 527

K Check here ▶ ☐ if the organization's gross receipts are normally not more than $25,000. The organization need not file a return with the IRS; but if the organization received a Form 990 Package in the mail, it should file a return without financial data. Some states require a complete return.

H and **I** are not applicable to section 527 organizations.
H(a) Is this a group return for affiliates? ☐ Yes ☐ No
H(b) If "Yes," enter number of affiliates ▶ _____
H(c) Are all affiliates included? ☐ Yes ☐ No (If "No," attach a list. See instructions.)
H(d) Is this a separate return filed by an organization covered by a group ruling? ☐ Yes ☐ No
I Enter 4-digit GEN ▶
M Check ▶ ☐ if the organization is **not** required to attach Sch. B (Form 990, 990-EZ, or 990-PF).

L Gross receipts: Add lines 6b, 8b, 9b, and 10b to line 12 ▶

Part I Revenue, Expenses, and Changes in Net Assets or Fund Balances (See page 17 of the instructions.)

1	Contributions, gifts, grants, and similar amounts received:		
a	Direct public support	1a	
b	Indirect public support	1b	
c	Government contributions (grants)	1c	
d	**Total** (add lines 1a through 1c) (cash $ _____ noncash $ _____)	1d	
2	Program service revenue including government fees and contracts (from Part VII, line 93)	2	
3	Membership dues and assessments	3	
4	Interest on savings and temporary cash investments	4	
5	Dividends and interest from securities	5	
6a	Gross rents	6a	
b	Less: rental expenses	6b	
c	Net rental income or (loss) (subtract line 6b from line 6a)	6c	
7	Other investment income (describe ▶)	7	
8a	Gross amount from sales of assets other than inventory	(A) Securities 8a	(B) Other
b	Less: cost or other basis and sales expenses	8b	
c	Gain or (loss) (attach schedule)	8c	
d	Net gain or (loss) (combine line 8c, columns (A) and (B))	8d	
9	Special events and activities (attach schedule)		
a	Gross revenue (not including $ _____ of contributions reported on line 1a)	9a	
b	Less: direct expenses other than fundraising expenses	9b	
c	Net income or (loss) from special events (subtract line 9b from line 9a)	9c	
10a	Gross sales of inventory, less returns and allowances	10a	
b	Less: cost of goods sold	10b	
c	Gross profit or (loss) from sales of inventory (attach schedule) (subtract line 10b from line 10a)	10c	
11	Other revenue (from Part VII, line 103)	11	
12	**Total revenue** (add lines 1d, 2, 3, 4, 5, 6c, 7, 8d, 9c, 10c, and 11)	12	
13	Program services (from line 44, column (B))	13	
14	Management and general (from line 44, column (C))	14	
15	Fundraising (from line 44, column (D))	15	
16	Payments to affiliates (attach schedule)	16	
17	**Total expenses** (add lines 16 and 44, column (A))	17	
18	Excess or (deficit) for the year (subtract line 17 from line 12)	18	
19	Net assets or fund balances at beginning of year (from line 73, column (A))	19	
20	Other changes in net assets or fund balances (attach explanation)	20	
21	Net assets or fund balances at end of year (combine lines 18, 19, and 20)	21	

(left margin labels: Revenue / Expenses / Net Assets)

For Paperwork Reduction Act Notice, see the separate instructions.   Cat. No. 11282Y   Form **990** (2002)

Figure 15.1 *Form 990*

The structure of an organization's funding can also have a dramatic impact on these figures. Those organizations that are fortunate enough to receive a small number of grants on an annual basis and derive the lion's share of their funding from these will have a significantly better cost structure than those organizations involved in soliciting funds from the general public. Not only will greater numbers of staff be required to administer fundraising from the general public, but the costs of communicating with an often diverse population of donors can be substantially higher (Sargeant and Kaehler 1998). Moreover, the sheer volume of transactions can add quite significantly to IT, data processing and even banking costs (Hind 1995).

Using fundraising ratios to compare between organizations could also be criticized on the grounds that such figures (unless averaged over a three- to five-year period) will fail to take account of large one-off contributions such as a particularly large grant or legacy income. A charity that might otherwise exhibit rather poor patterns of performance can thus be transformed overnight into one of the most efficient in the sector.

FACE, ACE AND FCE RATIOS

Having noted all these caveats a number of writers have nevertheless used financial reports to calculate a series of key ratios to compare the performance of non-profits. The ratio of fundraising and administration costs to total expenditure (FACE) is used frequently as a benchmark to measure the efficiency of charities. As Hind (1995) notes, there is a general perception that a FACE ratio of more than 20 per cent is unacceptable (i.e. a charity should spend at least 80 per cent of every £/$1 donated on the cause).

There would appear, however, to be little empirical evidence to suggest that 20 per cent is actually an appropriate benchmark to adopt. Hind argues that a low FACE ratio can be counter-productive, maintaining that the charity is not investing sufficiently in an administrative infrastructure to support its charitable work, nor is it making an adequate investment in fundraising to safeguard the charity's future if the FACE ratio is below 10 per cent. As a rough

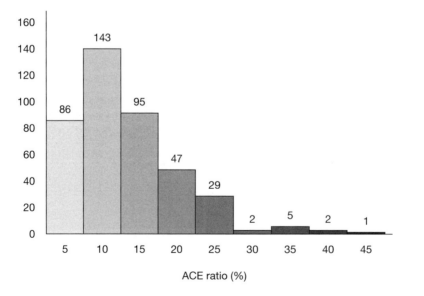

Figure 15.2 *Frequency distribution of administration costs to total expenditures (ACE) in 410 charities, 1992–1996*

Source: © Charities Aid Foundation. Reproduced with kind permission

304

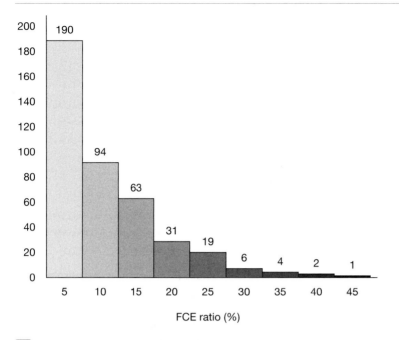

Figure 15.3 *Frequency distribution of fundraising costs to total expenditures (FCE) in 410 charities, 1992–1996*
Source: © Charities Aid Foundation. Reproduced with kind permission

guide Hind thus recommends that in other than exceptional cases, FACE ratios should lie somewhere within the range of 10 to 30 per cent. Again, it is important to remember that there is no justification for the numerical value of these limits.

Further insights can often be provided by splitting non-charitable expenditures into administration and fundraising costs. The percentage of administration costs to total expenditures is known as the ACE ratio, and in work by Sargeant and Kaehler (1999) 79 per cent of charities were found to have administration costs of no more than 15 per cent of all expenditures (see Figure 15.2).

The ratio of fundraising costs to total expenditures (FCE) may also be calculated and is obviously of particular interest to fundraisers. Averaging the performance of the Top 500 UK charities over the period 1992 to 1996, Sargeant and Kaehler identified that a high proportion (46 per cent) of non-profits claim to spend less than 5 per cent of their expenditure on fundraising (see Figure 15.3). Just as with the results from the US Form 990, these figures seem somewhat at odds with what we currently know about *actual* fundraising performance.

Descriptive statistics for each cost ratio calculated by Sargeant and Kaehler are provided in Table 15.1.

In previous studies the FCE ratio has been consistently shown to be a function of:

- *The size of the organization*: There seem to be economies of scale in fundraising activity that make it cheaper for larger organizations to raise funds than smaller ones. This is certainly true within the larger charities, although there is now some evidence to suggest that very small non-profits may also achieve higher levels of performance, presumably because much of the time necessary to raise funds in smaller organizations is 'donated' by volunteers.

Table 15.1 *Descriptive statistics of cost ratios (per cent)*

	Administration costs (ACE)	Fundraising costs (FCE)	Fundraising and administration costs (FACE)
Mean	10.4	7.8	18.2
Minimum	0.1	–	0.1
Maximum	42.8	40.7	57.8
Lower quartile	5.5	1.8	10.7
Median	9.3	5.7	16.2
Upper quartile	13.6	12.0	23.7

Source: Sargeant and Kaehler (1998). Reproduced by kind permission of the Charities Aid Foundation

- *The nature of the cause*: Work by Sargeant in both 1999 and 2003 has shown consistently that some categories of cause find it more difficult to raise funds than others. It would thus be unfair to compare the performance of a UK disability charity with that of an overseas aid organization. The former would tend to find it more difficult to raise funds than the latter, reflecting public interest in these causes in the UK. It thus seems likely that similar patterns will be reported in other countries where members of the public are perhaps more receptive to the message from certain causes because of current background levels of interest and concern.
- *Age/experience*: Those non-profits that are new to fundraising, or new to the use of certain techniques, will find that it takes time to establish a reasonable pattern of performance. Many techniques require investment over a period of many years before an adequate return on investment can be reported. Thus the move by a non-profit into the use of a new media or method of fundraising may adversely affect its aggregate fund ratios in the short to medium term.

There are of course many other factors that can influence the FCE, but these tend to have less marked effects on the ratio reported. Many of these are dealt with below.

FUNDRAISING PERFORMANCE

Not surprisingly, a variety of academic and professional studies have now been conducted into the issue of fundraising costs. In the USA, for example, a study by the Council for Advancement and Support of Education Study concluded from a study of fifty-one colleges and universities that the mean cost of fundraising was 16 cents on the dollar, the median 11 cents. Work in the UK by Pharoah (1997) examining the performance of the Top 500 fundraising charities reports that it costs between £0.01 and £0.51 to raise £1 with a mean of £0.08.

Against this backdrop a variety of bodies now stipulate 'acceptable' benchmarks of performance, with the Council of Better Business Bureaus and the Philanthropic Advisory Service currently specifying a 35 per cent limit on FR costs. It is interesting to note that despite these benchmarks, Steinberg (1986, 1991) famously argues that donors should not be concerned about fundraising costs at all. He notes that fundraising costs are sunk (i.e. spent) by the time the donor receives the solicitation and that as a consequence all the monies donated will actually serve to benefit the non-profit!

Of course the foregoing benchmarks are based on an examination of fundraising in aggregate and the returns accruing from various forms of fundraising are actually very different. The returns accruing from work with major donors, trust/foundations and corporates are, for example, considerably higher than those accruing from direct marketing activity.

The very nature of work with major givers makes the development of benchmarks for this type of fundraising problematic. It can take many years of cultivation before a sizeable donation may be offered, and for a charity new to this form of fundraising it may be two to five years before the activity becomes profitable. From work by Sargeant and Kaehler in the UK it would however be expected that every £1 of investment in major gift work should yield a return of £50 to £60 (when direct costs only are considered). In the USA where large capital and endowment campaigns are now an integral of the non-profit landscape the returns accruing from major gift activity are likely to be several multiples higher than this.

Corporate fundraising is also a complicated activity to benchmark. This is a function again of the staff time necessary to stimulate this category of giving, often accruing over many years. It is also a function of the various forms of gift that can be offered (e.g. gifts in kind, staff secondments and of course cash donations). Many of these forms of giving are difficult to place a monetary value on and hence the median return reported by Sargeant and Kaehler of £5 for every £1 invested must be interpreted with great care.

DIRECT MARKETING

A common mistake in attempting to benchmark non-profit direct marketing activity is to assume that all such activity is alike and to bundle all the costs and revenues associated with these activities together to calculate a single overall ratio. This approach is fundamentally flawed because it fails to draw a distinction between donor recruitment activity, where most charities lose money, and donor development activity, where significant returns accrue over time.

There are two other complexities unique to the UK where, as we discussed in Chapter 6, donors may be either committed or uncommitted. The latter offer only a series of occasional gifts in response to direct marketing solicitations, whereas the former are recruited to a regular monthly or yearly gift, which is deducted directly from their bank accounts. Given that the pattern of giving is markedly different, so too is the economics of this form of fundraising.

It should also be noted that in the UK charities are able to claim back the basic rate of income tax paid by the donor on any donation they might offer. This applies when a donor has paid income tax at or above the level of the gift (thus embracing most income earners) and where a declaration that this tax has been paid is offered to the charity. Thus in examining the performance of the fundraising function it will be appropriate to consider, at least in aggregate, the tax reclaimed by the charity. While one could argue that the level of tax reclaimed does not reflect performance, in fact UK charities must solicit the declarations and hence it is considered legitimate to include a consideration of these issues in attempting to benchmark performance.

Recent work by Sargeant *et al.* conducted in the United Kingdom in 2002/3 examined the use of direct marketing in fundraising in some detail. In the summary of their analysis that follows, the figures presented are based on a consideration of the direct (non-staff) costs *only* associated with each activity. Staff costs and tax reclaimed are reported separately.

Donor recruitment – direct mail

Their analysis began with the use of direct mail designed to recruit cash or uncommitted donors. The results for this form of fundraising are presented in Table 15.2. The immediate return

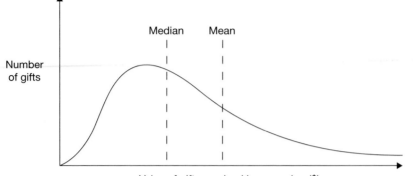

Figure 15.4 *Illustration of skewness*

Table 15.2 *Performance of direct mail cold recruitment (uncommitted or cash givers only)*

Measure	Mean	Std dev	Median
Return on investment	0.39	0.21	0.47
Cost per donor (£)	80.10	112.46	33.43
Average response rate (%)	3.83	6.02	1.70
Average cost per pack (£)	0.54	0.14	0.52

achieved by non-profits was a mere £0.39 for each £1 of investment undertaken. Not surprisingly as a consequence the cost of acquiring each new donor is relatively high and of the order of £33.40 per donor. It should be noted that performance data are often highly skewed – that is to say that most non-profits share a similar pattern of performance, but that a few have patterns of performance that are very different, skewing the distribution to the left or right. This idea is illustrated in Figure 15.4. Where results are skewed in this way the mean or average figure would be distorted, taking account as it does of the extremes of performance (or outliers) included in the sample. This effect is also illustrated in Figure 15.4. In this case a number of organizations had clearly encountered difficulties with this medium and were reporting very high costs as a consequence. In such circumstances the median (or middle) value is a better indicator of the 'typical' performance attained.

Data were then gathered in respect of 'reciprocal' mailings – once again designed to recruit cash or uncommitted givers. In the UK many charities swop lists of their lower value donors with other charities, a practice known simply as 'list-swops' in the USA. Table 15.3 reports the detail of the analysis. It is particularly interesting to note the enhanced ROI when considered in comparison to the ROI reported in Table 15.2. It is clear that non-profits find reciprocal mailings much more profitable than cold lists – at least in the short term. Not surprisingly the cost per donor is also much lower and the average response rate somewhat higher.

The performance of direct mail in the recruitment of committed givers is reported in Table 15.4. In this case the immediate return on investment (which in this case is calculated on the first year's income) is marginally better than would be the case for uncommitted givers. It should be noted however that the lifetime ROI (see Chapter 7) is likely to be significantly higher as the value of the ongoing commitment begins to accrue.

Table 15.3 *Performance of reciprocal mailings (uncommitted or cash givers only)*

Measure	Mean	Std dev	Median
Return on investment	1.41	0.52	1.23
Cost per donor (£)	11.24	2.62	11.07
Average response rate (per cent)	4.14	1.07	4.79
Average cost per pack (£)	0.41	0.12	0.40

Table 15.4 *Direct mail cold recruitment (committed givers only)*

Measure	Mean	Std dev	Median
Return on investment	0.81	0.77	0.49
Cost per donor (£)	146.14	126.33	118.34
Average response rate (per cent)	0.64	0.39	0.61
Average cost per pack (£)	0.47	0.03	0.47

Donor recruitment – other media

The results for other recruitment media are reported in Table 15.5. These show that charities achieve a healthy return on investment from DRTV. This probably reflects the fact that DRTV is now used in the recruitment of committed rather than one-off givers, and that changes in payment methods (namely the introduction of paperless direct debit (PDD)) are increasing fulfilment rates.

Also worthy of note are the figures reported for face-to-face recruitment, a relatively new method of donor recruitment in the UK. Face-to-face appears to be acquiring new supporters at a cost of around £63. Most charities would expect to achieve break-even on these (committed giving) recruits at around the eighteen-month point (not allowing for attrition).

Donor development performance

Table 15.6 presents data on donor direct mail programmes targeted at cash givers. Cash givers are typically sent four mailings per year, to which they respond on average at a level of between 7 to 8 per cent. This results in a somewhat disappointing return on investment of £3 for every £1 spent. However, it should be remembered that most UK charities now concentrate heavily on the recruitment, retention and development of committed givers. In many cases this may mean that the remaining cash givers are of a poorer quality than may have been the case in the past. It should also be remembered that some of the mailings sent may well be information communications such as updates and newsletters rather than direct appeals for funds.

Table 15.7 summarizes the data on the direct mail programmes designed for committed givers. It would appear that committed givers receive fewer communications throughout the year, and are far more profitable, though respondents reported a wide variation on return on investment. Again, some of the communications they receive may be informational rather than designed as appeals for funds. Many charities seek to upgrade the levels of the regular gift given by mail or telephone and the data may also reflect the results of this activity in part.

Table 15.5 *Returns from direct marketing media (£)*

Media	Mean	Std dev	Median
DRTV			
Return on investment	2.27	0.56	2.77
Cost per donor	115.46	56.47	139.47
Direct response press advertising			
Return on investment	0.61	0.58	0.58
Cost per donor	202.34	212.10	62.09
Press/magazine inserts			
Return on investment	0.87	1.01	0.26
Cost per donor	120.02	77.03	116.23
Face-to-face solicitation			
Return on investment	0.66	0.33	0.71
Cost per donor	63.67	20.97	62.54
Doordrops (unaddressed direct mail)			
Return on investment	0.56	0.46	0.35
Cost per donor	74.31	57.84	77.04

Table 15.6 *Performance of donor development mailings (uncommitted or cash givers only)*

Measure	Mean	Std dev	Median
Number of mailings received	4.86	2.80	4.00
Return on investment (£)	3.69	2.49	3.00
Size of donor base	51,122	76,249	17,500
Response rate (%)	8.2	2.3	7.5

Table 15.7 *Donor development mailings (committed givers only)*

Measure	Mean	Std dev	Median
Number of mailings received	2.88	1.45	3.00
Return on investment (£)	14.53	33.51	5.00
Size of donor base	45,439	61,322	12,500

Aggregate fundraising ratios

Finally, the research data allowed the researchers to calculate aggregate ratios for both recruitment and development that included both staff costs and any tax the organization was able to reclaim on donations received. Beginning with recruitment, the mean return on investment was found to be 0.95 with a standard deviation of 1.29, reflecting a highly skewed pattern of performance. Again, under these circumstances the median return of £0.44 for every £1 of investment is a more representative indicator of typical performance.

In the case of donor development activity the inclusion of tax reclaimed had a significant effect on the figures attained. To illustrate this we will begin by presenting the returns achieved inclusive of all direct costs but excluding tax reclaimed. In this case a mean return of £1.70 for every £1 of investment was reported. The standard deviation was found to be £1.27, the median value £1.26.

Finally, when all the direct costs associated with each activity (including staff costs) were included in the analysis together with the tax reclaimed, we find that donor development activity achieves a mean return on investment of £2.98 for every £1 of investment. In this case however the distribution was highly skewed with a standard deviation of £2.73 being reported. The median value is thus a more representative measure of typical performance and this was found to be £1.91 for every £1 of investment.

ENHANCING THE PUBLIC TRUST

As we highlighted in the introduction to this chapter, non-profits will be drawn to benchmarking as an issue for one of two reasons. First, they will be concerned about how their performance is perceived by donors or other stakeholders, and second, they will wish to assess the quality of their performance with respect to others in the sector, usually for the purposes of managing the fundraising function.

The first of these two motives for involvement in benchmarking activity can drive non-profits to present their performance in the best possible light, taking full advantage of the latitude that reporting conventions in either the UK or USA will allow. In essence, fundraisers need to ensure that they understand the 'rules of the game' at least as well as their counterparts in other organizations and can manipulate these to good effect. After all, if fundraisers in one organization adopt the practice of awareness recharging, there would seem to be no good reason why others with a similar justification should not do likewise.

Of course, this kind of practice does the donor no favours. He or she will have a legitimate and genuine interest in what performance is actually being attained and increasingly how much it costs a particular organization to raise a dollar/pound. The fact that 59 per cent of US non-profits find it appropriate to show no costs of fundraising at all should shame our whole profession. For anyone to believe that donors would be 'conned' into believing that this is actually the case is a nonsense. Such practices serve only to diminish donor trust and confidence in the work that fundraisers do and to make them ever more suspicious that the profession has something to hide. What is needed in both the USA and the UK is a concerted attempt on the part of the non-profit community to educate donors about the reality of fundraising costs and to develop some pride in the pattern of performance attained. While there may be an understandable temptation to downplay costs, fundraising continues to represent an excellent investment, achieving returns well above that which would be offered by any national stock market. It is the difference between saying to a $100 donor, 'we spent $90 of your gift on programmes and managed to keep fundraising expenditure down to $10' and saying instead, 'we spent $90 of your gift on programmes and guess what – with the other $10 we went out and got another $100'. Trade associations, government and sector umbrella bodies have a key role to play in facilitating this change in emphasis and in ensuring transparent and honest reporting of all the *actual* costs of fundraising.

OBTAINING BENCHMARKING DATA

For fundraisers seeking benchmarking data for the purposes of comparison, there are a number of institutions and studies that can assist in this process. In the USA organizations such as the

Better Business Bureau and Guidestar can provide aggregate data that may be manipulated to create an overall guide to a particular organization's performance. In the UK charities can approach the Centre for Inter-Firm Comparisons (which produces the fund ratios study) or the research team at the Charities Aid Foundation. There are also a number of academics conducting work in this field, including staff at the Centre for Voluntary Sector Management at Henley Management College, the Centre for Charity and Trust Research at South Bank University and the Indiana University Center on Philanthropy.

Uniquely, however, the sector has a strong history of collaboration between organizations and it may be possible for fundraisers to exploit their contacts with peers to determine how other organizations are performing in respect of certain categories of fundraising. While the data gleaned will undoubtedly be of immense value it should be remembered that different organizations will have different approaches to accounting for fundraising, and thus managers need to ensure that they are genuinely comparing like with like.

Whatever approach is eventually adopted we would recommend the process depicted in Figure 15.5. It begins with the fundraiser deciding what he or she intends to benchmark and why. We refer to this as the rationale for the benchmarking exercise, since it will drive what follows. The use to which the benchmarking data will be put will drive the choice of organizations that the fundraiser will want to compare its performance against. It may be that the organization is interested in organizations of a similar size, working with a similar category of cause or simply undertaking a similar pattern of fundraising activity. There is no one right approach here; the choice will be driven by the rationale for the exercise.

Having selected the cohort of organizations that will be included in the exercise it will then be necessary to gather the comparative data. These may be obtained from published sources (although be wary of the caveats we expressed above) or it may be obtained directly from the organizations themselves and either taken from their annual published accounts or internal management accounting data. Peer networks may be used for this purpose.

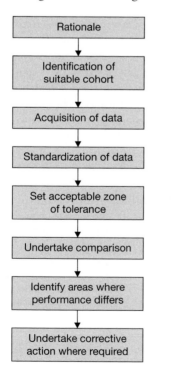

Figure 15.5 *Benchmarking process*

The next step is to examine how the data collected were assembled and to ensure as far as possible that the data across the whole cohort are standardized and hence reported in the same way. This will be particularly difficult in the case of published sources, but a telephone call to the non-profit can often clarify their policies on practices such as awareness recharging and so on. The researcher should also be sensitive to atypical dimensions to the results for particular organizations, such as the receipt of an unusually large legacy that can greatly distort reported performance. These would normally be omitted from the analysis.

When the data has been standardized the non-profit can then proceed to undertake the comparison and to examine its own performance against the cohort of other non-profits. In doing so it should be aware of the presence of any outliers in the sample and beware of skewed distributions as highlighted above. Comparison against the mean may produce misleading results if the distribution is skewed and the median may well be a better measure of central tendency.

If the number of organizations contained in the cohort is high there are a number of statistical tests that could potentially be employed to determine whether the performance of the organization relative to others is good, typical or poor. If the number of organizations is small, and in most cases with this kind of work it will be, then considerable care in interpretation is necessary. All too often, non-profits can conclude that their performance is considerably poorer than other players in the sector, when in reality, although performance does differ, the difference is negligible and certainly unworthy of serious management attention. For this reason some non-profits establish a 'zone of tolerance' where for a particular activity they agree that they will ignore variations of, say, plus or minus 10 per cent of the mean. Only when reported performance falls outside of that boundary do they identify why this might be the case.

Clearly, fundraisers can look at those aspects of their operations where they seem to be performing less well than the competition and seek to take corrective action. Equally, even where their performance is typical (or good) the analysis may highlight other non-profits that seem to perform very well in certain respects. A further investigation of why this might be so can be of considerable value, since there may be aspects of the professional practice of other organizations that could be copied or adapted for use. If, for example, a charity is found to be performing exceptionally well in the development of major donors, it may be that lessons can be learned from how they identify prospects, structure their approach, involve donors in the organization and ultimately make the ask. To obtain some of this information it may be possible to examine the trade press for reports on the actions undertaken, but more usually it will again be necessary to leverage the peer network that many professional fundraisers share in order to truly understand the reasons for a particular performance.

CHAPTER SUMMARY

In this chapter we have examined the critical issue of benchmarking and highlighted a number of ways in which non-profits can compare their performance with others in the sector. We have reviewed the drawbacks of using published accounts as the basis for comparison, notably that many non-profits fail to be open and honest about the realities of their fundraising costs. We have also examined differences in reporting conventions and policies that can serve to distort benchmarking results.

There are a number of factors that can drive reported fundraising performance, including the size of the charity, the nature of its cause, its past experience with particular techniques, the categories of funding sought and so on. Thus to be in a position to accurately compare the performance of particular non-profits it is essential that the fundraiser ensures that he or she is comparing like with like.

We have also reviewed the extant studies of fundraising costs and reported typical levels of performance, particularly within the context of the UK. While the chapter contains useful benchmarking data it must be appreciated that the returns we illustrate should be used only as a guide to the performance that may be expected by each medium. In many cases the experience of the charities participating in the study varied widely, making the establishment of industry benchmarks problematic.

We concluded by suggesting a process that non-profits could adopt to undertake their own benchmarking exercise and would recommend that the performance of the fundraising function is regularly compared against that of other, similar organizations. This will ensure that the non-profit maintains a consistent pattern of performance and does not miss any opportunities to improve the quality of its professional practice.

DISCUSSION QUESTIONS

1   What factors can influence the FCE ratio?

2   What is meant by the term 'skewness'? Why is it important to understand this term in relation to benchmarking activity?

3   A member of your Board has written to you complaining that it seems to cost your organization 5 cents more on the dollar to raise funds than other non-profits in the locality. How might you respond?

4   In your role as head of development at a US state university, prepare a presentation to the Board explaining how the university might seek to benchmark its fundraising performance against other non-profits.

5   A donor has written to you complaining that you spend too much on mailing him newsletters and other campaign materials. He feels that you should spend the money on raising money from Trusts/Foundations and corporates. How might you respond?

REFERENCES

Baily, A.L. and Millar, B. (1992) 'United Way: The Fallout After the Fall', *Chronicle of Philanthropy*, March: 1.

Charity Commission (2003) *Facts and Figures*, Charity Commission Website, 20 February.

Cordes, J.J. and Wilson, S. (2000) 'Costless Fundraising: Deconstructing The Evidence', Paper presented at ARNOVA Conference, New Orleans, Louisiana.

Cutlip, S.M. (1990) *Fundraising in the United States: Its Role in America's Philanthropy*, Transaction Publishers, New Brunswick, NJ.

Hansmann, H.B. (1980) 'The Role of the Nonprofit Enterprise', *Yale Law Journal*, 89: 835–898.

Henke, E.O. (1972) 'Performance Evaluation for Not-For-Profit Organizations', *Journal of Accountancy*: 51–55.

Hind, A. (1995) *The Governance and Management of Charities*, The Voluntary Sector Press, London.

Hyndman, N. and McKillop, D. (1999) 'Conversion Ratios in Charities in England and Wales: An Investigation of Economies of Scale', *Financial Accountability and Management*, 15(2): 135–153.

Palmer, P. and Randall, A. (2002) *Financial Management in the Voluntary Sector*, Routledge, London.

Pharoah, C. (1997) *Managing Finance in the Voluntary Sector – A Delicate Balance*, Charities Aid Foundation, West Malling, Kent.

Rooney, P. (1999) 'A Better Methodology for Analyzing the Costs and Benefits of Fund Raising at Universities', *Nonprofit Management and Leadership*, 10(1): 39–56.

Sargeant, A. and Kaehler, J. (1998) *Benchmarking Charity Costs*, Charities Aid Foundation, London.

Sargeant, A. and Kaehler, J. (1999) 'Returns on Fundraising Expenditures in the Voluntary Sector', *Nonprofit Management and Leadership*, 10(1): 5–19.

Steinberg, R. (1986) 'Should Donors Care About Fundraising?', in S. Rose-Ackerman (ed.), *The Economics of Nonprofit Institutions: Studies in Structure and Policy*, Oxford University Press, New York, pp. 347–364.

Steinberg, R. (1991) 'The Economics of Fund-Raising', in D.F. Burlingame and L.J. Hulse (eds), *Taking Fund-Raising Seriously: Advancing The Profession and Practice of Raising Money*, Jossey-Bass, San Francisco, pp. 239–256.

Chapter 16

Legal and ethical aspects of fundraising management

LEARNING OBJECTIVES

By the end of this chapter you should be able to:

■ Understand the legislative framework that impacts on fundraising.

■ Describe the principles of data protection.

■ Describe the requirements for legal/ethical charity advertising.

■ Describe other aspects of legislation pertinent to the USA and the UK.

■ Understand key ethical issues associated with fundraising practice.

■ Understand the rationale for codes of ethics and professional practice developed by professional fundraising bodies.

INTRODUCTION

Pick up a copy of any leading voluntary sector journal and you will inevitably find references to non-profits that have been felt to have acted inappropriately. Sometimes these actions may have been taken in violation of some legal requirement, but more frequently organizations are accused of behaving unethically, perhaps taking funds from a corporate donor with ties to dubious business practices in the Third World, or producing fundraising communications that are felt to be overtly shocking or even downright offensive.

Of course journalists writing for these media have a vested interest in highlighting what they perceive to be breaches of professional ethics or even fundraising law, since intense levels of public interest and concern mean that such 'bad' news makes great copy and copy that sells the journal or newspaper. While the voluntary sector contributes only a small proportion of GDP, it commands a high moral profile, leading to a disproportionate amount of media scrutiny and coverage.

Of course this is not necessarily a bad thing, since the agency role that non-profits play in dispersing funds donated by one group of individuals for the benefit of another requires that there be a high degree of public trust. Donors, who typically have no direct way of assessing how their funds are being used, must rely on their trust in the organization to reflect their wishes and to honour their obligations.

Managing public perceptions of the sector should thus be of immense concern to professional fundraisers. While they may exert little influence on the activities of other organizations they can at least ensure that their own professional practice reflects the highest possible legal and ethical standards.

In this final chapter we review these obligations and discuss the key facets of legislation that fundraisers in both the UK and the USA should be aware of. This legislation in effect sets the minimum standards that should be achieved in fundraising, but in no sense should be seen as reflecting desirable standards in each case. The law frequently says nothing about what most individuals would regard as a good professional standard likely to engender genuine levels of trust in voluntary organizations. It is this grey area between the minimum and desirable standards that is the domain of fundraising ethics and we deal with a number of key ethical issues, together with professional codes of conduct, later in this chapter.

DATA PROTECTION AND PRIVACY ISSUES

One of the most pressing and topical issues in fundraising is the question of donor privacy. The ever-reducing costs associated with owning and managing computing and data-processing power have brought database technology within the affordable price range of even the smallest non-profits. In the early years, much of what one could store on a database and the uses to which this might be put was unregulated. There have been numerous instances where personal data have been collected, stored and passed to third parties, resulting over time in some individuals being literally deluged with marketing and fundraising communications. This has impacted severely on the public trust and many charities have been criticized for failing to take account of legitimate demands for privacy in their various campaigns. Consumers and hence donors are no longer happy for organizations to store and manipulate personal information and to use this for the purposes of marketing and fundraising.

Of course it is very often commercial organizations and not non-profits that are the worst offenders. The overwhelming majority of non-profits have always acted responsibly and in a manner consistent with their overall ethos and mission. Nevertheless, some commercial enterprises have given the whole direct marketing industry a bad name by sending out high-volume, poorly targeted communications which simply irritate consumers and, by refusing to accede to legitimate demands, to curtail their activities. It is interesting to note that at the time of writing this is particularly the case for so-called SPAM e-mails which now account for over 50 per cent of the communications traffic initiated over the Internet and are a cause of enormous consumer indignation.

Inevitably when faced with what they regard as industry malpractice, politicians and legislators feel the need for intervention and will ultimately take steps to compel offenders to act in a more responsible way. What this means in practice is that many non-profits find themselves faced with new swathes of legislation designed to protect the public from sharp commercial practices. If you like, non-profits get caught up in the backlash against certain forms of activities. In this section we will consider both data protection and wider privacy issues in the USA and the UK. Readers in the USA will find European data protection legislation of more than passing interest. In many ways it represents the gold standard and may have an increasing role to play in influencing American legislators, who are still wrestling with how to deal with many of the same issues European law now addresses.

Data protection

In the European Union the community of nations has recently enacted new data protection legislation that offers new rights to consumers irrespective of the country in which they live.

These rights and hence the law have been interpreted slightly differently from one European nation to another, but the rules share a range of common features.

Using the UK as an example, the Data Protection Act 1988 was designed to bring the UK's regulatory framework into line with that now required by European regulations. It applies much more stringent controls over the use of personal data than was previously the case. Under the new Act all personal data (i.e. held about a particular individual) are now caught under the legislation. All organizations holding such data must register under the Act with the Data Commissioner and ensure that they follow the letter of the law in how they deal with such personal data. Interestingly the new Act contains provisions for both data stored on a computer in electronic format *and* data stored in other hard copy formats which would include paper files, notebooks and so on. Thus fundraisers involved in the solicitation of major gifts will, for example, find that the notes they make about each donor or prospect will now be caught under the Act. This is highly significant since under the Act anyone who has personal data stored by a third party (a non-profit) now has a number of specific rights:

- They may request the data controller (i.e. the individual managing the data in a non-profit) to supply a brief description of the personal data held, the purposes for which they are being held or are to be purchased, and the recipients to whom they are – or may be – disclosed.
- They may also request a copy of the personal data held and any information that may be available to the data controller in respect of how that data were acquired. This applies to all personal data irrespective of format and hence fundraisers must be aware that donors could conceivably request all the data the organization holds on them. This has the potential to be embarrassing if records are not strictly controlled, since in the authors' experience, fundraisers often record their own views on the individual, which may on occasion be unflattering!
- They may opt out of receiving further communications (see below) and charities must then 'delete' the individual from their records. In practice the individual's name and contact details will actually still be held on file to ensure that this obligation is met. Non-profits will need to ensure that should his or her name appear on any cold recruitment lists the organization may purchase that this is recognized and that the individual's wish not to receive further communication is still respected. This could not happen if the whole record was deleted since the non-profit would have no way of knowing that the individual had requested no further contact.
- Where the data are being processed to evaluate matters which relate to him or her directly, such as a credit check or an analysis of their performance at work, he or she also has the right to be informed of the logic involved in the decision-making process.

To control the potential for a spurious series of requests for information the Act provides that the data controller is not obliged to provide any of this information unless a request is made in writing and a fee paid. The Act allows data controllers to charge a reasonable fee for providing copies of any data held but controls the maximum amount that organizations are permitted to charge for this purpose.

The Act also provides individuals with the right to apply in writing to a data controller to prevent their information from being processed for the purposes of direct marketing. This is also a significant new right, and data controllers will need to ensure that subjects availing themselves do not have their data processed in this way.

The Act further creates a new category of personal data – namely sensitive personal data. This information consists of:

- The racial or ethnic origin of the data subject.
- His or her political opinions.
- His or her religious beliefs.
- Whether he or she is a member of a trade union.
- His or her physical or mental condition.
- The subject's sexual orientation.
- The commission or alleged commission of any offence.
- The proceedings for any offence committed or alleged to have been committed by him or her, the disposal of such proceedings or the sentence of any court in such proceedings.

The same rules apply as for personal data, but in addition a number of other restrictions are imposed on organizations holding or planning to hold one of these categories of data. One of the key restrictions is that data controllers must (with a few exceptions) seek the permission of the data subject for this information to be stored. Consent must now be given for the organization to hold the data. While one might think that the need for a non-profit to store such information is rare, many medical research charities hold information about an individual's health or medical circumstances. While this may be used largely for the purposes of service provision it can also prove invaluable in fundraising. Sensitive non-profits take care not to send fundraising messages stressing the plight of the victims of a particular disease to those whom they know are already sufferers. Some messages can be distressing and responsible organizations thus take considerable care to segment their audience. Under the new Act this will be made more problematic since they must now seek permission to hold these data.

From a fundraiser's perspective the Act has had two major impacts. The first is the requirement on non-profits to allow individuals to opt out of receiving further communications either from them, or third parties with whom their data may be shared. As a consequence fundraising communications now afford the donor the opportunity to decline further communication (see Plate 16.1) through what is known as an 'opt-out'. There is currently a debate raging around this issue since in some European countries practitioners have adopted a more stringent interpretation of the European Union legislation and compelled organizations to ask respondents to 'opt-in' to future communications.

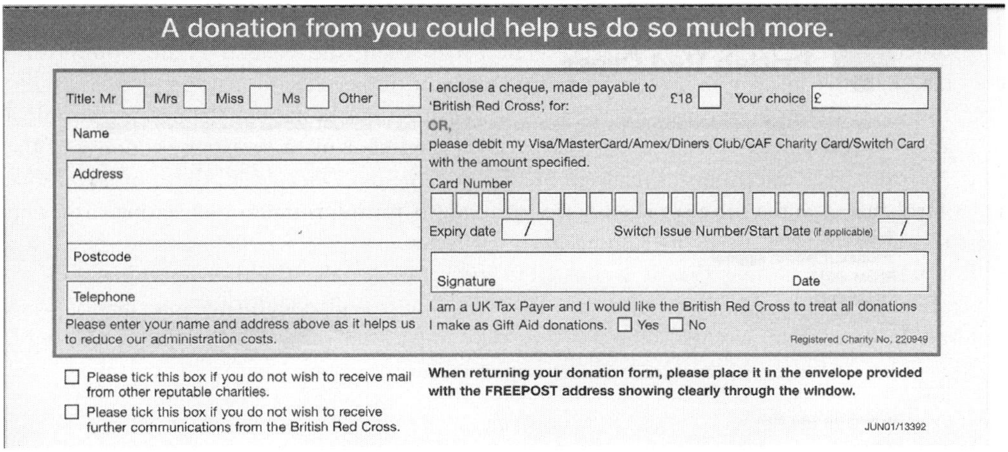

A donation from you could help us do so much more.

Title: Mr ☐ Mrs ☐ Miss ☐ Ms ☐ Other ☐

Name

Address

Postcode

Telephone

Please enter your name and address above as it helps us to reduce our administration costs.

I enclose a cheque, made payable to 'British Red Cross', for: £18 ☐ Your choice £

OR,

please debit my Visa/MasterCard/Amex/Diners Club/CAF Charity Card/Switch Card with the amount specified.

Card Number

Expiry date /   Switch Issue Number/Start Date (if applicable) /

Signature   Date

I am a UK Tax Payer and I would like the British Red Cross to treat all donations I make as Gift Aid donations. ☐ Yes ☐ No

Registered Charity No. 220949

☐ Please tick this box if you do not wish to receive mail from other reputable charities.

☐ Please tick this box if you do not wish to receive further communications from the British Red Cross.

When returning your donation form, please place it in the envelope provided with the FREEPOST address showing clearly through the window.

JUN01/13392

Plate 16.1 *Example of an opt-out*

Source: © British Red Cross. Reproduced with kind permission

This may sound like a small change, but individuals rarely take the time to read text in detail and only a small percentage will ever tick option boxes. What this means is that in countries in which an opt-out clause is adopted, the majority of donors can be legitimately contacted again, since few will avail themselves of an opt-out. In countries where opt-in is adopted the reverse is true and fundraising by mail can frequently become uneconomic since specific permission must be secured before subsequent communications can be initiated. In effect non-profits will have to write for permission to write!

The other key implication that arises from the Act is the extent to which it is legitimate for a non-profit to hold information for extended periods of time. The Act notes that data may only be held for a reasonable period without further consent being sought from the data subject. Sadly the Act is not definitive about what constitutes a reasonable period and only successive case law will clarify the true position. If a fundraiser secures a donation from a donor this year he or she is effectively granting permission to be contacted again, unless they specifically opt out of receiving further communication. Their consent may legitimately be implied by the fact that they have supported the organization. However, if, over the coming twelve months, the fundraiser tries in vain to secure a further donation, at what point does the donor's consent to be contacted expire? Would this occur after a further two, three, four or more mailings? The position is actually unclear, but it seems reasonable to speculate that this would take place after eighteen months to two years of further communications since most non-profits would describe the donor as being lapsed after this period. Writing to them thereafter would very likely be a criminal offence unless successive opportunities to opt out were offered in the communications they received. As the reader will appreciate, this is a technically complex and fast-moving area of legislation and professional fundraisers are well advised to seek periodic reviews of their practice from their legal team to ensure that their obligations under the Act are being met.

In the USA there is as yet no global Data Protection Act, or equivalent, although the SPAM issue may prompt federal legislators to reconsider these issues and to look again at the imposition of national regulations. In the meantime, the requirements for organizations to manage and manipulate data in various ways are a matter for state legislators, and fundraisers need to be aware of the specific legal requirements for both their 'home' state and any other states in which they may be soliciting funds. It is particularly important to beware of this if the organization is soliciting funds over the Internet since they may find themselves accepting funds from individuals residing in some states where the organization has not as yet met the appropriate legal requirements, such as registration.

Although there is no national data protection legislation, the Federal Trade Commission does take an active interest in privacy issues and many of these relate to matters of data protection. It has, for example, recently encouraged all organizations to honour the privacy promises they make to consumers. The FTC has also brought a number of cases under Section 5 of the FTC Act to enforce the promises made in privacy statements. Once again, those organizations soliciting funds over the Internet need to be wary of the promises their organization makes on the site and ensure that these are honoured to the letter.

It is also worth noting that it is the FTC that enforces the Children's Online Privacy Protection Act (1988), which prevents the collection of personally identifiable information from children without their parents' consent. This may impact on some non-profits dealing with children's issues and again the letter of the law must be respected.

Privacy issues

In the USA, there is increasing public concern over the use of telemarketing both to sell products/services and to solicit funds. Consumers who do not wish to receive telemarketing historically had only two ways in which they could rely on to stop calls being made. First they could rely on a voluntary system administered by the Direct Marketing Association, or second, they could notify each company separately. These systems were highly inefficient, and at the time of writing the FTC has just taken the step of launching a national 'do-not-call' register. This list is now legally binding on most telemarketers. The registry is available only for personal telephone numbers, not for business numbers. Telemarketers affected by the law are required to download phone numbers on the registry at least every three months and to ensure that they are not called thereafter.

Privacy is a central element of the FTC's mission and the organization is working hard to improve the way in which consumers are treated by the organizations with which they come into contact. The FTC encourages consumers to raise privacy issues with them directly and offers a toll-free telephone number to call for this purpose (1-877-FTC-HELP).

In the United Kingdom, as we noted above, the Data Protection Act offers wide-ranging new protection to consumers. In addition to this, they may also elect not to receive either unsolicited direct mail or telemarketing calls by registering their contact details with either the mail or telephone preference service respectively. (http://www.mpsonline.org.uk and http://www.tpsonline.org.uk. It is currently a legal requirement to abide by the telephone preference service stop list, while the equivalent mail list is good practice but not legally mandatory (this is, however, subject to debate currently). It is thus an offence for these individuals to be targeted with unsolicited telephone communications, and fundraisers must ensure that they carefully de-dupe any call lists they are proposing to use against the national stop list.

MAINTAINING COMMUNICATION STANDARDS

The appropriate management of personal data is not the only issue fundraisers must address. A further crucial concern is maintaining an appropriate professional standard in the communications that an organization generates. Dependent on the country in which a non-profit is resident it will face one of two distinct categories of control and regulation of this form of activity.

The first is statutory control within a country's legislative framework. Many countries have Advertising Acts that stipulate in great detail the boundaries of acceptable practice. The second approach is voluntary and self-regulatory in nature. In the UK a series of voluntary controls have been in existence for over forty years. At the core of these controls is the British Code of Advertising Practice and a number of different bodies established to ensure that this code is upheld. These bodies are funded by a levy on advertising expenditures (i.e. the industry itself) and put pressure on advertisers that contravene the Code of Advertising Practice to withdraw offending ads. The system for broadcast media is more robust, requiring pre-vetting of advertising materials before they are actually broadcast. This is not the case for non-broadcast media such as press advertising where the system operates retrospectively. That said, advertisers can ask that their material be vetted in advance of publication, but this does not guarantee that any subsequent complaints that may be received by the regulator would not be upheld.

For non-broadcast media the Advertising Standards Authority (ASA) oversees the code, while for all broadcast media such as radio and television it is now OFCOM (the Office of Communications). Both bodies work in very similar ways.

Taking the example of a press ad, if a member of the public suspects that an ad has contravened the code he or she may complain to the ASA which is then obligated to investigate the complaint and issue a ruling. If the ASA finds in favour of the complainant it issues a media notice ordering the offending ad to be withdrawn or, in the case of a direct marketing programme, to be terminated. Given that most suppliers of advertising space or materials are members of a trade association, the issue of a media notice is usually enough to ensure compliance. In the handful of cases where unscrupulous operators continue with activities that contravene the code the government may now intervene under the Control of Misleading Advertisements Regulations (1988) and issue an injunction preventing the activity from continuing.

In addition to responding to public complaints the ASA also conducts an ongoing programme of monitoring and currently scrutinizes more than 15,000 advertisements per annum (Fill 1995). While the code contains a number of specific guidelines for product categories (such as alcohol or tobacco), the general rule is that all advertising must be:

- legal;
- decent;
- honest;
- truthful.

How does one define each of these terms? The first is quite straightforward since the advertising of consumer credit, food, drugs and medicaments, for example, requires that certain information be provided in the communication if it is to be legal. The terms 'decent, honest and truthful' are less easy to interpret, particularly given that a certain amount of advertising 'puffery' is allowed by the code.

The advantage of self-regulation is that bodies such as the ASA can look at each individual ad and form a view of whether it meets these criteria, given the nature of the organization, the intended audience and what the ad is specifically intended to achieve.

In Plate 16.2 we reproduce an ad that appeared in a number of major national newspapers for a children's charity. It featured a baby sitting alone in squalid surroundings. Dirt covered the floor and walls; in his teeth the baby held a cord, which was tightened round his right arm to make a tourniquet; in his left hand he held a syringe as if to inject heroin. The headline stated 'John Donaldson Age 23'; the body copy stated, 'Battered as a child, it was always possible that John would turn to drugs. With Barnardo's help, child abuse need not lead to an empty future. Although we no longer run orphanages, we continue to help thousands of children and their families at home, school and in the local community.' The complainants objected that the advertisement was shocking and offensive.

In this case the ASA decided not to uphold the complaint. In reaching the judgment the ASA filed the following report:

> The advertisers believed the advertisement complied with the Codes. They said it was part of a campaign to raise awareness of their preventative work with children and young people; the campaign was designed to make people reconsider their opinions about Barnardo's work and the subjects depicted in each advertisement. The advertisers argued that they had not intended merely to shock. They said they had taken the precaution of researching the campaign twice among their target audience of ABC1 adults aged 35 to 55 and their supporters, staff and service users; they submitted the research findings, which they believed showed most people understood the advertisement's message and found its approach effective in changing opinions about Barnardo's work. The advertisers maintained that, because the consequences of drug addiction were potentially devastating, the stark image was justified as a means of raising public awareness of the potential dangers for disadvantaged children; they believed it was an effective way of making the point that Barnardo's could help keep them safe. Their consumer research acknowledged that some people found images of

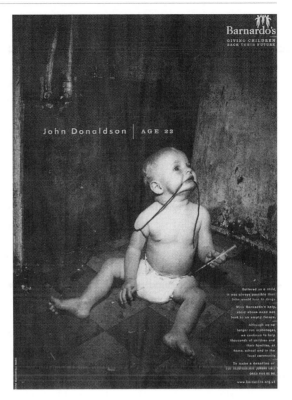

Plate 16.2 *Barnardo's advertisement*

Source: © Barnardo's. Reproduced with kind permission

alcoholism or drug abuse upsetting. They nevertheless maintained that an image based on the innocence of a child and potential pain in adult life communicated the message that Barnardo's was a contemporary charity with modern perspectives on child development. The advertisers submitted extracts from published research, which showed that disadvantaged and abused children were particularly vulnerable to emotional and behavioural problems in later life; they provided recent survey results that showed that parents and children found drugs worrying and frightening. They asserted that the child depicted had not been put at risk and that the advertisement was made with full parental awareness and consent. The advertisers said they had monitored public responses to their advertisement; they had received more supportive responses than complaints. The *Independent* (newspaper) said they had received less than five complaints and considered that the advertisement would not cause serious or widespread offence to their readers. The *Guardian* (newspaper) said they believed their readers would understand the advertisers' message and they had received no complaints. The *Scotland on Sunday* (newspaper) said they regarded drugs very seriously but considered that Barnardo's advertisement was compelling and justified. They said they had received no complaints. *The Times*, the *Scotsman*, the *Independent on Sunday* and the *Observer* did not respond. The Authority noted the advertisement had offended or distressed some readers. It nevertheless acknowledged that the advertisers had intended to convey a serious and important message. The Authority considered that they had acted responsibly by conducting research among their target audience to ensure the message was understood and unlikely to shock or offend. The Authority noted the picture of drug abuse was directly related to the advertisers' preventative work with children and considered that the target audience was likely to interpret the image in the context of the accompanying text. The Authority accepted the advertisers' argument that they had not intended merely to shock. It considered that, because the advertisers had used the image to raise public awareness of the seriousness of drug abuse and the action that could be taken to prevent it, the advertisement was unlikely to cause either serious or widespread offence or undue distress and was acceptable.

Plate 16.3 contains an example of an ad run for the baby charity Tommy's headlined 'Your 50p will keep a premature baby alive for 1.8 seconds. Please give generously.' It featured a cartoon drawing of a zebra in a hospital bed. Text at the bottom of the poster read: '£15 will help Tommy's put an end to miscarriage, premature birth and stillbirth.' The complainants, who interestingly comprised both members of the public and a competing charity BLISS, The National Charity for the Newborn, believed the advertisement misleadingly implied that contributions would be spent keeping babies alive.

In this case the ASA upheld the complaint and noted the following in its report:

The advertisers said the poster would not be used again because they had used all the poster space they could. They said the advertisement's message was that it was expensive to run a premature baby unit. They believed that by putting money into research to find a cause and prevent premature birth happening the NHS would be saved from the expense of supporting premature babies. The advertisers said the strapline '£15 will help Tommy's put an end to miscarriage, premature birth and stillbirth' made clear that donations funded their research into stopping premature birth. They provided a copy of their Memorandum of Association, which explained their funds had been directed at the prevention of premature birth. They maintained the topic of the advertisement was consistent with their dedication to raising awareness of the subject. They said that when readers called the number in the advertisement they were

Plate 16.3 *Tommy's advertisement*
Source: © Tommy's Campaign. Reproduced with kind permission

told at the start of the call that the donation helped provide funds for medical research into miscarriage, premature birth and stillbirth. The advertisers said they had received a lot of feedback about the advertisement but had received no complaints. They were surprised that readers had interpreted the advertisement in a way different from that intended.

The Authority considered that the claim misleadingly implied that donations would go towards the costs of supporting a premature baby. Because they did not, the Authority asked the advertisers to amend the advertisement and to take more care in future to make clear how donations would be used.

In the USA the FTC is the primary body with responsibility for overseeing advertising activity. The FTC's goal is to protect consumers from false claims, deception and misrepresentation. Where communication claims are alleged to be unfair or deceptive the FTC examines the materials to determine whether they are deceptive or likely to be deceptive in the way the public is likely to interpret them. It also considers the net impression of an ad and investigates the materiality of any claims that are alleged to be false. Finally the FTC will attempt to distinguish between 'puff' (or normal sales exaggerations) and genuinely deceptive ads. In recent years the FTC has had considerable clout. It can order the cessation of offending communication material, but it can also impose the tougher sanction of corrective advertising in cases where misleading claims have been made. This effectively compels the organization to repeat its communication, this time conveying the true picture to recipients. Indeed, the FTC has required some organizations to devote as much as 25 per cent of their communications budget to putting right any false claims that may have been made.

UK LAW

In the UK there are a number of other components of legislation that fundraisers need to be aware of in their professional practice. The most notable are described below.

Communication of registered status

The Charities Act 1992 requires that all registered charities must make their status clear in all communications. As the Act states:

> The fact that it is a registered charity shall be stated in English in legible characters –
> (a) in all notices, advertisements and other documents issued by or on behalf of the charity and soliciting money or other property for the benefit of the charity; (b) in all bills of exchange, promissory notes, endorsements, cheques and orders for money or goods purporting to be signed on behalf of the charity; and in all bills rendered by it and in all its invoices, receipts and letters of credit.
>
> (Charities Act 1992: 1-3-1)

From a fundraising perspective this means that all forms of fundraising communications and receipts must contain details of the charity registration number. Failure to include this information is an offence and it is likely that the Act would treat each separate instance as a separate offence, implying that, for example, a charity not printing its registration number on a mailshot comprising 10,000 units could be guilty of 10,000 separate offences.

Lotteries and raffles

Lotteries and raffles (e.g. where a charity may sell tickets for entry into a prize draw) have to be registered under the Lotteries and Amusements Act 1976. Local Councils are the registration authority for society lotteries for the purpose of raising funds for sporting, charitable or benevolent purposes. A typical society lottery would be raising funds for a local school parent–teacher association or a local amateur football club. Lotteries not promoted by societies or where the value of tickets for sale in a lottery exceeds £20,000 have to register with the Gaming Board of Great Britain and not with their local Council (see Plate 16.4).

For society lotteries there is a small initial registration fee (typically £35) payable to the local Council, and then, in order to remain registered, each society is required to pay an annual fee thereafter. Once registered, societies have to submit a return after each lottery showing the amounts collected, the amount spent on prizes and any expenses concerned with conducting the lottery. These returns are held for eighteen months and are available for public inspection.

Tickets sold as part of a registered society lottery must be properly printed and carry the details of the name of the society, the name and address of the promoter, the date of the lottery draw, the price of the ticket (which must not exceed £1), the name of the printer and the name of the local council with which the society is registered.

Plate 16.4 *Specimen raffle ticket*

Source: © National Eczema Society. Reproduced with kind permission

Street and house-to-house collections

In the UK it is not uncommon to see charity collections taking place on the high street of any major town or city. In many ways this is one of the most visible forms of fundraising many charities will undertake. Historically, charity fundraisers have also sought permission to call at the homes of individuals living in particular areas. Both these forms of fundraising require a licence and this is granted by the requisite local authority. There is typically no fee for this, but a formal application must be made if the activity is to be legal.

House-to-house collections are caught under the House To House Collections Act 1939 and the House To House Collections Regulations 1947. The Act requires that charities wishing to undertake this form of fundraising are licensed and that each promoter of a collection should exercise due diligence to ensure that all persons acting as collectors are 'proper and fit'. No person is permitted to act as a collector unless he or she has a 'Certificate of Authority', a prescribed badge; and, if money is to be collected, a marked collection box or a receipt book (with receipts and counterfoils or duplicates consecutively numbered). The amount donated, an indication of the purpose of the collection and a distinguishing number must be provided on the receipt. The Act also:

- prevents anyone under age 16 from acting as a collector;
- requires collectors not to annoy householders and to leave the property if requested to do so;
- requires the charity to furnish an account of the collection to the licensing authority.

Street collections are governed by the Local Government Act 1972 and the Police, Factories ETC (Miscellaneous Provisions) Act 1916. Once again the law requires collectors to obtain a permit. Collections may take place only on the day/time stipulated in this permit. Collections are required to take place in a manner that is not likely to annoy or inconvenience any person. In addition, collectors must:

- remain stationary;
- ensure that if they are working with others they should be at least 25 metres apart;
- carry a collecting box (which must be numbered consecutively and sealed in such a way as to prevent them from being opened without the seal being broken);
- place all monies in this collecting box and deliver the box unopened to the charity on completion of the collection;
- be unpaid. No payments may be made to collectors.

Those charities administering street collections must also provide an account of the collection to the licensing authority which must include a summary of the monies raised, the expenses incurred in connection with the collection, a list of collectors and a list of the amounts contained in each collecting box. The law also requires that the financial statement be certified both by the charity and a qualified accountant.

US LAW

Overview

In the USA the most pervasive legislation impacting on the fundraising profession is enacted and controlled at state level. Charitable Solicitation Acts are now commonplace and govern what fundraising may or may not be undertaken in a given state. This law also controls the activities of professional solicitors or fundraising consultants and again requires them to honour certain standards of behaviour. What follows is an overview of the matters typically dealt with by such Acts and should not therefore be relied upon as definitive information about the requirements of specific states. Fundraisers are therefore advised to consult the specific requirements of their home state, and any state in which they may be seeking to solicit funds, *before* undertaking such activities. Failure to do so may give rise to civil and/or criminal liability.

State legislatures that have created Charitable Solicitation Acts are generally keen to recognize the right of individuals and organizations to conduct solicitation activities. This is often the genuine starting point for charitable solicitation legislation. States are also keen, however, to protect members of the public from what may be described as sharp practice by requiring full public disclosure of the identity of persons who solicit contributions, the purposes for which such contributions are solicited and the manner in which the contributions are actually used.

State legislatures are also understandably keen to prohibit deception, fraud and misrepresentation in the soliciting and reporting of contributions.

Charitable Solicitation Acts frequently begin by requiring charitable organizations and sponsors to register if they wish to solicit funds in a given state. All chapters, branches or area offices will normally be required to register and must submit registration documentation. These registration documents must generally be renewed each year and maintained for as long as it is intended to raise funds. The initial registration form will usually be accompanied by:

1   A copy of the financial report or IRS Form 990 and Schedule A or Internal Revenue Service Form 990-EZ for the immediately preceding fiscal year. A newly organized non-profit with no financial history is required to submit a budget for the current fiscal year.
2   The name of the charitable organization, the purpose for which it is organized, the name under which it intends to solicit contributions and the purpose or purposes for which the contributions to be solicited will be used.
3   The name of the individuals or officers who are in charge of any solicitation activities.
4   The names, street addresses and telephone numbers of any professional solicitors or fundraising consultants who have agreed to act on behalf of the charitable organization, together with a statement setting forth the specific terms of the arrangements for salaries, bonuses, commissions, expenses, or other remunerations to be paid.

They must also supply a statement detailing whether the organization is authorized in any other state to solicit contributions and details of whether any officers associated with the organization have been convicted of criminal offences or have ever had registration documents revoked for whatever reason.

Each non-profit organization or chapter of a non-profit must accompany the documentation with a registration fee which usually varies depending on the level of donations the organization was able to attract in the preceding year.

Professional solicitors or consultants

As noted above, professional solicitors and consultants are normally covered under these Acts and are also required to register, declaring a range of personal information, including, interestingly, whether they or any of their employees are related to individuals associated with the charitable organizations they are proposing to work for. Professional solicitors must also file (and have approved) an appropriate bond which must be payable to the state, or to any person who may have a cause of action against them for any liability arising out of a violation of the Act.

This registration is essential, since not only are these individuals (or firms) obligated by law to register, it is also unlawful for charities to enter into a contract with solicitors or consultants that are not registered in this way.

In respect of fundraising consultants, regulations frequently stipulate that each contract or agreement between a professional fundraising consultant and a charitable organization must be filed with the state. Such agreements must be in writing, signed by two authorized officials of the non-profit and filed by the professional fundraising consultant at least five days prior to the performance of any service by the consultant. Solicitation under the contract may not begin before this filing has taken place.

These contracts must contain a statement of the charitable purpose for which the solicitation campaign is being conducted, a statement of the respective obligations of the consultant and charity, a clear statement of the fee that will be payable, a note of the effective and termination dates and a statement that the professional fundraising consultant will not at any time have control or custody of contributions.

In the case of professional solicitors, these individuals must file, no less than fifteen days before commencing any solicitation campaign or event, a solicitation notice. This notice will normally include:

1 a description of the solicitation event or campaign;
2 each location and telephone number from which the solicitation is to be conducted;
3 the legal name and residence address of each person responsible for directing and supervising the conduct of the campaign;
4 a statement as to whether the professional solicitor will at any time have custody of contributions;
5 the account number and location of each bank account where receipts from the campaign are to be deposited;
6 a full and fair description of the charitable or sponsor programme for which the solicitation campaign is being carried out as provided in the contract between the professional solicitor and the charitable organization;
7 the fundraising methods to be used;
8 a copy of the contract between the two parties.

Each contract between a professional solicitor and a charity must contain a variety of provisions, including:

1 a statement of the charitable purpose and programme for which the solicitation is being conducted;
2 a statement of the respective obligations of the professional solicitor and the charitable organization;
3 a statement of the guaranteed minimum percentage of the gross receipts from contributions which will be remitted to the charitable organization. If the solicitation involves the sale of goods, services or tickets to a fundraising event, the percentage of the purchase price which will be remitted to the charitable organization must be shown. Any stated percentage will normally exclude any amount that the charitable organization is to pay as fundraising costs;
4 a statement of the percentage of the gross revenue for which the professional solicitor will be compensated;
5 the effective and termination dates of the contract;
6 within ninety days after a solicitation campaign has been completed the professional solicitor must file a report of the campaign, including the gross revenue received and an itemization of all expenses incurred.

Each contribution collected by or in the custody of the professional solicitor must be solely in the name of the charitable organization on whose behalf the contribution was solicited.

These Acts also require all professional solicitors to maintain for a period of not less than three years detailed records of each campaign, including the name, address and telephone number of each contributor.

Disclosure requirements and duties of charitable organizations

Charitable organizations looking to solicit funds must typically provide a range of information to donors at the point of solicitation. This frequently includes:

1   the name of the organization and state of the principal place of business;
2   a description of the purpose for which the solicitation is being made;
3   upon request, the name, address or telephone number of the officer to whom any enquiries may be directed;
4   upon request, the amount of the contribution which may be deducted under federal income tax laws;
5   upon request, the source from which a written financial statement may be obtained.

Critically, states often require printed solicitations, written confirmations, or reminders of contributions to carry a specific statement, the precise wording of which is laid out in the Act. At the time of writing, in the case of Florida, the wording was as follows:

> A COPY OF THE OFFICIAL REGISTRATION AND FINANCIAL INFORMATION MAY BE OBTAINED FROM THE DIVISION OF CONSUMER SERVICES BY CALLING TOLL FREE, 1-800-435-7352 WITHIN THE STATE. REGISTRATION DOES NOT IMPLY ENDORSEMENT, APPROVAL OR RECOMMENDATION BY THE STATE.

Where the solicitation consists of more than one piece, as is often the case with direct mail, the statement must be displayed prominently somewhere in the solicitation materials. Many states now require a similar but differently worded statement, and hence those non-profits soliciting funds across the USA can find that lengthy compliance documents must be produced.

In addition to this statement, charities are obliged to conspicuously display the following information on every printed solicitation, written confirmation or reminder of a contribution:

1   the organization's registration number issued by the state;
2   the percentage, if any, of each contribution that is retained by any professional solicitor that has been contracted by the organization;
3   the percentage of each contribution that is actually received by the organization.

Once again, if the solicitation consists of multiple items this information must be displayed prominently.

Other requirements

Many states also have specific legislation that governs the solicitation of funds in certain environments, such as public transport. Licences are often required for this activity and the law frequently prescribes the detail of who may act as a solicitor, the disclosures they must make to potential donors and the manner in which a solicitation may take place. The aim of this legislation is typically to ensure that members of the public are not unduly inconvenienced by the solicitation process and that only right and proper individuals undertake these solicitations and manage the funds donated. In many ways, this legislation resembles that enacted in the United Kingdom to manage public collections. There are many striking similarities.

ETHICS IN FUNDRAISING

The study of ethics is essentially involved in determining right from wrong. Such decisions will be driven by an individual's own beliefs and values and those of the wider society in which they live. In Judaeo-Christian society, for example, these values may be derived from respect and compassion for the individual and a wider concern for the impact of one's actions on others. Ethics operate at a different level from the laws of a particular society since, as noted above, these laws frequently provide for only minimum standards of behaviour. They deal with the worst excesses of a society and with aspects of that society that are of wider interest and concern. They also reflect the prevailing view of the government, which one hopes in a democracy would in turn reflect the views of the majority of the members of that society.

Ethics by contrast operate at a 'higher' level. While a particular action may not be illegal, it may nevertheless be regarded by a given individual as wrong because it indirectly harms others, or is not in the best interests of the organization that employs them. It is this grey area beyond the realms of the law that is the domain of ethical judgements and where the fundraising profession has invested considerable time and effort to determine what does and does not constitute appropriate behaviour.

In our discussion of ethics it is not our intention to review the contribution of a procession of different philosophers. Rather, it is our intention to adopt a pragmatic approach and to introduce a range of common ethical dilemmas for fundraisers and two codes of conduct that have been established by the fundraising profession to provide guidance across the sector.

In reading what follows, it is important to bear in mind that there are no right or wrong answers in the domain of ethics. Some answers may be 'righter' than others, but ultimately professional fundraisers must make their own decisions about what is appropriate guided by the standards established by the bodies that represent the profession as a whole. In the USA, this is the Association of Fundraising Professionals (www.nsfre.org) and in the United Kingdom, the Institute of Fundraising (www.icfm.org.uk).

Current ethical dilemmas are discussed below.

Remuneration

The debate here concerns what constitutes appropriate remuneration for fundraising activity. Particularly at issue is whether fundraisers should be paid by salary or receive a commission for every donation they solicit successfully. Indeed, should this remuneration vary depending on the value of a particular gift? The payment of commission or bonuses has long been a practice of for-profit managers looking to retain and motivate their staff. Most managers do not have an ethical dilemma over whether to initiate a payment system of this type since the need to achieve sales and hence profit for the business is paramount, and bonuses can be a very effective motivational tool. However, in the context of fundraising the payment of bonuses is felt to be problematic since it could lead to undue pressure being exerted on donors to give. Fundraisers remunerated by commission would have a vested interest in persuading as many people as possible to give, even where it was clearly inappropriate for them to do so, or where their needs would be better served by giving to another organization in perhaps a very different way. This occurs because fundraisers have to make a living and if they are paid on commission the only way they can achieve this is to 'sell' ever more donors on making a gift. The security of a salary effectively removes this incentive and makes it less likely that fundraisers will feel under pressure to ignore the needs and wishes of the prospects they meet. They can, in effect, afford to take a longer term and more selfless view of the solicitation process.

Personal gifts

Many fundraisers become personally acquainted with their high-value donors and in some cases develop genuine and enduring friendships as a consequence. It is not uncommon under these circumstances for fundraisers to be presented by donors with often quite valuable gifts. The ethical dilemma here is whether such gifts should be accepted and whether the value should be retained by the individual or ceded to the non-profit. Again this is a complex area, because fundraisers should not seek to benefit from the relationships they have with their donors. The integrity of the relationship with the non-profit should be the first priority and it should always be maintained. That said, small gifts or tokens of affection may be acceptable, but of course the dilemma then becomes a decision over the point at which the value of such gifts begins to make them unacceptable. There are no right answers here and the safest solution is almost certainly to decline any personal gifts from donors, no matter how small they may be.

Privacy

Some fundraising techniques are regarded as more intrusive than others. Regrettably many of these techniques can also be highly effective forms of fundraising. Organizations and hence fundraising teams must therefore decide which techniques they believe it is legitimate to pursue. There are those who would argue that non-profits should not adopt any techniques that are in any way intrusive, but this is a gross simplification and only generates the further question: Who decides whether something is intrusive and how many people must hold the view before it is discontinued? In the USA the use of telemarketing agencies by non-profits to raise funds has generated considerable debate. Calling people in their own home at times that may not be convenient is a highly intrusive activity. While individuals have come to expect this practice of business organizations, there is a sense that non-profits should be more respectful of privacy issues. Again, though, this is not as straightforward as it may at first appear. If a school will cease to exist because of a lack of funds or local people are dying because of health or drug problems, there are few of us who would suggest that a non-profit should not attempt to raise funds to resolve these issues in every way possible. If one accepts this as a proposition, one then has to decide which causes and how great a need would warrant the use of intrusive techniques. This too, is thus an insoluble conundrum.

Efficiency

A further dilemma arises around the issue of when one should stop fundraising. Figure 16.1 illustrates the returns that organizations generate from fundraising at different levels of expenditure. Clearly this is a gross simplification of reality but it serves to illustrate the general experience of most non-profits. When expenditure is low on fundraising, organizations may not be investing enough to take advantage of economies of scale, or to achieve a significant enough media impact to overcome the clutter of other appeals. At this stage, point (A) in the figure, a dollar of investment may achieve only break-even or slightly higher returns. As expenditure rises the non-profit reaches a point where it achieves its maximum possible return on investment as economies of scale are eventually realized. Let us say that for the sake of argument the non-profit achieves a return here of $5 for every $1 of investment (Point (B) in the figure).

If the expenditure is increased still further the returns for each incremental dollar of expenditure then begin to fall. The reasons for this are manifold, but it often occurs because at a certain point it will become progressively more difficult for an organization to find additional new donors. It is still very cost-effective to raise funds, but the return begins to drop away to $3:1, then $2:1 and so on. This is represented as point (C) in the figure. The difficult ethical issue is that in pure economic terms the non-profit would be better off continuing to invest in fundraising to the point where marginal investment equals marginal revenue (i.e. to the point where an additional $1 raises exactly $1). This would maximize the income the organization

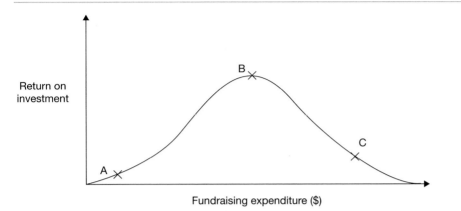

Figure 16.1 *Returns from fundraising expenditure*

was able to generate, but few donors would be happy with such a high percentage of their gift being spent on fundraising! Such a high level of fundraising expenditure, if adopted by all non-profits, would be likely to cause great offence and widespread public concern as fundraising messages began to dominate the media. It is thus rather more likely that an organization will decide to cease expenditure on fundraising at a point where the return for the incremental dollar is at a somewhat higher level. Of course, what this level should be is a matter for debate.

Appropriate corporate support

A number of non-profits have faced criticism when they have accepted gifts from companies that may be thought to be unsuitable partners, or indeed that undertake practices which directly oppose the mission of the non-profit. This issue is considered in detail in Chapter 11.

Distortion of mission

It is a fact that for most non-profits certain elements of what they do will be more attractive than others to potential funders. It is also sadly true that some of the most difficult and ground-breaking work will also be that which challenges donors and is therefore most difficult to raise funds for. A number of ethical dilemmas are then given rise to. First, the organization could be tempted to distort its mission to embrace other aspects of endeavour that are inherently more popular with donors. It may also be tempted to distort how the funds solicited are actually used. In other words, donors may be left with the impression that their gift will be used to support Project A, when in fact it will be used for the equally deserving but less popular Project B. Many within the fundraising profession would consider this to be unethical and the decision thus an easy one to resolve, but where projects share much in common and thus the distinction between them becomes blurred, it becomes a matter for judgement in respect of whether the donor is being substantially misled. This is frequently more of an issue in impersonal communications such as direct mail, where a mass audience is being addressed and hence campaigns may need to be generic.

ETHICAL CODES AND STANDARDS OF PROFESSIONAL PRACTICE

In the USA the Association of Fundraising Professionals (AFP) has strived since the early 1960s to foster high ethical standards among its members. The AFP as the largest fundraising

EXHIBIT 16.1 THE AFP'S ETHICAL CODE

AFP members aspire to:

- Practise their profession with integrity, honesty, truthfulness and adherence to the absolute obligation to safeguard the public trust.
- Act according to the highest standards and visions of their organization, profession and conscience.
- Put philanthropic mission above personal gain.
- Inspire others through their own sense of dedication and high purpose.
- Improve their professional knowledge and skills, so that their performance will better serve others.
- Demonstrate concern for the interests and well-being of individuals affected by their actions.
- Value the privacy, freedom of choice and interests of all those affected by their actions.
- Foster cultural diversity and pluralistic values, and treat all people with dignity and respect.
- Affirm, through personal giving, a commitment to philanthropy and its role in society.
- Adhere to the spirit as well as the letter of all applicable laws and regulations.
- Advocate, within their own organizations, adherence to all applicable laws and regulations.
- Avoid even the appearance of any criminal offence or professional misconduct.
- Bring credit to the fundraising profession by their public demeanour.
- Encourage colleagues to embrace and practise these ethical principles and standards of professional practice.
- Be aware of the codes of ethics promulgated by other professional organizations that serve philanthropy.

Source: Association of Fundraising Professionals. Reproduced with kind permission

professional body in the world has a large number of members who are encouraged to embrace shared values as a condition of membership. The AFP's ethical code is reproduced above.

The AFP also requires its members to abide by certain standards of professional practice. Violation of these standards may subject the member to disciplinary sanctions that can include expulsion. These standards are reproduced below. As you read through them, notice how many of the ethical dilemmas we alluded to above are expressly dealt with in the text.

In both the USA and the UK the professional fundraising bodies have simultaneously sought to meet the needs of donors and to deal with the most pressing ethical issues of the day, indicating explicitly the standards of care they should expect to receive. The US Donor Bill of Rights was created by the American Association of Fund Raising Counsel (AAFRC), Association for Healthcare Philanthropy (AHP), the Association of Fundraising Professionals (AFP), and the Council for Advancement and Support of Education (CASE). It has since been endorsed by numerous other organizations. The Bill of Rights is presented in Exhibit 16.3.

It is interesting to note how the fundamental themes of openness and transparency pervade this document and that in effect the professional bodies have created a mirror image of the standards of professional conduct to express these in terms of what these behaviours actually mean for donors. There are also moves to create an e-donors' charter to ensure that the key

EXHIBIT 16.2 THE AFP'S STANDARDS OF PROFESSIONAL PRACTICE

Professional obligations

1. Members shall not engage in activities that harm the members' organization, clients or profession.
2. Members shall not engage in activities that conflict with their fiduciary, ethical and legal obligations to their organizations and their clients.
3. Members shall effectively disclose all potential and actual conflicts of interest; such disclosure does not preclude or imply ethical impropriety.
4. Members shall not exploit any relationship with a donor, prospect, volunteer or employee to the benefit of the members or the members' organizations.
5. Members shall comply with all applicable local, state, provincial and federal civil and criminal laws.
6. Members recognize their individual boundaries of competence, and are forthcoming and truthful about their professional experience and qualifications.

Solicitation and use of charitable funds

7. Members shall take care to ensure that all solicitation materials are accurate and correctly reflect their organization's mission and use of solicited funds.
8. Members shall take care to ensure that donors receive informed, accurate and ethical advice about the value and tax implications of potential gifts.
9. Members shall take care to ensure that contributions are used in accordance with donors' intentions.
10. Members shall take care to ensure proper stewardship of charitable contributions, including timely reports on the use and management of funds.
11. Members shall obtain explicit consent by the donor before altering the conditions of a gift.

Presentation of information

12. Members shall not disclose privileged or confidential information to unauthorized parties.
13. Members shall adhere to the principle that all donor and prospect information created by, or on behalf of, an organization is the property of that organization and shall not be transferred or used except on behalf of that organization.
14. Members shall give donors the opportunity to have their names removed from lists that are sold to, rented to or exchanged with other organizations.
15. Members shall, when stating fundraising results, use accurate and consistent accounting methods that conform to the appropriate guidelines adopted by the American Institute of Certified Public Accountants (AICPA)* for the type of organization involved.

*In countries outside of the USA, comparable authority should be used.

Compensation

16. Members shall not accept compensation that is based on a percentage of charitable contributions; nor shall they accept finders' fees.
17. Members may accept performance-based compensation, such as bonuses, provided such bonuses are in accord with prevailing practices within the members' own organizations, and are not based on a percentage of charitable contributions.
18. Members shall not pay finders' fees, commissions or percentage compensation based on charitable contributions and shall take care to discourage their organizations from making such payments.

Source: Association of Fundraising Professionals. Reproduced with kind permission

EXHIBIT 16.3 THE DONOR BILL OF RIGHTS

Philanthropy is based on voluntary action for the common good. It is a tradition of giving and sharing that is primary to the quality of life. To ensure that philanthropy merits the respect and trust of the general public, and that donors and prospective donors can have full confidence in the non-profit organizations and causes they are asked to support, we declare that all donors have these rights:

I   To be informed of the organization's mission, of the way the organization intends to use donated resources, and of its capacity to use donations effectively for their intended purposes.
II To be informed of the identity of those serving on the organization's governing board, and to expect the board to exercise prudent judgement in its stewardship responsibilities.
III To have access to the organization's most recent financial statements.
IV To be assured their gifts will be used for the purposes for which they were given.
V   To receive appropriate acknowledgement and recognition.
VI To be assured that information about their donation is handled with respect and with confidentiality to the extent provided by law.
VII To expect that all relationships with individuals representing organizations of interest to the donor will be professional in nature.
VIII To be informed whether those seeking donations are volunteers, employees of the organization or hired solicitors.
IX To have the opportunity for their names to be deleted from mailing lists that an organization may intend to share.
X   To feel free to ask questions when making a donation and to receive prompt, truthful and forthright answers.

Source: © Association of Fundraising Professionals. Reproduced with kind permission

issues pertinent in the web environment will also be addressed specifically by the profession. It is important to note that all those wishing to develop a career in fundraising will be expected to honour this code in their professional practice.

CHAPTER SUMMARY

In this chapter we have provided an overview of the most topical legal and ethical issues that fundraisers need to address and take account of in their work. While it is impossible to provide a comprehensive review of pertinent legislation the most critical legal requirements have been described, notably those enshrined in the Data Protection Act 1988.

We have also provided a summary of key ethical issues and suggested that although there is no one right answer in respect of how these might be handled, the codes of ethics produced by the sector's professional bodies provide a significant source of guidance for dealing with these issues on a day-to-day basis.

All the documentation now provided in relation to standards and ethics is designed with the central aim in mind of enhancing donor trust in the sector. Trust lies at the very heart of voluntary organizations, and without it, the sector would find it impossible to secure funds. Donors must trust the non-profits they support to behave appropriately and in a manner consistent with their mission. Only by adopting and following both the letter and the spirit of these codes will fundraisers provide donors with the reassurance they need and begin to drive dubious professional practice out of the sector.

DISCUSSION QUESTIONS

1   Compare the ethical issues outlined in this chapter with the AFP Code of Ethics and Professional Standards. Are all these issues dealt with? How do the codes suggest that fundraisers should respond to these challenges?

2   Why is a donor bill of rights important? Is it not enough that fundraising professionals merely adopt and follow an appropriate code of professional practice?

3   Your Board has decided that since fundraising income has fallen this year it will 'borrow' funds donated by donors for another purpose to cover the day-to-day costs of running the organization. How should you respond?

4   What lessons can fundraisers in the USA learn from the Data Protection Act now implemented in the UK? Are there aspects of the Act that you believe would constitute best practice even though similar legislation does not exist in the USA?

5   In your role as head of fundraising you have been approached by an independent professional fundraiser who has worked as an agent for your organization in the past. She has told you that she has a donor willing to write a large cheque for $50,000 to support your organization. The professional fundraiser has indicated, however, that she would require a $5,000 finder's fee for soliciting this donation. How would you respond?

6   Many of the media in the UK have claimed that face-to-face street fundraising is unethical and is merely a form of social mugging. Do you believe this form of fundraising is ethical? Justify your response.

REFERENCE

Fill, C. (1995) *Marketing Communications; Frameworks, Theories and Applications*, Prentice-Hall, Englewood Cliffs, NJ.

Index